THE GERMAN PEOPLE

VOL. VIII.

HISTORY OF THE GERMAN PEOPLE at the
Close of the Middle Ages. By JOHANNES JANSSEN.

Vols. I. and II. Translated by M. A. MITCHELL and
A. M. CHRISTIE.

Vols. III.—XVI. Translated by A. M. CHRISTIE.

HISTORY OF THE GERMAN PEOPLE AT THE CLOSE OF THE MIDDLE AGES

By Johannes Janssen

VOL. VIII.

GENERAL CONDITIONS OF THE GERMAN PEOPLE FROM THE SO-CALLED RELIGIOUS PACIFICATION OF AUGSBURG IN 1555 TO THE PROCLAMATION OF THE FORMULA OF CONCORD IN 1580

TRANSLATED BY A. M. CHRISTIE

LONDON

KEGAN PAUL, TRENCH, TRUBNER & CO. Ltd.

BROADWAY HOUSE, CARTER LANE, E.C.

B. HERDER BOOK CO.

15-17 SOUTH BROADWAY, ST. LOUIS, MO.:

1928

SECOND IMPRESSION

TRANSLATOR'S NOTE.

These Volumes (VII. and VIII.) are translated from
Vol. IV. of the German [Fifteenth and Sixteenth Editions,
improved and added to by Ludwig Pastor].

Made and Printed in Great Britain by Percy Lund, Humphries & Co. Ltd., Bradford

CONTENTS

OF

THE EIGHTH VOLUME

BOOK II

INFLUENCE OF FRENCH CALVINISM AND SUCCESS OF
THE INTERNATIONAL REVOLUTIONARY PARTY DURING
A PERIOD OF INCREASING NATIONAL WEAKNESS, 1567-
1575.

BOOK III

HISTORY

OF

THE GERMAN PEOPLE

AT THE CLOSE OF THE MIDDLE AGES

BOOK II

INFLUENCE OF FRENCH CALVINISM AND SUCCESS
OF THE INTERNATIONAL REVOLUTIONARY PARTY
DURING A PERIOD OF INCREASING NATIONAL
WEAKNESS, 1567–1575

CHAPTER I

THE GERMAN PRINCE AND THE FIRST HUGUENOT WAR

THE Elector Palatine, Frederic III., was nearer akin to
French character and sentiment than were any of the
other princes of the Empire. He had grown up under
the influence of French culture and politics, and, as we
have seen, had adopted the religious views of Calvin.
At an early date in their proceedings he had become
initiated in the plans of the Huguenots, as we learn from
a letter of his to his son-in-law, Duke John Frederic of

Saxony, in which he said that he had received trustworthy information of a plot, in which the whole of
France was concerned, ' to massacre all the priests by
next Reminiscere Sunday.' If he could not look with
approval, he said, on a scheme of slaughter and insurrection, he knew not, nevertheless, what God might have
preordained concerning his principality in this and other
matters.   He bade the Duke keep this information
secret ; ' but as the scheme has been set on foot, and I
have been informed of it, it ought not to be kept hidden
from your grace.' [1]   Two years later, in May 1562, he
expressed his regret that the Huguenots at Lyons 'had
only expelled the priests and not massacred them.' [2]
At that time the first Huguenot war was raging in
France.[3] The Prince of Condé and Admiral de Coligny,
the leaders of the Huguenots, applied for help to the
Protestants of Germany and England.   At the end of
July they were expecting German troops to the amount
of 20,000 infantry and 10,000 cavalry, and, as the
Calvinist jurist, Franz Hotoman, informed the Elector
Frederic, they had promised to deliver over the city of

---

[1] Kluckhohn, *Briefe*, i. 126–127.

[2] See vol. vii. pp. 316, 317.

[3] Respecting the growth of Calvinism in France, De Meaux (pp. 41–42)
says : ' Ce qui accrédita le protestantisme, ce fut d'abord le courage de ses
sectateurs ; ce furent aussi les mauvaises mœurs de ses ennemis. La
maîtresse de François Ier avait favorisé les protestants ; la maîtresse de
Henri II les poursuivait. L'établissement public et en quelque sorte
officiel des maîtresses royales à côté du trône de France remonte à
François Ier. Le moment où la forte race des Valois allait avec ses
entours s'abîmer et se perdre dans une débauche effrénée, était précisé-
ment celui où elle se trouvait chargée de tenir tête à l'hérésie. Comment
Dieu et les hommes l'auraient-ils estimée digne d'une telle tâche ? Il est
permis de voir dans les guerres de religion et leurs horreurs le résultat et
le châtiment des folles joies de la Renaissance : des excès furent punis par
d'autres excès.'

Paris to the Germans in order to encourage them to flock in multitudes to their help.[1]

Coligny wrote on August 3, 1562, that the plunder of Paris had been planned in consequence of the enmity and cruelty shown to the Huguenots by so many of the Parisians ; owing to the scarcity of money the German cavalry troops were to live at the expense of the papists.[2]

Frederic and other princes who were friendly to the Huguenots, as, for instance, the Landgrave Philip of Hesse, lent them money for recruiting soldiers. But Christopher of Würtemberg caused King Charles IX. and his mother, Catherine de' Medici, to be informed, on September 20, that 'the King and the Queen were quite wrong in asserting that the princes of the Augsburg Confession had departed from their ancient friendship for the French crown ; it was calumny to say that they intended to lend help to those who were in arms against their Majesties.'[3]

Frederic considered it a mere matter of course to support the Huguenots. But when he learnt that troops were being enlisted for the royal army in the archbishopric of Treves, he wrote to the Elector of Treves that he must not allow General Roggendorf to supply the French King with German troops to put down his rebellious subjects ; if such things were permitted, all

---

[1] Kervyn de Lettenhove, *Les Huguenots et les Gueux : Etude historique sur 25 années du XVI siècle* (1560-1585), 6 tom. Bruges, 1883-1885 (i. 85, 86).

[2] Kervyn de Lettenhove, i. 502-504.

[3] See Barthold, *Deutschland und die Hugenotten*, pp. 397-398. The Landgrave Philip of Hesse had been the first and the most insistent in urging that help should be sent to the Huguenots, and he had led the way in contributing money also by giving 19,000 florins, when Frederic had still only consented to stand bail. See Heidenhain, *Unionspolitik Philipps von Hessen*, pp. 426 ff.

manner of misunderstanding and disturbance might arise in Germany, in opposition to the terms both of the religious and profane peace.[1] 'The Protestant Rhinegrave, John Philip, recruited Catholic and Protestant soldiers for the royal army against the Huguenots, and assured the Spanish ambassador at Paris that the Germans would fight for any one who paid them, without troubling themselves about the cause.'[2]

In September, Condé informed the German Protestant princes that Elizabeth of England would also come to the help of the Huguenots with money and men.[3] But it was only through betrayal of their country that the Huguenots would be able to obtain this help, just as in former years the Elector Maurice of Saxony and his associates had secured the help of the French King, Henry II., against Charles V. by betrayal of the Empire. In a compact of September 20, it was arranged that the Huguenots were to deliver up Havre to Queen Elizabeth, and hold out hopes to her of the possession of Calais.[4] 'Condé and Coligny are traitors,' said the Cardinal of Lorraine, ' for they have brought the English, the

[1] Kluckhohn, *Briefe*, i. 299-302.

[2] Barthold, p. 399. At p. 398 Barthold remarks that, 'While many distinguished, nominally Protestant, officers lent the service of their swords for forty years to the house of Guise and the Catholic League, and the Spaniards in the Netherlands, we find scarcely one distinguished Catholic who gave his support to the Huguenots or to the cause associated with them in the Netherlands. The adherents of the old Church, in every fresh political event, thought only of one final object : the victory of their own religion; to their mind the subject-matter of the great division was religion and nothing else. The followers of the reformed faith, on the other hand, incapable of grasping the situation as a whole, or else indifferent, could always manage to quiet their consciences with dogmatic or political considerations, whenever the prospect of higher pay or older personal claims induced them to go over to the ranks of the enemies of their Church. Our Rhinegrave is an example of this want of principle.'

[3] Kervyn de Lettenhove, i. 94.   [4] Barthold, pp. 406-407.

oldest and most inveterate enemies of France, into our country.' The English troops captured Havre and Dieppe ' for the glory of God and the fulfilment of the holy desires of Queen Elizabeth,' as they said. In Orleans Condé behaved as though he were the king of the Huguenots. He had coins struck out of the gold and silver vessels in the churches, and cannons made from the brass of the bells. In the districts south of the Loire, innumerable churches and cloisters were plundered and destroyed ; the sepulchres of the Norman dukes at Rouen were desecrated ; the bones of St. Irenæus and St. Martin of Tours were thrown into the water ; the statue of the Maid of Orleans, the liberator of France, was pulled down ; no single monument of art or antiquity was spared ; libraries were ruthlessly burnt down, among others the valuable one of Clugny, which contained from five to six thousand precious manuscripts. Monks and priests were tortured and put to death with the utmost refinement of cruelty. Three thousand French monks and nuns, said the Cardinal of Lorraine at the Council of Trent, were made to suffer martyrdom in the course of a few months, because they would not abjure their vows of obedience to the Apostolic See. Contemporary writers speak with horror of the frightful cruelty which, in the name of ' the pure Gospel' and ' the downfall of idolatry,' disgraced the land of France. But the Catholics also by no means abstained from cruelty. Prince Condé, supported by German troops, marched against Paris. He had no better success, however, in his contemplated conquest and sack of Paris than had the English in the attempted capture of Rochelle.[1] On December 19 the Huguenot

---

[1] Kervyn de Lettenhove, i. 96–112.

army sustained a defeat from Duke Francis of Guise, near Dreux, and Condé was taken prisoner. Coligny, who was elected general in his place, while waiting for reinforcements from England, left his German troops free to pillage and destroy everything around them.[1]

Meanwhile, in consequence of the declaration of some of the Huguenot nobles that they could not, with good consciences, take up arms against the King, a synod of sixty Calvinist preachers assembled at Saintes, and it was settled among them that ' recourse to arms was just, legitimate, and necessary.' [2]

In the eyes of the Calvinists, the leader of the Catholics, the Duke of Guise, was ' the greatest of tyrants and the worst enemy of God.' At the time of the conspiracy of Amboise, in the year 1559, the plan had already been made to extinguish the whole race of Guise. ' You pride yourself,' wrote John Sturm of Strasburg to Franz Hotoman, ' that no single member of the house of Lorraine and Guise will be left alive, and you appeal to a Bible text to prove that the whole of this family will be massacred.' In Geneva, the stronghold of Calvinism, the murder of tyrants was preached openly as a duty.[3] The Calvinist theologian Beza, who had been present at the battle of Dreux, and had instructed the town council to put all the leaders of the Catholic party to death, made a practice, after this defeat, of supplicating heaven in his sermons and public prayers to rid France of the Duke of Guise. Other preachers followed his example. An attempt at Rouen to assassinate the Duke ended in failure ; but at the

---

[1] Kervyn de Lettenhove, i. 119–120.
[2] *Ibid.* i. 98.   [3] *Ibid.* i. 34–37, 98, 114.

siege of Orleans he was mortally wounded by an assassin on February 18, 1563. The murderer, Jean Poltrot de Méré, after his capture, confessed voluntarily, in the presence of the Queen Catherine de' Medici, that Beza and Coligny had incited him to the commission of this deed. Chantonay, an ambassador of King Philip II. of Spain, reported that the murder had been resolved on by the court of the Elector Friedrich at Heidelberg ; but that Duke Christopher of Würtemberg had not given his assent to the plot. The English ambassador, Thomas Smith, wrote to Queen Elizabeth from Blois, on February 26, 1563 : ' Poltrot was instigated to the murder by Soubise, and kept up to it by Beza ; in the camp they are all praising and lamenting the Duke : he was the greatest general of France, indeed of all Christendom, equally beloved by the nobles and the soldiers.' [1] Coligny denied having incited Poltrot to commit the murder, and declared that he had only given him money to act as a spy ; but he considered the death of the Duke ' the greatest piece of good fortune that could have happened to the French monarchy, the Church of God, and above all to himself and his whole house.' [2] The Huguenot Hubert Languet (who later on acted for years as agent in Paris for the Elector Augustus of Saxony), in a letter to the latter's chancellor, Mordeisen, expressed his pleasure that Coligny had cleared himself in Saxony from the suspicion of having

---

[1] Kervyn de Lettenhove, i. 122–127 ; Barthold, p. 485.

[2] *Mémoires de Condé*, iv. 304. Beza declared the death of the Duke to be a judgment of God. ' Had I,' he wrote, ' in the heat of so righteous a war, known any way, either by ambuscade or by open violence, of ridding the earth of the Duke, I declare that it would have been a justifiable act on my part, as against an enemy in war, and I should not have sought to exonerate myself ' (Schlosser, *Theodor Beza*, pp. 172–173).

compassed the Duke's death out of ' family enmity.' It was more ' magnanimous' of Poltrot, he wrote, to have done the glorious deed by which he had saved his country from ruin, not from hope of reward, but of his own free-will.[1]

Suspicion of participation in the murder of the Duke rested on Catherine de' Medici. ' The Guises,' she said once to the Marshal Tavannes, ' had always aimed at becoming kings, until Orleans and I prevented it.'[2] The Queen forthwith entered into negotiations with the Huguenots. In 1561 she had asked the German Protestant princes whether she could reckon on their support if she accepted the Confession of Augsburg;[3] and now she was anxious to appoint Duke Christopher of Würtemberg governor-general of France; Christopher, however, rejected her offer.[4] She won over the Prince of Condé by means of the amorous intrigues of one of the ladies of her court, in consequence of which the Prince's wife died of grief.[5] On March 12, 1563, Condé concluded with Catherine a treaty which was signed on the 19th by Charles IX., and is known as the Peace of Amboise. By the terms of this agreement the reformed worship of God was to be allowed in the territories of the immediate feudatories of the King, except at Paris

---

[1] *Epist.* lib. ii. 239. Concerning Languet, see Geizer in the *Allg. Biogr.* xvii. 692 f. Blasel, *H. Languet* (Oppeln, 1872); O. Scholz, *H. Languet als Kursächsischer Berichterstatter in Frankrcich*, 1566-1572 (Leipzig, 1875) and Waddington in the *Rev. Hist.* xlii. 243 *sq.*

[2] Kervyn de Lettenhove, i. 130.　　　　[3] *Ibid.* i. 72-73.

[4] Sattler, iv. 193, Beil. No. 70.

[5] Kervyn de Lettenhove, i. 137-138; Barthold, pp. 511-512; v. Polenz, i. 247-248. Brantôme wrote of Condé: ' Le bon prince estoit bien aussi mondain qu'un autre et aymoit autant la femme d'autruy que la sienne; tenant fort du naturel de ceux de la race de Bourbon, qui ont esté fort d'amoureuse complexion ' (*Œuvres*, vi. 333).

and wherever the court happened to be residing. In the charter of this peace Condé was designated as a loyal subject and faithful servant of the King; but Elizabeth of England, on account of his breach of faith, called him a traitor and a wretch who only deserved to be cast to the dogs.[1] All the losses sustained by the Huguenots were made good to them, and for this purpose Catholic Church property to the amount of 900,000 livres was confiscated. Catherine looked on in person at the scandalous desecration of all the chalices, Mass vestments, and other articles of which the Huguenots took possession. Amid brilliant court festivals she drowned all thought of the miseries caused by the religious war, which a contemporary, Michael von Castelnau, depicts in the following words : ' Agriculture, hitherto more successfully pursued in France than anywhere else, is in a sorry plight ; villages and towns without number have been plundered and laid waste by fire ; the poor peasants are flying like frightened animals ; our tradespeople and artisans have forsaken their business and taken up arms ; the nobles are divided among themselves, the clergy are trodden down, nobody is secure of life or property ; robbery, murder, and assaults are of daily occurrence ; religion and piety have disappeared. Under the cloak of religion, blasphemers who deny God abandon themselves wholly to their own criminal lusts : the work built up by centuries of order and industry has been destroyed by the licence and wantonness of a few days.' [2]

The King was also obliged to pay the German soldiers who had fought with the Huguenots. True, they did not receive by any means the amount which

[1] Kervyn de Lettenhove, i. 140.   [2] *Mémoires*, livr. 5, ch. i.

had been promised them, but they took away with them 2,000 munition wagons filled with the unsaleable booty of which they had possessed themselves during a six-months' campaign. Incendiarism, devastation, and pillage marked their return journey, especially in the level country of Champagne and Lorraine. The country-folk were horror-stricken, wrote the Huguenot Hubert Languet, at the mere sight of a German hat. In a letter of June 29, 1563, he says : ' We are at length rid of the German cavalry, who, wherever they go, leave lamentable traces behind them.' [1] The Marshal of Hesse allowed incendiarism and pillage to be carried on in the archbishopric of Treves to the same extent as on French territory, so that, thirteen years later, complaints on the subject were still heard at imperial Diets.[2]

Coligny refused at first to agree to the terms of the peace ; he soon, however, became reconciled to the King and Queen, though on the condition, wrote the Spanish ambassador, that he should be allowed a free hand in the Dutch hereditary lands of the King of Spain. In co-operation with Catherine, Coligny exercised an important influence on the revolutionary rising in the Netherlands. Flanders, said Charles IX., belonged to him.[3]

---

[1] *Epist.* lib. ii. 248.   [2] Barthold, pp. 519–525.
[3] Kervyn de Lettenhove, i. 142, 169–170, 289.

CHAPTER II

THE REVOLUTION IN THE NETHERLANDS AND ITS REAC-
TION ON OTHER DISTRICTS OF THE EMPIRE UP TO
1568

AT the time of the abdication of Charles V., and all
through the first decade of his son Philip II.'s reign,
the German Netherlands were in a most highly flourish-
ing condition. What Æneas Sylvius had said of Augsburg in the fifteenth century, ' This town excels all
other towns of the world in riches,' might now be said
of Antwerp. More than 1,000 foreign mercantile houses
had been established there. As many as 2,500 ships were
often to be seen in the river Scheldt ; 500 came in regularly every day, and on market days as many as 800 ;
2,000 wagons, 10,000 peasants' carts drove every week
into the town, which, with its suburbs, counted 200,000
inhabitants. It was said that more business was trans-
acted at Antwerp in one month than in two years at
Venice, even in the most brilliant period of this city.
In the year 1560, the imports from Lisbon, merely in
sugar and spices, reached the value of 1,600,000 ducats ;
from Italy, in the same year, 3,000,000 ducats' worth of
silk, raw and manufactured, of camelot and gold stuffs,
were imported. The imports in German and French
wines amounted to 2,500,000 ducats ; in cereals from
the Baltic to 1,500,000 ducats. In 1556 the Italian
Luigi Guicciardini valued the English wool imported

to the Netherlands at 250,000 ducats, the cloth and
other stuffs at more than 5,000,000 ducats. In 1556,
also, cargoes of Spanish wool to the value of 600,000
ducats were imported to Bruges. But what specially
excited the wonder of foreigners was the fact that this
commercial activity and prosperity was not confined to
single towns, but was diffused through all the provinces.
'The whole country,' wrote the Venetian Cavalli, 'is
alive with commerce and brimming over with money, so
that everybody, however lowly in condition or limited
in capacity, is well provided for according to his circumstances.' In the towns of Courtray, Tournay, and
Lille, cloth is the staple manufacture ; in Valenciennes,
camelot ; in Brussels, beautiful carpets are made.
'These carpets,' says another Venetian writer, Soriano,
' show what artistic skill can do. As the masters in the
art of mosaic are able to produce pictures and copies of
various objects with little stones, so here, by means of
silk and woollen threads, the artisans are able not only
to give colour to their work, but also light and shade,
and to make the figures stand out in a manner that can
only be attained by the best painters.' [1] In these
wealthy provinces of Flanders there were no less than
300 towns, nearly 150 market boroughs, and 6,000 large
villages.

The politico-religious revolution ruined all this
prosperity, destroyed agriculture, trade, and industry,
laid waste the towns, and ' threw the country back for
a long period into a semi-barbaric state.'

Under the rule of Charles V. conditions had already
been ripening towards a tremendous revolutionary

[1] See Fischer, *Gesch. des teutschen Handels*, ii. 636 ff. and iii. 380 ff.,
430 ff. Höfler, *Betrachtungen*, pp. 6-7.

crisis. ' The inordinate love of luxury which prevailed in the country was sapping the deep religious feeling of the people, and bringing their morals to such a state of depravity ' that Queen Maria of Hungary, who had been Regent of the Provinces of the Netherlands for twenty-five years, wrote to the Emperor that she could no longer continue living among a people who seemed no more to have any reverence for God or man.[1] Matters grew very much worse in the reign of Philip II., who, unlike his father, was a stranger to the Netherlands ; Margaret of Parma, the Regent appointed by him, was, even in 1560, full of forebodings of the outbreak of a revolution.[2]

With the concurrence of the States-General, Charles V. had issued the most stringent penal edicts against the introduction into the Netherlands of the novel religious opinions promulgated from Wittenberg and Geneva. Nevertheless, this measure did not prevent the new doctrines gaining numbers of adherents, especially among the nobles, many of whom, ' deeply involved in debt,' thought ' to extricate themselves from their difficulties by the confiscation of church property,' and ' by the overthrow of the Spanish rule to set themselves up as sole lords and masters in the land.'

William of Nassau, Prince of Orange, the principal leader of the aristocratic party, had already before Philip's accession, by his squanderous living, incurred debts amounting to some 800,000 florins, and had by degrees brought himself to such a condition of financial need that he mournfully confided to his brother,

---

[1] Weiss, *Papiers d'Etat de Granvelle*, iv. 469.

[2] Gachard, *Corresp. de Marguerite de Parme*, i. 260. Respecting the commencement of the revolution in the Netherlands, and the grounds of discontent with the government after Philip II.'s departure from the country (August 1559), see M. Ritter, *Anfänge*, pp. 387 ff.

Count Louis of Nassau, that he was no longer in a position to keep up his household.[1]   As soon as the Prince of Orange found that he had been deceived in his hope of being appointed Governor of the Netherlands by King Philip, he began a systematic resistance to the Government ; in his ' Apology ' he boasts that from the very first he was determined to expel ' the Spanish breed ' from the soil of the Netherlands.   Although he had been brought up in the faith of the Augsburg Confession, he posed as a Catholic at the Court of Brusesls, and in 1561 he gave public expression to condemnatory remarks on ' the new unhallowed sects ' and their preachers, whom he denounced as bandits and traducers of the people   Unasked, he promised the Pope to withstand, with all means at his disposal, ' the heretical plague ' of Calvinism.   But when, in 1561, he married the Saxon Princess Anna, daughter of the Elector Maurice, he assured the Elector Augustus of Saxony of his own deep and sincere devotion to the Protestant faith, adding, however, ' that at present he did not dare allow this religion to be preached openly.'   His wife, he said, should carry on her Lutheran religion without let or hindrance ; she should have a Protestant preacher, and receive the Sacraments according to her own usage : their children, too, should be brought up in the Protestant faith.   Simultaneously with these assurances, he declared to King Philip that he had made it a condition of his marriage that his wife should embrace the Catholic faith, and that he would never consent to her

---

[1] Fuller details concerning the enormous debts of the nobles of the Netherlands in Juste, *Hist. de la Révolution des Pays-Bas sous Philippe II*, tom. i. 251 sv. The *Mémoire*, in Groen van Prinsterer, i. 37 sv. and *Oraniens Brief* i, 400. See De Gerlache, *Hist. du Royaume des Pays-Bas*, p. 71.

following any but the Catholic religion, and that not outwardly only, but in truth and sincerity. Religion was with him only a political means : religion, he said, was not worth a moment's thought if it stood in the way of acquiring profit, influence, or power. He told a friend in confidence at the wedding, that he did not want Anna to occupy herself in the dismal study of the Holy Scriptures ; he would rather that she read ' Amadis of Gaul ' and other entertaining books.[1] He made so little secret of the immorality of his principles that (according to a report of Duke Christopher of Würtemberg) at the convention of princes at Frankfort in 1558 he declared that ' the object of the institution of marriage was only to secure ascertained heirs ; otherwise it was no sin to have concubines as well as a lawful wife.' Christopher adds that the Elector Augustus of Saxony also heard similar utterances from the Prince of Orange.[2]

By his marriage with a Saxon princess, William of Nassau hoped to gain over all the Protestant princes to

[1] For these statements see Groen van Prinsterer, i. 93, 104, 119. Gachard, *Corresp. de Guillaume le Taciturne*, i. 430. Reiffenberg, *Corresp.*, pp. 260, 279. Prosper Levesque, *Mémoires de Granvelle*, i. 251. Raumer, *Histor. Taschenbuch*, Jahrg. 1836, p. 115. Concerning Orange's double-faced attitude in his marriage with Anna of Saxony, see especially H. Kolligs, *Wilhelm von Oranien und die Anfänge des Aufstandes der Niederlande* (Inaugural-Dissertation, Bonn, 1884) pp. 3-20. Even on May 13, 1566, Orange wrote to Pope Pius V.: ' It is my desire and my intention all my life long to remain the most humble and most obedient son of the Church and the Holy See, and to persevere in this devotion and this obedience as my ancestors did.' The text of this letter, and of a second of June 8, 1566, in which he again assured the Pope of his solicitude for the preservation ' of the ancient and catholic religion,' is in the Stimmen aus Maria-Laach, xxi. 219-220. In the same year, 1566, Groen van Prinsterer, 2, xviii., says positively of the Prince of Orange : ' Il étoit protestant de cœur et par conviction.'

[2] See M. Ritter, *Anfänge*, p. 410, note 2.

his revolutionary plans. 'This marriage,' wrote an
English agent on August 4, 1561, ' has been the making
of Orange.' [1] Hope was already high, in 1563, that ' the
fruit would soon ripen in Flanders.' On November 1
of this year, Count Louis of Nassau reported the conquest of Wurzburg to his brother William, and proposed
that the work of levying troops should be begun. More
than 400 nobles, he wrote, had entered into ' a league
and confederation' to stand by each other with person
and goods against all opponents, even against the
Emperor. The Prince of Orange must consider by
what means he could bring over to his side the captains
of horse who had served under Grümbach. The prince
approved of Louis's suggestion that he should have
himself named commander-in-chief of the Westphalian
circle, because it would then always be possible, without
exciting any suspicion, to have a good number of
soldiers in readiness.[2] In the same year, 1563, General
Count Günther of Schwarzburg sent word to the Prince
of Sondershausen that it was whispered secretly that the
Protestant princes, fearing that the Spanish King would
carry out the decrees of the Council of Trent, meant to
take the initiative and invade Brabant.[3] The following
year the Prince of Orange was most anxious that the
war between Denmark and Sweden should be brought
to an end as soon as possible, in order that Count
Günther and other generals ' may be sooner set free to
come to us, and discuss matters with us.' [4]

---

[1] Kervyn de Lettenhove, i. 71.

[2] '. . . on pourrait, sous ombre de cecy, avoir tousjours une bonne
quantité de gens de guerre à la main, sans aulcun soupçon, y mettant vous
et nous aultres quelque somme par an avecques ' (in Groen van Prinsterer, *Supplément*, 14*-15*).

[3] Groen van Prinsterer, i. 99.   [4] *Ibid.* ii. 22.

Meanwhile both Huguenot and English agents were busy in the Netherlands, stirring up sedition and carrying on their intrigues with Prince William. Pamphlets prepared in London were disseminated among the people, exhorting them to rise up against the tyranny of King Philip and of Cardinal Granvella, the first minister of the Regent.[1] The numbers of the sectarians had increased from year to year. Things had come to such a pass that sermons were sometimes preached to armed congregations. Here and there ' convents fell a prey to fire and pillage.' In the year 1564 the existence was discovered, at Bruges and Antwerp, of a sect whose preachers sanctioned the members having as many wives as they could feed ; four was the lowest number any of them possessed ; if the wives expressed any repugnance to the habits of their sect, the preachers had the right to put them to death. ' If no stand is made,' wrote the Bishop of Ghent on July 23, 1564, ' we shall have another Münster insurrection, and a much more terrible one indeed, for it will spread over several provinces. The anabaptist sects gain the largest following, and next to them the Calvinists, who are also fomenting sedition.' [2]

A few months before, on April 27, 1564, a French Calvinistic synod had met at Ferté-sous-Jouarre, and at the suggestion of Beza it had, besides other business, turned its attention to the affairs of the Netherlands. The decision of the majority had been that the time had come to resort to force and to organise an armed insurrection.[3]

---

[1] Fuller details in Kervyn de Lettenhove, i. 164-205.
[2] Heymann, *Epistolæ*, 62.
[3] Kervyn de Lettenhove, i. 206-207.

However, they did not yet proceed to arms.

After the Prince of Orange, in conjunction with Lamoral Count of Egmont, whom he had drawn into his revolutionary movement, had, in 1564, accomplished the recall of Granvella by Philip II., ' the ship of state was robbed of its pilot.' [1] The Regent became the plaything of the revolutionary party. A godless rule of the nobles set in. Everything in the land became prostituted to the greed of lucre : offices, dignities, privileges, were sold to the highest bidder ; even justice itself grew venal, and the King's treasury was pilfered. ' The lords and nobles of the court,' writes Pontus Paien, ' abandoned themselves to all manner of wantonness and luxury ; if now and then they got up early in the morning, it was in order to go to the chase ; the rest of the day was spent in drinking, the night in gambling and masquerades,' not to speak of worse doings.[2] Before long Calvinistic preachers began delivering seditious sermons in many places.

Even in Granvella's time the stringent religious edicts that had been issued had only been enforced in rare cases. The Prince of Orange and his adherents, in order to bring the Cardinal under the King's suspicion, had actually complained that he did not exert himself strenuously enough for the maintenance of the old religion and the extirpation of heresy.[3]

---

[1] See in *Schiller als Historiker* (Freiburg, 1879), S. 56–57, the favourable judgments, quoted by Janssen, of later Protestant historians respecting Granvella. Even Groen van Prinsterer rejects the reproaches raised against the Cardinal as unfounded, and rightly remarks : ' Le principal grief de ses antagonistes était, qu'il avait l'œil trop ouvert sur leurs desseins ' (*Archives*, i. 191).

[2] *Mémoires de Pontus Paien*, p. 60.

[3] *Mémoires de Granvelle*, ii. 33. Gachard, *Correspondance de Philippe II*, tom. i. 384. Groen van Prinsterer, i. 71 sv. See the

At a conference at Brussels the Bishops of Ypres, Namur, Ghent, and St. Omer, in conjunction with other theologians, addressed a petition to King Philip, in June 1565, begging him to soften down the edicts. It was represented to him that the object of the episcopal inquisition, the only one that existed in the Netherlands, was ' to admonish the people by gentleness and fatherly love, not by judicial severity.' But they met with no response from Philip. He continued to insist on relentless fulfilment of the edicts. These decrees, although the penalties were no longer enforced, afforded the revolutionary party a most convenient instrument for rousing the fury of the people. ' The Spanish religious tyranny,' it was said, ' grows worse every day, and finds its way to the most secret recesses of human thoughts.' Speeches and sermons on insurrection and on foreign help, on the King's faithlessness to his oaths, and on the subjects being consequently absolved from obedience, served more and more to inflame the people.

When, towards the end of the year 1565, fresh orders came from Philip with regard to the edicts, a request was made by some loyal subjects of the King, that these orders should not be made publicly known until the King had been apprised of the reception they were likely to meet with. But the Prince of Orange, who was only too ready to welcome the worst reception of the royal injunctions, declared that they could not postpone their execution without laying themselves open to reproaches from the King of penal obduracy. ' He carried his point with the Regent, and the command was forthwith issued that the governors of the

Actenstück Contre l'escript du Prince d'Oranges in the *Bulletins de la commission royale d'histoire* (Bruxelles, 1841), iv. 114.

different provinces and the courts of justice were to give every possible support to the episcopal inquisitors, and to carry out the instructions of the latter without any demurring. "We shall soon see now," the Prince said to an intimate friend, "the beginning of a remarkable tragedy." '[1]   In January 1566 he issued, for the provinces under his government, a stringent order in favour of the inquisition.[2]

Within a few months the flames of insurrection broke out.[3]

Count Louis of Nassau, in agreement with his brother of Orange, had already, in July or August 1565, commenced negotiations for forming a confederacy of nobles. In December a compact, which went by the name of the 'Compromise,' was signed and sworn to at Brussels, at first only by a few of the nobles, but later on several hundreds joined themselves to the number.[4] The revolutionary manifesto of the confederates, which soon appeared in print, was couched in the most virulent terms. It was aimed at the person of the King himself, who, it was declared, in spite of the solemn oath he had sworn, intended to introduce the Spanish Inquisition into the Netherlands, in order to enrich himself by confiscating the goods of his subjects.[5]

---

[1] *Vita Viglii*, p. 45.

[2] See H. J. Allard, *Een Plakkaat des Zwijgers ten gunste der Inquisitie* (8 Januari, 1565, stilo curiae = 1566), Utrecht, 1886.

[3] 'Depuis icelles [the royal commands] publiées par lettres de Son Alteze, escriptes aux evesques, consaulx et bonnes villes, c'est chose incroyable quelles flammes jecta le feu d'auparavant caché soubz les cendres' (Hopperus, *Recueil et Mémorial*, p. 62).

[4] See Ritter, *Anfänge*, pp. 416 ff.

[5] De Gerlache, in his *Hist. du Royaume des Pays-Bas*, i. 83 v gives an excellent analysis of the 'Compromise.'

The lower ranks of the population were drawn into the movement by a systematic distribution in all districts, towns, and villages of over 5,000 pasquinades and scurrilous pamphlets against the Church and the throne. Count Henry of Brederode, a man of wild, dissolute character,[1] who 'wanted to have the scoundrelly bishops exterminated like green [= young] dogs,'[2] set up a mart for revolutionary literature in his fortified town of Viane.

In March 1566 the Regent received fuller information concerning the alliances of the confederate nobles in France, England, and Germany, concerning the military strength of the league—which she was told could count on 35,000 men—and concerning the plan of attack which had already been drawn up. On April 5, Count Brederode, in the name and in the presence of some 400 nobles who, amid a surging crowd of the populace, had repaired to the palace of Brussels, handed over to the Regent a petition drawn up by Louis of Nassau, protesting against the Inquisition and the religious edicts, demanding their abolition, and recommending that an embassy be sent to the King and an assembly of the States-General be convened without loss of time. 'The Gueux' were sure of victory.[3]

Margaret promised to lay the petition before the King and to speak on its behalf ; she was all the more ready to do this as the petitioners had ' formed the resolution to

---

[1] Holzwarth, i. 258 ; Kervyn de Lettenhove, i. 269, 356, note.

[2] From a letter to the Prince of Orange's brother, Louis of Nassau (Groen van Prinsterer, i. 248).

[3] On the approach of the crowd, Count Berlaymont is said to have whispered to the terrified Regent : 'It is only a pack of beggars—ce n'est qu'un tas de gueux : ' hence the origin of the name.

undertake no innovations in religion, but to support the
old religion with all the authority they could command.'
Indeed, the confederates, although they were ' engaged
in secret intrigues' with foreign Protestants, and
although many of their number had openly apostatised
from the old Church, declared unanimously that the
maintenance of the Catholic religion was their real
object. Even·Louis of Nassau and the Prince of Orange's
intimate friend, Philip of Marnix, both of them decided
Protestants, stooped to this means of deception.[1]

The wheels had been set rolling.

The burghers of the town also formed a league
similar to that of the nobles. The members of it were
clad in grey, the colour of the ' gueux.' Frequent
meetings of the confederate nobles ' fanned the flames
of sedition.' Numbers of Calvinist preachers were
invited from Geneva and from France in order that
they might attack the popish blasphemy and all the
accursed papistical proceedings in churches and cloisters
with courageous language, and tear up all the venomous
plants by the roots. The activity of these men had
plentiful rewards. In Brussels and Antwerp the people
were plainly exhorted to take up arms. Antwerp,
which for years had been a centre of demagogic-religious
machinations, harboured within its walls a large number of native and foreign refugees and adventurers.
The league of the nobles applauded and encouraged
the ' sacred work.' ' Wild, anarchical sermons' were
preached to multitudes of listeners who had swarmed
from far and near. Ever since June and July, ' preachers
had been at work in all the provinces, learned and unlearned men from foreign parts, as well as renegade

[1] Groen van Prinsterer, ii. 84–85, 91; Holzwarth, i. 275–278.

clerics and monks born in the country, and even shoemakers, tailors, and other artisans; and one and all
admonished their hearers that now was the time of
harvest, that they must do away with all the jugglery
in the churches, with the priests and all their baggage.
Why not at once proceed to destroy all that belonged
to the service of idolatry, and divide the rich Church
treasures among themselves in this their hour of
need?' Placards and leaflets proclaimed that 'the will
of God demanded that the priests and monks should
be massacred;' 'no more pity should be shown to the
priests and monks than Elias had shown to the priests of
Baal.' 'The monks and the papists are delivered into
the hands of the children of God, as once upon a time
the idolatrous Egyptians were given into the hands of
the Israelites.'

In July 1566 nearly 2,000 armed nobles belonging
to the League of the Gueux assembled at St. Trond,
proclaimed universal freedom in religion, and delibe-
rated concerning measures for placing themselves in an
attitude of defence against the King. This meeting
was followed in August by all the worst horrors of
iconoclasm.

'From what passed at the gathering at St. Trond,'
says the Protestant historian Bor, 'there can be no other
conclusion than that this iconoclasm took place with the
knowledge and consent of the confederates.'

Count Brederode caused all the altars and images in
the church of Viane to be cleared away to the music of
drums   Count Culemberg was himself present at the
devastation of his church, held a carousal with his
company of plunderers on the ruins of the house of
God, and fed his parrot with the consecrated Hosts.

At Oudenarde the iconoclasts pleaded the orders they had received from the confederates, and showed their letters of instruction. At Leyden two nobles were at the head of the sacrilegious gang, and they wore the badge of the ' Gueux ' on their coats. The magistrate of Brussels proved to the Regent that Count Louis of Nassau and two of the Prince of Orange's nobles had endeavoured to stir up iconoclasm there also. The preachers co-operated with the nobles both at Ghent and at Antwerp. This last town was the theatre of all the escaped passions of the populace and its instigators, chief among whom was the preacher Hermann Modet, who had brought three wives with him. The cathedral of Our Lady 'was completely devastated, because it was contrary to the Word of God to preserve any idolatrous church decorations.' Altars were broken up ; images, organs, and painted windows mutilated or destroyed, pictures knocked in, embroideries torn, chalices, monstrances, and other costly treasures purloined, sepulchres torn open, corpses stripped of their ornaments, and the bones tossed about hither and thither. Bellowing out : ' Long live the Gueux ! ' the frantic mobs rushed from church to church, from cloister to cloister. These outrages went on for full three days and three nights, during which time there occurred much maltreatment of defenceless priests, monks, and nuns. ' There was not a single church or chapel,' says Wesenbeck, a Protestant informant, ' not a single hospital or cloister, in which everything was not destroyed.' In Flanders alone 400 churches were destroyed, and libraries innumerable, with all the valuable MSS. in them. ' Anything and everything is now tolerated in this country,' wrote the Regent to the King at Madrid, ' except the Catholic religion, and anybody calling himself or herself a Catholic.' [1]

' I cannot tell you,' wrote the King to Granvella on November 27, 1566, ' how deeply the ravaging and pillaging of the churches in Flanders has distressed and grieved me. No personal loss could cause me so much sorrow as the slightest offence to our Lord and the desecration of His holy images ; for His service and glory are dearer to my heart than everything else in the whole world.' [2]

For years past Granvella had again and again begged the King to come himself to the Netherlands in order to set right the anarchical condition of things, control and keep down the factions, and safeguard the people against the machinations of the demagogues. He had told Philip that it was being represented to the people in the most wicked manner, that the King was bent on abolishing all their privileges, and on introducing the Spanish Inquisition into the country : he must therefore come himself and undeceive his subjects, and teach them better, and when he came he must not bring Spaniards with him, but must be accompanied by a German retinue ; it was also highly desirable that a body of native troops of about five or six regiments, under native commanders, should be organised in the

---

[1] Fuller details and documents concerning these proceedings and the sources of information in Holzwarth, i. 344–377, 460–465 ; Janssen, *Schiller als Historiker*, pp. 80–85. For information concerning the skilful methods by which the people were incited to rebellion through foreign emissaries, and the organisation of the iconoclastic riots by the Confederates and the preachers, see Koch, *Untersuchungen*, pp. 70 ff. ; Kervyn de Lettenhove, i. 355–371. A more accurate list of the churches and art treasures that were destroyed is given by Rathgeber in the *Annalen der niederländischen Malerei*, pp. 196–199.

[2] Gachard, *Correspondance de Philippe II*, tom. 1, 489.

Netherlands. He had also advised Philip to enforce the
religious edicts with full rigour against the preachers
and the originators of public disturbances, but against
them only, and not against the harmless people who
were led astray, or those who were penitent ; it was
well, in the exercise of his prerogative, to have regard
to the privileges of the country and the nature of its
inhabitants.[1] But Philip had turned a deaf ear to him.
From the precincts of his Cabinet he had wanted to
carry on despotic rule like ' the mightiest sovereign of
the age.' Now again, when ' the deluge of revolutionary waters had swelled to overflowing,' and ' hundreds
of ruined churches and cloisters bore cruel witness to the
effects of the unfettered fury of the populace,' the
Cardinal once more tried all means in his power to
induce the King to come and restore order himself in
the Netherlands, and to win the hearts of the people by
a wise and conciliatory policy : though even now,
Granvella urged, he must as far as possible respect the
rights and liberties of the country, and rather let many
guilty persons go unpunished, than punish any who
were innocent, or merely victims of seduction. Among
this last class the Cardinal particularly specified Count
Egmont, who had only allowed himself to become a tool
in the hands of the Prince of Orange : ' To shed the
blood of one's vassals was to weaken one's own strength,'
he urged.[2]

Pope Pius V. also advised the King to go to the
Netherlands and take the management of affairs. But

---

[1] Granvella's *Briefe* in Groen van Prinsterer, 1, lxxvi, 151, 169;
Gachard, *Correspondance de Philippe II*, tom. 1, clxxii, 201.

[2] Granvella's *Briefe* in Gachard, *Correspondance de Philippe II*,
tom. 1, 518, 534, 560, 594, 599, and 2, li. With regard to Egmont, see
also 1, clxxiv; also Groen van Prinsterer, vi. 411, and *Supplément*, 43.

Philip would not listen to him either : he even flew into a rage with the papal legate on account of the Pope's interference.[1]   Now that his enemies in the Netherlands had taken up arms, he too had resolved, he said, to settle the question by the sword and to ' reduce the country to tranquillity by violence and terror.'   While refusing to pay any heed to the words of the Pope, who exhorted him, in the name of religion, to confine himself to peaceable measures, he lent a willing ear to the Augustinian Eremite friar, Fray Lorenço de Villa-vicencio, when the latter encouraged him in his warlike policy by reminding him that ' King David had no pity on the enemies of God ; he slew them all, and spared neither man nor woman.   Moses, too, with those on his side, in one single day sacrificed 3,000 of the children of Israel.   An angel, in one night, slew more than 60,000 of the enemies of God.   There had been no cruelty in these deeds ; it was merely that no pity had been shown to people who had no respect for the honour of God.   Your Majesty is a King like David, a leader like Moses, yea verily, an angel of God ; for so does Scripture call the kings and leaders of nations.   Enemies of the living God are these heretics, these blaspheming, sacrilegious, idolatrous men, these wild beasts, who will undoubtedly utterly destroy the sanctuary of God in the Netherlands, if timely measures are not taken to avert so sad, so deplorable a catastrophe.'[2]

After the fury of iconoclasm had subsided, ' a certain amount of tranquillity and order ' prevailed outwardly in the Netherlands, and a large number of the nobles

[1] Gachard, i. 488; Kervyn de Lettenhove, i. 470. See Holzwarth, i. 401.

[2] Gachard, 2, xliii–xlv.

withdrew ' from a movement which had led to such outrages ; many, indeed, returned loyally to allegiance to
the King.' Still, however, in January 1567, the reports
of the Regent to the King depicted the situation as a
hopeless one : things were growing worse and worse in
all the provinces. ' All the wealthy inhabitants were
leaving the country.' [1] The tranquillity of the land was
indeed only on the surface. At the beginning of December 1566, the heads of the Calvinist party, both preachers
and nobles, concluded treaties, at Amsterdam and
Antwerp, for resistance against Philip in case he should
lead an expedition into the Netherlands. They had
expectations of help from the Swiss, who should block
the Alpine passes against the passage of the King's
army ; from the English, who would find in the isle of
Walcheren and in Antwerp a basis of operations ; from
the French Huguenots, who were to take up a strong
position at Valenciennes. Encouragement also came
to them from Turkey. In the reformed consistory at
Antwerp a letter was read out from a Spanish Jew who
stood high in the estimation of Sultan Selim ; it ran as
follows : ' The Calvinists of the Netherlands were to
hasten on with all speed the accomplishment of the
conspiracy they had begun with such courage and
magnanimity ; the Grand Sultan was preparing for a
formidable enterprise, and in a short time the Ottoman
armies would give King Philip so much to do that he
would have no time even to think of the Netherlands.' [2]

---

[1] Castillo wrote from Antwerp on January 17, 1567, that most of the
rich people that he knew had gone away : ' La canaille presque centuplée,
la mélancolie et la défiance sur toutes les figures ' (Groen van Prinsterer,
Supplément, 44*).

[2] Fuller details in Holzwarth, ii. 101, 109-121 ; Kervyn de Lettenhove, i. 380-493.

The Flemish revolutionary party stood in close connection with the Grumbach-Gotha conspiracy.

After the defeat of this plot, the Emperor informed
the Spanish ambassador at his court that Grumbach's
papers, two large cases of which had been seized at
Gotha, revealed the full extent of the operations planned
by himself and his accomplices. They had aimed at
the ruin and extermination of all the princes of the
Empire, and, in justification of their intention, they
gave out that all that they had planned was meant for
the greatness and might of the Emperor, just as if for
his benefit they had intended to found an hereditary
monarchy and blot out for ever the memory of elections
and electors.

But, in spite of all this pretended zeal for his glory,
Maximilian went on: ' They had in reality only meant
to deceive him. A collection of terribly compromising
letters between them and the Flemish rebels had been
discovered, and he had cause to thank God fervently
that the troops had gone to Gotha at the time they
did. Had there been a delay even of a few months,
had they waited till the spring, as some had advised,
the conflagration would meanwhile have spread to
such an extent that there would have been no possibility
of stopping it.' [1] To King Philip himself the Emperor
wrote that he herewith sent him a confidential report
of the information derived from the entire collection of
Duke John Frederic's chancellery letters now in his
possession, and which showed that if the investment of
Gotha had been delayed by only one or two months,
the conspirators would have had time to muster a
sufficient body of soldiers to carry out their designs to

[1] Koch, *Quellen*, ii. 39.

the full ; and not only would they have invaded Germany
with overpowering forces and completely convulsed and
ruined the whole Empire, but they would also have
been able to give armed support to the rebellion in
Flanders. A simultaneous outbreak and a coalition of
the two movements had been resolved on : the two
revolutionary bodies would have worked into each
other's hands ' to such an extent that all the prisons
erected or contemplated by your Majesty could not
have broken their power and strength.' Maximilian
gave Philip reiterated assurances, based on his perusal
of the Gotha papers, that ' The Netherlands and the
outlawed princes had formed most extensive conspiracies together ; if they could have put an end to me
and to the King of Spain, they would not have stayed
their hands ; but God has mercifully preserved us by
means of this Gotha execution.' [1]

One of the most active of the conspirators was the
Prince of Orange's brother, Count Louis of Nassau.
' At the beginning of the troubles,' Count John of
Nassau wrote boastingly later on, ' this man was foremost
in pushing on the work, both in the Netherlands and
among some of the Evangelical Estates in Germany ; ' it
was notably through his instrumentality that ' the
Elector Augustus of Saxony and the old Landgrave
Philip of Hesse were influenced to look more favourably
on the Flemish cause.' [2]

During the siege of Gotha Count Louis had been
sent on business to the Elector Augustus by the Prince
of Orange. In the middle of February he wrote a report
to the Landgrave Philip of the negotiations between

[1] Koch, *Quellen*, ii. 40–43, and i. 54.
[2] Groen van Prinsterer, viii. 481, 491–492.

him and the Elector. The Elector, he said, had signified that ' the Prince of Orange must declare himself a believer in the Augsburg Confession, retain his governorship, and engage to manage the affairs of the country for the best interest of King Philip ; if thereupon ' the King went on with his warlike policy, that would be regarded as a sufficient declaration of war ; if the King complained of the Prince, the Elector would stand by the latter and stir up the King's anger ; when the waters began to overflow their channels, then they could learn to swim.' Augustus undertook ' to engage the army before Gotha not to fight in the interests of Spain.' On the Elector asking him if troops were already equipped, Count Louis showed him the muster-roll of over 6,000 cavalry and four regiments of infantry, to which Count Günther had pledged himself to add 4,000 cavalry. Augustus and Count Günther confidently expected that ' the whole of the troops before Gotha' would take service under the Orange princes, ' and, indeed,' Louis further added, ' the captains are adopting distinctive badges, and the Elector himself has asked for and volunteered to wear the wooden platter which is the badge of the Gueux.' [1]

These transactions did not remain hidden from the King. One of his commissioners wrote to him from the camp at Gotha on February 19, 1567 : ' Your Majesty has already been apprised of the fact that the Flemings are carrying on secret machinations in different directions, and that the two elder sons of the Landgrave of Hesse have already entered their service, and also Duke Julius of Brunswick, the son of Duke Henry. Count Louis of Nassau has been in the camp here the

[1] Groen van Prinsterer, *Supplément*, pp. 55*-56*.

last days for the purpose of enlisting soldiers. His special business was to arrange with the Elector that at the end of the campaign here, he (Augustus) should place his infantry and cavalry at the Count's service.' [1] When the Emperor remonstrated with the Elector on account of these transactions, Augustus flatly denied the charge, saying that he had nothing whatever to do with the rebellion in the Netherlands. 'Indeed, though it is true,' he wrote to Maximilian on March 29, 'that Count Louis of Nassau has been here in the camp and has had speech with me, nevertheless, as to any question of my supplying him or the Netherlands with any of the troops of the Holy Empire, he has not breathed a syllable to this effect, much less intimated that he was thinking of supporting a rebellion of subjects against their rulers.' Had the Count made any such request, Augustus went on, 'I should have answered him—of that your Majesty may be positively certain—in a manner consistent with my most loyal fidelity to your Majesty and with the duties of my office.' It would never, he added, enter his head to prescribe to other rulers laws and limitations for the treatment of their subjects, especially in matters of religion. 'It is, moreover, well known to your Majesty what my feelings are towards the whole house of Austria, and also towards the royal Majesty of Spain, and that ever since my rule began I have not only never acted in opposition to them, but have been glad to show them as much serviceable and friendly goodwill as possible. I beg, therefore, that your Majesty will not place any credence on such accusations against me.' He left it with the Emperor to consider whether it would not be well 'to issue a

[1] Koch, *Quellen*, ii. 36.

new order by which the cavalry before Gotha might be placed at the disposal of the King of Spain for better resistance against the rebels in the Netherlands.[1]

Thus the Elector Augustus, when only shortly before he had promised Count Louis ' to engage the army before Gotha not to fight in the interests of Spain.' On October 15, 1566, the Regent Margaret had already reported to Madrid that there was talk of a contemplated partition of the Netherlands. Count Brederode was to have Holland ; Gueldres was to be divided between the Dukes of Cleves and Lorraine ; Brabant was to be made over to the Prince of Orange ; Flanders, Artois, and Hainau to the King of France ; Friesland and Ober-yssel to the Elector Augustus of Saxony.[2] The Elector emphatically denied all knowledge of such a scheme : he had not the slightest share in ' such astounding conspiracies ; ' but, in spite of his protestations, ' all manner of rumours were in the air.' Again, in May 1568, the Emperor wrote to him : ' It is persistently rumoured in some quarters that your grace is in collusion with the Prince of Orange, and that you cherish the design of invading Friesland.'[3]

While the enlistment of troops was going on in several Protestant territories of the Empire to help Orange in the invasion of the Netherlands—still an integral portion of the Empire—the King of Spain, on the other hand, was authorised by the Emperor to recruit freely in German territory for resistance against the rebellious Netherlanders. For Philip II., as

---

[1] Groen van Prinsterer, *Suppl.* pp. 59*-63*.

[2] Gachard, *Correspondance*, i. 473.

[3] Groen van Prinsterer, iii. 218. In the year 1569 King Philip wrote : ' Je crois que c'est au duc Auguste et à Schwendi que nous devons la guerre ' (Gachard, *Corresp.*, ii. 54, note 1).

sovereign lord of a country whose seventeen provinces constituted the Burgundian circle, was, in Maximilian's estimation, ' a very important member of the Holy Empire : he contributed largely to the imperial revenues and he had a seat and a vote at the Diets. He had volunteered a considerable sum from his Spanish revenues for the last expedition against the Turks. He (Maximilian) could not allow a country which formed part of the Empire to be exposed to such frightful devastation, and he must take steps to put a stop to the ravages.'

In consequence of the favour shown by him to the King of Spain, Maximilian was denounced in Protestant leaflets as ' another Julian ' who had seceded from the ' Gospel.' [1] ' In all countries,' writes a chronicler of the year 1567, ' lampoons and libellous pamphlets were disseminated, unjustly accusing the Imperial Majesty of godless, infamous alliances with the enemies of Christendom.' [2] On the other hand, among the Protestant Estates it was rumoured abroad that in his Flemish policy the Emperor was only keeping up a semblance of friendship with Spain. He had said to Count Günther of Schwarzburg that he must have a regard for Spain because his sons were there, and because he expected large money aids from the King against the Turks ; ' if he issued severe mandates no attention must be paid to them.' [3] The Duke of Alva, who had been charged by Philip to punish with steel and with blood the ' high treason to God and the King ' committed in the Netherlands, entertained constant sus-

[1] See the poem, *Die Grabschrift*; Koch, *Quellen*, i. 38–42, and ii. 7-26, 165.

[2] Spangenberg, *Sächsische Chronika*, p. 708.

[3] Report in Groen van Prinsterer, *Supplément*, p. 58*.

picions of the Emperor's ' secret encouragement of the rebels.'

On his departure from Spain Alva received instructions ' to take prisoners all the leading men of the country who were either guilty, or under suspicion, and to make examples of them by the infliction of punishment.' [1] At the head of some 24,000 men the Duke advanced into the doomed provinces, and shortly after his arrival, on September 5, 1567, he organised his famous ' Council of Tumults,' the so-called ' Council of Blood,' which filled the land with terror, drove thousands of inhabitants into voluntary exile, and condemned other thousands to the hands of the executioner or to banishment. ' Every day,' Alva reported to the King on January 19, 1568, ' sees some of the rebels and originators of the risings brought to trial, examined, and punished by confiscation of goods.' When the question of a general pardon was raised Alva exclaimed : ' It would be premature ; it is out of the question ; first of all the towns must be punished, good round sums must be squeezed out of private purses, the royal revenues must be secured, the privileges altered. Before pardon can be proclaimed, fear must hover ruthlessly over the head of each individual, fear must bring the towns to the point of submitting to anything and everything, fear must wring larger sums out of those who are ready to buy themselves off, and fear must humble the Estates from the arrogance and presumption which would lead them to withstand the proposals with regard to the royal revenues.' [2]

Meanwhile the Empire ' had fallen into heavy

---

[1] Alva's letter to Philip, June 9, 1568, in Gachard, *Corresp.* ii. 29.

[2] Gachard, ii. 4-7. See Holzwarth, ii. 249 ff.

tribulation owing to the Flemish affairs ; preachers
and missionaries from the Netherlands were agitating
among the people.'

'The Netherlands,' wrote the town council of Cologne
on March 21, 1567, 'have come to misery and ruin of
person and goods in consequence of the seditious,
heretical preachers : all pious people should take warning
by what is going on ; but it seems that these same
preachers are gaining over the inhabitants of these
parts, especially of the town of Cologne, to their corrupt
doctrines.' [1]   Already, before the arrival of Alva, gangs
of sedition-mongers from Utrecht and St. Trond had
raised alarming disturbances in Cologne. They had
fixed on this town as the basis of their operations, and
they began an extensive enrolment of followers all
round the neighbourhood. Their recruits did enormous
damage by pillaging and levying contributions. Orange
himself, as part of his preparations for a campaign
against Alva, 'levied contributions on the people and
extracted money from the town council and the cathedral
chapter.' It was feared that the whole district of the
Lower Rhine would be drawn into the Netherlandish
disturbances. Alva wrote threatening letters complaining that the town council of Cologne 'gave lodging
and harbour to rebels who deserved punishment.' The
university and the ecclesiastical body required of the
council to issue stern prohibitive measures against
the swarms of sectarians who poured in daily from
the Netherlands : Anabaptists, Sacramentarians, Zwinglians, Calvinists, Libertines, and others ; the town,
they said, was threatened ' with tumult, danger, oppression, damage, heresy, corruption, and insurrection.' [2]

[1] Ennen, iv. 775.   [2] Ibid. iv. 838-844.

In the Duchy of Cleves, in the year 1567, a new king of the Anabaptists arose—the shoemaker John Wilhelmsen from Roermonde, who with a gang of 300 men went on for many years, spreading terror through the whole country by pillage and slaughter. He introduced polygamy, published a pamphlet entitled ' Von dem grossen und lästerlichen Missbrauch des unreinen Ehestandes,' [1] and prepared a new edition of Roth-mann's *Restitution oder Wiederbringung des rechten und wahrhaften Verstandes der vornehmsten Artikel des christlichen Glaubens, Lehr und Lebens.*[2] ' Stealing and pilfering,' he taught, ' were no sins, but, on the contrary, lawful actions in this new kingdom of God. All the goods of the earth were the property of Jesus Christ ; now, he and his followers were disciples of Christ, and had, therefore, a joint right in the goods of the earth.' [3]

' Ever since the beginning of the military proceedings in the Netherlands,' writes a contemporary, ' the Holy Empire has been in constant unrest, and the pestiferous vapours, for many years past diffused through all countries by the schisms in religion, the turbulence of the nobles and people, and the general decay of discipline, morals, and respectability, have been aggravated by all sorts of extraordinary rumours of formidable

[1] *Of the great and scandalous Abuse of the impure Institution of Marriage.*

[2] *Restitution or Restoration of the right and true Understanding of the principal Articles of the Christian Faith, Doctrine, and Life* Concerning this pamphlet see our remarks, Vol. v. 468.

[3] Bouterwek, ' Zur Wiedertäufer-Literatur,' in the *Zeitschr. des bergischen Geschichtsvereins,* i. 313–315. In the year 1574 the king of this new kingdom of God was betrayed, brought before a court of justice, with his gang, and in 1580 he was burnt alive at Cleve. See also Scholten, *Die Stadt Cleve* (Cleve, 1881), p. 592.

intrigues and conspiracies, plotted by the Evangelicals
against the Catholics and *vice versa* by the Catholics
against the Evangelicals.' [1]

It was reported that ' again in 1567 another gigantic
plot would come into operation against the Catholics : '
that ' the Margrave Hans of Brandenburg was enlisting
thousands of infantry and cavalry ; Poland and Sweden,
Mecklenburg and Anhalt, many counts, many of the
great nobles, all the malcontents, were in league together,
and that their intention was to exterminate the whole
body of Catholics, first of all Duke Albert of Bavaria.'
' And let this said Duke, and the Archbishop of Salzburg
and the Cardinal of Augsburg be well on their guard, the
Bavarian being chief head of the papists ; his grace of
Salzburg rich in gold and power ; his grace of Augsburg
the one who has sought most to contrive the ruin of
the Confession of Augsburg, and the exaltation of the
Popish Church.   Nobody will be spared ; fire, plunder,
expulsion, and ruin will overtake all alike.' [2]

Arrangements, in which France took a leading part,
were made at the same time for inciting the Protestant
Estates to rebellion.   In the spring of 1567 ambassadors
from the French King, Charles IX., appeared at the
different Protestant courts with warnings against the
hostile designs of the Catholic powers, and overtures
for an *entente cordiale* between the Protestant princes
and the King of France for mutual defence and protection.   A pamphlet emanating from France announced
that ' the Kings of Spain and Portugal, the Dukes of
Savoy and Bavaria, the Pope, and even the Emperor

---

[1] *Von Abnehmen christenlichen Glaubens und friedfertigen gott-
seligen Wesens durch einen Liebhaber der Wahrheit gestellt* (1571),
pp. 9–10.

[2] Kluckhohn, *Briefe*, ii. 73, note 1.

Maximilian had banded together for the extirpation of the Huguenots and Lutherans.' The Electors Frederic of the Palatinate and Augustus of Saxony were to be deposed, and the Emperor's two brothers put in their places; all princes who set themselves against the league were to be dethroned; all preachers who opposed it to be driven out of the country; the adherents of the new doctrines were to be compelled to attend the Mass or else rendered harmless by confiscation of goods, expulsion, and even punishment. 'A Rhenish patriarch' was to reinstate the Catholic Church all over Germany; Albert of Bavaria 'was to be the Pope's lieutenant and the clergy's commander-in-chief in this great work or war.' [1]

In all this there was not a word of truth. But all the protestations of the Emperor and of Duke Albert against so 'lying and venomous a report,' and all their efforts to organise strong proceedings against the inventors and disseminators of the falsehoods were utterly fruitless.

The Elector Frederic of the Palatinate was more willing than any of his colleagues to accept the French overtures. His peculiar position in the Empire as a Calvinist, and his constant fear that the Emperor might some day proceed to the execution of his sentence against him, drove him into closer relations with foreign powers. By his exertions an assembly was convened at Maulbronn in July 1567, and resolutions were framed by himself, Duke Christopher of Würtemberg, and the Margrave Charles of Baden, with a view to forming an alliance between all the Protestant Estates of the Empire

[1] *Auszüge* in Koch, ii. 135-137; Kluckhohn, *Briefe*, ii. 50-51. See v. Bezold, i. 21.

and France. The French King was actually to be allowed to enlist German troops, in the event of a foreign war, on condition of his promising ' not to let himself be incensed against the Evangelical princes in religious and other matters, above all in regard to the Council of Trent, and not to allow the decrees of this Council to be enforced in France.' [1]   On October 10, 1567, the Emperor wrote to Albert of Bavaria that the Elector Palatine and the Duke of Würtemberg had joined in a league with France and that watch must be kept over them. The Elector Frederic, he said on December 8, is behaving in his usual way ; he (the Emperor) had warned him faithfully and solemnly ; 'if he would not take the warning he would find himself sooner or later in the wrong box.' [2]

The point of chief importance to the Maulbronn confederates was to win over the Elector Augustus of Saxony to their decisions. But Augustus did not believe in the news of the dangerous plotting and planning of the Catholic powers ; it was ' nothing more,' he wrote, ' than the idle fancies and tales of some agitator who wished to excite mistrust and suspicion between the Emperor and the electors and princes. The banding together of all the Evangelical Estates would cause a great sensation and have very little effect, owing chiefly to the discord, divisions, and controversies between the different Estates in matters of doctrine and faith.   There was no doubt that it was these dissensions, more than anything else, which gave encouragement to the adversaries. ' To what extent they would be able to keep their deliberations secret,

---

[1] Kluckhohn, *Briefe*, ii. 66–67.
[2] *Briefwechsel*, pp. 176–177.

and what sort of co-operation and mutual help and
support might be expected before uniformity of doctrine
was accomplished, was easy to imagine.' [1]

Only once more did it happen that the Catholic
and Protestant Estates of the Empire made common
cause together, and that was at the time when Duke
Alva began to extend his military despotism to the
Empire also. On November 15, 1556, the Emperor
had authorised the King of Spain, by a public letter,
to enlist as many as 10,000 infantry and 3,000 cavalry
in-his dominions ; Alva had also been empowered by
an ordinance of the Imperial Privy Council to pursue
with his troops the rebels in those districts of the
Empire which were adjacent to-the Netherlands. On
the strength of this ordinance these troops, in April
1563, surprised the Bush-Gueux in the neighbourhood
of the village of Dalhem, near Erkelenz in the Duchy
of Jülich, scattered them in all directions, and inflicted
also all sorts of injuries on inhabitants of Jülich. The
Duke of Jülich-Cleve, who complained of this proceeding, was put off with empty excuses ; the Emperor
did not even enter a protest in favour of the sufferers. [2]
In addition to this, Alva, mixing himself up in the
innermost affairs of the Empire, espoused the cause of
the Archbishop of Treves in a quarrel between that
dignitary and the town, and admitted several hundred
arquebusiers within the city walls. Fear was entertained that Treves, ' a key of the Rhine and the Moselle,'
would be wrested from the Empire. [3] In consequence of
this proceeding the electors and a few other princes

---

[1] Kluckhohn, *Briefe*, ii. 80.   See Kugler, ii. 517-520.
[2] See *Zeitschrift des bergischen Geschichtsvereins*, vii. 97-103.
[3] Kluckhohn, *Briefe*, ii. 236.

sent an embassy to Vienna in September 1568 to solicit
the Emperor to take serious measures for putting a stop
to the Flemish disturbances so dangerous to the Empire,
and for the removal of the Spanish troops. Saxony
and Brandenburg were specially urgent in begging
Maximilian to take up arms himself for the protection
of the Imperial Netherlands ; they assured him that
all the Estates would stand by him collectively with
body and goods. They obtained the promise that a
deputation should be sent in the Emperor's name to
mediate between Alva and Orange, and that Maximilian's
brother, Archduke Charles, should go to Madrid as
ambassador to King Philip. In the Archduke's instructions it was stated that if the King did not alter his
procedure, the Emperor would not be able to resist the
pressure exercised on him in the Empire to induce him to
go to war : Philip was requested to clear away his foreign
troops from the Netherlands, to accept the Emperor
as a mediator for peace, and to look favourably on
an imperial embassy sent to Alva and Orange with a
view to procuring an armistice.

But Maximilian did not care for strong measures
in any one direction. He said frankly to the Spanish
ambassador at his court that the despatch of an archduke to Spain was only intended ' to stop the mouths
of the people.' Philip having become a widower in
1568, Maximilian bethought him of negotiating a close
family alliance with the King of Spain ; he ordered
the Archduke, already on his way to Madrid, to offer
Philip his (the Emperor's) eldest daughter in marriage.
Before even Philip had given his answer with regard to
the Netherlands the Emperor told him that he should
be content with whatever answer he gave ; he only

begged that it might be couched in such a form that he
could show it to the electors.

'What Maximilian heard from Spain was a bitter
pill to swallow.'

Philip rejected all foreign intervention. His answer
was as follows :—' In matters of religion he would never
tolerate anything that could be prejudicial to the Roman
Catholic religion, or its laws and institutions ; his
vassals and subjects had neither right nor reason to
complain of him on this score, still less were the German
princes entitled to do so. From the religious schism,
as experience had shown, anarchy, ruin, and misery had
resulted in all countries. In the Netherlands he had
been obliged to show an example by severe penalties in
order adequately to punish the unlimited and dangerous
insolence of popular agitators : sovereigns had absolute
power over their dominions. With the neighbouring
princes, who wanted to dictate to him what means of
defence he ought to select, he had always been on
friendly terms, and he had allowed their subjects every
possible freedom and opportunity for trade ; on several
occasions invasion of their territories would have been
fully justifiable on his part ; but each time he had
displayed moderation, and had forbidden any such
proceeding. He had not even taken strong measures
against the Count of Emden, who had given free passage
to the rebels when they made a forcible inroad into
Gröningen and Oberyssel, and allowed them facilities
for obtaining provisions. Although Duke Alva might
then easily have occupied his possessions in East
Friesland, he had abstained from doing so because this
small district belonged to the Empire and he did not
wish to give offence to the Emperor ; he had protected

the lands of Liège and Cambray, which the Prince of
Orange intended to devastate. It was in every respect
unbecoming to intervene on behalf of this Prince of
Orange, who, as vassal, as Governor of Holland, Seeland,
Utrecht, and Burgundy, and as member of the Council
of State, had broken every one of his oaths to his King ;
who had placed himself at the head of the insurrection,
and who was responsible for all the misfortune of the
Netherlands, for all the sacrilegious destruction of
churches, for all the deeds of violence committed against
God and against the King. So long as things remained
on their present footing it would be irreconcilable with
the royal dignity and authority that Frederic should
be pardoned and reinstated in his possessions. In a
special memorial to the Emperor, Philip expressed his
wonder and regret that Orange should have been able
to collect so large an army in Germany for the purpose
of using force against his prince and lord ; and that in
such an enterprise he should have received support
from princes, towns, and private inhabitants of the
Empire, and that the Emperor should not have had
power to prevent the calamity. No less did he deplore
the honour that had been shown to the rebel in sending
an archduke, the Emperor's brother, to Spain on his
behalf. What, however, grieved him most deeply,
Philip said to the Archduke, was the double-faced
attitude of the Emperor towards religion ; he warned
him not to omit the public acts which he owed to the
faith, to keep in the right and true way, and to fulfil
his duty as a Christian and a Catholic prince.

'The pill was bitter, but the Emperor gulped it
down.'

With regard to the Netherlands he answered the

King that his justification, exculpation, and explanation were grounded in the main on reason and right.
He did not, however, dare impart the contents of the
royal answer to the Elector word for word; by so
saying he drew on himself a reprimand from Philip.
No earthly consideration, the latter told him, ought,
under existing circumstances, to prevent him speaking
out his true opinion, nor could he, for the life of him,
understand why the princes of the Empire should be
angry at his making open confession of the Catholic
faith.   He then instructed the Duke of Alva to send an
exact copy of the answer to the Electors of Mayence
and Treves, in order that they might learn his true
opinions.[1]

With regard to religion the Emperor gave the King
the most positive assurances of fidelity to the Catholic
faith.[2]   But to the delegate of the Saxon Elector, on the
contrary, he spoke, in October 1568, of his sympathy with
the Protestants, and of how it had exposed him to
threats, not only from the Pope and the Spanish King,
but also from his own brothers; in fact he talked in
such a way that the Elector Augustus exhorted him to
acknowledge the Augsburg Confession publicly and
decidedly, and ' to defy the idolatrous monk at Rome
with all his followers.'[3]   The Elector Palatine Frederic
also urged him to introduce the profession of the true
religion at his court, and not to let himself be misled any
longer ' by the tools and members of the abominable
Satan,' but to withstand the ' Satanic importunities '

---

[1] Ritter, *August von Sachsen und Friedrich III von der Pfalz*,
pp. 338–349; v. Bezold, i. 37–40; Holzwarth, ii. 318–332.

[2] Koch, *Quellen*, ii. 100.

[3] Weber, *Des Kurfürsten August Verhandlungen*, p. 336.

of the papal legate at his court.[1] It had cost the papal
legate, Cardinal Commendone, considerable trouble to
gain admittance to the palace of this Emperor, who made
a show of his attachment to the Catholic faith. ' Is
it not a scandal,' Duke Albert of Bavaria had written
to Maximilian, ' that embassies from the Turks and
from other barbarous nations are welcomed with marks
of high honour, while all sorts of difficulties are thrown
in the way of receiving the legates of the Holy See ? ' [2]

With such duplicity the Emperor could not inspire
confidence anywhere. Duke Alva, in a letter to Philip
of September 18, 1568, gave unconcealed expression to
his contempt for Maximilian's weakness and deceitful-
ness, and said he suspected him of the design of con-
quering the Netherlands with the help of France.[3] . The
Spanish ambassador at Vienna was ordered by Alva to
signify to the Emperor that ' in order to cure the princes
of the Empire of their sympathy with the rebellious
Netherlands, Spain might at any moment instigate a
rising of the German nobility against Saxony, the
Palatinate, and other Estates ; it was only for the
Emperor's sake that this means had not yet been
resorted to, but it might perhaps become necessary.[4]

[1] Kluckhohn, *Briefe*, ii. 272-275.

[2] Wimmer, pp. 72 ff. ; v. Aretin, *Bayerns auswärtige Verhältnisse*,
p. 60.

[3] v. Bezold, i. 61-62.

[4] *Ibid.* i. 33-34. On Nov. 3, 1568, Granvella wrote to Philip II. :
'. . . Si les Électeurs du Rhin et d'autres princes allemands, malgré le
préjudice que leur a causé la première expédition du prince d'Orange,
persistent à le favoriser, le roi pourrait occuper leurs États jusqu'au
Rhin en les traitant comme rebelles à Dieu et hérétiques' (Gachard,
Corresp. de Philippe II, ii. 46).

CHAPTER III

GERMAN PRINCES IN THE PAY OF FOREIGN POWERS—
FRESH CAMPAIGNS IN FRANCE IN THE SECOND
HUGUENOT WAR—DEVASTATION AND ANARCHY IN
THE EMPIRE, 1567–1569

LITTLE confidence could be placed in the Emperor, and
little could the electors and princes trust each other,
as they were ' for the most part in the pay of foreign
powers,' from whom both they and their councillors
received considerable sums. France and Spain especially vied with each other in large bids to the princes,
whom they wished to use for their respective purposes.
' The French reckon on the dissensions in Germany,'
wrote the Venetian Giovanni Michiele in the year 1561,
' and they foster them by means of large pensions, which
they pay secretly to many of the princes, as, for instance,
the Count Palatine, the Duke of Würtemberg, the
Landgrave of Hesse, the Dukes of Saxony, the sons of
John Frederic, the Margrave of Baden, and others.' [1]
The yearly salaries which the French King bestowed
on his ' German pensionaries ' were calculated to amount
to 100,000 livres. [2] Margaret of Parma, the Regent of
the Netherlands, fixed the sum at an even higher
amount. When in 1566 she received 75,000 ducats
from King Philip for the German pensionaries, she wrote

---

[1] Tommaseo, *Relations des Ambassadeurs Vénitiens sur les Affaires
de France au 16e Siècle*, i. 444.

[2] See Groen van Prinsterer, iv. 69.

to Madrid that she had been informed that France paid
half as much again.[1]   Among the Spanish pensionaries
the following princes, although Protestants, were
included :—The Elector Joachim II. of Brandenburg
and the Electoral Prince John George, the Margrave
Hans of Brandenburg,[2] Duke Adolf IX. of Holstein,
who also received a pension from Philip's mortal enemy,
Elizabeth of England,[3] Duke Francis II. of Sachsen-
Lauenburg, the Dukes Ernest, Eric, and Philip of
Brunswick,[4] and the Counts of Schauenburg, of Schwarzburg, of Westerburg, and of Eberstein.[5]   In the pay
of France were the Saxon Dukes John Frederic and
John William with yearly pensions each of 13,000
florins,[6] and the Landgrave William of Hesse, who
received yearly 10,000 livres.[7]   Dukes Christopher and
Louis of Würtemberg also received annual foreign
pensions.[8]

The cleverest and the most unscrupulous of these
princely intriguers was the Count Palatine Georg Hans
of Veldeuz, a collateral member of the Palatine electoral
house.   He had been a pensioner of the French crown
since 1564, and in 1567 he wanted to lead the army of
mercenaries he had enlisted against the Huguenots, but
his offer was flatly refused, and he sought service for his
troops elsewhere.   He offered them at one and the same
time to the Prince of Orange against the Duke of Alva

[1] Reiffenberg, p. 219.
[2] *Ibid.* p. 11; v. Bezold, i. 59.   See Sugenheim, *Frankreichs Einfluss,*
i. 289.
[3] Groen van Prinsterer, iii. xxxii. 492.
[4] Reiffenberg, p. 159; Groen van Prinsterer, iii. xxxii.
[5] Lossen, *Kölnischer Krieg,* i. 99–100.
[6] Arndt, *Archiv der sächsischen Geschichte,* iii. 212.
[7] v. Bezold, i. 45, note 3.
[8] Sugenheim, *Frankreichs Einfluss,* i. 290.

and to the Duke of Alva against the Prince of Orange.[1]
He would have liked best to send them into the field
against his own kinsman, the Elector Palatine, and the
Emperor would have been glad if he had undertaken
the chastisement of this refractory subject.[2] When,
however, the execution of the sentence against the
latter fell through, Georg Hans denied having planned
it. In June 1566 he wrote to the Prince of Orange that
he was ' a born German prince, faithful to the Augsburg Confession,' and one who would not assist ' in the
abominable work of suppressing the true faith and establishing the idolatrous religion, especially against members
of the Holy Empire.' [3] The Count Palatine Wolfgang of
Zweibrücken, he said, had brought him to see that he
must not undertake an enterprise so unpleasing ' to
God and to his fatherland,' or ' expose his conscience
to the gnawing of the worm.' [4] Nevertheless, this same
Wolfgang had entertained similar plans the year before,
and had offered the King of Spain his services against
the Calvinistic Netherlands.[5]

Before the *entente cordiale* proposed by the French
Government to the Protestant princes in the spring of
1567 could be brought to pass, a fresh Huguenot war
had broken out in France ; and the Elector Palatine
Frederic, who was the most zealous co-operator with the
French crown, now bestirred himself hurriedly to help his
co-religionists against France. This prince, who considered himself a special instrument chosen by God for
the destruction of ' all popish idolatry,' and believed him-

---

[1] Groen van Prinsterer, iii. 172–173.
[2] Kluckhohn, *Friedrich der Fromme*, p. 327 ; v. Bezold, i. 32–33.
[3] Groen van Prinsterer, iii. 256 ; *cf.* iii. 172–173.
[4] *Ibid.* iii. 261–263.
[5] Philip's despatch of March 15, 1567, in Reiffenberg, p. 223.

self to be directly guided by the Holy Ghost, was anxious also to use all his energies in propagating 'the Holy Gospel' among foreign nations—that is to say, 'in converting the world to Calvinism.'[1]   A military spirit in politics had become dominant at the court of Heidelberg since the Augsburg Diet of 1566 ; it was not, however. Frederic, 'the pious Josias,' who was the ruling man ; politically he was entirely dependent on the guidance of his theologian Olevian and his two fanatically Calvinistic councillors, Christopher Ehem, 'the sworn enemy of the House of Austria,' and Wenzel Zuleger, to whom 'bitter hatred of popery' was ascribed as the highest praise.   'With Olevian and Ehem,' wrote the theologian Ursinus in confidence to his friend Crato, 'things are going just as you describe.   The reason of it is that Olevian rules Zuleger, and Zuleger rules Ehem, but Ehem rules Josias.'[2]   Frederic's second son, John Casimir, the chief supporter of the warlike policy, was in close connection with these councillors.

John Casimir had received no scholarly education ; he had only acquired the accomplishments of a knight. As a lad of fourteen he already distinguished himself at Nancy, at the court of Lorraine, by his love of drink. 'You will soon drink away your reason and understanding,' said his father to the fourteen-year-old boy.[3] 'I have been nothing but a poor knight's son all my life,' he himself wrote in his last years, 'and from my youth I have been fond of drinking wine.'   His nativity, the astrologers said, was cast under the planet Mars :

[1] '. . . n'ay trouvé au Prince Palatin que affections cherres de calviniser le monde . . .' (a letter of Leonhard von Ebbe to Louis of Nassau, March 2, 1573, in Groen van Prinsterer, iv. 71).

[2] Kluckhohn, *Friedrich der Fromme*, p. 431.

[3] *Idem, Briefe,* i. li.

as sister's son to Albrecht Alcibiades he had 'margravian blood and much margravian spirit.' He did, indeed, strikingly resemble this lawless incendiary ; he used to say that another Margrave and another Duke Maurice were greatly needed. Like Maurice and Albert, he, too, was wholly destitute of religious principles: he served the Evangelical cause because it suited his own interests.[1]

When, in the year 1567, the fight in the Netherlands began under Duke Alva, and the Prince of Condé raised the standard of rebellion in France, troops were recruited on German soil both for the King of Spain and the Prince of Orange on the one hand, and for the King of France and the Huguenots on the other. The bigoted Lutheran Duke, John William of Saxony, son-in-law of the Elector Palatine, as a pensioner of the French throne, set out with his troops, his wife accompanying him, to the succour of the 'popish monarch.' John Casimir, on the other hand, joined forces with Condé, and declared himself ready to put auxiliary troops in the field against the King. The Emperor sent a special ambassador to Frederic and John Casimir at Heidelberg to countermand the expedition to France, and ordered the troops they had levied to be disbanded on the strength of the Landfriede and the imperial plenary power ; but his protests were as fruitless as those made by some of the Protestant Estates. The Landgrave William of Hesse wrote to the Elector on October 22, 1567, that no help must be given to the Huguenots, for it was a false statement that the war was in the cause of religion. He had heard that Condé was trying to deprive the King, to whom he had pledged

[1] See the admirable character sketch of Casimir in v. Bezold, i. 13–17.

his faith, of his country and his subjects, and to declare himself king. He could not see that such conduct was a matter of religion or taught in the Gospel; it ought rather to be looked on as a public and punishable act of rebellion and high treason. If they supported such a movement ' the papists would crow over them and declare that now it was plain to see what was their object in this pretended religious war; they would make it a reason, not for making an attack, but for the formation in their defence of the long-rumoured league, and in the persecution by fire and sword of all the members of the Protestant religion.' To the Elector Palatine's councillor Zuleger, who was anxious to carry out the expedition, William and his brother Louis answered ' they must be careful not to introduce into the Empire evils of all sorts which they would not be able to get rid of without the greatest danger and difficulty; also they must not run the risk of provoking great potentates, for whom all the princes of the Augsburg Confession put together would not be a match.' [1]

In December 1567 the military expedition to France began with a frightful devastation of the Count Palatine Wolfgang's territory of Zweibrücken; the poor inhabitants were made to atone for the hostile attitude taken up by the Count Palatine at the Diet of Augsburg against his Calvinist cousin Frederic. Casimir's undisciplined

---

[1] Kluckhohn, *Briefe*, ii. 115–142. William wrote also to the Prince of Orange on Nov. 1, 1567, that ' the affairs of their co-religionists in France had more the aspect of a rebellion than a reasonable remonstrance ' (Groen van Prinsterer, iii. 128–129). ' Omnes humores nostræ reipublicae sunt in maximo motu,' he wrote to Christopher of Würtemberg on Nov. 12, 1567 : ' Deus avertat, ne inde fortis et indissolubilis sequatur apoplexia ' (Kluckhohn, ii. 127, note 2).

soldiers, about 11,000 men, behaved in France also, both to friends and foes, like ' German barbarians,' and the Huguenots themselves were glad ' to be rid of their friends.' After the conclusion of the peace of Longjumeau (March 23, 1568) matters had nearly come to a battle between the troops of John Casimir and those of his brother-in-law, John William.[1]

The Peace of Longjumeau lasted only a few weeks. The Huguenots took up arms again, and they and Charles IX. recommenced levying troops ' on the soil of the Holy Empire, where everything was to be had for money, and where the Emperor was only a shadow.' In order to secure freedom for recruiting in the domains of the ecclesiastical electors, Charles IX. told these princes that he had only granted the Huguenots religious liberty until he had the means of bringing them to obedience.[2] The Prince of Condé entered into alliance with Elizabeth of England. In 1563 this Queen had called Condé a scoundrel who deserved to be thrown to the dogs, because he had violated the compact made with her ;[3] now, as a return for fresh help, she instructed him to place in her hands the ports of Brittany and Normandy. Condé, so Hubert Languet understood, had promised the Queen to put Calais in her hands also.[4] In Germany Condé and Coligny found ' staunch supporters ' in the Elector Palatine Frederic and the Count Palatine Wolfgang of Zweibrücken. Wolfgang had for years past zealously opposed the ' accursed, insurrectionary, Calvinistic sect,' with which, he said, ' no Christian ought to hold communion ; ' but when, in August 1568, the Prince of Condé and Coligny held

---

[1] v. Bezold, i. 29.   [2] Kervyn de Lettenhove, ii. 174.
[3] See above, p. 9.   [4] *Epist.* lib. i. 73; Kervyn de Lettenhove, ii. 174–177.

out advantageous prospects to him, he declared himself
ready to support the Calvinists, and pledged himself
to bring up to them in September 6,000 German cavalry
and three regiments of infantry. Formerly a most
bitter opponent of the Calvinist Elector Palatine, he
now became reconciled with Frederic, received a loan
from him, and, on his recommendation, obtained from
Elizabeth the promise of considerable subsidies.[1]

Deeds of fearful plunder and devastation, similar
to those which in 1567 had been perpetrated in Wolfgang's territory during John Casimir's expedition to
France, were now enacted by Wolfgang's lawless hordes
in Alsace and the neighbouring bishoprics. In order
to revenge himself for former attacks and to forestall
fresh ones, the King of France wanted to transplant
the war into the Empire. At the commencement of
the winter of 1568 the Duke of Aumale began to treat
the districts of Veldenz, Strasburg, and the Palatinate
as hostile territory. In February 1569 Georg Hans
of Veldenz, in a letter to the Margrave Charles of Baden,
described as follows the acts of pillage of the French,
and their outrages against men, women, and children :—
' All the inhabitants fled from the villages ; on one day
as many as eighteen children were found dead in a
street ; and still every day women and children are
found dead in the forests. Besides which they strangled
many of the men, and often roasted their feet in the
fire in order to get money from them. In consequence
of all this misery we went with a safe-conduct to the

---

[1] Bachmann, *Herzog Wolfgang's Kriegsverrichtungen*, pp. 25 ff. See
K. Menzel, *Wolfgang von Zweibrücken, Pfalzgraf bei Rhein, Herzog in
Baiern, Graf von Veldenz, der Stammvater des baierischen Königs-
hauses*, 1536–1569. Compiled with the help of Schwartz's *Literary
Leavings* (Munich, 1893), pp. 502 ff.

Duke of Aumale, who gave us the comfortable assurance
that no harm should befall us. He added, however,
that he had no control whatever over his soldiers, as they
had not been paid for a long time, and he was therefore
obliged to shut his eyes to what was going on. Moreover, the captains had been directed, on their return
march, to ravage the German lands in the same way
that the Germans had devastated France, and to bring
back with them well-laden wagons. These orders
they executed so faithfully that from one village alone
they carried off eighty horses and 600 head of cattle,
besides everything else they found there; after which
they burnt down the village, and they treated other
villages in like manner.'[1] A French agent who was
taken prisoner disclosed that there was a design hatching
at the French court 'for the conquest of Germany.'
France wished to join with Spain in a military attack
on the Empire; Philip II., however, was by no means
in favour of an extension of French dominion in the
direction of the Rhine. Nevertheless, the Duke of
Alva placed troops at the disposal of the French King,
but forbade him to take part in an attack on the
Empire.[2]

From all directions reports came to the Emperor
of 'the lamentable situation of the Empire, and of the
acts of violence, depredation, and cruelty of the troops
as they passed through the country,' and of the 'gar-
tenden Knechte' or Quartierer—that is, disbanded soldiers
—who loafed about in large gangs, quartered themselves
among the peasants or in small towns, and committed
the grossest excesses. In their train were often all
manner of 'vagabonds, beggars (of both sexes), gipsies,

[1] Kluckhohn, *Briefe*, ii. 295, 296.   [2] v. Bezold, i. 52–53.

jugglers, and so forth.' They were not satisfied with pillage, robbery, and murder, but they also set fire to the ripe cornfields. In Bavaria ' these infamous proceedings' went to such lengths that Duke Albrecht repeatedly issued orders for a general hunting down of the criminal gangs. It was decreed by a ducal mandate of May 1, 1568, that ' on the fifteenth day of every month all wardens, judges, and constables are to join together in pursuit of these ill-doers ; ' in later mandates it was stated that all who were caught were to be sent to the galleys, or punished by hanging.[1]

' Equally numerous and general were the complaints of extortion practised on subjects, and of the decay of trade and industry and the scandalous fraudulence of countless numbers of merchants.' George Ilsung, provincial governor of Suabia, who was sent round the Empire by Maximilian to obtain a loan of 40,000 florins on ' fair and certain security,' complained bitterly in a letter from Augsburg on December 21, 1569, that despite all his efforts he had nowhere been able to obtain any money : ' I have discovered that numbers of merchants here, of good standing, have openly defied the regulations of the Mint and the constitutions of the Empire, and within the last four months have sent more than 500,000 florins, at 50 per cent. interest, in a lump sum to Venice, to be thence transmitted to Turkey. The result is that not only here at Augsburg, but also at Nuremberg, there is such a scarcity of money that all trades are at a standstill ; no merchant can carry on dealings with another, or procure any money. This state of things is not only injurious to the common welfare of Germany, but also

---

[1] Westenrieder, *Beiträge*, viii. 295–300.

to the whole of Christendom.' Merchants who send good German coin out of the country must, in due time, get it back by bills of exchange. Hence such a rise in bills that honest traders are unable to get into their hands the money due to them abroad for German goods and necessary for carrying on their trade, except by losing 6, 7, or 8 per cent. on their bills. Through the neglect of the authorities it has come to this that 'neither is there any cash in hand nor are any bills on this place accepted! More thalers and florins are procurable at Constantinople and Alexandria than in the whole Roman Empire : the Turk is able to make war on us, not with his but with our money, freely and openly conveyed to him for the sake of filthy lucre.'[1]

The Bishop of Augsburg, Cardinal Otto von Truchsess, wrote from Rome to Duke Albert of Bavaria on January 29, 1569 : ' There is no doubt that disturbances of no slight nature are to be feared in the Empire, and all the more so because his Imperial Majesty has gone on so long shutting his eyes to the true state of things, instead of joining with your Grace and other loyal and peace-loving princes to preserve peace and right in the Empire.' The adversaries, as is plain to see, are not simply concerned about ecclesiastical property, ' they have designs also on the imperial crown, sceptre, and majesty, and the fatal policy of temporising, dissembling, sitting still and doing nothing, affords them encouragement and opportunity.' ' It is assuredly time that we should awake out of sleep, and, with God's grace, do our part in the matter. Thank God there is still so much strength

---

[1] Transactions of the Diet of 1570, i. 529-531, in the Frankfort Archives.

and opportunity at hand, that we shall be quite well able to protect and defend ourselves against all unlawful aggression, if only we set to work with manly courage and resolution. It must come to this in the end, and we are in a much more advantageous position now for taking the bull by the horns than we shall be later on if we let ourselves become further weakened and humiliated by continued procrastination. The intrigues carried on against us, both within and without the Empire, are well known, and our antagonists are growing daily more audacious, defiant, powerful, and insubordinate : their arrogance has reached such a height that they stop at nothing that it occurs to them to do. ' By the truth of God,' Otto complains again on February 12, ' there is more favour shown now at Vienna to the Turks than to the priests, be they legates or bishops. This is what things have come to.' ' Is it not lamentable that in Vienna every sort of proceeding against the true religion is allowed, and the authorities think to grow happy and rich by conceding, conniving, tacking, and temporising ? It is terrible. Would to God I could spend an hour or two with your Grace and confer with you on all these things. The pious Pope has formed a good plan, and has the best will and intentions. But he has no experience. There is no doubt, however, that if an earnest appeal were made by the Catholics to his Holiness, he would give them the necessary help, counsel, and support. Verily we have slumbered too long, and it is high time to make an end of dissensions and to band together with the few who are true-hearted and steadfast. Of these, within and without the Empire, there are still a good number, and they would be able to make no small show of strength.

The opposite party do not let the grass grow under their feet : with them to think is to do. If they are not afraid of acting on the offensive, why should the loyal party fear to act on the defensive, while the opportunity is there, and the necessity is plain as a pikestaff to our eyes ? The dastardly timidity, the cowardly prudence, the nervous anticipation of danger, which are exhibited, only improve the position of the enemies and encourage them to proceed to greater lengths. Whereas, if they saw that some few of us were preparing to withstand them, their insolence and audacity would be more likely to abate. If the two highest chiefs and the remainder of the Catholic potentates could all be united together, the game would be won. But if some of them should not agree to this, methinks that the remainder, who are truly God-fearing men, ought to have no scruples in joining forces together, as many of them as are able, in so righteous a cause, and that, trusting in God Almighty, they should as much as possible devote their combined intelligence, resources, and personal services to the business of defence. It would be a Christian venture, even if a hazardous one. But to do nothing, to sit still and wait for others to act, to be faint-hearted and frightened, to be without counsel and resources, to give the adversary the chance of further encroachments, to fear our enemies more than God, what else is this but to throw the game away ? ' [1]

In his answer to this letter the Duke declared himself in full agreement with the Cardinal ; ' but,' he said, ' what are we and other true-hearted Catholic princes and Estates to do, when, as your Grace knows, things are all at sixes and sevens ? ' In Vienna, where, according

[1] Wimmer, pp. 84-89.

to the Cardinal's statements, little trust is placed in the Catholic party, and the other party is petted and toadied, they will doubtless soon find out on what a tottering foundation they are building, and will repent of the course they have taken ; ' but as things are, there is nothing to be done but to commend the matter to God. For if help and counsel does not come to us from above, we cannot see how human power and understanding are to aid us any longer. To his Holiness the Pope we look for all that is gracious and fatherly. If also in these difficult and dangerous times any disaster should befall us, we should not cease to appeal for help and counsel to his Holiness, in the confidence that he would not desert us, seeing that we have never given anybody cause for enmity, except in the matter of religion.' Hinting at the Emperor, Albert said emphatically that the Cardinal knew who was the obstacle to a league such as he proposed, ' and we should cut a sorry figure if we solicited the great potentates to this effect, when there was little chance of any good result, and all sorts of danger in the undertaking.' The Elector Palatine, he said, was openly calling on the neighbouring governors of circles to unite in preparing for war against the King of France on behalf of the Empire, and to make an attack simultaneously from three directions.' ' Whether they will respond to the call, and whether the project will be accomplished, time must show. Of the arrogant behaviour of the Elector, however, your Grace can well judge. In short, these people wield an authority greater even than that of the Emperor himself, and this state of things becomes worse and worse the more we give in to them.' [1]

[1] Wimmer, pp. 90–91.

The Palatine court was in a turmoil of activity.
The Elector Frederic, guided by his councillors, supported the Prince of Orange with enormous sums of
money, endeavoured to enlist the Elector of Saxony
and other Protestant princes in a new expedition planned
by John Casimir against France, and made strenuous
efforts to effect an alliance with England. His desire
was that England, Denmark, Sweden, and the Protestant
princes of the Empire should form themselves into ' a
great league against the papists ' for the protection of
the evangelical faith. England was to furnish most of
the money, Germany the chief supplies of troops. The
English Queen, Elizabeth, was to give security for a
considerable sum of money for the equipment of a
formidable military force against ' the enemies of the
Gospel.' The Elector Palatine's councillor, Ehem,
hoped further to gain the support of France in the
fight against Alva, and was desirous also of utilising the
rebellion of the Moriscoes against Spain. At the
instigation of the Elector Frederic ' an evangelical
convention ' was held at Erfurt in September 1569 for
deliberation respecting this league. But Brandenburg
and Saxony hesitated as to the advisability of such an
alliance, partly because Elizabeth was not in agreement
with the Augsburg Confession, partly because they did
not approve of joining in a confederation which had the
appearance of being directed against the Emperor and
the Empire. The Elector Joachim II. of Brandenburg declared that there was nothing whatever to
warrant them in fearing that the Catholics would commit a breach of the Pacification of Augsburg. A proposal brought forward by a Huguenot delegate for a
' perpetual league,' defensive and offensive, with the

German princes, and the German Imperial and Hanseatic cities, with concurrence of England, Scotland, and the northern kingdoms, was also rejected at Erfurt.[1]

At the same time, so it was reported to Duke Albert of Bavaria, there were some resolutions passed at Erfurt. ' The delegates who represented the electors and princes at Erfurt,' wrote Albert to Duke Alva on November 21, 1569, ' believe certainly that the Kings of Spain and France, the Pope, and others of their adherents have already banded together against the Protestants, and that both the said monarchs have resolved that, as soon as the King of France has overcome and put down his rebels and enemies in France, they will turn their attention to an attack on the Count Palatine and Prince-elector Frederic and on others besides who have opposed his Majesty.'

Thereupon, those assembled at Erfurt had agreed, so he had heard ' from a trustworthy source,' that, if they saw good reason to believe that this course was really to be pursued, they would co-operate to the very best of their ability to afford succour to those who were in danger of aggression, and all who were unwilling to join with them they would either compel to do so, or else they would in some way or other disable them and render it impossible for them to help the other side. For this purpose every elector and prince was to get together as much money as possible, and, indeed, several princes had already borrowed considerable sums at a high rate of interest. ' In the northern districts the cry goes everywhere that the evangelical Christians

[1] Neudecker, ii. 168–181. Heppe, *Geschichte des deutschen Protestantismus*, ii. 196-203. Ritter, *August von Sachsen und Friedrich III*, p. 333. v. Bezold, i. 54 ff.

must not be deserted, and that they can be helped with a good conscience. Preachers are exciting and incensing the people from the pulpits, telling them that the papists have prepared a bath of blood for the evangelicals, and warning them to beware.' 'And all this is everywhere firmly believed. Many of the delegates have in consequence advised their lords not to delay any longer, but to equip themselves betimes, and to take the initiative. After all only one issue is possible : priest after priest must be dislodged until the bishoprics are in the hands of the laity. Provision may thus be made for the children of many poor princes, peace and union maintained, and the pure Word of God further propagated.' [1]

Fearing the Calvinists' league and war schemes, Duke Albert of Bavaria exerted himself most strenuously to strengthen the league of Landsberg, a defensive alliance both of Catholics and Protestants. Now, again, as in former years, he hoped to persuade the Lutheran Elector of Saxony to join this confederacy ; the confederates were also anxious to win over the Elector of Brandenburg and the Duke of Würtemberg. With the same object Albert sent an embassy to the three ecclesiastical electors, and to the Bishops of Münster, Liège, Strasburg, and Spires, and made an attempt also to draw the Burgundian circle and Lorraine into the league. [2] 'We are hard at work,' he wrote on December 18, 1569, to Duke Alva, 'strengthening the Landsberg defensive alliance, inviting, with a view to warding off all suspicion, both the adherents of the Augsburg Confession and those of the old Catholic religion,' as

---

[1] Sugenheim, *Bayerns Zustände*, pp. 574–575, note 14.
[2] v. Bezold, i. 63–64.

the object of this union is ' the general preservation of
the Public Peace and the Religious Pacification.' But
the admission of the Netherlands and of Lorraine was
objected to even by the Catholic members of the league ;
and the Emperor, to whom Duke Alva, at Albert's
suggestion, had appealed through the Spanish ambassador at the Viennese court, spoke decisively against
the accession of the Netherlands. ' At first,' wrote the
Spanish ambassador to Alva, ' the Emperor thought
the plan good and reasonable, but after closer deliberation with some of his privy councillors, he repudiated it
altogether.' Maximilian actually gave orders to Duke
Albert, as the latter wrote complainingly to Alva,
' not even to mention the matter at a meeting of the
confederates at Vienna, pointing out the great danger
that might otherwise arise.' [1] This letter threw Alva into
a violent rage. The imperial answer, he said in a letter
to King Philip, ' stirred my bile more strongly than
beseems a man of my position negotiating with so great
a sovereign as the Emperor is. In truth, I am at a loss
to know what I am to say.' ' On the one hand the
Emperor ties your Majesty's hands to prevent your
retaining possession of your dependencies ; on the other
hand, he says that he cannot resist the insolence of the
rebels. He suffers the Protestants to go on forming
their leagues, and shows interest and pleasure in them,
letting himself be entirely led by the Elector Augustus.
His councillors are one and all humble servants of the
Elector, and will do nothing but what pleases him.' [2]

Maximilian, however, was no longer at that time

---

[1] Sugenheim, *Bayerns Zustände*, p. 576.

[2] Letter of Jan. 15, 1570, to Philip, in Gachard, *Correspondance de
Philippe IV*, tom. ii. 119.

under the influence of the Saxon Elector.   The intimate
relations between the two men had cooled down since
Augustus, although discouraging the comprehensive
plans of the Palatine court respecting the league, had
nevertheless entered into closer connection with this
alliance.

For years past a family alliance with the electoral
house of Saxony had been contemplated at Heidelberg.
In the year 1568 the Elector Frederic took steps to
obtain for his son John Casimir the hand of the Princess
Elizabeth.   The Elector Augustus was tricked into
giving his consent to his daughter's betrothal.   In the
first place he received an assurance from the Landgrave
William of Hesse that John Casimir ' was not at heart
in favour of Calvinistic doctrine ; ' and, secondly, John
Casimir himself signed a declaration concerning the
Lord's Supper, purposely couched in such equivocal
language that the Elector, little versed in theological
questions, believed it to contain ' a complete, cate-
gorical, and straightforward statement of the Lutheran
doctrine.' [1]

The Venetian ambassador reported on January 20,
1569, that the projected matrimonial alliance between
Saxony and the Palatinate displeased the Emperor very
much, and that the accession of Denmark and Sweden
to the league of the German princes was apprehended.[2]
How dark and sinister was the shadow cast by this
alliance, the Emperor discovered when, in November
1569, he sent an embassy to Dresden to treat with the
Elector of Saxony concerning a Diet which he had
summoned to meet at Spires, and to beg Augustus to

---

[1] Kluckhohn, *Ehe Johann Casimir's*, pp. 85-96.
[2] v. Bezold, i. 43, note 3.

attend it in person. Augustus sent word to the deputation that he ' was prostrated by bodily infirmity, and
that his room was full of oils and ointments.' The
messengers were dismissed with a letter of *congé* in which
the Elector ' bluntly refused ' to appear at Spires. The
Saxon councillors told the ambassadors that ' things
were in such a dangerous plight that the Elector would
not think it at all advisable for him to leave the country
and to incur so great an expense ; besides which the business, on account of which the Diet had been convened,
was not of sufficient importance to cause the Elector
to take such a long journey abroad. Moreover, what
should he be able to do out there all by himself, when
the Elector of Brandenburg was too old and decrepit
to attend the assembly, and no one knew what the
Count Palatine Frederic meant to do ? They would
not be able to settle much with regard to religion at
Spires, for the Catholic Estates would not conform to
the Augsburg Confession, nor would the Confessionists
come round to the Catholics. As regarded religion,
therefore, the meeting would be attended by bad
results ; its only aim was probably to create dissensions
among the electors.' [1]

In the course of December the Emperor made another
attempt to soften the Elector's temper. He informed
him through a delegate that he purposed ' paying his
Grace a visit in person to speak to him confidentially,
in the full conviction that the proposed conversation
would be both agreeable and satisfactory to him. He
begged the Elector to fix the time and the place

---

[1] *Relation der Kaiserlichen Gesandten Busla Felix von Hassenstein
und Dr. Timotheus Jung*, Copie im *Frankfurter Archiv, Reichstagshandlungen de anno 1570*, tom. ii. 115–124.

for the interview.[1] The request met with no response.

The Elector of Brandenburg also gave very unsatisfactory answers with regard to the Diet. Repeated appeals were made to him through imperial delegates who begged him, if he was prevented by illness from coming himself, that he would at any rate send the electoral prince John George as his representative ; but Joachim could not be prevailed on to accede to the Emperor's wishes. ' Affairs in the Empire were in such a dangerous state,' he said, ' that nobody knew what the following spring might bring forth.' The Elector Palatine Frederic was still less willing than the others to give in to the Emperor.[2]

' Imperial commands and requests,' Maximilian complained, ' are scarcely worth a brass farthing with many people. All is anarchy and insubordination. What is to be done ? '

The military commander-in-chief, Lazarus von Schwendi, was called upon to answer this last question. Before the Emperor went to Spires he commissioned Schwendi to prepare a memorandum of advice on the perilous position of the Empire, and the best means for ameliorating it.

[1] *Kaiserliche Instruction für Georg Prowskowsky, Freiherrn zu Proskaw dd. Prag, 1569* . . . *Dec.*, Copie *loc. cit.* fol. 138-140.

[2] *Commissarien-Relation von Brandenburg vom 9. December, 1569.* Reports of Count Henry of Starhemberg, of Jan. 16, 1570, from Cölln on the Spree, and of Count Ulrich of Montfort, of Jan. 25, from Spires. Copies *loc. cit.* fol. 125-131, 160-163, 173.

CHAPTER IV

THE DIET AT SPIRES IN 1570

On March 5, 1570, Lazarus von Schwendi sent the Emperor the advice he had asked for, in a document entitled ' Discurs und Bedenken über jetzigen Stand und Wesen des heiligen Reiches, unseres lieben Vaterlandes.' [1] He added an exhortation that Maximilian would proceed to the work in good earnest; for the world, in its present wicked state, could not be governed by kindness only. ' Excessive liberty, licence, and insubordination,' he wrote, ' have now reached such a pitch in Germany, that they cannot be altered, corrected, and improved by mild and gentle measures only, and without recourse to the terror of the law and the authority of rulers.'

The Empire ' was now nothing more than an empty title and dignity; ' the Emperor could barely protect himself and his loyal Estates from insurrection, violence, and open injustice. The Estates were full of distrust, one against the other, and in consequence of the schism in the Church, which was the worst of all the evils, ' the German Government had become a prey to the inroads of foreign nations.' If, owing to this most deplorable schism in religion, which was producing more and more division of hearts and minds, more and more unruliness

---

[1] ' Discourse and Reflections concerning the present Condition of the Holy Empire, our dear Fatherland.' (Translator.)

and impiety, the distracted Empire might never be
restored to its pristine glory, there were, nevertheless,
means at hand by which the threatened ruin of common
nationality might be averted. The Emperor was
humbly entreated to carry these means into practice,
in conjunction with the leading Estates of the realm
and all true lovers of the Fatherland.

In matters of religion Schwendi was often very far
from clear ; and in questions of faith he was anything
but a strict Catholic. He revealed himself, indeed, in
the light of a vehement opponent of the Popes, whom
he charged, in bitter language, with the destruction of
the Empire. He insisted, at the outset, that the oaths
imposed on the bishops and the clergy by the papal see
must be abolished by ' an imperial decree binding the
whole Empire.' Further, the Emperor, as the highest
ruling authority in Germany, must himself constrain
the bishops and the clergy to fulfil their vocations more
worthily, and to do away with the many abuses that
existed. The adherents of the new religion must be
made to conform to the Augsburg Confession, and must
not be allowed to encourage among them any novel
doctrines and sects. The state of things in the new
religionist districts appeared to him altogether hopeless.
' The change of religion,' he wrote, ' has been accompanied
in many places with so much anarchy, licence, subver-
sion of necessary discipline and ceremonial, and such
an insufferable spirit of presumption and discord has
grown up among preachers and teachers, that each individual goes by the light of his own private judgment,
everybody strikes out a fresh path, and anathematises
everything and everybody else : hence arise unutterable mischief and scandal, and endless schisms and

sectarianism.' To remedy this state of things, Schwendi
advised that the Protestant rulers should consent to
some uniform system of Church organisation ; that they
should prescribe to their preachers a precise code of
doctrine and ordinances to be by them closely observed
under pain of punishment ; and that they should also
place the preachers under ' some sort of authorised
control and legislation.' The habit of reciprocal reviling
and slandering from pulpits and in print must be
sternly prohibited ; no sectarian book or pamphlet,
aimed at the Catholic faith or the Augsburg Confession,
must be allowed to issue from the press without the
previous sanction of the official authorities. Whereas
there was no hope at present of any reconciliation between the dissentient creeds, it was above all essential
that the terms of the Pacification of Augsburg should
be faithfully observed on both sides. All alliances
between Estates of the Empire and foreign powers must
be strictly forbidden by an Imperial Recess, and those
independent private leagues of Catholic and Protestant
Estates, which afforded foreign nations easy opportunity of interference with German affairs, must be
formally interdicted.

With regard to ' external politics and secular administration,' Schwendi advised first and foremost that
the Emperor should at once make provisions for a
successor to the crown, so that there might be no interreg-
num after his death. Another pressing need was that
measures should be taken for accelerating the procedure
of the Imperial Chamber. At the present time this
court ' was a mere name and shadow of justice ; '
plaintiffs appealing to it could either get no redress at
all, or only after long delays and infinite trouble. Old

unsettled law cases were left to accumulate, while fresh ones arose year by year, so that, if matters were not improved, complete chaos would be the final result.

Thoroughgoing reform was also needed in the military department. The unbounded licence of the German soldiery, and the levying of troops by foreign potentates, gave reason to fear the most sinister consequences ; and, indeed, ' German strength and manhood ' were already more at the service of foreign countries than of the Emperor and other established authorities. This state of things was destructive to all law, discipline, loyalty, and love of the Fatherland. ' Wild and brutal licentiousness ' was making havoc among the people of Germany. Foreign nations, by means of the mercenaries they recruited, were able to carry on all sorts of intrigues in Germany, and to kindle civil wars in the Empire. ' Germans are completely sold to foreign nations, at whose pleasure, for the sake of lucre, they let themselves be stirred to hatred against one another, and scrupled not to send their own countrymen to the shambles, so that nowadays nothing is held more cheap than German flesh and blood : ' and the German nation has consequently fallen into utter contempt with all other nations, and the Empire has completely lost its reputation. It is therefore imperatively necessary that an imperial decree should be framed, forbidding any foreign potentate to levy troops on German soil without the consent of the Emperor and the Electors. Special and definite military laws must be enacted for infantry and cavalry soldiers. All councillors of electors and princes must be forbidden in future to receive service-money and pensions from foreign potentates.

Reform was also needed in the government of the

circles. The Emperor must be the permanent Governor-General of all the circles, and a prince of the Empire should be nominated chief-lieutenant under him. An arsenal must be erected in each circle, and at Strasburg, or some other place, there should be an imperial arsenal, maintained at the national expense and furnished with the necessary complement of artillery and munition for field fighting and sieges. Each circle must also have its own military coffer. If the Emperor, the Electors, and the princes could once recover control of the military strength of Germany there would not only be nothing to fear from these foreign powers whose ' might, without German reinforcements, was manifestly very slight ; ' but the foreigners, on the contrary, would fear the Empire : the Emperor and the Electors would be in a position to come forward as arbiters and peace-mediators in the wars of these foreigners. But if the Imperial Government thought best to continue that policy of ' endless diets, despatches, and embassies,' by which alone it had hitherto sought to assert and protect its laws and prerogatives—thus becoming the laughing-stock of the world—the result would be constant inroads in the Empire, now at this point, now at the other, until at last it lost everything it possessed. Was not the King of France, for instance, being left in the tranquil possession of all the imperial territories that he had unlawfully acquired, whereas there had been a good opportunity of recovering these during the French civil war ?

By means of the new governmental system proposed for the circles, and by keeping up adequate military storehouses, Germany would also always be in readiness for sudden defence against its most dangerous enemies, the Turks. For the completion of the fortification works on the Hungarian frontier, the Estates must place liberal sums at the Emperor's disposal; for if the Turks got possession of this frontier, Germany would be plunged up to the ears in irremediable danger, tribulation, and ruin. In all the previous wars against the Turks it was not men so much as experience and military skill that had been wanting. The maintenance of a certain number of regular soldiers, at the expense of the Empire, would be a good way of keeping the nobles constantly occupied against the Turks and of securing a supply of experienced military commanders.

Another most important step was once more to assign a worthy sphere of activity to the knights of the Teutonic Order. This order had been established for the purpose of combating the infidels, and it had formerly done good knightly service in this cause. For a long time past, however, its members had lain idle, had been useless and profitless to the Fatherland and to Christianity, and had busied themselves solely with their domestic affairs. They must now be reclaimed for the service of the Emperor and the Empire, and be employed to conduct military operations on the Hungarian border, in like manner as the Knights of St. John at Malta carried on warfare at sea. If a place of residence were assigned to them in Hungary and all the territory that had been conquered there in open fight were made over to them, the Knights ' would not only acquire more manliness and uprightness, but also more self-control and better discipline than was characteristic of warfare in the present time.' The order would then become, as it were, a school of knightly training for the young nobles; its ranks would be joined by many honourable people not belonging to the order, and from these, in the event of war, the best generals and captains would proceed.

In conclusion, Schwendi recommended that the Emperor and the Estates should take special measures for preventing the Netherlands from becoming separated from the Empire, and handed over to a foreign rule, with forfeiture of their traditional rights and liberties. It would be well to endeavour to bring these provinces under the protection of the Pacification of Augsburg. Great care must also be taken to avoid any untimely attacks or inroads on the part of the Empire, by which foreign nations might be provoked to embark on open war.[1]

Armed with this ' Discurs und Bedenken,' Maximilian betook himself to Spires.

While he was on the journey, the marriage of the Count Palatine, John Casimir, with the Princess Elisabeth of Saxony was solemnised at Heidelberg on June 5, 1570. Besides the Elector Augustus and his wife Anna, there were present at the festivities the Margraves George Frederic of Brandenburg-Anspach and Charles of Baden-Durlach, the young Duke Louis of Würtemberg, the Landgraves William, Philip, and George of Hesse, Duke Adolphus of Holstein, and a number of counts, barons, and nobles accompanied by large retinues. ' Royal magnificence' was displayed on the occasion ; there were ' splendid banquets with as many as 200 dishes, and costly wines, native and foreign, the

---

[1] Copy in the Frankfort Archives, *Reichstagshandlungen de anno 1570*, tom. i. 126-171. See *Zeitschrift für Gesch. des Oberrheins.* Neue Folge, 8 (1892), 408 f. Respecting Schwendi's religious attitude see Janko, *Lazarus von Schwendi* (Vienna, 1871), s. 141 ; Hopfen, pp. 109 ; Maurice, p. 360 ; Kluckhohn, *Allgemeine deutsch. Biogr.* xxxiii. 400.

best that could be imported from abroad ; besides all manner of jousts, knightly sports, masquerades, and other delectable kinds of ineffable merry-making and amusement, so that all was mirth and rejoicing.   No expense was spared, and the young Countess Palatine was bedizened with jewels, chains, rings, and precious stones as though she had been more even than a king's daughter.' [1]   The Venetian ambassador, in his account of the festivities, dwelt specially on the splendour of the Electress Anna, who, he said, at the dance in the evening had had eight of the most distinguished gentlemen to dance in front of her with torches, whereas the Empress, on such occasions, generally had only two.[2]

For such 'outrageously magnificent festivities' as these, which were little in keeping with 'the general distress of the times,' the princes had ample time to spare, but they had no leisure for the transaction of affairs of state in the near-lying town of Spires.   The Elector Augustus did not appear at all at the Diet ; the Elector Frederic was present at the opening, but went straight back to Heidelberg afterwards, and only now and then took part in any of the transactions.   Of the other princely guests at the wedding, several hurried back home as soon as the festivities were over.

The Catholic party feared that an opposition diet had been held at Heidelberg, and that resolutions against the Emperor and the Pope had been passed.[3]

The Diet was opened at Spires on July 13, 1570. In the Emperor's opening address, which was read to

---

[1] *Curieuse Nachrichten*, pp. 43–44.
[2] v. Bezold, i. 70, note 1.
[3] Cf. Kluckhohn, *Friedrich der Fromme*, p. 344.

the assembly by the imperial secretary, Andreas Erstenberger, it was said that everything in the Empire was 'as
it were out of joint;' the well-being of the nation was
paralysed, general decay was at hand. Of good laws
and regulations there was no lack; peace regulations
and penal ordinances had been framed at Diet after
Diet, by committee after committee, but none of them
had been attended to. 'Insubordination and lawlessness
were more and more gaining the upper hand, so that
neither law nor ordinance, neither admonition nor command were heeded, and among many people, both of
the upper and the lower classes, but especially among
military captains, there was no longer any respect for
authority, nor any love of the common Fatherland.
One and all, they followed the bent of their own wills and
inclinations, and acted solely with a view to personal
gain, regardless of the interests of the weaker brethren.
It had come to this, that almost every man, even commoners and private individuals, intrigued and negotiated
on their own account with foreign nations, and accepted
appointments from them; nay, more, for the profit of
foreigners as well as their own, they inveigled and recruited horse and foot soldiers within the Holy Empire,
and, unprovoked, led them in imperial territory
against other estates, rulers, and subjects; they looted
and levied contributions as barbarously and ruthlessly
as if they were not Germans in their own country and
among their friends, but hostile invaders in a foreign
land.

With its 'military system thus in a state of utter
disorganisation,' the Empire could not possibly continue
to exist; if unlimited freedom of enlistment was allowed
to go on, foreign potentates would in the future secure

a footing on German soil. It was therefore imperatively necessary, for the restoration of peace and
justice, that the daily increasing insolence of the German
soldiers should be restrained, and the prowess and
chivalry of the German knights of old be as much as
possible revived. Care must be taken that in future
no recruiting of troops be carried on in Germany, by
foreign kings or princes, without express permission
from the Emperor, and military laws must be enacted
for the direction of the soldiers, both infantry and
cavalry. On the strength of Lazarus von Schwendi's
memorandum of advice, the Emperor demanded that
' for the better maintenance and enforcement of the
Public Peace a military commander-in-chief should be
appointed, a general armoury or arsenal erected in each
circle, and money stored up in readiness for a sudden
emergency.' [1]

With regard to the ' external situation of the Empire,'
it was manifest that ' partly through open violence
from abroad, partly through intrigues and fighting at
home, partly also through wilful and deliberate secession
of the Estates, the Empire was becoming daily more
and more circumscribed and mutilated, and, moreover,
so terribly weakened in its members, its population,

[1] 'Kaiserliche Proposition vom 13. Juli 1570,' in the Frankfort *Reichstagsacten*, 74, fol. 45–84. According to the Protocol in the Frankfort
Archives, *Reichstagshandlungen de anno 1570*, tom. ii. 343–605, the
Emperor arrived at Spires on June 18 (see Häberlin, viii. 175, and Koch,
Quellen, ii. 56), and waited for some of the Electors and princes till
July 13, when the opening of the Diet took place. After the imperial
secretary, Andreas Erstenberger (the author of the 'Autonomia') had read
out the ' Proposition,' Maximilian addressed a personal charge to the
assembly, saying that as in his ' Proposition ' he had asked for nothing
' but what would tend to restore and maintain in the Empire salutary
peace, tranquillity, and order,' he hoped that the Estates would apply
themselves loyally and seriously to the task.

its authority, jurisdiction, and prerogative, that, unless some crucial measures of reform were instituted, nothing short of complete dismemberment and ruin could be the final issue. The Estates were once more adjured to take to heart the extreme importance of the measures proposed, and to consider how best to act in order to avert the impending ruin of the Empire.[1]

But the Emperor met with no response.

The proposed prohibition of foreign enlistment in the Empire provoked violent opposition from the Protestant Estates, who had no intention of being in any way hindered from helping ' the distressed Christians ' in France, in the Netherlands, and even in Germany itself. The Frankfort delegate wrote that ' they would never consent to German liberty being curtailed and restricted to such an extent as this ; for it was easy to see to what injury, disaster, and ruin the persecuted Christians might be exposed in foreign lands, or even in the Holy Roman Empire, if they could obtain no adequate relief or succour in case of having to resist aggression.' [2]

Ehem, chancellor of the Elector Palatine, interpreted the proposed prohibition as an attempt ' to tie the hands of the Germans by unconscionable fetters and impositions.' [3]

' If freedom of recruiting were withdrawn from the Empire,' said the Count Palatine George Hans, ' it would be as good as robbing the nation of its entire substance.' [4]

The delegate of Duke John William of Saxony

---

[1] *Reichstagsacten, loc. cit.*   [2] Koch, *Quellen*, ii. 64.
[3] Kluckhohn, *Briefe*, ii. 403.
Reichstagshandlungen (in the Frankfort Archives), ii. 446.

declared that the only explanation of the matter in his eyes was that the clergy wanted to deprive the laity of their freedom and to cut off their provisions. His sovereign lord was the appointed officer of the French crown, and he wished to remain in his post.' [1]

The Ecclesiastical Estates and Bavaria had spoken in favour of the imperial charge, but ' the timidity of the Catholics again came immediately to the surface.' The Bavarian delegate withdrew from the business ' because it had come to his knowledge that suspicions of a most sinister nature were afloat, viz. that they were plotting against German liberty, and trying to promote one religion more than another : ' he would, rather, he said, have nothing to do with the matter ' than help to augment such mistrust and suspicion.' [2]

It was in vain that the Emperor proposed not to be himself the sole judge in the question of enlistments on a large scale, but to act with the advice and concurrence of the Electors. ' The whole affair ' turned on the insignificant resolution that foreign enlistments should not take place without ' petitioning '—that is to say, without informing the Emperor.

The remainder of the imperial proposals also ' went the way of all flesh.' Maximilian had said in his address that he thought the Estates would see for themselves that the present governmental system of the circles did not insure to the Empire adequate protection and security against foreign foes. Recognising this so fully himself, he wished to improve matters in this direction by the appointment of a governor-general and a lieutenant-governor, and by erecting armouries

[1] *Reichstagshandlungen*, ii. 448.   [2] *Ibid.* ii. 447.

and magazines and providing a military coffer. The advantage to the general well-being of the state that would accrue from these measures would be so great and instantaneous, that the necessary cost of the work ought not to act as a deterrent. The proposed governor-general and his lieutenant would only be appointed in urgent cases, when danger was threatened from some enemy, and the whole expense of their maintenance would only fall on the imperial treasury when war was going on. By the establishment of separate treasuries in the different circles he contemplated remedying the regularly recurring evil of having to begin collecting money for carrying on war at the very time that it was urgently wanted for use.

The Estates, however, were of opinion that the present constitution of the circles would be quite adequate ' if it was better carried out.' It would be a very serious matter to keep any considerable number of soldiers ready for service in the circles. As for the creation of arsenals in all the different circles, it would be impossible to fix on convenient places whence, in case of need, the artillery and ammunition might be brought up with sufficient speed, let alone the fact that by such an arrangement the Estates would no longer be masters of their own artillery. A governor-general could not be appointed ' without violation of the Religious and Profane Peace, because he would without doubt be favourable to the one religion, unfavourable and injurious to the other.' [1]

' Just as the military system was left remaining in its old, unsatisfactory condition, so was it also with the legislative system, for the most necessary improvement

[1] Koch, ii. 62-63 ; Häberlin, viii. 196-197.

of which the Emperor asked the assistance of the Estates.'

The Frankfort delegate, Charles of Glauburg, wrote on September 13 : ' They are now in a leisurely manner beginning to deal with Dame Justice; and whereas this worthy matron is suffering from the ill-usage of many years past, and has been very badly doctored, and her complaint now seems almost incurable, nobody knows how to set to work with at least an appearance of earnest ; it appears that two hours were to be spent regularly each day by the deputies of electors and princes in discussing this point.' [1]

This, however, was nothing new. ' At each successive Diet, from time immemorial, complaints had been heard from members of the Imperial Chamber, and from its assessors, of inadequate pay, or of remuneration withheld, and of excessive business, while the Estates and private individuals on the other hand had complained of tardy, inadequate justice.'

Thus, at the Diet of Augsburg in 1566, the judges and magistrates had complained that considerable sums of money due for the maintenance of the courts were outstanding, and that the payment of salaries and fees could not be enforced. But they had added that, even if they were paid these arrears of salaries, they would still be in need, owing to the enormous increase of prices in every department of life in and around Spires : not only had fruit, wine, and all provisions mounted to half again of their ordinary price, but the burghers had raised house rent, tradesmen and artisans the price of their goods and their labour, to such an extent that the salaries of judges and assessors of the

[1] *Reichstagsacten*, 74, fol. 15[b].

Imperial Chamber no longer enabled them to live con-
formably to their position, and many of them were
obliged to draw on their own private means. Moreover, legal cases had multiplied so enormously that the
present staff of ministers of justice was no longer sufficient for all the work that had to be done. In consideration of these statements the Diet had then decided
that ' to the twenty-four existing assessors eight more
should be added in order that the cases pending in
the court should be more speedily brought to a satisfactory issue.'

Nevertheless, during the four years which had
elapsed since then, ' litigious cases had grown even
more numerous and complicated.' The number of
' unsettled lawsuits amounted in 1570 to nearly 5,000,
not including the innumerable fiscal cases that were
still pending.' ' With regard to the officers of the law
it was complained that they were most dilatory in the
performance of their duties, so that witnesses often
died before a case came on, and many aggrieved Estates
and subjects were thus deprived of means of bringing
forward evidence.' If no remedial measures were
adopted, the Emperor intimated to the Estates, the
administration of justice would come to a complete standstill.

Once more the magistrates' bench was augmented
by nine new members; ' but how little even this sufficed
to meet the want was shown by the annually reiterated
complaints through the following five-and-twenty years,
during which the constant cry of the law officers was
that they had twice as much work to do as in bygone
years; for whereas formerly they only attended the
courts of justice three times a week, now they were

obliged to go every day, and both in the morning and the afternoon.'

From the inspectors the officials of justice ' received for the most part good testimonials as to knowledge and efficiency in work, but strange things occurred sometimes which provoked a large amount of ridicule and derision.' [1] For instance, in the case of an old lawsuit between the Monastery of Heilsbronn and the Bishop of Würzburg, which had been left unsettled for thirty years, the Imperial Chamber suddenly summoned the abbot, the prior, and the monks of Heilsbronn, either to appear themselves in court or to send a representative, while as a matter of fact there had been long since no abbot, no prior, no monks, and indeed no monastery of Heilsbronn.[2]

' But if the internal condition of the Empire showed up lamentably at the Diet, it was worse even with its foreign position.'

' We had to endure more and more derision from foreigners concerning German want of unity and power ; more taunts about the bishoprics and other imperial territories which we had allowed France to get and keep possession of, about the submission of Prussia and Poland and of Livonia to the Muscovites.' ' But there was no help anywhere, and they did not want to spend any more time over these matters at the Diet.' The Frankfort delegate, in his report of the proceedings on September 29, said : ' With regard to the recovery of lost territory they will not waste much time : the idea is that it will be enough if we can

---

[1] *Von Rechts- und Justizsachen* (Augsburg, 1682), s. 23, 119. See Häberlin, vi. 266–270, viii. 229–252, and xix. 344.

[2] Muck, ii. 423.

manage to keep what we have got ; as to getting back
what has gone, it would be a very difficult matter.' [1]

With regard to Prussia, the Grandmaster Hund
von Wenkheim brought forward the claims of the Order
against the King of Poland and begged for advice as to
how this monarch was to be moved to recognition of
the claims ; he asked that the sentence against Prussia
which had been confirmed by the Imperial Chamber
should be enforced. But ' he spoke to the wind.' It
was out of the question, the Estates decided, to think
of making any hostile appeal to the King of Poland,
who in such a case was quite likely to ally himself with
the Turks ; moreover, he was himself a powerful
sovereign and able to put several thousand cavalry in
the field. The best plan would be for the Emperor to
try once more to enter into friendly negotiations with
the King of Poland, who would undoubtedly ' not
object to such a course ; ' a day should be fixed for a
meeting, and if then these conciliatory measures failed
the Emperor must devise some other method for meeting
the emergency.' [2]

' It is highly to be wondered at,' wrote the Würtemberg delegate, ' that, on the question of the recovery
of Prussia, the Grandmaster should have been opposed
by the lay princes also, notwithstanding that in 1559
the Estates adhering to the Augsburg Confession had
voted as one man in favour of this same motion, and
had also unanimously declared that the Margrave
Albert the Elder ought to be suspended.' [3]

Neither did the loss of Livonia rouse the Estates ' to

---

[1] *Reichstagsacten*, 74, fol. 28.

[2] *Reichstagshandlungen de anno 1570*, tom. i. 482[b], 487. See Schmidt,
Neuere Geschichte, iv. 191-193 ; Koch, *Quellen*, ii. 70-71.

[3] Koch, *Quellen*, ii. 73.

any serious decision.' On November 2 the Electors
notified to the council of princes that ' as regards these
foreign powers that had usurped dominion over imperial
possessions—such as Poland, the Muscovites, Sweden,
and France—after giving the matter their serious consideration, they had come to the conclusion that, in
view of the present disturbed condition of affairs, and
of divers weighty obligations imposed on the Empire,
it would be impossible at this time to carry this matter
of recuperation through effectually.' The whole council
of princes fell in with the views of the Electors. It
was the same old story, said the Grandmaster. Again
and again the Estates had been admonished by the
Order of the danger threatened by Russia, and had
been appealed to for help ; but ' they had never re-
sponded ; they had always chosen to imagine the
dangers further and further off. Now the evil was at
the door.'

While the Estates were debating and deliberating
at Spires, the Czar Ivan IV., in conjunction with Duke
Magnus of Holstein, whom, in January 1570, he had
nominated King of Livonia under Russian suzerainty,
had commenced the siege of Reval. The Emperor
warned the Estates that there was no doubt but that
' the Czar was maintaining the band of pirates who for
some time past had been roving round the Netherlands,
and that it was to be feared that he might suddenly
and unexpectedly bear down upon the Estates bordering
on the sea.' It was desirable, therefore, to take into
consideration by what means the Muscovite aggressions
might be encountered and the entire loss of Livonia
averted. But ' in this respect again nobody would
stir.' The Estates replied that in these inauspicious,

heavily-burdened times they could not advise any
extensive action.   It would never do to make an attack
on so mighty a potentate as Ivan ' for the sake of a few
individual Estates : ' he must not be provoked and
brought down upon the Empire, especially as it was not
positively known whether the laying siege to Reval
implied ' any design on the Empire.'   At the same
time it would be well ' to keep careful watch on the
proceeding,' and the Emperor was advised to procure
' trustworthy information' regarding it.   If it should
transpire that the Muscovite and the Duke ' had designs
on the Empire,' the Emperor would then do well to
notify to the Duke, through a deputation, that as a
Prince of the Empire and a Christian by birth, he must
break off his connection with Russia ; if he refused
to obey, the armed strength of the Nether- and Upper-
Saxon circles must be called out against him.   A deputation should also be sent to the Czar to solicit him, as
a Christian, to maintain a neighbourly attitude and not
to seek to appropriate any appanage of the Empire.
Such measures would, no doubt, have a conciliatory
effect on him.   But if, in spite of this amicable appeal,
' signs of sinister intentions on his part should still be
observed,' the Emperor would then be at liberty, ' in
order further to consider the matter, to summon a
meeting of deputations.   The maritime towns should
be instructed to take good measures for fortifying their
seaports ; the neighbouring powers must be requested
not to strengthen the enemy by supplying him with
war materials ; and the town of Lübeck must be cut off
from all supplies, ' not, however, until the existence of
hostile intention had been established, so that the
Muscovite might not get scent of the preparations and

be thereby further incited to enmity against the Empire. Denmark also, in view of its claim on Poland, and Sweden, on account of Reval, should also be solicited to enter into friendly negotiations.' [1]

Mecklenburg and Pomerania, alone among the Estates, voted at Spires for resolute action against the Czar. Seeing that there was no chance of anything being done, they had at any rate entered their protest to the effect ' that if any evil should befall the Empire, which might God forbid, they at least had done their loyal best in uttering a warning.' [2]

Defeat also attended the Emperor's plan for ' maintaining the sea coasts and the maritime power of Germany,' viz. to appoint an admiral of the seas to protect the Baltic provinces and put a firm check on further loss of territory by means of a German fleet. The council of princes were in favour of leaving the matter to the Emperor ; but the Electors declared on December 8 that ' the " Admiral " question was a weighty and far-reaching one, and could not be left in the Emperor's hands, at any rate at present.' [3]

Maximilian's demand for an imperial subsidy for

---

[1] *Reichstagshandluugen de anno 1570*, tom. i. 482–484 ; tom. ii. 391, 544 ; *Reichstagsacten*, 74, fol. 34–85. Duke Alva had shown astute judgment when he urged the Estates ' to forbid any further consignment of cannons, armour, guns, and other implements of war to Russia ; for if Russia was to have at her disposal the military experience and the military resources of Europe, she would certainly one day become a terrible enemy, not of the Empire only, but of the whole West (Altmeyer, *Hist. des relations commerciales et diplom. des Pays-Bas avec le Nord de l'Europe pendant le XVIe siècle* [Bruxelles], p. 375).

[2] *Reichstagshandlungen*, tom. ii. 391.

[3] *Ibid.* ii. 601. The princes said at their meetings : ' To equip a fleet is the business of a king—it is a true saying that not even a single ship can ever be sufficiently equipped, much less a whole fleet.' The Emperor's proposals concerning the appointment of an admiral in Koch, ii. 63.

the maintenance of the garrisons in the border fortresses and for building new frontier fortifications was met at first with unanimous opposition. Afterwards, however, consultation was held as to the possibility of raising a new tax for this purpose.

But what fresh article was to be taxed? A tax on salt, the Austrian ambassador said, had been rejected on a former occasion because ' many a poor man used more salt in the course of the year than did the richest, and such a tax would fall unequally.' In the Austrian dominions an attempt had been made to tax wine, but in that too there had been ' little justice : ' it had been the same also with an income tax that had been introduced, when it had been left to each individual to estimate his income ' conscientiously ' and to pay 5 per cent. on it; ' consciences had proved so elastic that much injustice had crept in.' It was suggested that the least extortionate and most equitable course would be to impose a tax on buildings, to be contributed by all classes, including the lay and spiritual princes, in a definitely fixed ratio. The proposal, however, was unanimously opposed by the council of princes, and the idea of a tax was finally rejected.[1]

The debates as to what other aid might eventually be given to the Emperor occupied three weeks. What was finally proposed for mitigation of the evil was like a few drops of water on a hot stone.[2]

As a precaution, in case of sudden danger from the Turks, the princes consented that the Emperor should be empowered, in such an emergency, to summon a Diet, ' without consulting the Electors ' (albeit without pre-

[1] *Reichstagshandlungen*, tom. i. 469.
[2] See chap. v. 98–101.

judice to their rights and privileges), which Diet should meet either at Ratisbon or at Augsburg, in four weeks from the date of convocation, and should take into consideration 'the means of saving his Majesty's Christian hereditary dominions.' The Electors, on the other hand, insisted that Maximilian ought first to inform them of any such pressing need 'in order that matters might be brought forward, discussed, and settled according to the usual procedure.'[1]

'The question of the reconquest of the bishoprics wrested by France was much discussed at intervals during the whole term of the Diet, but also without any practical result; for in this case, as in the matter of Russia, no serious action could be contemplated.' The sole conclusion arrived at by the Estates was that the Emperor should solicit France in a 'neighbourly manner' to restore Metz, Toul, and Verdun. He was advised to represent that the Estates 'could easily have compelled France to make this restitution, but that out of Christian pity they had spared that grievously distressed kingdom, and that they relied on just restitution being made.'[2]

During the transactions at the Diet Charles IX., on August 8, had concluded with the Huguenots the Peace of St. Germain-en-Laye, had granted them a complete amnesty, reinstatement in their possessions, free exercise of their religion, admission to public offices, and four important fortresses as places of refuge for a term of two years. In a secret article of the treaty the King of France had guaranteed to the Huguenots 2,000,000 livres for repayment of the sums

[1] *Reichstagshandlungen*, tom. ii. 597, 599-600.
[2] *Ibid.* tom. i. 482ᵇ.

raised in Germany and England for the purpose of
levying troops for Condé and Coligny.[1]

A Huguenot delegate brought the news of this treaty
of peace to the Protestant Estates at Spires, and read
out a letter of instructions from the Huguenot leaders
in which the latter acknowledged that they owed this
peace 'to the support given by the Count Palatine
Wolfgang and to the favour and help of other electors
and princes who were adherents of the Augsburg Confession;' they were ready, they said, to prove their
gratitude by action, and begged that an influential
deputation of the Augsburg Confessionists might be
sent to Charles IX. to solicit him to continue in unbroken
observance of the treaty.[2] The Protestant Estates
agreed to do this, and to remind the King through the
deputation ' of the ancient and longstanding friendship,
good understanding, and neighbourliness that had
existed between his royal Majesty and his Majesty's
laudable ancestors on the one hand, and the German
Electors and princes on the other.' In order to give
still greater proof ' of their loyal and sincere affection '
the Electors and princes offered in all friendship and
respect to ' stand by him with counsel and assistance '
in case of ' anybody molesting or making war on him ; '
and, they added, ' they felt confident that his royal
Majesty would serve them in the same friendly manner
if they should find themselves in need of help.' [3]

In December 1570, shortly after Charles IX.'s
marriage with the Archduchess Elizabeth (a daughter
of the Emperor), the deputation was accorded a solemn

---

[1] Kervyn de Lettenhove, ii. 209.
[2] ' Instruction,' translated in the *Reichstagsacten*, 75, fol. 119–121.
[3] *Ibid.* fol. 125–128.

audience at the French court. Their spokesman, Hubert Languet, offered congratulations to the royal couple, protested vehemently against ' the intrigues ' of the ' Bishop of Rome,' and reiterated on the part of the princes the promise ' to render the King substantial help if, in the maintenance of the treaty of peace, he encountered opposition from the enemy.' [1]

A Huguenot agent informed the Tuscan ambassador that the princes, in communications addressed to the Huguenots, had advocated the participation of France in a war against the Pope ; and that the Emperor also was endeavouring to move the King of France to embark on a war of this sort, which war was also to be directed against Tuscany.[2]

Regardless of the protest entered by the imperial ambassador, Count Arco, Pope Pius V. had raised Duke Cosmo de' Medici to the rank of Grand Duke of Tuscany, and on March 5, 1570, had caused him to be solemnly crowned.[3]

Maximilian bitterly resented this proceeding. He was completely powerless against all the enemies of the Empire who, ' openly and unopposed, possessed themselves at pleasure of territory belonging to the Empire,' and scandalously spurned all imperial rights and prerogatives : he was powerless against France, Spain, Russia, and other ' formidable potentates ; ' with regard to the Pope, however, he was determined, at any rate, to show himself mighty in words. He said to an ambassador of Queen Elizabeth of England, the most bitter enemy of the Apostolic See and the Catholic

[1] See Kluckhohn, *Briefe*, ii. 408, note 1, and v. Bezold, i. 76, note 2.

[2] See v. Bezold, i. 77–78.

[3] v. Reumont, *Gesch. Toscana's*, i. 242. See Turba, *Venet. Depeschen*, iii. 497 f.

Church, that it was his intention to ' bring back the insolent Bishop of Rome to apostolic ways.' ' In a campaign against Rome,' he added, ' the German princes would not leave him in the lurch.' [1]

Without doubt the Protestant princes, the Lutherans as well as the Calvinists, would have supported him to the full extent of their power ' had open war been declared with the object of making a clean sweep of the Antichrist.' ' We are all fighting against the demon,' the Prince of Orange proclaimed in 1569, ' that is to say, against the Antichrist at Rome. We must flee from the darkness of Egypt, the papacy. God is calling the faithful of all nations to unite under His banner.' [2]

In the Protestant camp there were not wanting those who declared it to be the most sacred duty of the Emperor and of the secular Estates to march against Rome without delay, and that, not only with a view to putting an end to the Pope's dominion, but also to getting rid of the ecclesiastical princes and electors. The theologian Matthew Judex was foremost in urging on the Protestants to such an undertaking. ' Our Lord and God,' he wrote, ' is kindling in the camp the courage of His soldiers, He blows the trumpet-blast of battle, and with no uncertain voice He calls us to take vengeance on the enemies and to massacre them whole-sale. For the greater the fury hurled at them, the better He is pleased ; no amount of cruelty can be sufficient to avenge their crime and to punish it as it deserves.' And not only must all the ministers of the Divine Word combine against the Antichrist, but ' all persons whatsoever who wield political power, high and

---

[1] v. Bezold, i. 75.   [2] Kervyn de Lettenhove, ii. 187.

low alike, are in duty bound to pay him back, sword in
hand, in double measure, what he has meted out to
them.   The Pope has lifted up his head over Emperor,
kings, princes—yea, verily, over the Holy Roman
Empire ; he has trampled the greatest monarchs under
foot ; he has stirred up the bloodiest tumults against
the Empire, and to feed his idolatrous worship he has
plundered the whole world.'

Vengeance similar to that wreaked on the Pope was
also to be dealt out to all ' ecclesiastical authorities,'
to ' bishops, cardinals, mass-priests, monks, and nuns ; '
they must be compelled to renounce their ' worship of
idols, their blasphemy, their Baalism, and their murder-
ing of souls,' they must be treated ' as thieves and
robbers, and deprived of all political power and dignity ;
and all Church emoluments and property must be taken
from them.'

So wrote the theologian Judex, who was instructor
of youth at the university of Jena.   And even this
programme of chastisement was not enough, in his eyes,
for the Pope, the bishops, and the whole body of Catholic
clergy.   According to the laws of God, according to the
rights of nature and of the state, he went on, all holders
of political power must further take into consideration
' what particular mode of punishment by death was
merited by those seditious and infamous men who had
assailed and oppressed the majesty of the Emperor, of
kings and of princes, and all persons holding civil
authority, who had been convicted as fiendish murderers
of bodies and souls, as sacrilegious plunderers of churches,
and of the whole world, as sodomites, fornicators, and
destroyers of all chastity and decency.'

Everybody was convinced that these men were

guilty of all these crimes : they must therefore be slain with the sword as men who had arrogated to themselves power in defiance of the command of Christ, they must be hung and stretched on the rack like robbers, they must be burnt with fire like sodomites.

In support of all he said, Judex quoted passages from Luther's pamphlet, 'Das Papsthum vom Teufel gestiftet' (the papacy founded by the devil). Luther had depicted the modes of punishment he recommended in those pictures which had been printed first at Wittenberg, and a second time at Jena. In these the Pope and the cardinals are seen hanging on the gallows, or on a cross, while devils hover round them, seize hold of their souls, and carry them off to hell. The inscription runs : ' The merited reward of the most satanic Pope and his cardinals.' ' As a pendant to this, Luther exhibited another picture in which Pope Clement IV. appears as an executioner, with sword in hand, cutting off the head of Conradin, son of the Emperor Conrad IV., and King of Sicily and Naples, with the inscription : ' The Pope returns thanks to the Emperor for immeasurable benefits.'

' Herein,' says Judex, ' we have unmistakable evidence that all rulers, high and low, act in a right and praiseworthy manner when they take vengeance on the papacy ; when they abolish the idolatry and all the sodomitish atrocities of the papists, deprive them of all political jurisdiction and Church property, transform the pseudo-bishoprics into secular principalities, and transfer abbeys, commendaries, and suchlike larvæ of the Antichrist from the hands of pseudo-clerics into the keeping of offcials who know how to rule and administer.'

' On the other hand,' Judex goes on, ' all rulers, high or low, are reprehensible in the extremist measure if, instead of acting in the manner pointed out, and repaying the papacy with double coinage, they bolster it up, protect and defend it ; for in so doing they are defying the commands of God : " Go ye forth and pay him back double what he has given you," and " Destroy all the places in which the heathen have set up their idols." If they do not punish the Pope and extirpate the bishops they commit their own souls and the souls of their subjects to the tender mercies of those ravening wolves who can do nothing else but rend and strangle (John x., Matthew vii., Acts xx.) as on the slaughtering-bench. Rulers like these are no better than bawds and harbourers of the lowest specimens of humanity, and prostituters of their subjects' virtue and modesty. The houses of the priests are nothing else than common brothels.'

All rulers, Judex concludes, must follow the example of Jehu, Josias, and others, who destroyed all idolaters and idolatry with fire and sword.[1]

The possibility of a military campaign against Rome had already, in 1568, been mentioned confidentially to the Elector Palatine Frederic by an imperial councillor.[2] But, in spite of Maximilian's threats against ' the insolent Bishop of Rome,' arms were not resorted to against him.

A very different war soon engrossed the attention of the world.

---

[1] *Gravissimum et severissimum Edictum,* &c. (see above, p. 285, note 1) in Schlünelburg, xiii. 375–389. Planck, iv. 207, note, calls this piece of writing ' a veritable curiosity.' There are very many more similar pathological curiosities, as we shall see.

[2] Kluckhohn, *Briefe,* ii. 255

In February 1571 Pius V. expressed his pleasure to the Emperor at learning that he had declared himself ready to form an alliance with him (the Pope) against the Turks. He told the Emperor that if he would consent to concluding the treaty in that same year he would place money and troops at his disposal, and he asked for fuller information as to where he should send the troops. He added that he had also sent ambassadors to the King of France and to other sovereigns and princes to negotiate concerning a universal league. ' We must endeavour,' wrote the Pope, ' to unite the whole world against the arch-enemy of Christianity.' [1]

[1] In the Archives of the Vatican, Pii V. *Brevia*, 19, fol. 380. For the information derived from these archives, I am indebted to the kindness of Dr. Gottlob at Rome (now Professor at Freiburg in Switzerland).

CHAPTER V

TURKISH WARS UP TO 1572

THE might of the Turks was steadily increasing. At the death of Sultan Solyman II. in the year 1566 more than two-thirds of Hungary were in their hands, and Central Austria was menaced with an invasion from them. In 1566 Maximilian led an army of over 60,000 men into Hungary; but through his own military incapacity, the want of able and intelligent generals, and the lack of discipline among the troops, he had been 'doomed to see the whole brilliant armament broken up to his shame and to the sport of the enemy of the Christian name.' It was of no avail to the valiant Nicholas Zriny that he held out so long in the siege of Szigeth. After his heroic death on September 7 the fortress fell into the hands of the Turks. Gyula also, with the whole district appertaining to it, was lost to the Emperor. Mutinies among the troops, insubordination and treachery among the captains 'brought everything to ruin.' Maximilian wrote from the camp near Raab, on September 29, to Duke Albert of Bavaria that he could do nothing 'with the deceitful people.' 'God knows that I am working myself well-nigh mad in the midst of the distracted state of things. There's no end to what I might write. In short, when we had more men we could not bring them up to the scratch and now the numbers are so greatly reduced that it is

necessary to proceed very cautiously : it's all very
well for those to talk who know nothing whatever of
the circumstances.' On October 18 he complains that
' the Bohemian and Silesian troops, and others also,
have gone off against his orders ; he has scarcely 800
horse left ; towards the end of the month the imperial
subsidy will lapse, and he is quite incapable himself
of maintaining the mercenaries any longer. I am
further compelled to inform you, with deep distress,
that my brother Ferdinand also withdrew from the
field last Tuesday, in spite of all my remonstrances and
appeals and his sense of honour, and so forth. Nothing
I could say was of any use.' [1]

This protracted and costly war had almost drained
the imperial finances. In 1568 Maximilian was obliged
to agree to pay Selim II. an annual tribute of 30,000
ducats, while ' every year he had reason to fear an
invasion of his hereditary dominions and further inroads
into the Empire.'

At the Diet of Spires Maximilian had represented
to the Estates that the only means of keeping themselves in readiness against another Turkish invasion,
and utilising as a first line of defence the small remnant
of Hungary left to the Empire, was by erecting a strong
line of border fortification. If they did not wish
deliberately to draw down the arch-enemy upon Germany they must forthwith set to work to continue the
fortification works already begun, the yearly cost of

[1] *Briefwechsel*, pp. 161–163, 165, 166–167. Respecting the part
played by the Archduke Ferdinand II. of Tyrol in the Turkish campaign,
and the Emperor's accusation, see Hirn. ii. 291–295. For an account of
the whole war, see Huber, pp. 257 ff., where the special literature of the
subject is carefully catalogued. See also Turba, *Venet. Depeschen*, iii.
s. xxx. and 324 ff.

which amounted to 1,000,000 thalers. He could not himself defray the expenses from his own hereditary dominions, for there was no sovereign in Christendom who had such an extensive frontier to maintain. The nation was, moreover, bound to give substantial help to the border principalities, after all the aggression and misery they had suffered from the Turks. The imperial frontier and that of the Archduke Charles of Styria together made up 200 German miles in diameter and 300 in circumference.

Along these boundary lines there were ninety-six strongholds all garrisoned by German and Hungarian cavalry and infantry. Even in times of peace the defence of this frontier employed 21,000 men, whose maintenance spread over the whole year. Their regular pay amounted to 1,400,000 florins annually, which sum was doubled when additional strength was rendered necessary by threatened invasion. If the Estates persisted in refusing the required aids, the Emperor said, he could only commit the matter into the hands of the Almighty ; if, however, an invasion of Germany by the Turks did indeed occur, he at any rate could not be blamed for not having given timely warning.[1]

After this imperial declaration the Estates passed a resolution to the effect that all and any Turkish subsidies formerly voted to the Emperor, and not yet spent, should be used for building fortifications ; besides which twelve *Römermonate* (war contributions)[2] should be granted, to be paid up in six instalments by the year 1575. But ' the result of this resolution was, for the

---

[1] Koch, *Quellen*, ii. 66–67.
[2] Contribution of the Estates of the German Empire to a common war. (Translator.)

most part, a lamentable failure,' in spite of the severe
penalties decreed at Spires against 'procrastinating
Estates.'

In the year 1566 also, penalties of the same sort had
been decreed, and, nevertheless, George Ilsung, imperial
administrator of Suabia, in response to the Emperor's
request for a report respecting 'the aids collected,'
stated on May 3, 1750, that there were still arrears
amounting to 538,000 florins. He said that he received
daily complaints from the different Estates of the
manner in which they had been utterly ruined by
military insurrections, plundering, and levying of contributions, by bad crops and famine prices ; in addition
to all which, their subjects, for similar reasons, could
no longer perform their yearly services, still less pay
the customary taxes. Whenever he reminded the
Estates of their outstanding debts, he said, he received
angry answers. The Elector Palatine, for instance,
had written openly to him that he had protested against
the tax, that he still owed 44,000 florins, but would
not even contribute half that amount.

In the Upper and Lower Saxon circle some of the
princes refused to give any help at all, and 'sent angry
messages to the effect that they could not obtain any
supplies themselves, much less could they contribute
supplies elsewhere.' The Electors of Saxony, of Brandenburg, and of Cologne, and the town of Lübeck had
not paid up a single farthing (*heller*) at the end of April
1570 ; the town of Hamburg, which ought to have
contributed 8,640 florins, had only paid 220. 'There
are some quite well-intentioned ecclesiastical Electors,
Princes, and Estates,' Ilsung wrote to the Emperor, 'who
declare that if no way is found for bringing the dis-

obedient Estates to pay their quotas, they too will not
in future give any more help, by whatever name it
be designated. They say that they have frequently
found that these disobedient Estates are much more
honoured at court than they are themselves, that they
obtain all that they want, whereas the obedient ones
have to go to the wall, and can get no satisfactory
hearing or redress in their difficulties.'

'The greatest obstacle of all to procuring aids for
the Turkish war was the manner of life of all the
Estates, both spiritual and temporal, with but few
exceptions; the whole of their incomes and all the
substance of their lands and people were disgracefully
dissipated in pomp and splendour, and they existed
solely on the sweat of their poor distressed subjects
and the yearly taxes extorted from the latter. Whether
God Almighty will suffer this state of things to go on
for ever, and will not look down in pity on the miserable people, whose prayer goes up to Him daily, time
will show.'

Ilsung further pointed out to the Emperor that out
of the imperial aids contributed for the Turkish war
he had lent over 270,000 florins for private imperial
expenses, and had not yet been paid back; while all
the time the disbanded soldiers, for whose payment
alone this sum of 270,000 florins had been granted
by the country, had not yet been fully paid, though
it was three years since they had been discharged; this,
he added, reflected great discredit on the whole Empire.[1]

---

[1] The Emperor's despatch to Ilsung from Prague, April 5, 1570.
Ilsung's answer of May 3, 1570, and his statement of accounts, also the
statement of accounts of Thomas of Sebottendorf. Copies in the Frankfort
Archives, *Reichstagshandlungen de anno 1570*, tom. ii. 223-225 ; tom. i.
195-214, 286, 303-306.

'Is it not enough to drive one mad,' asked Lazarus von Schwendi in 1570, 'that in face of the greatest danger and necessity all the world is cold and indifferent, while princes and lords, regardless of the fact that the hereditary enemy draws nearer and nearer, spend their days in wild, unchristian revelry, in debauchery and extravagance, and actually dare to cheat their wretched subjects out of the money collected for Turkish aids? They that are going to fight against the enemy drill themselves into drinking and vice. It seems verily as if everything was going to rack and ruin.' The Electress Maria of the Palatinate had already written some time before to one of her sons-in-law, 'Eating and drinking and carousing is not the way to overcome the Turks.'

'The poor people were fleeced down to the marrow of their bones' in order ostensibly to raise money for the Turkish war. 'But lords as well as subjects will soon be beggars all. The poor are crying to Heaven for vengeance against us, and our Lord God will surely hear their cry. Our poor subjects say they would gladly give the money if they were only sure that it would be used against the enemy. But the money is flung to the devil, and the Turk presses further and further into Germany.'[1]

In a pamphlet of the year 1570, called 'Aufruf zum christlichen Heerzug wider die Türken' ('A Summons to a Christian Campaign against the Turks'), it says: 'The extent of the horrors that are to be feared if the hereditary enemy invades the Empire can well be estimated by those who are acquainted with the conditions in Hungary and in other countries, both in peace and war, that are occupied and oppressed by the

---

[1] Kluckhohn, *Briefe*, i. 722, 737.

barbarians. It has been credibly calculated that even
in times of peace the Turks carry away yearly from
the imperial hereditary lands as many as 20,000
Christians whom they subject to the most inhuman
slavery, not to speak of the endless plunder and destruction which they perpetrate. Words cannot describe
the atrocities they are guilty of in the shape of murder,
tearing off limbs, slow roasting by fire, brutish immorality, and so forth. And all this during so-called
peace. How will it be in time of war ? ' In time of
war, the Emperor stated, ' the bestial fury of the Tartars
manifested itself in deeds of such brutal abomination
to men and women, both old and young, as no honourable person can write or speak of. Some of them went
so far as to devour the flesh of young persons who were
plump and in good condition, and to make dainty dishes
out of the fat of young children and the breasts of
young women.'

In this *Aufruf* it was said that ' all Christians of
high and laudable aims and intentions should make it
their business to defend the Empire with all their might
and to punish and avenge these deeds of wickedness.
But, alas, there is no one in the Empire who will strike
the first blow ; each waits for the other, dissension
continues rampant, and in the end we shall all be
ruined.' [1]

Ever since the victory gained by the Ottoman
corsair chieftain, Chaireddin Barbarossa, over the
Christian fleet off Prevesa, the Turks had carried on a
rule of war and devastation in the Mediterranean ;

---

[1] *Aufruf zum christlichen Heerzug wider die Türken* (1570), s. 3, 5,
9 ; Koch, *Quellen*, i. 86–105, and the annotations, pp. 105–109. See
the *Aufruf* of Neser von Fürstenberg, pp. 30, 40, 43.

they were threatening Italy from Hungary and Greece, and by their enterprises against Malta and Cyprus they were spreading universal terror. 'I demand Cyprus of you,' wrote Sultan Selim to the Senate of Venice in 1570; 'will you surrender it willingly, or will you wait for me to use force? Beware of driving me to unsheathe my indomitable sword, for the war that I shall let loose against you will be a terrific one; do not rely on the extent of your treasury, for your gold will flow away like a running stream.'

Venice could not embark unaided on a war against the Ottoman might; Charles IX. of France was in league with the Turks; King Philip II. of Spain was engrossed with the Flemish revolution, and, moreover, full of well-grounded suspicion against the Venetians, who at critical moments had frequently proved themselves to be 'Christian Turks.'

At this juncture Pope Pius V. stood forth as the saviour of Christendom.

Since his accession in 1566 he had been unwearied in his endeavours to organise a war against the Turks. On March 9 of that year he had represented to the faithful believers the danger with which all Christian states were threatened. He granted a jubilee and enjoined penitence and alms-giving for the expedition. 'Away with religious dissensions in face of the common danger!' was his appeal to the Protestant princes of Germany; 'we are seeking you out, as a good shepherd seeks his wandering sheep, in order to bring you back to the fold: nothing but a universal league can save us.' He tendered support to the Order of the Knights of Malta, helped to fortify the Italian sea-coast towns, paid the Emperor monthly remittances for the cam-

paign going on in Hungary, and negotiated an alliance
between Maximilian and the Kings of Spain and France.
In the year 1567 he exacted tithes and other taxes
from the monasteries for the Turkish campaign. Since
the Turks, he wrote to Philip II. on December 8, 1567,
intended to attack Malta the following spring and were
fitting out a fleet of unheard-of magnitude, he would
send the Grandmaster a contingent of troops as well
as money aids : he begged the King of Spain to do the
same.[1]

When the attack on Cyprus occurred later on, ' the
Pope had but one thought by day and by night, namely,
how he could manage to bring about an alliance between
himself, Venice, and Spain, and also unite the other
Christian powers for the same object.' ' When I
received permission,' writes the Venetian ambassador,
Michael Soriano, ' to treat concerning an alliance with
Spain, and when I communicated the fact to the Pope,
he held up his hands to Heaven and gave thanks to
God ; he promised to give his whole mind and thoughts
to this business.' On July 1, 1570, the first transactions took place at Rome between the plenipoten-
tiaries of the Pope, of Spain, and of Venice ; but during
the first months the Pope did not succeed in effecting
a coalition of the two maritime powers. While the
negotiations were going on the Pope heard of the
Emperor's threatening utterances against himself, and
also of the fears entertained of an attack on the Church
hierarchy by the German Protestants and the French
Huguenots, and in August he despatched the knight
Jost Segesser, captain of the Swiss guard, to the Catholic

[1] In the Archives of the Vatican, Pii V. *Brevia*, cod. 12, fol. 19, 49[b],
56[b], 92, No. 175 ; Pii V. *Epistolæ*, 13, fol. 53.

cantons of Switzerland, to obtain from them the promise of a contingent of 4,000 or 5,000 men in the event of a raid on the Holy See. Segesser was instructed to lay stress on ' the disturbing and alarming proceedings of the new religionists in Germany and France,' and especially on the extensive preparations of the Turks. But ambassadors from the French King frustrated this measure of the Pope by open and secret opposition to the levying of troops in Switzerland for the service of the Pope or the Christian Turkish league. Charles IX., who shortly before had renewed his treaty of friendship and commerce with the Sultan, not only rejected the Pope's invitation to join a league against the Turks, but endeavoured to persuade his new Protestant friends, the Queen of England and the German princes, that the negotiations going on in Rome were aimed more against the Protestants than against the Turks.[1]

The negotiations at Rome had come to a standstill because the maritime powers could not arrive at an agreement about their contributions, or about the admirals, or on the question whether, if one of the powers should violate the terms of the agreement, ecclesiastical censure should be passed on it. Soriano gave it as his opinion that ' any one who was so devoid of sense of honour as to forsake the league would not be afraid of censure.' The Signoria (Senate of Venice) would not hear of a clause respecting violators of the treaty being inserted in the charter of the treaty;[2]

---

[1] v. Segesser, ii. 86–89.

[2] 'Negociatio et conclusione di Lega . . . scritta d. Michel Soriano,' in B. Sereno's *Commentari della guerra di Cipro* (Monte Cassino, 1845), pp. 393–417. Concerning the transactions respecting a league against the Turks between Pius V., Philip II., the Emperor, and Venice, 1570–1571, see Schwarz, i. 178 f., 183 f., and Turba, *Venet. Depeschen*, iii. 490 f., and the passages quoted there.

they wanted to keep their hands free for the commission of treachery later on. Already the news was flying into Rome that Nicosia, on the Island of Cyprus, had been taken by the Turks on September 9, and that, in violation of the terms of capitulation, 20,000 men had been butchered in cold blood. And yet the settlement of the league was still delayed. Not till May 21, 1571, was the Pope able to congratulate King Philip II. ' The Holy League ' was at last an accomplished fact. According to its terms 200 galleys, 100 transport ships, 50,000 infantry, and 4,500 cavalry were to be marshalled against the Turks and against the Moors of Tunis, Tripoli, and Algiers ; half the expenses were to be defrayed by Spain, one third by Venice, and a sixth part by the Pope ; Don Juan of Austria was to be nominated commander-in-chief ; no one of the three allied powers was to conclude peace without the consent of the others. On May 24 the league was solemnly ratified. Although at the beginning Pius V. had had neither ships nor arms, he nevertheless succeeded in fitting out twelve galleys for the war. He also enlisted the forces of the other Italian states for service in the common undertaking.[1] Again and again he implored the Emperor and the Doge of Venice to work together zealously for the reform of the clergy. God, he said, would only answer the prayers of holy priests for victory over the hereditary enemy.[2]

The hope cherished by the Pope that the Emperor would join the league, as indeed the latter had given

---

[1] In the Archives of the Vatican, Pii V. *Epistolæ*, 16, fol. 36ᵇ, 52, 98, 103, 104. See *Epist.* 15, fol. 136ᵇ, 138ᵇ, 158ᵇ.

[2] Archives of the Vatican, Pii V. *Brevia*, 12, fol. 49ᵇ ; *Epist.* 16, fol. 38.

him reason to expect,[1] was not fulfilled. The King of France, a few days after the conclusion of the league, towards the end of May 1571, sent the Bishop of Acqs, François de Noailles, an apostate from the faith, to Constantinople in order to obtain help from the Sultan, either in the shape of a loan or of subsidies, for the war which he (Charles IX.) contemplated waging against Philip II. in the Netherlands.[2] Noailles, who also advocated a close alliance with Elizabeth of England,[3] was instructed to manœuvre in Venice with a view to bringing about the secession of the Republic from the league.[4] On his way to Constantinople he witnessed in Venice the universal rejoicing of the people over the great victory which the Christian fleet, under Don Juan, had gained over the Turks at Lepanto on October 7.

The Pope burst into tears at the news of this victory. ' There was a man,' he said, ' sent from God, and his name was John.' The Spanish poet Cervantes, who fought and was wounded in this famous action, called the day of the Battle of Lepanto ' the most glorious day in the century.'

The Turks, who had flattered themselves that the Christians would never again dare to encounter them in open fight, saw their fleet annihilated, 210 of their 250 galleys either taken or sunk, and an incalculable amount of booty fall into the hands of the conquerors.

The hitherto overweening power of the Turkish Empire was shattered to such an extent that the Pope, full of the most ardent projects, hoped in a few years to see the arch-enemy completely expelled from Europe.

---

[1] See above, p. 95.   [2] Baumgarten, p. 200.
[3] Baumgarten, p. 196.   [4] Martin, *Hist. de France*, ix. 290.

On October 27 he sent an exhortation to Duke Albert
of Bavaria begging that now at any rate, after so glorious
a triumph, he would exert himself to the utmost to
bring about the union of the Empire with the holy
league; he also admonished all the other princes of
the Empire to unite in this ' sacred cause.' On October 24 he wrote to the King of Poland, on December 17
to Savoy, Mantua, Lucca, Genoa, Ferrara, Parma,
and Urbino, asking for help and support.[1] In the
Duke of Urbino he found a zealous and clear-sighted
ally. ' War against the Turks,' the Duke said, ' is
all the more desirable now, since they have at least
sustained a defeat, and we are masters of the sea. The
war, therefore, should be proceeded with this very
year, and carried on mainly at sea through the fleet.
If we wait till we have persuaded the Emperor to invade
Hungary jointly with us we shall miss the advantageous combination of fleet and army. In Hungary we
shall not be able to drive the enemy to an engagement,
for they have extensive territory there into which they
can withdraw, and fortresses which will check our
advance. Besides which, the armies of even the principal allies, of the Pope, Spain, and Venice, would not
be sufficient in Hungary; the Emperor is only contributing a small contingent, and from the princes,
especially the Protestant ones, there is not much to
be hoped. It is the prevalent opinion that the Protestants do not look with friendly eyes on the progress
of our cause, and that they have it in their power to
hinder it. Once more I say the war should be carried
on where the army and the fleet can co-operate, and
where we ourselves are masters of the situation—that

[1] Pii V. *Brevia*, 19, fol. 421, 583 ff.

is to say, in the Levant. If the Turks are attacked
at the same time by the Emperor in Hungary, and also
by Russia and Poland, possibly even in Africa also, so
much the better. The great thing is to begin operations
at once; merely to defend oneself is not to fight; he
who wishes for victory must resolutely strike the first
blow. The first point of attack must be Gallipoli,
since the conquest of this place would open up to us the
Straits of the Dardanelles.'[1]   On February 16, 1572,
the Pope urged the Grandmaster of the Knights of
St. John to have his triremes in readiness in March
in the Straits of Messina.[2]

But no more great deeds were accomplished.

The French King, Charles IX., led by his mother,
Catherine de' Medici, became the betrayer of Christendom.

It was utterly in vain that the Pope, on December 12, 1571, addressed himself imploringly to Charles,
to Catherine, and to the French nobles, beseeching
them to join the league against the Turks.[3]   The
French court was all in favour of a close alliance with
the Turks. Immediately after the battle of Lepanto
the King of France had proposed to the Sultan to enter
into alliance with him, and endeavoured to obtain a
separate treaty of peace for Venice. Noailles had
been instructed, ' with his accustomed skill,' to incense
the Porte against Spain ' in order to shorten the horns
of this overbearing power.' As soon as France had
declared war against Spain, Turkish ships were to
appear on the French coast, in order to threaten the
Spanish coasts. Noailles urged the Duke of Anjou to

---

[1] *Cod. Ottobon.* 2510, fol. 205 ff.   [2] Pii V. *Epist.* 16, fol. 215ᵇ.
[3] Pii V. *Epist.* 16, fol. 191–203.

begin war on Philip II., telling him that his ' first trophy '
would be ' the whole of Lombardy.' [1]　On February 5,
1572, the Pope wrote to Charles IX. that he was confident that the allied powers would win still further
glorious victories over the arch-enemy ' to their own
eternal honour, but to the eternal shame of your Majesty,
if you still hold aloof from this league.　This shame
would be all the greater if, as we can scarcely believe,
it is really true that the rebels against the Catholic
religion have in mind to upset this most sacred undertaking, and to use armed force against the allies.　We
must further declare that we are by no means pleased
at your Majesty's having sent that Acqs, who calls
himself a bishop, on an embassy to the enemy of
Christendom. ' [2]

Philip II. was kept closely informed of all Charles IX.'s
dealings with Constantinople, with the Huguenots,
with the heads of the Flemish revolution, and with
Elizabeth of England.　He had to fear simultaneous
attacks from the allied forces of England and France
in Flanders, in the Pyrenees, and on the Atlantic Ocean,
and was therefore unable to send any substantial number
of troops to the Levant in the spring of 1572.　Venice
was already concluding alliances at Constantinople.　The
Turks never again, it is true, quite recovered from the
defeat they had sustained at Lepanto ; faith in their
invincibility at sea had for ever disappeared ; but the
fruits which might have been expected from that
glorious victory of 1571 were lost by the allies.　Broken-
hearted with disappointment, Pius V. died of grief on
May 1, 1572.

[1] v. Segesser, ii. 131 ; Baumgarten, pp. 196–198.
[2] Baumgarten, p. 198.

His successsor, Gregory XIII., exerted himself with equal zeal to form a new extensive league of Christendom against Islam. Late in the evening of May 13, in the first hours of his pontificate, when the echoes of the 'Te Deum' in St. Peter's had hardly died away and the ceremony of doing him homage was but just over, he began negotiating with the Spanish representative concerning a fresh Turkish war.[1] 'His Holiness is busily engaged with preparations for the league,' wrote the Cardinal-bishop Otto of Augsburg from Rome to Duke Albert of Bavaria, on February 21, 1573; ' we hear all day long in Rome the drums and trumpets of the captains who are " recruiting soldiers." ' [2] But then followed the perfidious treachery of Venice, who concluded peace with the Sultan, ceded him the Island of Cyprus, for the sake of which the war had been begun, and promised to pay the Porte the sum of 100,000 florins for three years. This betrayal plunged the Pope into the most profound misery. ' You have heard,' he said to the assembled cardinals on April 8, 1573, ' what the Venetians have done, in violation of their promise, in violation of their oath. Half fearing this disaster we repeatedly pressed their envoy on the subject, but he always assured us that the Venetians would abide firmly by the league. We have tendered them help, we have spared no outlay, we have sent our nuncios now to this prince, now to the other, to fire their zeal. This very year the King of Portugal wanted to join the league, and was ready to contribute ships

---

[1] In the *Codex Barberini*, xxxvi. 20, fol. 40. Kindly contributed by Herr Schwarz, chaplain to Campo Santo in Rome (now in Berlin). Respecting the ineffectual endeavour of Gregory XIII. with regard to the Turkish war, see the documents in Theimer, i. 67–79.

[2] Wimmer, p. 96.

and troops for commencing the war. Now all is useless. Let us pray to God to turn away His wrath from us and to have pity on His Church.' [1]

France, as Charles IX. bragged at Constantinople, 'continued to be the chief ally and supporter of the Sultan.' Through the scandalous policy of the French King the Parisian court was for a long while the centre of the international revolution, where friends and foes were alike deceived and betrayed.

[1] In the *Codex Barberini*, see above, p. 112, note 1.

CHAPTER VI

FRENCH DESIGNS ON THE NETHERLANDS AND THE
EMPIRE—PROCEEDINGS OF THE INTERNATIONAL RE-
VOLUTION PARTY UP TO 1574

SINCE the peace of St. Germain-en-Laye the Huguenots
had been the dominant party in France; the leaders
held the King so completely in their power that they
considered him to all intents and purposes one of themselves. 'Catherine de' Medici,' said the papal nuncio
to the Spanish ambassador Alava in October 1570,
'does not believe in God; nor do any of those by whom
she and the King are at present surrounded.'[1] The
transactions with the Turks had already commenced
when Catherine set negotiations on foot with a view
to a permanent alliance with England through the
marriage of her third son, the Duke of Anjou, and
Queen Elizabeth of England. This marriage, it was
hoped on the Protestant side, would lead to the triumph
of Protestantism throughout the whole of Europe.
'If Anjou is tractable,' wrote the English minister
Cecil in March 1571, 'he will be able, with the help
available from the German Empire and elsewhere, to
become the knight-conqueror of the whole papacy.'
From utterances of Charles IX. the English ambassador at Paris had derived the greatest encouragement:
he was confident that the French King himself would

[1] Baumgarten, pp. 33-34.

rise up against Rome.[1]   Catherine was furious at finding
that Anjou would only agree to the English marriage
on condition of being allowed free exercise of the Catholic
religion.   This was all nonsense, she wrote to the
French envoy in London on July 25, and her son had
probably been put up to it by his favourites ; but she
should revenge herself on these favourites.   Lignerolles,
the chief of them, was murdered soon afterwards.
Catherine added, in her letter, that if she did not carry
her point she would transfer her efforts to her youngest
son, the Duke of Alençon, who would not make so many
difficulties.[2]   In order to bring Anjou to the scratch,
Catherine endeavoured to obtain from Elizabeth the
promise that he might at any rate practise his religion
in secret, telling her ' that she would be certain soon
to succeed in converting him.'   But Elizabeth would
not consent even to this.[3]   The matrimonial scheme
fell through.   Notwithstanding its failure, however, a
treaty was concluded between England and France on
April 19, 1572, for mutual support in case of either
power being subjected to aggression for any reason
whatever.   Charles IX. was most anxious to secure the
support of England in his intended operations against
the Netherlands.

The conquest of the Netherlands had been meditated
by the Huguenots immediately after the conclusion of
the peace of St. Germain-en-Laye, contemporaneously
with the plan for a marriage between Margaret, the
youngest sister of Charles IX., and Prince Henry of
Navarre, one of the Huguenot leaders.   The Prince of

---

[1] Kervyn de Lettenhove, ii. 270.

[2] *Recueil des Dépêches, Rapports*, &c. (London, 1838-1840), tom. vii.
234.

[3] Baumgarten, p. 61.

Orange's brother, Louis of Nassau, had established
himself as a pirate chieftain in the town of La Rochelle,
the actual headquarters of Coligny; from the French
harbours he molested and plundered the ships of Spanish
merchants and sold the booty he got from them in the
open market.[1] Philip II.'s complaints of these proceedings at the French court were utterly fruitless.
'I shall support the Prince of Orange,' Charles IX.
declared, in March 1571, to the ambassador from Florence; 'I shall occupy myself solely with the affairs
of Flanders.' He entered into correspondence with
Orange, and Louis of Nassau, with Coligny, held out
to him hopes of help from two lay electors in his enterprise against the Netherlands. While Orange and
his brother, in their public appeals, persistently declared
that 'the freedom and independence of the Netherlands' were the sole objects of their exertions, they
allowed themselves to be drawn into a most disgraceful
territorial bargain with Charles IX., a bargain which
even their worshippers branded later on as infamous.
With the foreknowledge of the Prince of Orange, Louis,
in July 1571, submitted to the King, in a private interview, a plan for the partition of the Flemish provinces:
Flanders and Artois were to be given to France, Zealand
and Flushing to the English, while Holland, Brabant,
Gueldres, and Luxemburg were to become an appanage
of the Empire under the Prince of Orange, who was to
be raised to the rank of 'Elector of Brabant.' Louis
communicated this scheme to Walsingham, the English
ambassador at the French court, and enjoined him to
use his influence to procure for it Queen Elizabeth's
approval; he pointed out that through Zealand Eliza-

[1] Kervyn de Lettenhove, ii. 290–291, 292, note ; Baumgarten, p. 153.

beth would hold the key of the Netherlands, and, by an alliance with German princes, would be able to oppose any dangerous attempt at aggrandisement on the part of France. Walsingham accordingly recommended the plan to his sovereign, and also advised the participation of England in the ' great concern.' He wrote to London that the German princes who intended to co-operate were wise enough to foresee that if France got possession of all the provinces of the Netherlands, she would be much too powerful. It was for this reason that the division had been planned : Louis of Nassau had been ' chosen by God as an instrument for His glory.' He therefore begged respectfully that the Queen would at any rate encourage him to go forward, ' so that the fire which has begun to burn may become a great one, and that we may be benefited by its heat.' [1]

Charles IX. was wholly absorbed in dreams of great conquests, and he entered into close alliance with Coligny, whom he invited to the French court at Blois in September 1571. The Huguenot leader met with a most brilliant reception from the King, was loaded with money and tokens of honour, and even favoured with ecclesiastical benefices, among others an abbey with a yearly rental of 20,000 thalers. He was appointed Privy Councillor to the King and commander-in-chief of the forces which were being equipped for the conquest of Flanders. But it was not solely to the Netherlands that Coligny's attention was directed.

In common with all the leaders of the international revolution, both crowned and uncrowned, Coligny aimed above all at the ' destruction of Catholic Spain

[1] Juste, *Hist. de la Révolution des Pays-Bas*, ii. 251-256. See especially Kervyn de Lettenhove, ii. 301-321.

as one of the great powers ; in all his actions this was
the dominant motive.' For this purpose he kept agents
actively employed both in England and at the Protestant courts of Germany, and also at Constantinople ;
carried on secret relations with the Moorish chieftains
in Spain, and exerted himself to destroy the sources of
Spanish wealth in the West Indies. He also endeavoured to incite the Protestant cantons of Switzerland
to ally themselves with France against Philip II.[1]

In the autumn of 1571 Charles IX., in response to
the overtures which had been first made to him by
Protestant princes,[2] sent a skilful diplomat, Caspar von
Schönberg, to the Elector Augustus of Saxony, to pave
the way for a ' defensive alliance ' between France and
the Protestant Estates of the Empire. Schönberg was
to begin by stating that the King, on account of the
Pacification of Augsburg, to which nevertheless he
intended to remain true, apprehended all manner of
annoyance from the Pope and his followers. His
Majesty of France entertained special feelings of friendship for the houses of the Palatinate, of Saxony, Brandenburg, Hesse, Brunswick, and Würtemberg, and was
particularly anxious to maintain amicable relations
with them : in return for any protection, help, and
support they might be ready to afford him, he would
do everything in his power for them, no less than for
his own crown and kingdom. Augustus replied that
he would confer with other princes on this important
matter, and if the ambassador would return in a month
or two he would then treat with him further on the

---

[1] Kervyn de Lettenhove, ii. 325–333 ; v. Segesser, ii. 132.

[2] *Instruction für Schönberg an den Kurfürsten von Sachsen* in
Groen van Prinsterer, iv. 1*: '. . . sur les offres qu'il luy faisait le
premier . . .'

matter. On October 2, 1571, Charles IX. gave audience
to an agent of the Elector Palatine Frederic, and
instructed him to inform his Lord and his Lord's friends
that he (Charles) would gladly enter into alliance with
him, and that the time had come for settling all the
details of the agreement. The agent, Doctor Junius, a
Calvinist preacher, answered that it would be necessary
also to draw Queen Elizabeth of England into the league,
and the King declared himself fully agreed to this proposal. With this message Junius went back to Germany,
accompanied by Philip Duplessis-Mornay, one of the
most active and keensighted of the Huguenot agitators,
who had orders to repair to the Prince of Orange ' in
order to assure him of the King's willingness to assist
him.' [1] Soon afterwards, before October was out,
Schönberg, armed with an autograph letter from the
King, and with letters of credit from Queen Catherine
de' Medici and the Duke of Anjou, reappeared at the
court of Dresden to push on further the negotiations
respecting the league.

Schönberg had ' great schemes ' in his head. ' Only
the noble crown of France,' he said encouragingly to
the Duke of Anjou, was worthy of the Empire.[2] Louis
of Nassau had held out to the King, as the great prize
of war, the prospect of the imperial throne for the
house of Valois, and had told him, moreover, that ' the
overtures did not proceed from himself but from those
who had power and authority to make them.' [3]

The Landgrave William of Hesse pointed out to
Queen Catherine ways by which her favourite son Anjou
might attain to the Roman crown, but at the same

---

[1] Kervyn de Lettenhove, ii. 334–335. [2] Groen van Prinsterer, iv. 16*.
[3] Groen van Prinsterer, iv. 84*: Kervyn de Lettenhove, ii. 344.

time he spoke reproachfully to the Elector of Saxony of the Elector Palatine's friendship with France. Frederic was, in truth, more open to French allurements than were the other princes, and he was bestirring himself very zealously in furthering the transactions with regard to the Franco-German league.[1]

'The Roman Empire,' wrote the Landgrave Wilhelm to the Elector Frederic, 'stands on the feet, part of iron and part of clay, of which the Prophet Daniel speaks.'[2]

The Catholic Estates, the ecclesiastical ones especially, entertained 'the profoundest mistrust of the Elector Palatine's intrigues.' They accused Frederic of plotting their extermination,[3] and, indeed, Frederic's own chancellor, Ehem, declared on one occasion that it had been the Elector's intention 'to annex the Bishopric of Worms at any rate to the Palatinate.'[4] 'The priests are afraid of losing their authority and sustenance,' so an electoral councillor had said some time before. It was all very well, they said, for Saxony and Hesse (who discountenanced the scheme) to talk, for they 'had already eaten and digested their share.'[5] Frederic, who was supporting the rebellious Netherlands and provoking the King of Spain by other acts of violence, feared on his part an attack from Alva.[6] Duke Albert of Bavaria wrote to the Emperor on July 10, 1572, that the Elector had given Philip II. grounds for a military invasion, because it was 'through his Calvinistic preachers, whom he had sent in large

---

[1] *Schönberg's Correspondence* in Groen van Prinsterer, iv. 1*-9*; cf. iv. 269. *Die Bündnissverhandlungen*, in Kluckhohn, *Briefe*, ii. 427–437, 444 ff. See v. Bezold, i. 86–87, and Ritter, i. 436 ff.

[2] Kluckhohn, *Briefe*, ii. 477.   [3] v. Bezold, i. 92, note 1.

[4] v. Bezold, i. 442, No. 293.   [5] *Ibid.* i. 65–66, note 4.

[6] *Ibid.* i. 84, note 4.

numbers into the Netherlands, that all the disturbance there had arisen.' Whereas the Catholic Estates were threatened with danger from the Protestants, Albert begged that Maximilian ' would exert the authority of his imperial office, which was all that the small handful of Catholics had to rely on.' [1]

Among the Protestant Estates, however, there was no agreement whatever. Duke Julius of Brunswick declared that the German princes had no right to make alliances with foreign potentates. ' He has acquired these opinions,' wrote Schönberg, ' in the school of his brother-in-law, the Elector Joachim II. of Brandenburg.' The Elector John George of Brandenburg, who had succeeded his father Joachim on January 2, 1571, was in favour of sending reinforcements to the French King, but he did not wish to conclude a formal alliance with France without the Emperor's consent. Such a proceeding, he said, would engender mistrust and confusion, and give rise to the formation of a counter alliance. His father had always refused to take part in such alliances, and had also forbidden them in his will. Such was John George's answer to the proposals of Ehem, the Elector's ambassador, viz. that each of the three Electors should, in case of war, furnish Charles IX. with 1,000 horse and contribute 40,000 florins for their equipment and pay ; in return for which they would demand from the King 3,000 horse and a regiment of Gascony arquebusiers, together with pay for six months. Augustus of Saxony, also, was not inclined to place an auxiliary army at the disposal of France, but only to pay subsidies. The Elector Frederic was consequently obliged, in May 1572, to content himself with telling

<hr>

[1] Kluckhohn, *Briefe*, ii. 468–469.

the French ambassador at Heidelberg that they must hope for a more satisfactory result on the occasion of future negotiations. Meanwhile ' affairs in France had grown ripe for explosion.'

Next to Coligny, Count Louis of Nassau stood highest in the King's favour. He was in receipt of a pension of 120,000 francs. Through his influence the marriage contract between Margaret, sister of the King, and Prince Henry of Navarre had been ratified on April 11, 1572. ' I give my sister,' Charles IX. had said, ' not only to the Prince, but to the whole Huguenot party, as a token that I espouse them all.' [1]   On May 11 he wrote to Noailles, his ambassador at Constantinople : ' You will have the goodness to inform the Sultan that I have equipped a fleet of men-of-war under pretext of defending my harbours and sea coasts, but in reality to disquiet the Catholic King,' Philip II.,' and to stimulate the courage of the Flemish *Gueux de la Mer,* who have already taken possession of Zealand and completely convulsed Holland. I have concluded a league with England, which has roused the Spaniards to most bitter jealousy ; this same effect has also been produced by the understanding I have entered into with the German princes.' [2]   At the same time Charles IX. assured the Catholic King that he was attached to him in the most sacred fidelity, and that he would do all in his power to retain the Netherlands in loyalty to Spain ; his intercourse with Louis of Nassau, he added, had no other motive than the desire to induce Louis to enter the service of Philip. He gave the same assurances to the papal nuncio.[3]

---

[1] Kervyn de Lettenhove, ii. 347, 363.   [2] Noailles, *Henri de Valois,* i. 9.
[3] Kervyn de Lettenhove, ii. 355.

The *Gueux de la Mer* whom Charles IX. thus encouraged in their enterprises, and whom the Prince of Orange supplied with letters of marque, were, even on Protestant showing, ' the most abominable pirates of any age, men of such ferocity in plunder and destruction, and of such fiendish cruelty, as were scarcely met with even among the Turks.' They consisted, for the most part, of the scum of all nations, and they attacked indiscriminately every vessel that came in their way—whether Spanish, German, English, French, Danish, or Swedish—if it offered any prospect of booty. Under the pretext of introducing everywhere ' the true and genuine Word of God according to Calvin's doctrine,' they pillaged and destroyed churches and cloisters, and perpetrated against Catholic priests, monks, and nuns deeds of cruelty and atrocity such as the histories of nations seldom have to record.[1] At the same time the ' Buschgensen ' (*Gueux Sauvages*) committed depredations on land, and threw whole provinces into terror and consternation by their unparalleled cruelty.[2]

Alva's rule of terror must bear a very great share of responsibility to blame for all these atrocities. ' It was as if the King and the rebels,' writes a contemporary, ' had joined together to bring all the bloodshed they could on the Netherlands, and to destroy all the prosperity of the provinces.' Innumerable lawsuits and prosecutions, in which, according to the law of the

---

[1] Altmeyer, *Les Gueux de la mer et la prise de Brielle* (Bruxelles, 1863). See Holzwarth, ii. 492 f.; Kervyn de Lettenhove, ii. 408, sv.

[2] Wynckius's work, *Gensianismus Flandriæ Occidentalis*, gives the most gruesome details. For a study of Calvinistic art in the invention of modes of torture, designed especially for monks and priests, see the *Theatrum crudelitatum Hæreticorum nostri temporis* (with pictorial illustrations), Antverpiæ, 1588.

period, the torture was employed, were set on foot by
the ' Council of Blood ; ' condemnations were followed
up by confiscation of property, which plunged thousands
of victims into destitution and despair. ' The cries of
thousands of widows and orphans,' wrote the loyal
citizen Viglius, ' are going up to Heaven.'

Philip II. violated the oath he had sworn on receiving
the allegiance of the Netherlands, when, in spite of all
Cardinal Granvella's expostulations, he gave licence to
Alva to load the people with new, burdensome, and
most unjust taxes. ' Regardless of the essential differ-
ence between the two countries, Alva endeavoured to
apply the Spanish system of finance to the Netherlands,
and in March 1569 issued decrees for a tax of the one
hundredth penny (or one per cent.) on all property real
and personal ; of the twentieth penny (or five per cent.)
on every transfer of real estate ; and of the tenth penny
(or ten per cent.) on every article sold.' This tenth
penny especially excited general indignation ; the
Estates protested that whereas commodities often
changed owners ten times in the week, such a tax was
tantamount to confiscation of goods. But all remonstrances, whether from the Estates or from the Council
of State, went unheeded. The bishops implored the
King and Alva to rescind these taxes, which fell most
heavily on the indigent and the poor. ' The bishops,'
Alva answered, ' understand nothing of the matter :
they have been stirred up by the town magistrates.'
On March 24 the Bishops of Ypres, Ghent, and Bruges
addressed themselves again to Philip, declaring that the
tenth penny would lead to the depopulation of the
country and the interruption of all trade ; it was irreconcilable with justice and incompatible with the true

welfare of the State. Even should the Estates have
agreed to it, which was very doubtful, they knew well
from the writings of ecclesiastical teachers that when a
law was unjust and was repudiated by the people, the
King was in conscience bound to repeal it.[1] But Philip
would not give in. Alva maintained that this tax was
not different from the Spanish Alcabala, from which, in
his town of Alva only, he had drawn 50,000 ducats
yearly. ' In Spain,' so Granvella reported, ' Alva's rule
is much discussed. It is said that he will not dare to
go back there, for he is so greatly detested that the
Spaniards would move heaven and earth in order to
extirpate utterly the house of Toledo.' [2]

Commerce came altogether to a standstill in the
Netherlands. It was of no avail now that Alva was
ready to rescind the tenth penny on corn, meat, wine,
and beer, and on the raw materials for manufacture ;
nobody would work any longer ; there was dearth of
the most ordinary commodities of existence. The next
disaster was the rupture of commerce with England.
Queen Elizabeth had kept back some sums of money
due to the Spanish crown, and Alva consequently let
himself be persuaded to interdict all English trade,
which was the most lucrative source of profit in the
Netherlands, and to lay an embargo on all English
ships and commodities. From this time the centre of
commerce between England and Germany was withdrawn from the Netherlands and removed almost entirely
to Hamburg. The Netherlanders were face to face with
the melancholy prospect of complete commercial ruin.

' The universal discontent, or rather despair which

---

[1] Kervyn de Lettenhove, ii. 394, 398, 400.
[2] *Ibid*. ii. 407.

prevailed,' wrote Granvella, ' was the mightiest weapon in the hands of Orange, of the Gueux pirates, of the rebels, and of all the enemies of the King.'

On April 1, 1572, the sea Gueux succeeded in capturing the strongly fortified town of Briel, the capital of Zealand, through which they secured an important centre of operations. The churches and monasteries in the town were plundered and destroyed, crucifixes and images of saints trampled under foot and burnt, and nineteen priests put to death by torture. Briel was to become a second La Rochelle. The number of clerics murdered in Briel amounted to 184.

Without waiting for the arrival of the 1,200 cavalry recruited in Germany, Count Louis of Nassau, in agreement with Charles IX., entered the Netherlands in May, whereupon the King incited the Prince of Orange to take up arms also in conjunction with the Count Palatine, John Casimir. The French freebooters who served under Count Louis and other leaders took possession, at the end of May, of the Flemish towns of Valenciennes and Mons; 8,000 Frenchmen were to unite with the English soldiers who intended to effect a landing on the Flemish coast. The insurrection broke out in Holland, Zealand, Guelders, and Friesland; numbers of towns were compelled by violence to go over to Orange. Priests, monks, and nuns suffered terrible tortures at the hands of the Calvinists. At the capture of Gorkum on June 27 the Gueux registered their oath with all due formalities, that no injury should be done to any of the clergy; nevertheless, nineteen of the latter, simply for the crime of not abjuring their faith, were put to death after undergoing the most excruciating tortures, and their corpses were torn to pieces and dishonoured by the soldiers. 'These idolaters and god-makers,' as they were called by the Calvinists, died as heroes for their faith, with a constancy equal to that of the martyrs of the early centuries.[1]

While Alva was prosecuting the siege of Mons, the Prince of Orange came across the Rhine with 7,000 German cavalry and 17,000 infantry. He promised 'freedom of religion and conscience,' but his troops also inflicted the most cruel deaths on numbers of priests and monks.[2] With the knowledge of Charles IX. a body of Huguenot nobles and 6,000 French irregulars, under the command of Genlis, had come up to the relief of Mons; 2,000 English troops had also arrived in Flushing, although neither France nor England had declared war against the sovereign of the Netherlands. On July 17, 1572, the forces under Genlis were annihilated by Alva; Genlis was taken prisoner, and among his papers was found a letter from Charles IX. to Louis of Nassau, in which the King announced his intention of using all the means at his disposal to set the Netherlands free from the dominion of Spain.[3] At the same time Philip II. received from the French King the warmest assurances of sincere friendship, together with expressions of unutterable regret that certain vassals of France should have attached themselves to the Flemish rebels. 'I answered him,' Philip wrote to Alva on August 2, 'as if I fully believed these assurances.'[4]

---

[1] See Holzwarth, iii. 23–51.

[2] Kervyn de Lettenhove, iii. 65. 'Mes gens,' wrote Orange, 'se sont plus attachés aux prestres et moynes,' in Groen van Prinsterer, iii. 482.

[3] The letter of April 27, 1572, in Gachard, *Correspondance de Philippe II*, tom. ii. 269.

[4] Gachard, *Correspondance*, ii. 271, No. 1151.

Coligny threatened the Spanish ambassador at the French court that if he did not procure the free release of the French who had been taken prisoners in Flanders, he would be killed in Paris, and no Spaniard would any longer be sure of his life in France.[1]

Mons was forced to capitulate. Strong reinforcements from Germany were on their way to Alva. Queen Elizabeth, who had begun to hesitate as to breaking openly with Spain, recalled the English ships and troops from Flushing.

Now came the moment when Charles IX. was forced to make a decision. Coligny and other Huguenot leaders reiterated incessantly that no time should be lost in declaring war against Spain. Duplessis-Mornay represented to the King that a more favourable moment for striking could not be expected : the Emperor was held in check by the Turks, the Pope too was involved in the Turkish war, the Protestant princes would be at the service of France; ' Germany,' he said, ' which has smitten us in times past, now holds out to us the hand of friendship, and invites us to join her in a league which will sap the strength of the Spaniards on the one hand, and double ours on the other.' For France, he said, war was necessary in order to provide an outlet for all the corrupt and superfluous blood which would otherwise produce some fresh disease in the body political.[2] ' You must begin war against Spain,' Coligny said threateningly to the King, ' or we shall feel obliged to begin something against your

---

[1] Baumgarten, pp. 204, 206 ; Kervyn de Lettenhove, ii. 497.

[2] '. . . pour vuider tant de sang corrompu et superflu, qui pourroit créer quelque nouvelle maladie au corps de vostre estat, il fault ou saigner, ou pour le moins esventer la veine, entreprendre, dis-je, une guerre ' (Du Plessis-Mornay, ii. 20–37).

Majesty.'[1]   Charles IX. allowed himself to be talked over ; preparations were set on foot, and ' every hour orders were sent out for cavalry and infantry.'[2]

But Catherine de' Medici took fright at the threatening situation and declared that she would only support the Prince of Orange if England and the German princes also joined in the war.

At an interview in Cassel in June 1572 the Elector Augustus of Saxony, the Count Palatine John Casimir, in the name of his father, the Elector Frederic, and the Landgrave William of Hesse agreed together to furnish the French King with 3,000 cavalry in case of need, and to pay their expenses as far as to the frontier. Schönberg was again despatched to the princes with instructions drawn up on August 10 ;[3] fresh negotiations were also begun with England.

Coligny, nevertheless, pressed for a decision. He did not scruple to tell Queen Catherine that he would no longer obey her commands. At the council-board of the King he said that he intended to redeem his promise to the Prince of Orange and to back him up through his friends, his relations, and his servants, and if need be with his own person.[4]   On August 11 Orange wrote to his brother Louis that Coligny had informed him that nearly 12,000 arquebusiers and 3,000 cavalry were equipped, and that he was ready to take the field himself with these troops.[5] Catherine de' Medici seemed to have lost all influence over the King, who was completely

---

[1] Kervyn de Lettenhove, ii. 505.

[2] Report of the Venetian ambassador, Giovanni Michiele, in Albèri, ser. 1, vol. iv. 283 *sqq.*

[3] Kervyn de Lettenhove, ii. 514.   [4] Baumgarten, pp. 211–220.

[5] Groen van Prinsterer, iii. 490.

governed by Coligny, and it was already rumoured that she was going to be sent back to Florence, and that the Duke of Anjou also, the enemy of the admiral, was to be removed from the court.[1]

On August 18 the marriage of Margaret with Henry of Navarre took place. ' The time draws near,' wrote the Florentine ambassador, ' when the Huguenots intend to strike a tremendous blow. When the festivities are over, most of the Huguenots will withdraw and meditate on the means by which to safeguard their own interests, in case the King should not change his mind ; it is considered certain that they are all admirably armed and mounted, and in readiness to assemble at a moment's notice for a march against Flanders.' Military preparations had been made in nearly all the provinces : from 30,000 to 40,000 were awaiting Coligny's orders.

Meanwhile, Catherine and the Duke of Anjou had made a plan for getting the admiral out of the way, and they hoped to be able to throw the blame on the Guises and on Alva. The shot fired at Coligny missed ; 700 or 800 Huguenot nobles, with the Prince of Condé at their head, went to the Louvre to demand justice from the King. On August 23 the Huguenots formed the resolution to take possession of the Louvre on the following day, to massacre the Royal family, and to proclaim Henry of Navarre King.

Such was the course of events which led up to the horrible massacre of St. Bartholomew's night. It was not as a religious body that the Huguenots were to be extirpated, but as ' a party of politico-military conspirators.' In the provinces also the persecution

[1] Kervyn de Lettenhove, ii. 518.

instituted by the atheistical Catherine de' Medici was of an essentially political nature.[1]

The horrors of the night of St. Bartholomew rent asunder for a time the threads which had united the French King with the Protestant princes. The Elector Augustus of Saxony, in particular, was determined to have nothing more to do with France, but at the same time he also discountenanced any further participation in the ' Calvinistic conspiracy ' of Orange. ' If we are to speak the truth,' he wrote to the Elector Palatine Frederic on October 10, 1572, ' it has at all times been repugnant to us that Germany should have made common cause with foreign intrigues of this sort.' Augustus disapproved of every kind of separatist league among the Protestant Estates ; for in Germany, he said, there was nothing to fear from their Catholic fellow-princes so long as they, the Protestants, did not infringe the fundamental principle of the Pacification of Augsburg ; this treaty obliged the Emperor and all the Estates to espouse the cause of any prince who was unexpectedly attacked by foreign powers.[2]

Lutheran clergymen, even in the principality of Nassau, zealously opposed the policy of supporting Orange. The Superintendent Bernhardi at Dillenburg was imprisoned for having said that the Prince of Orange's war was unchristian, that the troops which

---

[1] Fuller details in Kervyn de Lettenhove, ii. 521-598 ; Baumgarten, pp. 224-237.

[2] Kluckhohn, *Briefe*, ii. 468, 534-538. Caspar von Schönberg, who had been managing the league transactions with the Protestant princes, met with no further response after St. Bartholomew's night, and the Saxon Elector, in October, refused to receive him, and only vouchsafed him a written answer. See Turba, *Venet. Depeschen*, iii. 543.

had been led into the Netherlands were melancholy victims, and that the whole enterprise was but the work of Calvinists.[1] It was thought in Lutheran circles that if Orange 'could gain favour and riches from Spain, he would not concern himself much about religion and the holy evangel.' [2]

And, sure enough, in the year 1572 the Counts John and Louis of Nassau presented themselves to Salentin, the Archbishop of Cologne, and begged of him that, as nearest neighbour to the Netherlands, he would use his influence with the King of Spain to procure for their brother, the Prince of Orange, the grant of an annuity equal to what he had lost through the confiscation of his property. 'If the King,' they said, ' agreed to this, the Prince would be ready to withdraw voluntarily from the Netherlands, and would never set foot in the country again. He promised further to deliver up to the King all the towns that had risen in rebellion, and to re-establish the Catholic religion in them.' [3]

---

[1] Keller, *Nassau*, p. 399.

[2] '*Warnung vor rebellischen Conspirationem unter dem Schein des Evangelii* (1572),' C².

[3] '. . . entregaria a S. M. todas las villas rebeladas, con el esta-blecimiento de la fee católica en ellas.' The Archbishop caused this pro-posal to be laid before Duke Alva, who, however, would not agree to it (Gachard, *Corresp. de Philippe II*, tom. 3, 140). Orange sent for one of the most renowned professors of the university of Louvain, Elbert Leoninus, and confessed to him, according to the account given by the professor to Morillon, ' qu'il est misérable et que ses gens luy comman-dent plustost que luy à eulx,' ' que à la longue il ne se polroit soubstenir, et il luy confessa que cela sçavoit-il bien et que, s'il polroit obtenir la grâce de son roy et du pape, il se mettroit à deux genoulx pour recepvoir leurs commandements.' Morillon, who related this to Cardinal Granvella on December 16, added : ' A ce que je veois, il se feroit catholique pour ravoir son bien.' (Would that Philip might agree to the request !) (Kervyn de Lettenhove, iii. 195-196.) Philip would not yield in any point, and Alva's rule of terror ' went on. ' Illa militum intolerabilis licentia,' wrote the Bishops to the King on May 13. 1573, 'ac injustitia et concussiones,

This last promise might not be very difficult to fulfil, as the bulk of the people in the Netherlands had remained true to the old faith. Even ten years later, Orange said in a despatch to the burghers of Ghent, ' it was only too true that in the Netherlands, especially in Flanders, there was not a single town in which the Catholics were not in a majority, and were only kept down by the magistrates and by force of arms.'[1]

In September 1572 Louis of Nassau made an offer to Duke Alva of joining his troops to those of his brother of Orange, and of invading France ' to the great profit and advantage of the King of Spain.' Alva rejected the offer with the words : ' I know Louis of Nassau to be a very wicked man ; I see that he is not satisfied with being traitor to his own side, but wishes to betray the opposite side also.'[2] ' Orange and his brother,' said the French councillor of state Jean de Morvilliers, in April 1573, ' would rather set the whole world by the ears than rest satisfied with a small income.'[3] On the other hand, the theologian Beza called Count Louis a ' champion of God.'

It was at the Palatine court that negotiations with

aliæque injuriæ vehementer etiam animos populi catholici alienatos pæne ad desperationem multos adduxit.' The theological faculty of the university of Louvain also courageously admonished the King of his duty. Just as the bishops had before rightly objected to the seven penal edicts against the heretics (see above, p. 19), they refused now to have any part in Alva's violent inquisitional measures. Alva's successor Requesens also complained at Madrid of the bishops on April 8, 1575 : ' La plupart des évêques sont de braves gens, mais ils n'ont pas le courage de faire exécuter la moindre chose en matière de religion. Je ne pardonne à aucun des hérétiques, mais à quoi cela sert-il si les évêques ne les dénoncent pas ? En tout ce que je fais, ils croient voir l'Inquisition ' (Kervyn de Lettenhove, iii. 91–93, 472).

[1] See Koch, Quellen, ii. 201.   [2] Kervyn de Lettenhove, iii. 75.
[3] Groen van Prinsterer, iv. 63*–64.

France were first resumed. The Count Palatine, John Casimir, assured a French plenipotentiary ambassador, in the spring of 1573, that he was sincerely attached to the house of Valois. He expressed his deep regret that in the second Huguenot war he had allowed himself to be misled by the representations of false counsellors into entering the field against the King: God, he said, was his witness that he had not the slightest desire now to lead troops again against the Huguenots. On the contrary, he would much rather be appointed general of five or six thousand German cavalry, which the King could make use of as he liked.[1] Louis of Nassau, when Alva rejected his proffered services, had again resumed relations with Charles IX., and in the year 1573, at the time of the Easter fair in Frankfort-on-the-Main, he entered into fresh negotiations respecting the Netherlands with the French agent, Schönberg. Whereas he had shortly before declared that he wished to go to France in order to avenge the massacre of St. Bartholomew, he now, in return for secret or open support of his brother Orange, offered the French King, by whose orders the Huguenots had been butchered, the Dutch provinces of Holland and Zealand. The Prince of Orange, however, wished to retain these provinces in his own keeping, recognising the King only as their ' Defender and Protector ; ' but he was ready to hand over to the French crown all other conquests which he might make in the Netherlands with French help. The King was to pay down 300,000 florins as the price of the bargain. Charles IX. was willing to make the purchase. True, his treasury was completely exhausted, but he was ready at resource ; he would

[1] v. Bezold, i. 104–105.

organise a raid on Catholic church property; the Grand
Turk also, for the sake of injuring Spain, would contribute
3,000,000 crowns yearly.[1] Count Louis also succeeded
in obtaining for Orange the support of the electoral
court of the Palatine. In the month of May there
seemed a prospect of a Nassau-Palatine military expedition;[2] the project, however, was not realised.
Zuleger, one of the councillors of the Palatine Elector,
had other plans in his mind for the partition of the
Netherlands. On November 8, 1572, he had suggested
to Orange to contrive that Zealand and Holland should
fall into the hands of Queen Elizabeth of England, in
order that this sovereign might be 'complete mistress
of the sea.' And then, with the help of English money,
one of the Elector's sons would openly bring him reinforcements by land.[3]

Schönberg had still more important concerns to
settle with the Protestant princes.

He made known to Count Louis that Charles IX.,
although aware that, as the son-in-law of the Emperor,
he would derive 'all manner of advantage' from the
elevation of the house of Austria, would nevertheless
prefer, for the sake of 'the general welfare,' that 'a
Protestant prince should be elected King of the Romans,
whereby not only would the freedom of election be
maintained, but all kinds of ever-recurring grievances
might be got rid of.'

The house of Austria had almost come to think
that the Empire belonged to it by right of succession,
and not by the free settlement of election. 'If the
Protestant princes again overlooked the Austrian game

---

[1] Kervyn de Lettenhove, iii. 211-220.   [2] v. Bezold, i. 104-108.
[3] Groen van Prinsterer, *Suppl.* 135*.

and allowed a popish prince to be chosen as King of the Romans, they might end by finding themselves in a dangerous predicament, and be surprised by an unexpected onslaught from their antagonists. Added to this, the house of Austria was at present in such a lamentable state of financial exhaustion that without contributions from the nation it would be unable to maintain the imperial prestige. Even as it was, the Estates of the Empire could not, ' without extreme detriment to the German nation at large,' furnish the requisite supplies for any length of time, and if a King of the Romans was again chosen from the Austrian line, there would be still further encroachments on the national purse, ' the taxes would be increased and would become permanent.' For these reasons the King of France was ready to do all in his power to further the election of a Protestant prince ; he would not only pledge himself to ' helping in a becoming manner, but would also guarantee a considerable sum of money for the expenses of the election.' [1]

At the time of these overtures France ' had already forestalled the house of Austria and secured precedence in Poland.' Henry of Anjou, brother of Charles IX., had been elected King there on May 9, 1573, and the Habsburgian candidate, Archduke Ernest, was left in the cold. The new Polish King, like Charles IX., was also anxious, ' for the sake of the general welfare,' to see a

---

[1] These proposals, Schönberg wrote to Count von Retz, were submitted to the princes, ' pour leur faire couler dans le cueur quelque bonne opinion de nostre sincère volonté en leur endroict. Car cela donnera un honnête prétexte à nos amis de nous pouvoir mettre sur les rangs, comme ils sont délibérez de faire, estants tout asseurez que les princes s'accorderont aussi peu de prendre ung d'entre eulx, que les Polonnois se sont peu accorder à prendre ung Piaste ' (Groen van Prinsterer, iv. 110).

Protestant prince raised to the royal throne of Germany ; he pledged himself, Schönberg said, to render every possible help in this direction.   The King of Spain and his adherents were the only enemies the princes would have reason to fear ; but a new German king (when once he was elected), supported by France and Poland and the Protestant Estates, would be a match even for Spain and all her friends.   If, however, instead of a German prince, the Estates of the Empire should prefer to place the King of France on the German throne, he (Charles) would then relieve the Empire of all payment of subsidies, would protect all the liberties of the Empire, and bring about a lasting peace with the Turks. ' It was imperatively necessary that the Protestant Estates should come to an amicable understanding with France and Poland, in order to be able to cope with the ' perfidious intrigues ' of the King of Spain in Germany.[1]

' Is there any one ignorant of the fact,' wrote Schönberg in September 1573 to Count von Retz, ' that there is nothing but the weight of France's help which can support the Protestants against the Catholics, who are backed up by the house of Austria, the Pope, and all the Italian powers ? ' [2]   The Protestant princes, so said the Councillor of State, Jean de Morvilliers, in April 1573, in a memorandum for Catherine de' Medici, were doing all they could to spread mistrust and enmity between France and Spain ; ' their tranquillity, their greatness, their security, and the possibility of establishing their religion everywhere ' depended on war between these powers. The yearly salaries paid by France and German princes

---

[1] Despatch of Louis of Nassau to the Hessian Kammermeister, Simon Bing, dated August 28, 1573, in Groen van Prinsterer, iv. 97–107.

[2] Groen van Prinsterer, iv. 113.

had amounted under Francis I. to 10,000 livres ; now
they amounted to 100,000, and they had grown into
regular annual tribute ; after having been paid voluntarily in the first instance, they were now demanded as
a right, however bad the condition of French finances
might be ; it was never possible to satisfy the princes :
they were wholly made up of greed and covetousness.[1]
But the princes, be it said, were very ready also to
serve France. Schönberg gave what he considered
the highest praise to the Landgrave William of Hesse
when he wrote of him to the Duke of Anjou that ' the
fleur de lys ' was engraved on his heart, and that he
was the inveterate foe of all the foes of France.[2]

At the French court hopes had long since been
cherished that the acquisition of Poland would secure
the attainment of the imperial crown and the establishment of a universal French monarchy. ' We must
secure Poland at any price,' Schönberg had said before
the election of Henry of Anjou, ' in order afterwards to
mount higher.' France and Poland, in conjunction
with the Turks, wrote Blaise de Montluc, could hold all
the rest of Europe in check. At the death of the
Emperor the Roman crown also must accrue to one
of the royal brothers, and, in view of this, Henry of
Anjou must marry the daughter of a powerful prince of
the Empire, without respect to religion. All prophecies
had concurred in foretelling the advent of a new and all-
powerful Emperor Charles from the dynasty of France.

Schönberg's proposals with regard to a French

---

[1] Groen van Prinsterer, iv. 59*, 61*, 69*. To John Casimir's confidential friend, La Huguerye, the Prince of Orange said in 1574 that he
was having recourse to every means ' pour mectre en mauvais menage les
deux roys de France et d'Espaigne ' (La Huguerye, i. 279).

[2] Groen van Prinsterer, iv. 54*.

alliance and a French election met with serious consideration from the Elector Palatine Frederic and his
son John Casimir, and the ' Palatines ' forthwith proceeded to draw up an election capitulation for the
foreign royal house.[1]

At this same date the Counts Louis and John of
Nassau were engaged in plotting with the Calvinistic
counts and lords in the Rhenish district the formation
of a military league which was to effect the secularisa-
tion of the Rhenish bishoprics.[2] The Elector Frederic
pronounced himself ready to take the command-in-
chief and to appoint his two sons, John Casimir and
Christopher, his lieutenant-generals. ' Our League of
Counts,' wrote Louis and John to their brother on
October 22, 1573, ' is very promising ; not a few counts
only, but electors and princes, towns and noblemen, the
King of France even and his brother, the King of Poland,
and above all our co-religionists in Poland, are in treaty
with us about it.' [3] The Elector Frederic hoped ' at
any rate to gain the bishopric of Worms ' for the Palatinate.[4] The Bishop of Spires, it was reported, had just
found a wife for himself ; the Archbishop of Mayence,

---

[1] v. Bezold, i. 111–115. See pp. 85, note 3, and 119, note 1. Groen van
Prinsterer reckons it among the merits of the Prince of Orange that he
attempted to wrest the imperial crown from the house of Habsburg and
to transfer it to the house of Valois ; he considers that he was anxious to
save Christendom from the religious and political despotism of the house
of Habsburg (*Archives*, 8, xlii).

[2] v. Bezold, i. 100, 128–129. La Huguerye, who goes beyond the
mark in his statement of figures (see Lossen, *Kölnischer Krieg*, i. 213*,
note), says of the ' League of Counts : ' ' . . . affin d'asseurer et nouer la
négociation, led. sr. électeur les asseura d'estre leur chef et de leur donner
au besoing ses deux filz, Casimir et Christofle, pour ses lieutenans
généraux aux armées. Et fut ainsy l'affaire résolu et tenu pour faict, et
toutes leurs promesses et signatures mises ès mains dud. sr. électeur '
(*Mémoires*, i. 166–167).

[3] Groen van Prinsterer, iv. 224.   [4] v. Bezold, i. 442, No. 293.

Daniel von Brendel, was looked upon as a partisan of the Protestants; as for the Archbishop of Cologne, Salentin von Isenburg, who was not a priest, the Elector Frederic 'was thinking of securing him by means of a wife and a pension from France : ' he intended, if the Archbishop came round to Protestantism, giving him his own daughter in marriage.[1]

In the winter of 1573 the Elector Palatine's chancellor Ehem and John of Nassau began negotiations with Salentin on this matter. The Archbishop had rendered assistance to Duke Alva, and was in receipt of a Spanish pension, although, according to Ehem's account, ' he was ill-disposed towards Spain,' thought nothing of the Pope, and hated the priests, especially the Jesuits ; besides which he had ' a proud spirit,' was ' avaricious and grasping owing to his poverty,' and meant ' very soon to have a wife.' But Salentin would not go over to Protestantism ; if the Protestant Estates, he said to the negotiators, would take him under their protection without requiring him to change his faith, he would marry and retain the archbishopric. While the nego-

---

[1] v. Bezold, i. 130–131, 442, note 2 ; Lossen, *Kölnischer Krieg*, i. 211 ; in La Huguerye, i. 202–204, fuller details on the negotiations of the Palatine Elector 'avec les évesques du. Rhin, pour les faire prendre femme, et, avec les armes, leur asseurer leurs éveschez en patrimoine perpétuel.' ' Et desjà avoit gaigné l'évesque de Speire, qui avoit sa femme toute trouvée ; de l'évesque de Mayence, ilz en avoyent bonne espérance ; de celuy de Trefves, ilz n'en faisoient poinct d'estat, sinon *pour en faire ung butin*. Mays la peine se trouva aux deux évesques de Colongne et de Liège, près duquel on gaigna ung commendeur qui le gouvernoit du tout, luy donnant espérance de luy faire espouser la damoiselle de Bourbon, qui estoit à Heydelberg . . . et près de celuy de Colongne, qui estoit lors Salatin, comte d'Izembourg, comme celuy de Liège, de la maison de Grosbech, son mareschal, avec de grands moyens; offrant led. sr. électeur aud. évesque de Colongne sa fille en mariage et de luy conserver l'évesché et électorat héréditaire en sa maison. Et estoient, quand je fus dépesché, ces négociations en bons termes.'

tiators were in Cologne, a nuncio brought to the Elector the papal confirmation of his election. 'It was a strange business,' wrote Ehem, when he and Count John, with the nuncio and his attendant Jesuits, dined together at the electoral table, and ' one of them commended the Elector to our Lord God, while the other relegated him to the devil.' The nuncio met with a very unfriendly reception from Salentin, and was almost immediately dismissed without any ceremony, and almost with insult. Salentin remained in alliance with Spain, but with regard to the French pension offered him, he said that ' French crowns ' were dearer to him than Spanish ' *Königsthaler* ' ; at the same time he was ' a German, and had the interest of the Fatherland at heart; ' he had also ' always been a promoter of German liberty.' [1]

Concerning Salentin also at that time these words might be quoted : ' O thou poor, much abused German liberty, thou that art for ever paraded on the lips of thy princes, and, nevertheless, art so lamentably betrayed by them to foreign lands ! There is no more faith and loyalty left. They juggle and plot, and conspire right and left, at one and the same time with sovereigns who are opposed to each other, but none the less they expect to be regarded as honourable men and protectors of the poor deceived and betrayed people. The imperial dignity and reputation does not count for a farthing with them.' [2]

This was especially the case at the court of the Elector Palatine.

[1] Documents in Groen van Prinsterer, iv. 337–341, 342–345. ' Ueber Salentin's gleichzeitigen Verkehr mit den Spaniern ' (Gachard, *Corresp. de Philippe II*, tom. ii. 395, 444–446).

[2] Franzosentrutz, Bl. 3.

The Emperor had written to apprise the Elector
Frederic of the fact that, at Philip II.'s solicitation, he
had promised to help his hereditary lands of Nether
Burgundy in maintaining the attitude of defence that
had been forced on them, by sending them a consignment of several hundredweights of powder, partly out of
the imperial arsenals and partly bought up from other
places ; he begged that the Elector would be friendly to
the imperial and royal servants of Spain, entrusted
with this convoy, on their way through the Palatinate.
But on October 6, 1573, the sons of the Elector, John
Casimir and Christopher, attacked the powder transport on the open highway, threatened the officers with
the gallows, refused to read the imperial letters patent
which they carried with them, and sent fifteen wagon-
loads ' up to heaven in smoke.' [1]

Maximilian's complaints about ' contempt and defiance of imperial authority and dignity were utterly
useless.'

Fresh extensive schemes of alliance began to be set
on foot. In the middle of October negotiations were
begun concerning a gigantic confederation in which
England, Scotland, the German princes, the Netherlands, and the Swiss Protestant cantons were to join.
The English Queen gave her approval to the terms
proposed by the Elector Palatine for a league with the
Protestant princes, but wished that the Kings of Sweden
and Denmark should also be drawn into it.[2] Charles IX.
offered sums of money for an expedition into the
Netherlands, and John Casimir received the money at
Metz for the Nassauers.[3] They had now got ' all that

---

[1] Despatches in Kluckhohn, ii. 598–607 ; cf. v. Bezold, i. 127–128.
[2] Kervyn de Lettenhove, iii. 283, 294.   [3] v. Bezold, i. 109–110.

was wanted for beginning the ball.' 'You will have it,' Schönberg had written to Count Louis on September 29, ' and you will get it in a lump sum of ready, money, and at the time and the place that you wish.' [1]

The Elector Frederic again hoped to interest the Elector Augustus of Saxony in his project for a league. In November John Casimir was commissioned by his father to impress on the court at Dresden that it was necessary to support the Prince of Orange. The French King had given 100,000 crowns, and there was reason to hope that the Queen of England would do as much, for ' by the seizure of Spanish ships, by sending munitions and soldiers, and also by loans of money, even though these were small services and performed through a third hand,' she had shown herself favourably inclined to the cause. Elizabeth had been solicited to deposit 200,000 or 300,000 crowns in safe places in the Empire. In addition to this, negotiations were going on with Salentin of Cologne with a view to weaning him away from the Duke Alva and procuring for him a French pension, and France had already made a handsome offer. The Elector of Mayence also had made most extensive promises to the Counts of Nassau : ' he would help to further their cause, regardless of his Imperial Majesty, in order that the matter might be brought to a good issue.' As, moreover, ' the league with the Scotch had been set going, there was all the more reason for putting their hands to the plough.[2] In December Louis of Nassau wrote to Orange that the Elector Palatine had attempted to take the new Stattholder of the Netherlands prisoner on his way to Holland.[3]

[1] Groen van Prinsterer, iv. 207.   [2] Ibid. iv. 127*-131*.
[3] Ibid. iv. 278.

'Regardless of the Imperial Majesty,' and in spite of all remonstrances, Frederic's son, the Count Palatine Christopher, at the beginning of 1574, 'equipped cavalry and infantry troops, openly before all the world,' with a view to a campaign in the Netherlands. The Elector, however, 'for a long time pretended not to have any knowledge of his son's enterprise.' 'It seems not a little strange to us,' the Emperor wrote to Frederic on February 26, 'that your Grace's sons, now this one, now the other, notwithstanding that they reside to a great extent at or close by your Grace's court, and ride in and out almost daily with your people, should engage in proceedings of this sort, which are not only in direct opposition to our imperial laws, and to the constitutions of the Empire, but are also injurious and vexatious to numbers of peace-loving estates, and that all the while their doings should be unknown to your Grace.' If the Elector could not put a stop to these goings on by virtue of his paternal authority, the Emperor urged, he might at any rate do so as governor of the circle.[1] If the Germans kept out of the quarrels in the Low Countries 'peace would undoubtedly follow of itself,' wrote John of Hoya, Bishop of Münster, on February 28, 1574, to the Landgrave William of Hesse, 'for we see that Flanders, Brabant, Hainault, and others of the King's provinces, which have continued in submission to the ruling authorities, have remained in a peaceable condition.' The people of Holland and Zealand might recover a like condition of peace, if they would return to the obedience and allegiance they owed. Pending such an issue, however, there would always be danger

---

[1] Kluckhohn, *Briefe*, ii. 630-631.

of the outbreak of a troublesome war which, if other
powers joined the King of Spain, might easily plunge
the Germans into such peril that their children's children
would still have cause to lament over it.[1]

The Count Palatine Christopher's expedition was
got under weigh, but affairs took a disastrous turn.
On April 14, 1574, the German troops were almost
entirely cut down by the Spaniards on Mooker Heath ;
Christopher and the Counts Louis and Henry of Nassau
were killed in the battle.[2]

A few days before this battle Charles IX. had promised the Elector Frederic to help his son Christopher
with a definite sum of money.   The death of the King
of France, which followed on May 30, 1574, altered the
attitude of the Palatinate towards the French court.[3]

Fresh disturbances broke out in France, and the
Count Palatine tried to turn them all to his own advantage.   By treaties which he concluded on June 1, 1574,
with the Prince of Condé and other Huguenot leaders
and their allies, he not only obtained large enough
money indemnities for a fresh expedition to France, but
also the prospect of acquiring the German bishoprics of
Metz, Toul, and Verdun.   John Casimir himself was to
undertake the command of the German auxiliary troops.
In the event of the Count Palatine, or other Estates of
the Augsburg Confession, being attacked during the

---

[1] Groen van Prinsterer, iv. 350.

[2] Account in Gachard, *Corresp. de Philippe II*, tom. iii. 51–53.

[3] Blaise de Montluc says, in his commentaries, after the death of
Charles IX. : 'J'oserois dire que, s'il eust vescu, il eust fait de grandes
choses, et aux despens de ses voisins eust jetté la guerre de son royaume ;
et si le roy de Pologne [later on Henry III.] eust voulu s'entendre avec
luy, et mettre sus les grandes forces qu'il pouvait tirer de son royaume,
tout leur eust obey, et *l'Empire eust été remis en la maison de France* '
(*Collection*, xxii. 549).

campaign, French soldiers, in addition to the German
troops, were to hasten to the rescue, even before the
French campaign had begun.[1] The treaties, as the
Emperor pointed out in a despatch to the Elector
Frederic, were expressly directed against the Catholic
Estates.[2] The war was not to be brought to a close
until John Casimir had got possession of the three
bishoprics; the French allies engaged to defend him
and his heirs against any attempt to disturb him in the
possession of these dioceses.[3]

At the imperial court ' the incessant machinations
of the Palatines' aroused the most intense bitterness.
The imperial councillor Erstenberger, in a letter to Duke
Albert of Bavaria on May 22, 1574, exclaimed : ' May
the Almighty vouchsafe us grace and power to put an
end to these ruinous anti-German proceedings, and
may He punish the authors of the evil as they deserve!
These are the glorious fruits of the reformed, blood-
thirsty religion, which is spreading like cancer through
nearly all lands, and which will hereafter bring irremediable disaster on rulers and subjects ! ' [4]

Augustus of Saxony also, who had repeatedly
rendered help to the Elector Frederic and his son-in-
law, John Casimir, broke off all friendship and connection
with them, and condemned unreservedly the French
policy of the Palatinate. He wrote to the Emperor
on September 9, 1574 : ' If I am asked as an Elector of
the Empire to give my advice on the matter, I cannot
say or counsel otherwise than that it would be necessary

---

[1] Kluckhohn, *Briefe*, ii. 719–720.
[2] *Ibid.* ii. 719, and also v. Bezold, i. 146, note 1.
[3] *Ibid.* ii. 720–721.
[4] *Ibid. Friedrich der Fromme*, pp. 475 to S. 408, note 12.

to enforce against it the constitutions and recesses of the Empire, since I cannot but consider that, by virtue of the oath I have taken, I am more strongly pledged to the Empire than I am bound by any tie of relationship.[1]

The Elector Augustus at that time declared himself openly one of the bitterest opponents of Calvinism, and this in consequence of events which call for a somewhat detailed exposition, because they led to a violent revulsion in the ecclesiastical conditions of Saxony, and were of the deepest significance for German Protestantism in general.

For the better understanding of these circumstances it will be necessary first to consider in fuller detail the clerical conditions of the Palatinate as they developed after the Diet of Augsburg in 1566.

[1] Kluckhohn, *Briefe*, ii. 722.

CHAPTER VII

CALVINISM IN THE ELECTORAL PALATINATE SINCE THE TIME OF THE AUGSBURG DIET OF 1566

THE Augsburg Diet, from which both Catholics and Lutherans had expected ' the destruction of Calvinistic poison in the Palatinate,' ' only served to diffuse it more widely and to carry it into many other towns and territories, so that,' thus Tilmann Hesshus complained, ' there was reason to fear that the whole of Germany would be infected with the venom, and that the holy Luther's pure doctrine, which alone had the power of salvation, would be completely rooted out.' The sole glimmer of comfort that Hesshus could discern was that the Elector Palatine ' still encounters formidable (God grant it may be invincible) resistance in his own land from the strong, valiant spirits, the preachers, the Estates, and the people' of the Upper Palatinate. ' Would God,' he exclaims, ' that they may never again bow down the knee before this blasphemous Calvinism, this most abominable invention of the devil, this Calvinistic Baal and all the hellish swarm of vipers that he engenders!' [1]

The Lutheran Provincial Estates of the Upper Palatinate, backed up by the Stattholder Louis, eldest

---

[1] In the *Warnung vor rebellischen Conspirationen unter dem Schein des Evangelii* (1572), D[3].

son of the Elector, opposed every alteration in the
Augsburg Confession, and raised serious complaints
respecting the squandering of Church revenues. All
immovable goods, they had already some time ago
objected, had ' been given away for a mere song, and
the movable property had been made away with.'
' All the gold and silver treasures and all the furniture
of the cloisters had been carried off, and the buildings
had been allowed to go to such ruin that the wind and
the rain now had free passage through them, and they
had become in great measure uninhabitable. But
what was still more to be regretted was that the old
religious foundations providing for nobles and commoners, and for the poor especially, had been suppressed.
The Elector was exceeding the limits of his prerogatives.
Just as he had no power to impose laws, taxes, and
imposts without the consent of the Estates, so he had
no right—still less right indeed—to inflict anything
burdensome on his subjects in ecclesiastical matters
which affected the salvation of their souls. If, however,
they were assured that they would be exempted from
any innovations in their churches, they were ready to
act in a way wholly unprecedented in their part of the
country, and which would be a matter of astonishment
to foreign lands, viz. to undertake the whole burden of
the debts of the principality.' But the Elector Frederic
stood out for unconditional obedience. He was not, he
said, introducing any unnecessary innovations, and in
necessary reforms and the ' doing away with disorder,'
he would not allow himself to be dictated to. The
proposal with regard to the debts he approved of
entirely, but he could not agree to the conditions
annexed : if the Estates persisted in these stipulations

he should be driven to the conclusion that they were not
thoroughly in earnest in making this offer.[1]

In order to procure free scope for the Gospel, Frederic,
at the time of the Augsburg Diet of 1559, had insisted
that the people must be left free to choose one or other
of the religious creeds sanctioned by the Pacification of
Augsburg ; the poorer classes, he said, had been badly
provided for in the terms of this Peace ; it was only fair
to allow them the same freedom as was accorded to the
upper classes, to princes, and to lords.[2]   In the case of
his own subjects, however, he did not practise what he
preached. The Lutherans in his territory, who demanded
to be left in undisturbed enjoyment of their faith and
their religious ordinances, were allowed as little freedom
in this respect as were the Catholic inhabitants.   ' My
subjects and their consciences belong to me,' he said ;
he would therefore ' do the needful for them.' [3]

The Elector had summoned a Provincial Diet for
November 3, 1556, and at a preliminary meeting, held
in Heidelberg, his councillors begged him not to trouble
himself about the opposition of the Provincial Estates,
' not to allow them to dictate to him, but to withstand
them firmly and not carry on disputations with them ;
if they appealed to the Augsburg Confession, they
should be told that the Elector would do nothing
contrary to the Word of God, and consequently nothing
contrary to the Augsburg Confession which was grounded
on the Word of God.' With regard to the altars and
images still left in the Lutheran churches of the Upper
Palatinate, the theologian Olevian moved : ' that ido-

----

[1] Wittmann, pp. 28–32. The Countess Palatine Elizabeth to the Landgrave William, on May 22, 1563, in Kluckhohn, *Briefe*, i. 400.

[2] See above, p. 40 (n. 3).

[3] Wittmann, p. 49.

latry must be abolished, even if with fire and sword; it would be well if all the idols and images were publicly burnt.' Another member of the council was of opinion that it would not be expedient ' to burn the idols openly on the market-place ; it would be better to collect them together in rooms and burn them as firewood.' A third opinion was that ' Idolatry was infecting the reformation, and must therefore be tackled in earnest ; a little leaven leavened the whole lump, but idolatry must first be eradicated from the hearts of the people by good preachers, and then they could get rid of the idols as we have done down here' in the Lower Palatinate. It did not seem judicious, this speaker said, to ' make a wholesale clearance' of all the Lutheran preachers who were opposed to the innovations, as they would require 350 church and school officials in the Upper Palatinate, and there were ' not more than seven good ones' in the Lower Palatinate : ' if these were to be sent to the Upper Palatinate, the Lower would be left destitute.' The remonstrances of one of the electoral councillors who said that ' the question was a very grave one, and that frequent changes in religion were dangerous,' were disregarded.[1]

Immediately on his arrival at Amberg the Elector placed his own preachers in the principal churches of the town, and also filled secular posts with officials of the Calvinistic faith. When the Provincial Estates complained of this, Frederic answered : ' those who could not agree with their rulers in the matter of religion might leave the country and go elsewhere ; he was not bound to consult anybody as to how the ministerial offices were to be filled, and he would not allow his hands to

[1] Wittmann, pp. 37–40.

be tied in this respect either; the Heidelberg doctrine was in conformity with the Augsburg Confession.' On another occasion he said that ' the Augsburg Confession was compiled from the divine scriptures, although there was a good deal of idolatry in it.' A religious conference held by his orders between his Calvinist preachers and the preachers of Amberg only served to increase the mutual bitterness of spirit. The Amberg preachers in their sermons called their opponents ' godless heretics, unchristian, seducers, sectarians, agitators, wolves, devil's teachers, sacramentarians, fanatics, desecrators of the Sacrament, and iconoclasts.' Frederic put his foot down, and sternly forbade any more of this ' storming and raging ' in future, and issued a decree enjoining ' the abolition of idolatry.' Under the head of ' idolatrous ' were classed ' surplices, communicants' napkins, the rite of exorcism at baptism, Latin hymns and chants, the ringing of the Angelus, *the agony of Christ*, and the curfew bells (morning, noon, and night), images and crucifixes ; ' even the beards of the Lutheran preachers were in danger of being declared idolatrous.[1]

The Provincial Estates were strengthened in their resistance against the Elector's attempts at innovation by a written manifesto of the Emperor, in which they were urged ' to hold themselves, as they had done hitherto, aloof from the dangerous sect of Calvinists, especially from their doctrine of the Eucharist ; in all political matters, however, to show obedience to the ruling authorities. Maximilian hoped, he said, that their reigning sovereign did not intend to tyrannise over their consciences, in opposition to the letter of the

[1] Wittmann, pp. 40-53.

Pacification of Augsburg, and to set aside the system of Church organisation established by the Elector Otto Henry ; if, however, the Elector Frederic should go to such a length as this, they (the Provincial Estates) must then appeal to the Pacification of Augsburg, which allowed both the upper and the lower classes of the Empire, to belong either to the old religion or else to the Augsburg Confession, but did not sanction their adopting any other opinions or joining any sect they liked. The Elector was furious at this interference on the part of the Emperor. He sent word to the bearer of the manifesto that he was to return home forthwith, and in a letter to Maximilian he deprecated ' this your Imperial Majesty's arrogant assumption of power.' He had not, he said, been convicted of any sectarianism or heresy, and he was astonished that the Emperor should recommend Otto Henry's Church system to the Provincial Estates, since this code, according to the appendix, which deals with adding to or subtracting from it, did not bind its followers to the letter of the text; and since Otto Henry himself, in his lifetime, had introduced all sorts of things which were not contained in the code.[1] Frederic reprimanded the Provincial Estates for having accepted the Emperor's unbecoming document, and most sternly forbade their making any answer to it.[2] But he could not break their ' hard heads.' They told him plainly that all that had happened so far had been done in opposition to their will, and that if the worst came to the worst they should take advantage of the right of emigration granted them by the Religious Peace.

---

[1] Kluckhohn, *Briefe*, i. 706, 717–719.
[2] *Ibid., Friedrich der Fromme*, p. 275.

'I wish my lord your father and all his false prophets were far away again,' wrote the Lutheran
Countess Palatine Dorothea, widow of the Elector
Frederic II., to Frederic's daughter Dorothea Susannah,
on December 20, 1566; 'I wish I could get the whole
business out of my head; but there is so much misery
that it is not easy to dismiss these things from one's
thoughts. Nothing has yet been secured with respect to
religion. Our party are still in power, thank God.
Three weeks ago the provincial deputies were allowed to
go home, and before their departure they told your
father plainly that they would not adopt his religion, and
should go on protesting against his Grace in this matter.
Thereupon your father waxed very angry and ordered a
beadle to shut them all up in the hostel, where they
were kept for three or four days. Afterwards they were
summoned to the court, where the chancellor delivered
them a long lecture with fierce threats of punishment
by sword and otherwise.' 'A heavy fine has been
imposed on them, which they are to pay by the holy
day of the three kings, and they are bargaining with
usurers, merchants, Jews, and heathen fiends. Where
they will betake themselves no one can find out:
rumour says, to Basle. In short, it does not enter
into your father's reckoning to stand by his land and
his people; all he thinks of is to fleece them to the
skin, and get all he can out of them, and leave them
pining in misery. And this is what he is taught by
the God he believes in, and by his unchristian conscience.' [1]

At the first sermon preached by the Calvinist
ministers the people 'fled from both churches with great

[1] Kluckhohn, *Briefe*, i. 738–741.

tumult and uproar.' [1] It was only Frederic's presence
that saved the preachers from acts of violence. When,
however, one of them had the audacity to declare that
the people of Amberg would not lie down to rest before
the Elector had had some of their heads chopped off,
the populace collected together in mobs in different
parts of the town and Frederic had great difficulty in
preventing the alarm-bell from being sounded.[2] The
renewal of the order to smash and destroy all images in
the churches of the Upper Palatinate caused general
fury and indignation. In many places even the magistrates refused to obey. The Countess Palatine Dorothea,
in a letter to the Duchess Dorothea Susannah on March 18,
1567, tells her that ' when the monastery at Amberg
had been stormed, and the crucifix carried about with
much vile, abusive language, an imperial envoy had
come up and had said : " The Elector had better take
warning by his son-in-law, Duke John Frederic of
Saxony ; what had happened in Saxony might happen
also in the Palatinate, for he knew that the Emperor
would not allow this work to go unavenged." The
electoral councillors had at first been minded to put the
ambassador in prison, but on second thoughts they
had given orders that the iconoclastic work should
be stopped. The new preachers also had begun to
lose courage. Carpenters and masons had refused to
help in the destruction of images. " One carpenter
came forward and said it was a sin ; then one of the
new preachers came forward and said : to leave the
images in the church is a greater sin than any curses or

---

[1] Count Palatine Reichart to Christoph van Württemberg; Kluckhohn, *Briefe*, i. 712.

[2] Wittmann, p. 54; Kluckhohn, *Briefe*, ii. 927.

imprecations one could utter." What beautiful sort of teaching this all is you can well imagine.'[1]

But no amount of opposition could shake the Elector from his purpose. The Calvinist preachers set over the parishes of the Upper Palatinate had to endure mockery and scorn, torments, dangers, and ill-usage of all sorts ; there could be no question of any beneficial pastoral labour. Under such circumstances the lawlessness and profligacy of the people increased everywhere in an alarming degree. All persons who refused to have their children baptised according to Calvinistic rites were compelled to undergo rigorous punishment— were sometimes even put into prison. Severity of this sort only made the people more obdurate.[2] But it was the Calvinistic doctrine of the Eucharist which provoked ' the strongest abhorrence.' It availed nothing that the Elector assured the deputies of the Council of Nabburg, as he had often assured others, that his doctrine of the Sacrament ' was altogether based on the divine Word, whereas Luther, to whom they everlastingly referred, was so undecided on the subject that he had changed his opinions about the Sacrament four times.'[3]

' In numbers of places things went the length of an insurrection : ' ' there was no end of scandalous and abusive language from the pulpits.' Frederic complained to the Landgrave William of Hesse, in 1575, that ' the Lutheran preachers publicly condemn and vilify our doctrines and those who believe in them, and ourselves also, and incense our subjects against us, and stir them up to rebellion.' ' Only lately, again, our leading councillors have been subjected to the same

---

[1] Kluckhohn, *Briefe*, ii. 12–13.   [2] Wittmann, pp. 56–57.
[3] Wittmann, p. 63.

insulting treatment they have often experienced before ;
several hundreds of ruffians, with weapons in hand,
have collected together and mobbed our lord high
steward, mocked and jeered at him, and in addition,
during the sermon, they have thrown stones into the
churches.'[1] Heidelberg theologians were of opinion
that it was necessary to resort to measures of war.
In the year 1575 it was said that Amberg was about to
be invaded by an armed force. But the Palatine
nobles—so the bigoted Lutheran lady, Elizabeth,
Countess Palatine, wife of John Casimir, wrote to
Dresden—had declared that ' they would not go with
the troops to the Upper Palatinate, for they had no
intention of fighting against God.'[2]

' Added to all the heavy troubles with the stiffnecked people of the Upper Palatinate, and their
mutinous revolts,' the Elector and his land ' were
pestered with other lamentable dissensions in matters
of religion, which led in the end to a bloody tragedy.'

It seems from the account of Silvan (one of their
number) that a certain group of clergymen, Adam
Neuser, pastor of the Church of St. Peter at Heidelberg,
John Silvanus, preacher and inspector at Ladenburg,
Jacob Suter, pastor at Weidenheim, and Matthias Vehe,
deacon at Lautern, had been strongly influenced by
the writings of Erasmus of Rotterdam and Sebastian
Franck, and had conceived ' doubts of various kinds
respecting the mystery of the Holy Trinity.' They
took to compiling their sermons ' in such a manner as
to avoid all mention of the Trinity and of the Incarnation of Christ.' Silvan published a treatise entitled
' Of the one true God and the Messiah Jesus of the true

---

[1] Kluckhohn, *Briefe*, ii. 927.   [2] *Ibid.* ii. 836-837, 843.

Christians, as opposed to the false god in three persons, and the double-natured idol the Antichrist.' 'Christ,' he said, 'is only styled God on acount of His heroic virtues, like Hercules.' The four men made up their minds to escape to Transylvania. Adam Neuser composed a letter to the Sultan, which, however, he afterwards annulled and did not send. This letter was to the effect that, as a preacher and teacher at Heidelberg, he had considered the question of ' the many and various changes and dissensions in the Christian religion, in which there were now as many creeds as there were individuals.' For this reason he had discarded all teachers and exponents of Holy Scripture, and by means of original research he had come to the conclusion that Christ was not the son of God, and not of the same substance with the Father, but that there was only one God, as the Alcoran also taught: from study of the Alcoran he had discovered that the Mohammedan faith was grounded on the Gospel of Christ. The Turkish Empire was that of which Daniel had prophesied that it should rule over the whole world. Neuser called on the Sultan to invade Germany, and promised to help him by disseminating his religion. If the Sultan, he said, wished to enlarge his dominion, now was the opportune moment, while ' the Christian preachers were all at variance with each other, and the common people were beginning to waver in their faith.' 'Everybody was now heard complaining that all that their priest said was full of falsehood and uncertainty.' In addition to which the lower classes were so heavily oppressed by their rulers that they ' openly longed for the coming of the Turks.' [1]

---

[1] The documents in Arnold, ii. 1125-1136. See *Unschuldige Nach-*

This letter, with other suspicious writings of the four preachers, fell, in 1570, into the hands of the Elector, who forthwith caused the offenders to be put in prison, and subjected them to an inquisitorial trial. The Heidelberg theologians, Olevian, Ursinus, Boquin, and others expressed their opinion, in a comprehensive memorandum, that Neuser and Silvan were blasphemers of God who deserved capital punishment. Death by stoning, however, which the Mosaic law prescribed for blasphemy, was no longer in force in Christian legislation ; they must be executed by the sword or by hanging. Previous to their execution the prisoners must be subjected to torture in order to extort from them the names of their associates, among whom there were said to be men of high standing and repute.[1]

Meanwhile, Neuser saved himself by flight, became a Mohammedan, and met with an unfortunate end in Turkey. He is reported to have said to an imperial ambassador at Constantinople that ' in order to guard oneself against Arianism, one must be on one's guard against Calvinism.' [2] Silvan, on the other hand, renounced his erroneous opinions, and made recantation both in written statements and in conversations with two theologians. He was not, however, set free. Frederic solicited the advice of the Elector Augustus of Saxony and of his political councillors, all of whom concurred in recommending capital punishment; in

richten zum Jahr 1702, pp. 799-804, and Lessing, *Zur Geschichte und Literatur* (Brunswick, 1774), iii. 121-194. We take this opportunity of remarking that Döllinger, ii. 460, confounds John Silvanus with Stephen Sylvius.

[1] Kluckhohn, *Friedrich der Fromme*, pp. 380–381, and 474, notes 5 and 6.

[2] ' Qui non vult fieri Arianus, caveat ne fiat Calvinianus.' See Mylius, *Predigten vom Türken*, p. 38 ; Leuchter, p. 224.

consideration, however, of the offender's recantation, they advised that the sentence of death by fire should be commuted to death by the sword. 'Such a terrible case of blasphemy and a crime of such enormity must be punished most severely as an example and warning to others.' [1]

With his own hand Frederic wrote out the sentence passed on the prisoners, adding to it the words : ' He believed he had also the Holy Ghost, who in these matters was a master and instructor of the truth.' Suter and Vehe, who had been misled by the others, were let off with banishment ; Silvan was beheaded on the market-place of Heidelberg on December 23, 1572.[2] Martin Seidel, a teacher at the *Pädagogium* at Heidelberg, who also belonged to the Antitrinitarians, fearing a like fate to Silvan's, took refuge in flight. His doctrine was that ' Christ was not the Messiah ;. He had only been a true expounder of the laws of nature, and whoever obeyed these laws as explained by Him fulfilled all the claims of religion prescribed by God.' The Elector's confidential councillor, Thomas Erast, at that time rector of the university of Heidelberg, and who had helped zealously in converting the Palatinate to Calvinism, came under suspicion of heresy with the divines, on account of his close connection with Silvan and Neuser, and was summoned to give an account of his faith before an inquisitorial commission presided over by the Elector.[3]

' From the horrible Heidelberg Arianism ' the

---

[1] Kluckhohn, *Briefe*, ii. 424–425.

[2] Fuller details in Wundt, i. 88–154. Kluckhohn (*Friedrich der Fromme*, p. 382) erroneously makes March 23 the date of Silvan's execution.

[3] Hautz, *Die erste Gelehrtenschule*, pp. 22–25.

Lutheran theologians tried to prove that ' the Calvinism of the Palatinate led direct to Mohammedanism.' [1]
Jacob Andreä, Chancellor of the University of Tübingen, complained in sermons which he preached at
Memminger and published in print, that the Heidelbergers were not only Calvinists, Nestorians, and
Arians, but also ' on the road to falling into the horrors
of the Alcoran.' The Calvinists, he said, were ' the
most lying scoundrels on the face of the earth.' [2] Philip
Nicolai, Lutheran preacher at Unna in Westphalia,
wrote with equal virulence : ' The Calvinistic dragon is
pregnant with all the horrors of Mohammedanism ;
the monster is in league with the Turks.' [3] ' The
electoral Palatinate is the abode of every kind of
abomination.' [4]

George Mylius also, professor of theology at the
university of Jena, referred in his sermons to the
' Calvinistic rabble at Heidelberg ' who were intriguing
with the Turks, as a proof that ' this impious Calvinism
was nothing else than a preliminary measure for introducing Mohammedanism and the Alcoran.' [5]

In all these attacks and accusations against ' the
Heidelbergers and their venomous kindred in many
other districts of the Empire ' the great concern of the

[1] An anonymous pamphlet under the above title, 1573.

[2] See Kluckhohn, *Friedrich der Fromme*, pp. 396–397. Arnold, ii. 8.
On January 3, 1574, Ursinus wrote to Bullinger : ' Nota sunt vobis nova
convitia Schmidlini (J. Andreä) quibus nos Arianismi et Mohametismi
accusat, classicum canens, ad nos tanquam proditores et hostes ecclesiæ
et patriæ, et novos quosdam Turcos in media Germania exortos, *armis
opprimendos* ' (In Heppe, *Gesch. des deutschen Protestantismus*, 2 Beil.
p. 140).

[3] Arnold, ii. 8.

[4] Cited in the pamphlet, *Wider die Teufelskinder, eine frumme
Ermahnung*, p. 23.

[5] *Zehn Predigten vom Türken*, pp. 37ᵇ–38.

theologians and preachers ' was to preserve the true teaching of the Gospel, at any rate in Saxony, where by means of Luther, God's chosen instrument, the pure Gospel had first been introduced ; and to root out all the countless devil's seeds of Calvinism scattered all over the ground, and to do all in their power to drive the Elector Augustus to take part in this godly work.' [1]

[1] *Wider die Teufelskinder*, pp. 27–28.

CHAPTER VIII

ECCLESIASTICAL CONDITIONS IN SAXONY—CRYPTO-CALVINISM AND ITS OVERTHROW

IN the duchy of Saxony, Duke John William, as soon as he had entered into possession of the land taken from his brother John Frederic after the execution at Gotha, set himself up as ' an angel of the pure doctrine of Luther.' All theologians who did not hold pure, unalloyed Lutheran opinions were deprived of their posts at the university of Jena and compelled to leave the duchy. Among those appointed to the vacant offices was Tilmann Hesshus, who regarded the Duke as a new Constantine or Theodosius, as a second Charlemagne. The formulæ of doctrine, hitherto obligatory in the land, were pronounced ' false, misleading, and objectionable,' and a new ducal religious edict, of January 16, 1568, was presented to all preachers for their signature ; those who refused to sign it were expelled from the country. The Flacians of Jena made a fresh violent attack on the Wittenberg divines in a treatise ' On Justification and Good Works.' The Wittenberg divines defended themselves in a counter-treatise, drawn up by Nicholas Selnekker (who on expulsion from Jena had taken refuge at Wittenberg) and written with so much force of conviction that nobody could have supposed that the author would immediately afterwards become a valiant champion of

the Flacians against Wittenberg.[1]   The pulpits again
resounded with insults and invectives, with ' snarling
and biting,' more virulent even than before ; in taverns,
' at guest-tables and at wine parties,' the mysteries of
religion again became the subjects of disputation ;
booksellers found it profitable to publish as many controversial and libellous pamphlets as possible. [2]

In order to bring about a reconciliation between the
theologians of Wittenberg and those of Jena, the Elector
Augustus and Duke John William arranged for a
religious conference to be held at Altenburg.   This
assembly, which began in October 1568, and lasted till
March 1569, only produced ' still more terrible discord.'
' It even set the heavens in agitation.'   While it was
going on the Electress Anna received intelligence of all
sorts of wonderful phenomena that had occurred :
there had been ' frequent conflagrations in the castle, in
the council house, in the college ; there had been several
great downfalls in the church ; the Uhu had screeched
in the castle and in the church ; the great crows had
cawed in a horrible manner ; another time all the dogs
in the castle had begun to roar ; ' ' three pinnacles on
the castle of Leuchtenberg near Kahla had been on
fire, but the fire had not been a natural one.' [3]   The
theologians of the duchy of Saxony demanded the
destruction ' of all the chief writings of Melanchthon ; '
those of the Saxon electorate, on the other hand, urged

---

[1] See Gillet, *Crato*, i. 379–381.

[2] Sixt, *Paul Eber*, p. 79.   On January 10, 1568, Caspar Peucer wrote to
Crato : ' Typographi se ad judicia et affectus hominum accommodant hujus
sæculi, qui non utiles et bonos, sed maledicos et contentiosos libros requi-
runt.   Talibus jam et præla occupantur et implentur fora ac tabernæ ac
personant pulpita, convivia, congressus.'   Gillet, *Crato*, i. 381, note.

[3] v. Weber, *Anna*, pp. 305–306.

that ' these writings had in part been composed and printed during the lifetime of Luther, of blessed memory, and had been praised and loved by him.' [1] John William, who was president of the conference, declared that in the whole of his life he had never seen such disgraceful behaviour on the part of theologians. ' They had begun the transactions in the name of God, and had then proceeded to scolding and jeering as though it were question of a comedy.' [2] Each party published its own versions of the conference (fourteen whole weeks of which were taken up with the sole discussion of the article on justification), and each endeavoured to persuade the world that it had won an incontrovertible victory, and to expose the atrocious heresy and the signal overthrow of its opponents.[3] Paul Eber, the superintendent-general of Saxony, who came back from Altenburg broken down in soul and body, complained bitterly that ' the Church was torn in pieces by the fierce and irreconcilable dissensions of its teachers ; that the unhappy consciences of the people were perplexed and misled on every single point of doctrine, and that they were sinking more and more into epicureanism. The Elector's subjects, oppressed and ground down in every direction by new burdens and intolerable taxes, and almost reduced to beggary, were beginning to call down curses on those for whose preservation they were bidden from the pulpits to pray.' [4]

' What creed is there,' asked Andreas Dudith in 1569, discussing the general situation of Protestantism : what creed is there that one can believe in, seeing that

---

[1] Sixt, p. 85.   [2] Wilkens, p. 135.
[3] Heppe, *Geschichte des Protestantismus*, ii. 206-207.
[4] Sixt, pp. 79, 81 ; Gillet, i. 385, note 48.

not only each separate Church claims to be the only true
one and anathematises all the others, but that theologians also contradict themselves day after day, and
reject to-day what they taught yesterday, and that it
is impossible to feel sure to-day what will be thought
of any given religious opinion to-morrow ? Formerly
such dissensions as these were put a stop to either by
councils or by papal decrees ; but what councils, what
authority, what laws can silence disputes nowadays
when licence and lawlessness prevail everywhere ? '
' Are we going to pretend,' he concluded with reference
to the persecution and punishment of all who thought
differently, ' that the weapons of our warfare are
spiritual and not carnal ? Are we going to maintain
further that consciences must not be coerced in the
matter of faith, that they must be left in freedom ? ' [1]

The result of the Altenburg conference had been to
make the Elector Augustus of Saxony a still fiercer
enemy of all the Flacians, and he issued a mandate
proclaiming that all preachers in the electorate of
Saxony who would not affix their signatures to a formal
condemnation of Flacianism were to be expelled from
the land. Augustus had already in 1567 made a signal
example of his feudatory, Count Wolf of Schönburg,
who had shown favour to the Flacians and had called
a religious edict of the Elector unchristian. He not
only deprived him of his fief and ordered him to quit his
territory, but caused him to be incarcerated in the
' Kaiser ' at Dresden, a dungeon which, according to the
account of the warden, had not been cleaned out for so
long that ' now the stench was so horrible that nobody
would go into it to clean it ; ' the Count would ' certainly

[1] Gillet, *Crato*, ii. 271-272.

be suffocated there.' After a few days the prisoner became so rigid in the face and in other parts of his body, that there seemed great danger of suffocation, and he signified to the chancellor and the councillors of the Elector his willingness to make an apology, to pay a large money fine, and to sell his possessions, 'provided he were left free to follow his conscience.' Augustus, however, would not agree to this stipulation, but insisted on unconditional submission. 'Even if the Count dies in the dungeon,' the Elector wrote, 'it will affect us no more than if we had had a dog hung; and if he does die in prison, our orders are that his corpse shall be left there and bricked over.' In order to escape from death the Count at last made the penitent declaration that he had acted from a spirit of obstinacy, and he begged forgiveness for the 'crime he had been guilty of.' [1] In the year 1570 the Elector had a cannon cast with the inscription :

> Die Flaciane und Zeloten
> Sind des Teufels Vorboten.[2]

The Flacians, Nicholas Selnekker wrote in 1570, court

---

[1] Fuller details respecting the execrable treatment of the Count in Distel's *Flacianismus*, pp. 27 ff. The prayer which Hieronymus Haubold, rector of the provincial school of Schönburg in Geringswalde, made his pupils repeat, during the imprisonment of the Count, is very significant of the religious conditions of the time : ' Wilt Thou then no more look upon us nor listen to us ; wilt Thou indeed forget us ? Who will sing praises unto Thee in his life, who will give Thee thanks in hell ? Go to, if Thou lettest us be covered with shame, then must Thou too be covered with shame ; if Thou lettest us be downtrodden, then wilt Thou too be downtrodden ; how canst Thou suffer this ? ' (S. 37, note 1.)

[2] ' The Flacians and the zealots are the devil's forerunners.' See Schmidt in Riedner's *Zeitschrift für die historische Theologie*, 1849, pp. 73 ff. Also ' Ergänzungen von Th. Distel ' in *Archiv für die sächsische Gesch.*, Neue Folge, iv. 367 ff. For the Flacian cannon-balls, on which there were also rhymed inscriptions, see the same Archives, vii. 320 ff. ; Distel, *Flacianismus*, p. 15.

the favour and approval ' of the lower classes, pander to
the profligate, unthinking masses, and this leads not only
to extraordinary and disgraceful wrangling, discussion,
riots, and murder in taverns and ale-houses, and at all
convivial meetings, but it also produces all manner of
revolt against and contempt for the holy ministry of
the Church and the regular authority of the State.'
' Almost all churches and parishes are loud with the
noise of lewd, disorderly yells and shouts occasioned by
these uncontrollable insurrections.'

' The congregations delight in hearing all this, and
they add fuel to the fire to make the flames all the
fiercer. From day to day the people grow more and
more depraved, and it is greatly to be feared that
everything will rapidly go to rack and ruin.' [1]

Duke John William became alarmed, in 1570, lest the
Elector Augustus should resort to armed force against
Jena on account of the conduct of the Flacians who denounced him openly as a renegade heretic, a tyrant, and
a Mameluke of the worst description. He begged the
Landgrave William of Hesse, in view of the possibility
of such an event, to fortify him with good advice,
telling him that the theologians of Wittenberg and
Leipsic had already published a libellous pamphlet
invoking secular aid against the Flacians. The burghers
of Jena declared that if the Elector appeared before the
town with his troops they would deliver the theologians

---

[1] *Christliche Verantwortung*, A—C, D⁴. 'The theologians of Jena,' he
writes, ' scream and rant publicly from the pulpit, at court, and anywhere and everywhere: Selnekker, Schelmlecker. . . .' In particular, the
Jena professor, Joh. Friedr. Celestinus, ' had attacked him in the most
virulently hostile manner.' Selnekker, in revenge, called this man ' a
venomous serpent, a bacchant, a ranting devil, a shameless madman,
a scoundrelly liar,' and so forth. L², N.

over to him; the students, on the other hand, assumed a threatening attitude in defence of their teachers. The following placard was seen one day at the street corners : ' All students who do not come ready armed to the market-place in the evening will be reckoned as men of straw.'

The Elector Augustus, having, as he said, been told by some of his councillors that they had themselves heard him publicly prayed against at Weimar in the presence of the Duke of Weimar, wrote to the Emperor on May 20, 1570, begging his Majesty not to be displeased if he planned some means by which to put a stop to the offensive proceedings of the Duke and his theologians. Maximilian's answer, according to the Landgrave's account, was that ' if the Duke would not listen to his remonstrances, he must leave him to look out for himself.' [1] At the Diet of Spires in 1570 the Elector succeeded in carrying through a resolution to the effect that the sons of the captive Duke, John Frederic, should be restored to their paternal inheritance under his (the Elector's) tutelage, and thus Duke John William was deprived of half of his territory.

Meanwhile, on the strength of the decree of a sovereign prince, Protestantism had acquired a fresh domain in Northern Germany.

Duke Henry the younger of Brunswick-Wolfenbüttel had died on June 11, 1568, and his son and successor, Duke Julius, had declared himself in favour of the Augsburg Confession, had inhibited the exercise of the Catholic religion everywhere in his dominions, and

---

[1] Heppe, *Geschichte des deutschen Protestantismus*, ii. 297, 317–330 ; Gillet, *Crato*, i. 402.

confiscated all church and convent property. He had
had a new code of doctrine, a ' Corpus Doctrinæ,' drawn
up for Brunswick by the superintendent of the place,
Martin Chemnitz, and the Tübingen chancellor, James
Andreä, whom Duke Christopher of Würtemberg had
placed at his service for a time. The Duke was of
opinion that ' the Holy Ghost could work quite as
effectually through two men as through a number,'
and that therefore these two theologians were quite
sufficient for the Turk.[1] The new Church regulations
were published in 1569, and submitted to every preacher
and schoolmaster for signature. All who refused to
sign were obliged to leave the land.[2]

James Andreä, who had been commissioned by Duke
Christopher to take in hand the task, so often attempted
by the Protestant princes, of establishing ' general
harmony among the evangelicals,' prepared a formula
of concord on the five articles of justification, good

[1] Hachfeld, pp. 57 ff.

[2] The first edition of the Church Ordinances was bought up again,
because at p. 67, where the baptismal ceremonies are prescribed, the
words in the Apostles' Creed, ' who was conceived by the Holy Ghost '—
' suffered under Pontius Pilate '—' of the Father Almighty,' were left out
' by mistake ' (Stübner, *Histor. Beschr.* p. 46). In contradiction of this
statement, Koldewey, in the *Zeitschrift für Niedersachsen*, 1887, p. 260 ff.,
and in the *Theol. Studien und Kritiken*, p. 61 (1888), shows convincingly
that no mistake occurred, but that these passages of the Creed were
omitted intentionally, since the *interrogatio de fide* in the rite of baptism
—the subject here in question—does not keep quite strictly to the text
of the Creed. He is not so successful in arguing against a withdrawal of
the first edition, and claiming that the first and second editions were
sold out. Moreover, when, on the ground of this solitary instance,
he makes a general complaint against Janssen's use of original documents, his objection is altogether unjustifiable, as has been recently
pointed out in the *Histor. Jahrbuch*, x. 860; indeed, four Protestant
scholars—two of them theologians—take the same view as Janssen.
Before Koldewey, moreover, no one had ever raised an objection against
this view.

works, the adiaphora, free-will, and the Sacrament.
He met with zealous encouragement in his work from
Duke Julius and the Landgrave William of Hesse.
Augustus of Saxony also interested himself in the
matter, accorded him a friendly reception, and gave
him letters of introduction to the theologians at Wittenberg and Leipsic. Concerning these theologians Andreä
had written to Duke Christopher on September 27,
1568 : ' Some of them are open and avowed Zwinglians,
but they are still friendly and courteous, as they have
no authority and keep silence.' [1] He was hopeful at
that time of coming to an understanding with them,
and he made no opposition to their principal demand
for recognition of Melanchthon's 'Corpus Doctrinæ,'
which was the standard of teaching in the Saxon
electorate : on the contrary, he pronounced it to be a
thoroughly orthodox volume.[2] In Weimar he met with
' open reviling.' The court preacher Irenäus declaimed
' most virulently against him from the pulpit, and
Hesshus declared in sermons that Andreä had a work
in hand which proceeded from the devil, and that he
wished to warn everybody against it as against the devil
himself.' [3] In a letter to the Elector of Saxony he gave
a list of fifty-four insulting names which the Weimar
theologians had applied to him, either openly or in
written statements, sent by them to Duke Julius of
Brunswick and the Landgrave William of Hesse.[4]
Martin Chemnitz, in conjunction with whom he had

----

[1] Kugler, ii. 531.

[2] Heppe, *Gesch. des deutschen Protestantismus*, ii. 247 ff. ; Gillet, i.
396, 397. ' Melanchthon's *Corpus Doctrinæ* was printed originally (1559)
merely as a book-dealer's speculation, and was only later on invested with
authority under the title *Corpus Misnicum* ' (Mönckeberg, p. 190).

[3] Heppe, p. 2 ; Beil, S. 72.

[4] See Calinich, *Kampf des Melanchthonianissmus*, p. 22.

compiled the Brunswick Church Ordinances, would have little to do with his scheme for a formula of concord. He called Andreä a 'new apostle who wanted to prescribe novel articles of faith.' Alarmed at Andreä's connection with the Wittenbergers, he wrote in the spring of 1570 to Mörlin: 'They mean to put down the controversies with force and with fists. They intend to slay and quarter all the Flacians, and their adherents after them. And after that there will be peace and tranquillity.' [1]

But a breach between Andreä and the Wittenbergers was at hand. By Andreä's exertions a convention of theologians had been summoned at Zerbst in order to deliberate on means by which the existing authority of Melanchthon's teaching could be maintained side by side with that of Luther.[2] During the transactions

---

[1] Hachfeld, pp. 106–107.

[2] A letter of the Landgrave William of Hesse (May 8, 1570) to the theologians and councillors deputed to Zerbst is worthy of notice. He had had, William writes, a vehement discussion with the theologians, who wanted to set Luther's books up as sacred. He had told them that there were 'coarse, abominable *errores* to be found in them. They had answered that it was possible Luther might have erred in his first writings before he had become perfect; but afterwards, when he had attained perfection, his books were *ne in apice quidem* to be censured. Thereupon we asked them " *quo tempore* this his perfection had begun ; whether *circa annum tricesimum*, when he had written *librum de matrimonio*, or if it had happened 'circa annum quadragesimum,' when he had written *Hausenwurster*, 'indignum plane theologo librum,' as they themselves were obliged to allow ; or if it was 'circa annum quadragesimum quartum,' and thus in his last year, when he wrote *de libero arbitrio*, the very things which they now dared to reject, and published the little work in which he said they ought not to become reconciled with Duke Henry ? " This enigma they were not able to solve ' (Neudecker, *Neue Beiträge*, ii. 283–284). The chief cause of the Landgrave's animosity towards Luther is revealed in a letter of the Countess Palatine Elizabeth to her mother, the Electress Anna of Saxony. She and her husband, John Casimir, she wrote on July 21, 1575, were on a visit to William at Cassel : 'He began talking to me of Dr. Luther, and he denounced Dr. Luther as a scoundrel,

on the occasion of the promotion of several doctors of
theology, in May 1570, a disputation took place at
Wittenberg in which avowed Calvinistic dogmas were
defended and the doctrine of ubiquity taught in Würtemberg was fiercely attacked. Andreä, who had gone
from Zerbst to Wittenberg to be present at the ' Promotion,' repudiated ' the disputed propositions as unchristian and Mohammedan,' and left the place ' with
strange threats that the whole of Saxony ought to
write against this university, that the Wittenbergers
were Zwinglians or Calvinists.' The Heidelberg Calvinist, Thomas Erast, wrote to Bullinger: ' It is publicly known through the Wittenberg theses that our
party are masters of the pulpits and schools there.' [1]
The Wittenberg printer, Hans Luft, said that ever since
1567 he had no longer known what to do with the
Lutheran writings ; whereas, if he had printed twenty
or thirty times more Calvinist books, they would all
have been bought up at once.[2]

The most prominent and at the same time the most
influential of the Wittenberg Crypto-Calvinists was
Caspar Peucer, professor of medicine and history.
After the death of his father-in-law, Melanchthon, he
had been unanimously elected Rector of the university
and entrusted by the Elector with its whole internal
management. As physician to the Elector he was
frequently at the court of Dresden, where he was treated

for he had persuaded his father to have two wives, and he made Dr.
Luther out to be very wicked. Then I said it was not true that Luther
had done this. Then the Landgrave said he had his own handwriting
which proved it. I answered back that they could very well have forged
his writing without his knowing anything about it.' The Landgrave
fetched the written statement, but Elizabeth would neither read it nor
hear it read (v. Weber, *Anna*, pp. 401–402).

[1] Gillet, *Crato*, i. 407.   [2] Anton, i. 57.

with such high distinction that on one occasion he actually stood sponsor to an infant prince. George Craco, the Elector's privy councillor and confidential adviser of many years' standing, was also the tried and trusted friend of Peucer, and agreed with him in all questions of religion.[1] In his capacity of Curator of the university Craco pushed forward Peucer's proposals for filling the chairs at Wittenberg, and thus the Melanchthonians, or Philipists as they were called, gained completely the upper hand. At Dresden the court preacher Christian Schütz was notably their champion. John Stössel also, superintendent at Pirna, was among the zealous partisans of Crypto-Calvinism.

In the year 1571 there appeared, in the name of the Wittenberg theological faculty, a new Catechism, in which the doctrine of the Eucharist differed from that in Luther's Catechism, in which there was no mention of participation through the mouth in the body and blood of Christ, and which taught, in diametrical opposition to the Würtemberg dogma of ubiquity, that the body of Christ was circumscribed by a space in heaven. In the preface written by Peucer the wish was expressed that this manual of religion, compiled and abridged from Melanchthon's ' Corpus Doctrinæ,' might serve as a stepping-stone for the more advanced pupils in the Latin schools and Gymnasia, between Luther's Catechism and the higher theological studies. Peucer, who had become chief inspector of the higher schools, wrote himself to the Rector of the ' Schulpforte,' [2]

---

[1] Craco (it was thus he spelt his name, not Crakow or Krakau) was not the Elector's chancellor, but his privy councillor and financial adviser. See Kluckhohn in v. Weber's *Archiv für sächs. Gesch.* vii. 144, note.

[2] A famous school in Saxony, near Naumburg, and the oldest and

enjoining him to procure the necessary number of copies for his own educational institute, and to make the pupils commit to memory the passages printed in large type.

The new Wittenberg Catechism provoked the most vehement opposition.[1] The Brunswick theologians declared it to be a falsification of the Divine Word, and called it a sacramentarian book.[2] The Jena theologians, Wigand, Hesshus, John Frederic Cœlestinus, and Timotheus Kirchner talked of a 'new incursion of devilish spirit.' In a pamphlet they published entitled ' *Warnung vor dem unreinen und sacramentarischen Catechismus Etlicher zu Wittenberg*,' they drew attention to the fact that the Wittenbergers had already before given expression to abominable heresies and blasphemies. 'They want to make an end of Luther, that is to say of his teaching, and at the same time to appear innocent of doing so;' their teaching is 'falsehood, seduction, perversion of the holy Testament; it's nothing but deceitful jugglery, with which they hope to befool Christendom.'[3]

The Wittenbergers, in self-defence, published in the year 1571 the 'Wittenberger Grundfeste,' in which they not only paid the Flacians back in their own coin, but

most renowned of the three old Saxon (so-called) *Landes* or *Fürsten Schulen*. (Translator.)

[1] Printed at Wittenberg, published at Leipsic, it was reprinted twice in the same year, 1571, and twice again in the following year. Klose, *Der crypto-calvinistische Catechismus*, in the *Festprogramm* of the Hamburg Gymnasium, 1856.

[2] Calinich, *Kampf*, pp. 55–57. The Lutheran clergy of the town of Hanover accused the Wittenberg theologians in 1575 of having, ' at the instigation of the devil, troubled the Church in which they were brought up and reduced it with their venomous doctrines ' (*Zeitschrift des histor. Vereins für Niedersachsen*, Jahrg. 1870, p. 207).

[3] *Warnung*, B, C³. See Calinich, *Kampf*, pp. 40–55.

also vehemently denounced the Würtemberg and Nether-Saxon theologians. They said that 'nearly all the leading articles of Christian doctrine had been falsified with wicked, malicious pertinacity by that execrable brood of Flacians;' that the unfortunate youth of the land had been misled and deceived by them; that the novel Brenzian doctrine of ubiquity was a fresh piece of Schwenckfeldian extravagance, a wilful desecration of truth, which God could not possibly allow to go unpunished : ' if men held their tongues, the stones would at last begin to cry out.' Martin Chemnitz, 'the new Aristarchus at Brunswick,' whom Brenz had defended, 'had been bitten by three mad dogs—pride, envy, and ingratitude.' [1]

Against the ' Wittenberger Grundfeste ' Chemnitz set up another creed, for which he obtained the approval of the Nether-Saxon Churches. Lüneburg alone kept aloof, the local superintendent Goedemann having declared it to be 'disastrous for each Church and each preacher to set up a separate creed.' [2] The Jena theologians were even more incensed than they had been before by the ' Grundfeste.' The Wittenbergers, they reiterated in 1572, ' trample Luther's doctrine under foot, laugh at it, ridicule it, anathematise it in the most scandalous manner, jeer at Christianity, mock Almighty God in heaven. It is from the Frenchmen Calvin and Beza that they have learnt all these falsehoods. Melanchthon was in conspiracy with Calvin and Bullinger, those sacrilegious enemies of the Testament of Christ.' They alone (the Jena divines) possessed the true, unalloyed doctrine, and they wanted to keep free from all ' the extravagancies and errors of the Pope,

[1] Planck, v[b]. 578–583.   [2] *Ibid.* v[b]. 584.

the Turks, the blasphemers of the Sacrament, the Schwenckfeldians, Servetians, Arians, Antinomians, Interimists, Adiaphorists, Synergists, Majorites, Enthusiasts, Anabaptists, Manichæans, and other sects.' It was their duty to condemn all their opponents. ' If we are not flagrantly to condemn false doctrines and teachers,' they said, ' because they are so numerous, then you must not condemn the papists who are much more numerous than the sacramentarians—no, nor the Turks either. Shame on thee, thou unworthy Christian, does the Word of God teach thee all this ? ' [1]

The Wittenbergers knew well how to talk round the Elector Augustus, who was a man of no culture or learning, and who was incapable of forming an independent judgment on dogmatic discussions. They assured him that it was utter fraud and spitefulness on the part of their opponents to accuse them of digressing from Luther's teaching. At their desire the Elector summoned a convention of theologians at Dresden, and at this meeting a new form of confession called the *Dresden Consens* was drawn up, and the doctrine of the Wittenbergers again publicly stated.[2] The Heidelberg professor Ursinus wrote to Bullinger in 1572 : ' The Elector does not in the least understand the matter, but he has promised to support the Dresden Consens, and not to sanction anybody's expulsion in the name of Zwinglianism and Calvinism, as they call it. He has also said that he was pleased that we and his theologians were not far from agreeing together.' [3]

On March 3, 1573, Duke John William died. At the

---

[1] Von den Fallstricken, A⁴, D³⁻⁴, F³, G⁴.
[2] Calinich, *Kampf*, pp. 75-87.
[3] Heppe, *Gesch. des deutschen Protestantismus*, 2 Beil. p. 138.

beginning of his reign he had made a will which had been confirmed by the Emperor, appointing the Elector Augustus his executor. Later on, however, he had altered this will and named the Count Palatine Louis and Duke Albert of Prussia his executors, and he had forbidden any changes to be made in the ecclesiastical conditions of his land. Augustus, nevertheless, instantly assumed the government and issued orders to expel the theologians Hesshus and Wigand from the country. A general inspection of churches was instituted. Under threat of eviction all the preachers were obliged to sign a ' Revers ' to the effect that they were willing to accept Melanchthon's Corpus Doctrinæ and the Dresden Consens, that together with the unaltered version of the Augsburg Confession they would accept the altered version also, and that they would keep clear of the Flacians. Within a few weeks, nine superintendents and 102 preachers lost their posts for refusing to sign this document. For want of better substitutes many of the vacant places had to be filled up with young Wittenberg stipendiaries.[1]

Among the number of those who were evicted was Caspar Melissander. As a supposed Flacian he was driven away into misery and want, notwithstanding that the widowed Duchess Dorothea Susannah went down on her knees before the Elector to intercede for him.[2] The Duchess herself received orders to leave the castle at Weimar forthwith, otherwise she and her children would be deprived of all food and drink, and everybody would be forbidden to take them the least

---

[1] Löscher, *Hist. Motuum*, iii. 156 ff.; Galetti, *Gesch. Thüringens*, v. 222; Gillet, i. 434.

[2] Anton, pp. 68-69.

particle of bodily nourishment. She was also informed that she must sign Melanchthon's Corpus Doctrinæ, and not receive the Sacrament without the Elector's permission. An imperial warrant authorising her to retain, in both her jointure districts, pastors and schoolmasters of her own religion, was treated with contempt; the electoral government decreed that there must be no independent religion in the land, or else the unity of the faith would again be destroyed by Flacianism. Weimar became the scene of intense agitation and excitement. In the parish church, according to Wigand and Hesshus, the devil, accompanied by the Saxon preacher Mirus, appeared in bodily shape to the faithful believers, wearing a most horrible form, so that ' his picture was taken by many of them several times, and at last it was printed.' [1]

Flacianism, so its adherents said, became ' the public victim to be sacrificed on the cross.'

In Thuringia and in Saxony—in the county of Mansfeld especially—its cause was contended and battled for, not only in the field of literature and in the pulpits, but also in ale-houses and market places, where bleeding scalps often testified to the fierceness of the encounters. Mere schoolboys even would join in the ' Flacian' street fights. ' Scarcely a single household was any longer at peace or unity.' Hesshus and Wigand had set themselves up as decided antagonists of Flacius. They showed up the monstrosity of his doctrine that ' original sin constitutes the substance of man,' by pointing out what extravagant and preposterous conclusions must follow from such a premiss, and the result was that ' a large proportion of the people came

[1] Wilkens, pp. 189–192.

gradually to the opinion that it was their duty to seize
pikes and poles and turn out these devilish villains and
divide their goods.' 'I have demonstrated more than
half a dozen times,' Hesshus exclaimed, 'that Flacius
says : "It is the devil who made and created man ; the
devil is the human potter." ' According to the teaching
of the Flacians, said Wigand, 'original sin is an intelligent animal ; it can laugh, talk, sew, work, read, write,
preach, baptise, administer the Sacrament ; for it is
the substance of man that does all these things ; Christ
took on Himself the substance of man, therefore He took
on Himself original sin.' [1] Several preachers from
Eisleben and other towns made the same complaints of
Flacius and of his friend, Cyriacus Spangenberg, deacon
at Mansfeld, and accused them of teaching that ' man
had been created by Satan, that is, was baptised in
the name of the Holy Trinity and favoured with God's
grace, that women in a state of pregnancy carried live
young devils about with them.' [2] The Counts Volrad
and Carl von Mansfeld were zealous adherents of the
Flacians ; the first-named had a printing press erected
for Spangenberg and caused his writings to be distributed at the church door.[3] For this act of partisanship
they were hooted in the streets by the opponents of
Flacianism, and the windows of their castles were
smashed in. During the sermons of the ' Substantialists' appointed by these counts as preachers at
Eisleben, there was always, as they themselves complained, ' such storming, rioting, banging, thumping,
blustering, and pelting with stones, as had scarcely ever

[1] Preger, *Flacius*, ii. 348, 352-353.
[2] Account of Report on Spangenberg's *Bekenntniss* (Eisleben, 1573),
B, L³, O² ff.
[3] *Unschuldige Nachrichten* (1712), p. 315.

been experienced even from Sacramentarian fanatics, iconoclasts, anabaptists, or seditious Münzer peasants.' The widow of a count of Mansfeld ' had a hand in the game, and helped the cause on lustily, and wanted to get the credit of doing it all out of Christian zeal side by side with the "Accidence" priests of Eisleben.' The principal agent in the propagation of ' the pure doctrine ' was a squire of Ramelburg, a tax collector, who had had a child by the sister of his wife, and had put an end to it. The Counts Hans Georg, Hans Albrecht, and Hans Hoyer were on the side of the anti-substantialists. At their instigation the feudal lord of the county, the Lutheran administrator of Magdeburg, on the last day of 1574, ordered a troop of cavalry and infantry to march from Halle into the Mansfeld district. Plundering and ravaging, the troops forced their way into the houses of the preachers, and robbed the burghers of Mansfeld of their arms and ammunition. Spangenberg managed to escape, but his sick mother was thrown mercilessly out of her bed, and his fine library was looted and destroyed. Every single burgher was tried and examined as to his faith. Thirteen town councillors and twenty-six or twenty-eight burghers who would not abjure the doctrine which had been preached to them were put into prison, where for weeks they were tortured by cold, hunger, and the threats of the executioner. Everybody was enjoined to conform to the faith of the Administrator of Magdeburg. The recreants were removed to Halle, the town councillors in wagons, the burghers following on foot behind them, walking two and two, fastened together with hand-screws.

But the worst fate was reserved for the preachers,

who were obliged to leave the country in the depth of
winter. In addition to this, many of them were subjected to the greatest indignities. One of them, whose
books and household furniture had been thrown out
into the street, had to spend a rainy night with his
children under the open sky. Bodily ill-usage also was
not seldom resorted to. One burgher, who spoke up
for the doctrine of substantialism, received a blow from
the fist of one of the counts, which made the blood
gush out. The burghers were told that if they did not
conform they would be deprived of the right of pasture
for their cattle, and that the whole of the valley would
be laid waste by fire. The deceased relations of the
counts were disinterred and buried again in places to
which no suspicion of ' substantialist heresy ' attached.
The schism in the family of the counts augumented still
further the tyranny practised on their subjects.[1]

While the persecution of his adherents was going
on in Mansfeld, Flacius died in want and tribulation at
Frankfort-on-the-Main, on March 11, 1575, hunted down
like a baited boar by the Elector Augustus, ' that
adiaphoritish and sacramentarian satrap.'[2]

What most distressed him and his friend Spangen-

---

[1] *Gewisse newe Zeitung von der newen vorhin unerhörten Hallischen
Inquisition und trübsäligen Zustand der Kirchen zu Manssfeld*, printed
by G. Scherer, *Triumph der Wahrheit wider Lucam Osiander* (Ingol-
stadt, 1587), pp. 110-133. See Planck, 5ᵃ, 404-436. Richard, *Licht und
Schatten*, pp. 128-129. The execrable procedure, however, did not, as
Richard implies, originate with ' savage papistical bigots.'

[2] After his death James Andreä, ' the preacher of conciliation,' wrote
that he did not doubt ' *quod nunc cum omnibus Diabolis coenaturus sit
Illyricus, si modo domi sunt, et non asseclas ejus, Spangenbergium et
reliquos, passim comitantur* ' (Planck, 5ᵃ, 345, note 148). Hesshus
described Flacius as a man ' qui triste et horrendum exemplum profli-
gatisimæ petulantiæ, projectissimæ impudentiæ et inauditæ pertinaciæ
ediderit,' &c. (pp. 404-405).

berg through the whole of the dissensions was the
behaviour of the Wittenberg theologians towards the
doctrine and the memory of Luther. Those men,
Spangenberg wrote, had not only departed from Luther's
teaching in ten or eleven articles, but they had spoken
of him himself in the most abominable manner. ' They
say Luther was a *Philauticus*—that is to say, a man
who did not think much of anybody except himself,
and whom nothing pleased but what he himself said
or did. Item, a *Philonicus* and an *Eristicus*, a scolding
old hag, who was always in the right, who would not
credit anybody with anything good, who would give in
to no one, who sought nothing but his own glory, and
could not endure a rival. Item, a *Doctor Hyperbolicus*,
the sort of teacher that made a camel out of a flea, who
said a thousand things and only meant about five of
them, who plunged into the arena, whether the cause at
stake were God's truth or not. Item, they call him a
Polypragmonicus, who meddled insolently with everybody's trade, who always went beyond his orders, and
took upon himself business that in no way concerned
him. Item, an *Ostentator ingenii*, a showman of his
own self, parading his great mind without necessity
and having no wish but to be admired. Item, a *Stoic*,
a bully who lived as he pleased, and held others down
in tyrannical bondage.' [1]

The Palatine Elector's privy councillor, George
Craco, had spoken of the banishment of the Flacians
in tones of assured victory,[2] little dreaming that the

---

[1] *Warhaftiger Bericht von den Wohlthaten die Gott durch Martinum
Lutherum seliger, fürnämlich Deutschland erzeygt und von der schänd-
lichen Undankbarkeit für solche grosse Gaben.* See Lengenbrunner,
Erinnerung, 7 a.b.

[2] Menzel, ii. 471.

triumph of the Wittenbergers and all the Crypto-
Calvinists in Saxony was not to be of much longer
duration. Since the appearance of the Wittenberg
Catechism and the *Grundfeste* the opposite party had
become ' mightily strengthened ' at the Dresden court.
Superintendent Greser wrote to his son-in-law Selnekker :
' The court preacher Wagner has heard the Elector
say that he would give 20,000 florins if he could undo
the printing of those books, and that it would require
very little encouragement to make him drive all those
villains to the devil.' [1]   On the death of Wagner the
Wittenberg party did not succeed in getting one of their
adherents appointed court preacher in his place ; on
the contrary, side by side with Christian Schütz, George
Listenius, a strict Lutheran and a zealous advocate of
the doctrine of ubiquity, was nominated to the vacant
post, and entrusted by the Elector with the education
of the electoral prince, Christian.   Listenius began a
fierce campaign in his sermons against the Wittenberg
divines and his colleague Schütz.   On this account, as
he wrote later on, his life became in danger, but, he
added, he had nevertheless put his opponents to shame,
and this was ' as great and divine a miracle as could be
found anywhere in history, and one that would not be
forgotten as long as the world lasts.' [2]

As early as Christmas Day, 1573, ' it became publicly
known that the Elector no longer felt any love for the
Wittenbergers.'   ' It's my belief,' he had said on this
same day to Schütz, ' that there are as big rogues to be
met with at Wittenberg as anywhere else.   I have been
forced to hear a great deal about this Catechism from

[1] Löscher, iii. 158.
[2] Kluckhohn, *Sturz der Cryptocalvinisten*, pp. 95-96.

my kinsmen, but I do not intend for the sake of three persons to expose myself, my land, and my people to the dangers of sacramentarianism. I cannot suffer that people should abuse my favours, nor allow any one to act the Elector in my place ; for I mean to be sole Elector. I can truly say that in all the world there are no more fickle and inconstant people than the priests.' [1]

Augustus had a lofty idea of his importance and dignity in ecclesiastical matters, as was markedly shown in a picture partly designed by himself. In the year 1566 he employed the painter Henry Göding the elder to decorate the outside panels of the triptych and the predella of an old altar with paintings. The picture of the descent of the Holy Ghost, now in the town church at Wittenberg, in which Luther appears as St. Peter, was one of this set. In the representation of the Last Supper the apostles are portraits of Luther and of some of the Elector's court retinue, but the Elector himself sits in the middle and represents the Saviour instituting the Sacrament of the Lord's Supper.[2]

The court preacher, Christian Schütz, wrote once to the Elector that on his entry into Weimar ' it had seemed to him as if the Divine Majesty itself was before his eyes.' [3]

The final catastrophe was the publication in January 1574, under the title of ' Exegesis,' of a theological treatise on the dogma of the Eucharist,[4] which so plainly

---

[1] Heppe, *Gesch. des Protestantismus*, ii. 419–420.

[2] *Beschreibende Darstellung der alten Bau- und Kunstdenkmäler des Königreichs Sachsen* (Dresden, 1882, Heft i. 88–89). In the mural decorations of the Church of the Virgin at Pirna Luther was painted as the evangelist Luke, and Melanchthon as Mark (Heft i. 63).

[3] Calinich, *Kampf*, p. 177.

[4] ' Exegesis perspicua controversiæ de cœna Domini.'

upheld Calvinistic teaching as the only true and tenable doctrine, that its diametrical opposition to Lutheranism could not but be obvious to the most poorly instructed laymen.[1] This treatise did not emanate from the Wittenbergers themselves, but was the work of the Silesian physician, Joachin Curäus, a former pupil of Melanchthon ; [2] the Wittenbergers, however, commended it, distributed it among the young students, and sent copies through their own agents into distant regions. Notwithstanding that this pamphlet had been published without the name of the author or printer,

[1] Planck, 5[b], 606.

[2] Heppe, *Gesch. des Protestantismus*, ii. 422–423 and 467 ff. Even at that time, as Curäus complained, the Catholic belief in transubstantiation was still spread through the whole of the Saxon people. 'Etiam a doctis,' he wrote in 1574, 'non facile exuitur. Populus vero . . . *auribus et oculis hæret in panis intuitu*; illum veneratur animo gestu et *adoratione*' (Heppe, ii. 386, note). The *ecclesiastical ministry* at Rostock complained in Jan. 1569 to the Duke of Mecklenburg that their congregations at public meetings came forward as defenders 'of the popish doctrine of transubstantiation, which had with great difficulty been refuted by Dr. Luther;' and that they 'raised again the subject of the miracles at Sternberg' (Wiggers, 'Der Saliger'sche Abendmahlstreit,' in Niedner's *Zeitschrift*, 1848, p. 620). A leading argument of the Calvinists, as Lutheran divines said, was 'that if the Lutheran belief concerning the Sacrament was maintained, the popish horrors of sacrifice, procession, and adoration could not logically be rejected' (*Kurz Bekenntniss*, handed in at Torgau, 1574, H[3]). The Calvinists, wrote Backmeister, called the Lutheran form of communion a 'diabolica manducatio' (a devilish eating); they call us 'cannibals and blood-suckers' (*Christliche Anleitung*, p. 89). Similarly, in the Confession handed in at Torgau, complaint was made that all the Sacramentarian writers 'calumniate us abominably, and say that the partaking of Christ's body through the mouth is a Capernaite or cyclopean act of cannibalism' (Bl. H[26]). What else are the Lutherans, they ask, than cannibals, Capernaites, blood-suckers, eaters of God and Thyests, who conceive of the holy banquet as an ordinary, corporeal, physical meal, in which the mouth, throat, and stomach all take part? They make themselves a seven-inch-long god of bread baked, cooked, roasted in the oven; they devour it with their mouths, biting and chewing it, and carrying about small particles of it in their teeth until they putrefy (Wilkens, pp. 63–64).

and that it bore a French or Genevese press-mark, and although it had been intentionally set about that it came from a foreign press, it soon became known that it had been printed and published by the bookseller Vögelin at Leipsic, a friend of the Wittenbergers.

The Elector flew into a violent passion on learning the truth from the old Count Ernest of Henneberg, who told him at the nuptials of some prince that his theologians, who up till then had concealed from him the fact that they were Calvinists at heart, had now openly declared their tenets in the new book they had published. ' If he knew,' he wrote, ' that he had even one Calvinistic vein in his body he would wish that the devil tore it out.' [1]

After a secret consultation with the Provincial Estates an inspectoral visitation of the universities of Wittenberg and Leipsic was decreed. Vögelin confessed to being the printer of the pamphlet, was sentenced to pay a fine of 1,000 florins, and esteemed himself fortunate even in being able to escape from Saxony almost in a state of beggary.[2]

It was necessary to use even greater severity against Peucer, Craco, Schütz, and Stössel, for numbers of secret letters found upon them showed that they had been in conspiracy with the people of Heidelberg and with the Swiss, and that they had said many damaging things about the Elector. Schütz and Stössel had talked of things which they had recommended to the Elector in confession, they had complained of the petticoat government of the Electress Anna at the court, had praised the ' Exegesis,' and had pronounced

---

[1] Planck, 5ᵇ, 617.
[2] Hospinian, fol. 23ᵇ ; Calinich, *Kampf*, pp. 112-113.

the sudden imprisonment of the physician Hermann, Peucer's son-in-law, a piece of tyranny. Craco had disclosed some of the Elector's intentions, and had shown as little sense of honour in his talk about the Electress Anna. The Elector was especially incensed by a letter of Stössel to Schütz, which had fallen by mistake into the hands of the court preacher Listenius, and by him had been delivered to Augustus. This letter contained an injunction to Schütz to try to win the favour of the Electress : ' If we only had Mother Anna on our side we should soon win over my lord also.' In another of these letters Peucer had comforted Schütz with the words : ' The truth, which so many rivers of blood in France and Belgium have not been able to drown, will finally triumph in these lands also.' [1]

In April 1574 the Elector caused Craco, Peucer, Stössel, and Schütz to be put in prison, and summoned a considerable number of the knights and landed proprietors to Torgau. He told them of all the rash, secret, and cunning intrigues that there were going on, of all the dark, sinister plotting and manœuvring to undermine the truth, and to establish strange sacramentarian doctrines in the country. He said that ' he had been wickedly and scandalously deceived by the four scoundrels who were in prison ; he had taken them for pious, honourable men, but he had found out from their conduct that they were quite the opposite. Owing

---

[1] Extracts from the letters in Löscher, iii. 167–171 ; Peuceri, *Historia Carcerum*, pp. 103 *sqq.* See Gillet, i. 449–452. Kluckhohn, *Sturz der Kryptocalvinisten*, pp. 104–107. In a letter to the Duchess of Mecklenburg of June 3, 1574, the Electress Anna expressed the opinion that the early death of her son Adolphus was a judgment of God on the Elector for having allowed an arch-calvinist like Peucer to be the child's godfather (v. Weber, *Anna*, p. 378).

to these false, lying scoundrels, he said, he himself and
his pious land had unjustly come under suspicion of
having abjured the pure doctrine of Luther and taken
up with Calvinism.   The long-protracted schism in
this land was solely due to the fact that these secret
Calvinists had not chosen to proclaim their tenets openly,
otherwise a stop would soon have been put to their proceedings, and the foul vermin would not have been
allowed to settle down in the land.   The venomous
plant must now be torn up by the roots.'   Calvinism,
he went on, which they had tried with all their might
to introduce all over the land, had deluged France and
the Netherlands with blood, and no one would persuade
him but that the Calvinists had hoped to bring about
a like bloody consummation in Saxony, however godly
and pious they might make themselves out to be.[1]

A court of inquisition, appointed by the Elector,
drew up ' the Torgau Articles,' which all theologians
were henceforth to be required to sign : all obdurate
ones who refused to do so were to be arrested.   The
theologians of Leipsic and Wittenberg were summoned
to Torgau to give a plain answer—Yes or No—to the four
questions : Whether they agreed in their hearts to the
doctrine of the Sacrament as set forth in these articles ;
whether they renounced from their hearts, as terrible
and injurious heresies, all the errors of the old and
the new Sacramentarians enumerated in the articles ;
whether they accepted everything in Luther's writings,
including (and especially) all that he said concerning
the Sacrament in his pamphlet against the heavenly
prophets, and in his ' Kurzer und Letzter Bekenntniss '
(' short and last confession '), and considered it all the

[1] Hutter, cap. 8, fol. 68 ff ; Calinich, *Kampf*, pp. 128–131.

expression of the real, only, and eternal truth of God; and finally whether, from their hearts, they condemned the execrable 'Exegesis' of the Wittenbergers as a sacramentarian book, and would engage henceforth to combat and oppose all the extravagant theories contained in it.

The Leipsic theologians all signed the articles. Among the Wittenbergers, on the other hand, the Professors Widebram, Cruciger, Pezel, and Moller refused their assent; in particular, they said, they could not accept as gospel truth all that was contained in Luther's controversial writings. 'Luther's books,' they said, 'were not positive. Sometimes he wrote one way, sometimes another; besides which there were dirty spots and objectionable things in his controversial writings.' Cruciger bluntly called the articles ' a medley of all sorts of things which Luther himself, had he been alive, would not have signed.' [1]

The four theologians and the two professors of the philosophical faculty, who had refused to sign, were sentenced to imprisonment as state criminals, and later on banished from the country.[2]

On June 20 the court of inquisition submitted to the Elector a proposal for a general visitation, in order to root out the last remnants of sacramentarianism. It was suggested that for each university Augustus should nominate four men as ' reformers and inspectors,' who should be commissioned to examine not only into political matters and intrigues, but also, and principally, into ' the religious teaching in each and every profession.'

---

[1] Respecting the ambiguity of the Torgau Articles, see Heppe, *Gesch. des Protestantismus*, ii. 430 ff.; Calinich, *Kampf*, pp. 140, 145.

[2] See Hospinian, *Hist. Sacram.* ii. 380.

Without their permission no MS. was to be printed, nor any suspected book offered for sale.[1] Even in the country high roads in Saxony, so the Landgrave William of Hesse was informed, Calvinists were hunted down.[2]

'Pure doctrine, justice, and freedom have triumphed,' so the Elector's privy councillor Lindemann announced. In celebration of this triumph Augustus had a medal struck, on which he himself figures as an armed hero. In his hand he holds a pair of scales; on the heaviest side of the balance lies the Child Jesus with the inscription 'Omnipotence;' on the other side, with the inscription 'Reason,' sit the four Wittenberg theologians, who, with the help of the devil depicted above their heads, are vainly endeavouring to bear down the scale with their weight.[3] Augustus found other ways also of giving artistic expression to this victory of truth. At a large display of fireworks in honour of Maximilian's visit to Dresden with his Empress and his sons in April 1575, four symbolic figures were introduced into the show. One of these represented Hercules in the act of killing the Hydra. The features of Calvin were noticeable in this presentation, and the following inscription appeared: 'As Hercules finally conquered the many-headed monster with fire, and taught it how to die, so Augustus, Duke of Saxony and Elector, the hero of glorious renown, will, with God's help, crush and overcome the perfidious secret brood of Calvinists that have crept into these lands.'[4]

There was not much that was 'glorious' in the Elector's behaviour towards the four former favourites

---

[1] Calinich, *Kampf*, pp. 167–172.
[2] Rommel, *Neuere Gesch. von Hessen*, i. 591.
[3] Tentzel, *Saxonia numismatica*, p. 137.
[4] Gillet, i. 465–466.

whom he had put in prison. The privy councillor
Craco was thrown into the filthiest dungeon of the
Pleissenburg at Leipsic. The governor of the castle,
George Richter, who, in pity for his wretched condition,
had endeavoured to procure a modification of the terms,
was, by order of the Electur, denounced as a rogue in
front of the castle, and then horsewhipped to the gate
of the town by the hangman. In Gotha, on a former
occasion, Craco had looked on pitilessly at the tortures
of the Chancellor Brück,[1] and now he himself was
stretched on the rack for four whole hours. He died
(March 16, 1575) with mangled limbs on a miserable
layer of straw.[2] With utter contempt for truth the
Elector assured his son-in-law, the King of Denmark,
in a letter, that Craco had died of starvation by his own
will. In another part of the letter he actually indulged
in a coarse joke about the wretched victim.[3] The
Superintendent Stössel begged for pardon, and swore
' henceforth to preach pure Lutheran doctrine.' ' He
looked so terrified and white and trembling,' the Elector's
private secretary relates, ' that I verily believe if his
cheek had been cut it would not have bled.' Hopes
of mercy and grace were held out to him in consequence
of his apology ; nevertheless, in spite of the Elector's
promise, he was retained a prisoner in the castle of
Senftenberg until his death in 1576 ; his opponents tell
all sorts of tales concerning his state of desperation and
the terrible death he suffered.[4] The court preacher
Schütz declared himself willing to abstain from all

---

[1] See vol. vii. pp. 396-399.

[2] Hospinian, 39ᵇ; Weine, iv. 123-124. Fuller details in Kluckhohn,
Sturz der Kryptocalvinisten, pp. 110-127.

[3] Kluckhohn, *Sturz*, p. 127.

[4] Calinich, *Kampf*, pp. 178-182 ; von Helbach, pp. 257-259.

further writing and plotting, to give up preaching and the office of preacher, and to observe the conditions of confinement to his own house imposed on him. The Elector, however, would not extend any such mercy to him. He said that Schütz was an 'artful, wanton, wavering, venomous, wicked priest, who deserved bodily punishment.' He was condemned to twelve years' imprisonment.[1]

But Peucer was put to worse torture than any of them because ' he would not abjure the doctrine of the Sacrament which had been rooted in his heart for thirty-three years, and adopt Luther's doctrine instead.' Year after year he was left pining in a damp, dirty dungeon, and, by order of the higher authority of the Leipsic Burgomaster Rauscher, was constantly harried with injunctions ' to desist from his devilish errors.' Rauscher read out to him the Elector's decision, which ran as follows : ' Since these are matters which I dare not leave unpunished, nor indeed would wish to pass over, Peucer must die ; but I grant him this much, to choose for himself the kind of death he prefers.' ' When I read him out this verdict,' Rauscher reported, ' his tongue became lively, it twirled and twisted to express that he had not deserved this from your Electoral Grace.' He ' went through a hard struggle and shed tears of agony at the thought of what was before him, but it was impossible for him, he said, to act against his conscience.' ' I answered,' Rauscher goes on in his report, ' that if your Grace did not carry out the sentence of death upon him, he would be subjected to durance still more vile ; for your Grace could not possibly allow him to go on thinking himself cleverer and better

[1] Calinich, pp. 137, 173-177.

O

versed in the Holy Scriptures than yourself and all
the distinguished theologians who have searched into
and pondered over this article; our Lord God,' I
told him, 'will not construct a special heaven for him.'
He was told that the Electoral conviction would be
forced upon him with red-hot tongs ; that he would
be confined in a subterranean dungeon in Hohen-
stein, where he would become a prey to worms and
filth, that his corpse would be thrown out into the
place where dead animals lay, and that his children
would be driven out as beggars. Rauscher also pronounced over him, in the name of the Elector, a solemn
curse from a thousand demons if he did not alter his
opinions and assent to the doctrine which the Elector
and his theologians had recognised as the truth. With
bitter tears Peucer again referred to his conscience,
' but pledged himself at the risk of his life never again
as long as he lived to speak to anybody about these
articles, still less to dispute about them. If they meant
to take his life, he said, let them do it quickly, for he
was already half dead, and would far rather be put an
end to at once than live on in such misery and torment.'
No single book, not even the Bible, was vouchsafed
to the prisoner. The costs of his imprisonment swallowed up his small means. His wife Magdalena, Melanchthon's daughter, died in September 1576 of grief and
want.

On Peucer's remarking once to Rauscher that ' the
misery of his wife and children affected him much more
deeply than his own,' Rauscher answered him ' that
he need not trouble himself any more about his wife,
for she was dead.' ' He then broke out in complaints
and reproaches, saying that we had killed her by our

ill-treatment of himself.'[1] When the Emperor begged the Elector to release the prisoner, saying that he would take him into his service, Augustus answered that ' he could not spare him,' for he wanted to force him into conversion. Peucer remained in prison without a single word of consolation, suffering constantly from illness, and distracted with grief for his motherless, deserted children. In addition to the Burgomaster Rauscher, the theologians Selnekker and Andreä also exerted themselves to bring about the conversion for which the Elector was so anxious.[2] Selnekker did not

---

[1] *Historia Carcerum*, p. 350 ff. The pastor, Paul Pfeffinger, to whom Peucer had made a private confession, was desired to reveal what had been said to him. Pfeffinger, however, honourably refused to do so (p. 338). Further details in Calinich, *Kampf*, pp. 202-247 ; Arnold, ii. 19 ; Henke, *Peucer und Krell*, pp. 31-33. See there, pp. 38-40, the list of authorities consulted for the account of Peucer. The *Apologia*, composed by Peucer during his imprisonment, published by Hermann Müller in the *Zeitschrift für preussische Gesch. und Landeskunde*, xiv. (Berlin, 1877), 90-135, 145-191. ' At a time when evangelical faith had been completely deteriorated by a method of inquisition which was in most glaring contrast to the principles of Protestant conformity to scripture,' says the publisher (pp. 91-92), ' the whole procedure against Peucer shaped itself into a veritable tragedy, as he himself shows in many passages of his writings.' The Protestant Wagenmann says at the end of an article on Peucer in the *Allgemeine deutsche Biographie*, xxv. 555 : ' But whatever may be the judgment passed on the nature and measure of his offence, there is nevertheless no doubt that the treatment he was subjected to, above all the personal behaviour towards him of the Elector and the Electress and their accomplices, descended to a depth of injustice, brutality, and wickedness which were all the blacker because perpetrated under the hypocritical cloak of religious phraseology and zeal for the Church. In spite of all attempts at whitewashing from old and new orthodoxy, the history of the so-called Crypto-Calvinistical discussions, and with it the story of Peucer's persecution, remains one of the darkest pages in the history of the Lutheran Church, and indeed of the history of culture in the sixteenth century.'

[2] While Peucer still stood in favour, Andreä had represented to the mother of the Electress, and to other courts also, that ' Robbers who had only been guilty of a few murders were put to death, but that Peucer had ruined thousands of souls ; he was poisoning the soul of the Elector ;

find it such a difficult matter to regulate his faith
according to the wishes of the secular authorities.
' With all his heart,' he wrote once to the Elector, ' he
was ready to crawl on all fours to Dresden in order
to clear himself by all means of the suspicion which
Augustus entertained against him.[1]

The Elector even had recourse to the occult art of
geomancy in tracking out secret Calvinists and their
' villainies.' On May 26 he asked some questions in
his dotting-books (*Punctirbüchern*) respecting Andreas
Freyhub, professor of theology at Leipsic, on whom
he looked with suspicion in spite of his recantation.
From a ' root-number ' he came to the conclusion,
' because the number (representing dots unintention-
ally made) indicated quarrelling and envy, that Freyhub,
an obstinate, self-willed man, reckless and inconsistent,
had been led, probably at the instigation of the Heidelberg idol and its worshippers, to wreak his vengeance
on the hated Doctor Selnekker. And once having
come to see through the spectacles of his instigators,
he, great talker and brawler that he was, volunteered
with more relish to dispute, quarrel, and brawl after
the manner of the wretches of his kind.' It was also
' clearly shown by this figure that he was meditating
flight, and meant to take his wanderer's staff into another
land, and to leave behind him the stench of a runaway
apostate, unless some barrier were placed across his
path that he would stumble up against.' To the further
question, ' Has Freyhub also held correspondence with
Doctor Peucer during his imprisonment ? ' the figures

he lay like a watch-dog at the door of his apartment, and would let no one
in who professed a faith differing from his own ' (Henke, *Peucer und
Krell*, p. 24).

[1] Planck, 5[b], 600, 601, note.

answered in the affirmative. ' From this root-number
I conclude that the two desperate villains have carried
on a great deal of writing and intercourse by messages,
and I have come to this conclusion for the reason that
this number says emphatically " yes," and it is the most
constant and the very best of the numbers.   There is
no doubt whatever that they have carried on a great
deal of secret knavery, and that it has been going on a
long time.'   Punishment must therefore follow.   On
this same day, May 26, at ten o'clock in the evening,
Freyhub was conveyed to the Pleissenburg, and shortly
after sent into exile.[1]

Towards the ' idol of the Calvinists at Heidelberg,'
the Elector Frederic, Augustus conceived intense hatred,
and the antagonism which grew up between the two
Electors became of far-reaching significance for the
general political and religious history of the Empire.

[1] Richter, *Die Punctirbücher*, pp. 22–23 (how the art of ' dotting ' was
carried on, see pp. 16–17).   Respecting the treatment which the electoral
chancellor, Kysewetter, and the judge (*Hofrichter*), Jan von Czeschaw,
experienced as Crypto-Calvinists, see Kluckhohn in v. Weber's *Archiv für
sächsische Gesch.* vii. 144–174.

CHAPTER IX

ANTAGONISM BETWEEN THE ELECTORS OF SAXONY AND
OF THE PALATINATE—THE COUNT PALATINE JOHN
CASIMIR IN THE CHARACTER OF A NEW GIDEON—
CONDITIONS IMPOSED BY THE ELECTOR PALATINE
FOR THE ELECTION OF A NEW GERMAN KING—1575

THE Elector Augustus did not entertain the slightest
doubt that Craco, 'that desperate scoundrel,' had
intended, after the pattern of the Huguenots and the
Netherlanders, to institute a political revolution under
the cloak of religion. Craco and the chancellor Ehem,
he was convinced, were the real originators of the
objectionable war policy of the Palatinate.[1] The
Elector Palatine, Frederic, on the other hand, wrote
that 'many would regard the change of conduct in
Augustus, who by his present actions was condemning
everything of which he had formerly approved, as
shameful and dishonouring.'[2] He had interceded on
behalf of the prisoners, but had been harshly rebuked
by Augustus; Frederic and his theologians had nothing
to do with the Augsburg Confession, Augustus had
said; he would do well not to trouble himself about
things which did not concern him, but to keep a closer
watch over his own councillors, who had already shed
a great deal of innocent blood, and, if he did not take
care, would again lead him into waters which it would

---

[1] v. Bezold, i. 135–136.   [2] Kluckhohn, *Briefe*, ii. 706.

be impossible for him to swim out of. On Frederic's remarking in a letter that there was still much in Luther's Church which was closely akin to popery and which needed reform, he received answer that if he and his theologians regarded the Lutherans as papists, they must not take it amiss if they were told ' what was the tendency of Calvinistic teaching, as exemplified in the Netherlands and in France.' In a letter in which Frederic said it was not he who had led the expeditions to the Netherlands and to France, and that he had not been able to hinder it, Augustus made the marginal note : 'Even a child of three years old must be able to see and understand what plotting has been going on at Heidelberg for some years past ; and were not all those conspiracies an inveigling of subjects against their rulers, ' as indeed their proceedings and wars clearly show ' ? [1]

The antagonism between the two Electors became intensified when, in June 1575, Prince William of Orange contracted a marriage with the Huguenot Princess Charlotte of Montpensier (who was living at the court of Heidelberg) before he had obtained a separation from his wife Anna, a niece of the Elector Augustus and the Landgrave William of Hesse. The Prince of Orange had repudiated Anna on account of conjugal infidelity. She had been kept under restraint, and the Landgrave William had even thought it advisable to have her secretly immured and to spread a report that she had died.[2] Through Orange's new marriage her shame had become publicly known to the world, to the disgrace

---

[1] Heppe, *Gesch. des deutschen Protestantismus*, ii. Beilagen, pp. 19, iii. ; Calinich, *Kampf*, p. 139 ; Kluckhohn, *Briefe*, ii. 713–714, 890.

[2] Orange approved of this plan (Groen van Prinsterer, v. 192).

of the Saxon and Hessian houses. The Elector Frederic was well-nigh driven mad by the scandal; 'he was as one demented,' the Landgrave William said.[1] Augustus was incensed by this shameful marriage, and again called geomancy to his help. He discovered from his dotting-book that Orange's new wife had been a harlot, that from her youth up she had been versed in the arts of lying and stealing, and that, having escaped from a convent, she had come ' to the sacred house of Heidelberg, where she had been welcomed with honour and distinction in virtue of her Christian religion and her pure, blameless life and character, and whence she had united herself by marriage with the chief of all scoundrels and sedition-mongers, who was not worthy of a better wife, and had entered into a conjunction of whores and villains.[2]

Augustus was also greatly enraged at this time respecting his son-in-law, John Casimir, ' who ill-used his wife and was always engaged in foreign intrigues.'

The fulfilment of the treaties which John Casimir had concluded in June 1574 with the leaders of the Huguenots [3] had been prevented by the transition of the government of France to Henry III. New treaties, however, had been arranged. On April 11, 1575, the Count Palatine agreed with an ambassador of Elizabeth of England, that in return for a money aid of 150,000 crowns he would lead 15,000 to 16,000 men into France, would take the advice of an English agent in conducting the war, and would not conclude peace until he had

---

[1] Groen van Prinsterer, v. 300.

[2] Richter, *Punctirbücher*, pp. 30–31. See Raumer's *Histor. Taschenbuch*, Jahrg. 1836, pp. 159 ff.; Kluckhohn, *Briefe*, ii. 841, note 2; and *Friedrich der Fromme*, pp. 411–417, note 21[a].

[3] See above, pp. 144–145.

given Calais into the hands of Queen Elizabeth.[1] The
Prince of Orange being at this time in treaty with
France, John Casimir discovered that 'Orange had
no zeal for religion, that he was actuated solely by
avarice, and that his behaviour would be determined
by self-interest alone.'[2] In July 1575 the Prince of
Condé received at Heidelberg from the hands of the
Elector 50,000 crowns, which Elizabeth had contributed for a fresh civil war in France, and he sent the
Queen of England his thanks for her support 'in so
holy an enterprise.'[3] Henry III., in the month of April,
had made very extensive concessions to the Huguenots,
granting them complete freedom of religion, and the
possession of all the towns they had taken. Bearing
in mind the saying of Theodore Beza, 'Freedom of
conscience is a diabolical dogma,'[4] the Huguenots had
stipulated that no religious tenets but their own and
those of the Catholics were to be tolerated in France;
all others were to be severely punished. Henry had
agreed to this condition also. He had furthermore
consented to 'a reform of the Catholic Church,' and he
had humbled his royal dignity so far as to accept the
Queen of England as arbitress in all his disputes with
his subjects. But even these concessions did not satisfy
the Huguenots. They further demanded the towns of
Lyons, Metz, and Amiens[5] as places of refuge. As,
however, John Casimir had promised to deliver Calais
into the hands of the English, he himself was to be

---

[1] Kervyn de Lettenhove, iii. 489.   [2] La Huguerye, i. 292-294.
[3] Kervyn de Lettenhove, iii. 536.
[4] 'Libertas conscientiarum diabolicum dogma' (Beza, *Epist. theol.*
[1573], p. 21). See Paulus, *Die Strassburger Reformatoren und die
Gewissensfreiheit*, p. 102.
[5] Kervyn de Lettenhove, iii. 490-492.

rewarded with Metz. And not Metz only. In a treaty arranged in September between him and Condé, the 'chosen head of the reformed Churches in France,' it had been decided that he was to bring into the field 8,000 cavalry and 8,000 Swiss, besides artillery, in return for which he was to be appointed administrator for life of the three bishoprics of Metz, Toul, and Verdun, with full and free enjoyment of all the temporalities of the said bishoprics, without any exceptions ; he was to be free to introduce the reformed religion into these dioceses, and to employ Huguenots only for garrisoning the towns.[1] John Casimir said that, in view of the advancement of the Palatine house, these three bishoprics must be given to none but himself.[2]

In a supplementary treaty Condé and his allies pledged themselves to support the Elector Frederic, in case of need, personally and at their own expense, with 6,000 arquebusiers and 2,000 French cavalry ; in return for which the Elector promised to send 6,000 German cavalry under the command of John Casimir, if Condé and his allies should require fresh reinforcements after peace had been concluded. On the other hand, the Elector, as usual, conveyed his assurances to the Emperor that he had had nothing whatever to do with his son's expedition, and had neither given money nor any other help towards it.[3]

On December 4, 1575, John Casimir entered the field. 'Ah, my most beloved mother,' wrote his wife Elizabeth on December 29 to the Saxon Electress Anna, 'it is my lord's own father who has been the cause of

---

[1] Kluckhohn, *Briefe*, ii. 919–921, and also v. Bezold, i. 164-165, note 2.

[2] v. Bezold, i. 164.

[3] Kluckhohn, *Briefe*, ii. 921–922 ; v. Bezold, i. 166.

my lord going off to fight ; for the old man has been
talked round by the learned doctors and the priests,
and has come to think that my lord will be elected
King. I never heard anything so foolish in all my life.
Ah, if only he would be content with what God has
bestowed on him ! I have heard from the great high
steward himself that my lord's father has spent all the
money he possesses on the war in the Netherlands and
in France, so that if the Palatinate should be attacked,
or be in any danger, there would be no means of help.
They blame my lord's father very much because he will
not approve of the expedition, and they care less than
nothing for the Emperor. They do nothing but defy
the Emperor and my father. I hear it all going on,
and my heart is nigh to breaking. They seem to think
they may do just as they like ; nobody dares thwart
them. I said once to my husband that they will end
in bringing the Emperor down on them for their defiance ;
I said that my lord knew very well what trouble he had
got into before. Whereupon my lord answered that it
was because he had an unmerciful Emperor that he
was acting in this way ; all that he had had in his mind
before and had not succeeded in accomplishing, he now
meant to carry completely through, and also to visit
the Emperor with chastisement. This is the way they
are always talking. They stir up misery and disaster,
and they will soon have enough of it. May God over-
rule all things for the best ! ' [1]

John Casimir's troops did not wait till they got
into France to begin their frightful devastations. In
Lorraine, at the very outset of the march, the princely
hordes distinguished themselves by plunder and incen-

---

[1] Kluckhohn, *Ehe Johann Casimir's*, pp. 122–123.

diarism. Hans von Schweinichen, who accompanied Duke Henry of Liegnitz on this marauding campaign, says of John Casimir : ' Wherever his army halted for the night and left the next morning, he caused their quarters to be set on fire, so that when the inhabitants got up in the morning they were greeted by the sight of ten or twelve villages all in flames ; and it was enough to make one weep one's heart out, for it was such a fertile and beautiful country, that it was grievous to see it all destroyed in this way.' [1]

This campaign was called ' a holy crusade ' for the extermination of the ' Antichrist of Rome.' In honour of John Casimir, Doctor James Theodori had composed a 'Christian and spiritual lamentation ' which was to be sung to the tune of

> O Mensch, beweine deine Sünde gross
> (O man, bewail thy sins so great),

and which was a prayer that God would release the wretched, persecuted Christians in France and the Netherlands from the tyranny of the Antichrist, and that He would destroy and exterminate the Antichrist with all his godless followers.' [2]

Still more frightful was the incendiarism and plundering on French territory. Between Condé and John Casimir there existed no sort of understanding, and their armies, ' exempt from all military discipline, were free to ravage like hordes of barbarians.' The whole area between Orleans and Paris was laid waste.

In April 1576 peace was concluded with the throne of France. ' In his conduct throughout,' John Casimir wrote to his wife, ' he had sought nothing else than the

---

[1] Schweinichen, i. 174.
[2] Kluckhohn, *Friedrich der Fromme*, pp. 373 and 473, note 17.

advancement of God's glory and the welfare of his
fellow-creatures.' [1] The three bishoprics on which he
had counted as his share of the spoils did not fall to
his lot, but he obtained rich compensations instead.
He received the command of a French company and
of 4,000 German cavalry, a yearly salary of 40,000
francs, the duchy of Etampes, and nine lordships in
Bourgogne, and finally the duchy of Château-Thierry,
' the best of the lot,' the yearly revenues of which were
reckoned at 20,000 francs. He set to work at once to
stamp out the Catholic faith in the duchies of Etampes
and Château-Thierry, and ' to establish the preaching
of the Divine Word.' The King had engaged to pay the
Count Palatine 1,700,000 francs for the German troops.
As, however, the money was not at once forthcoming,
the lawless troops compensated themselves on their
return march by fresh abominable plunder of the French
people. John Casimir entered Heidelberg on August 25
as a triumphant hero, decked with a crown of golden
laurel leaves ; in his train his army brought numerous
wagon-loads of rich booty. In speeches and sermons
he was celebrated as ' an ornament of Germany and
Gaul,' as a new ' Alexander the Great,' as a second
' Gideon and Joshua.' He was flushed with the hope
of achieving similar triumph in the Netherlands in the
character of ' a champion of religion ordained by God.' [2]

The Countess Palatine alone experienced no joy in
her husband's triumph. She wrote to her mother that
the peace concluded in France had no reality in it, for
the King had already made a secret statement to the
effect that ' he meant to fight it out to the bitter end

---

[1] Kluckhohn, *Ehe Johann Casimir's*, p. 124.
[2] v. Bezold, pp. 168 ff., 181-182; Kervyn de Lettenhove, iii. 633.

and not to make a present of his kingdom to the Count
Palatine.' He had said also that neither he nor his
brothers intended to keep to what they had promised
the Count Palatine, but that as soon as they had got
on their legs again they should visit the Palatinate.
And they cannot be blamed for this, ' for in verity my
lord had no good grounds for marching there. We
used religion as a cloak for our shame, but now it is
manifest why we did it all—namely, that we might fill
our hands with booty. We want to dictate to other
potentates how they are to govern their countries, and
we cannot even govern our own.' To her father Elizabeth wrote : ' They praise my lord as the noblest prince
under the sun. They say also, " Our Lord God has
called him to the work." But that I cannot believe,
and will not allow myself to think. We have a terribly
good opinion of ourselves. My lord often says, and my
lord his father, that the Emperor and all the Electors
will be in terror of my lord, and will attend to all that
he advises and act accordingly. So fearfully grand
we are in our talk, your Grace would not believe it.
This all pains me so much and grieves my heart more
than I can say.' [1]

The Emperor and the Ecclesiastical Electors were
living in terror of violence from the Count Palatine,
who was ready equipped for war. Their chief fear was
that he would make a raid on the Archbishopric of
Cologne,[2] as indeed he did later on.

The measure of strength with which the Palatinate
credited itself was realised in 1575, when Maximilian
made known to the Elector his long-cherished wish to

[1] Kluckhohn, *Ehe Johann Casimir's*, pp. 127-128.
[2] v. Bezold, i. 182, note 1.

secure the succession to his eldest son Rudolph. The Elector Frederic would have preferred that no election should take place during the lifetime of the Emperor, in order that, in the event of a vacancy on the throne, the Palatine imperial vicariate should come into power and have the opportunity of using its influence for the propagation of Calvinism. At any rate Frederic intended that the new king should be bound over by an election capitulation ' to suppress the popish Antichrist with all his godless followers, and to promote the advancement of the dear Gospel.' The Elector was as strongly opposed as ever to granting any toleration to the Catholics, and as zealous in his endeavours to force his Lutheran subjects in the Upper Palatinate into Calvinism. At the very time of the French military campaign, an armed invasion was being planned at Heidelberg against the Upper Palatinate, and the theologian Ursinus expressed his astonishment that the same people who had engaged themselves to carry war into France had not the courage to forbid their own subjects to appoint such dangerously hostile preachers as the Lutherans.[1]

The Stadtholder of the Upper Palatinate, Count Palatine Louis, the son of the Elector, was a decided opponent of his father's Calvinistic tenets, and had expressed his opinion on the ' disputed religion ' to his father in a manner that caused the latter to say ' Louis was more insolent and wicked, and more violently opposed to him than the Augsburg Confessionists themselves had been at the Augsburg Diet of 1566.' [2] But, whenever the Catholics were in question, father and

[1] Kluckhohn, *Friedrich der Fromme*, pp. 393-394.
[2] *Ibid.*, *Briefe*, ii. 874.

son were in full agreement. They would neither suffer
the Catholics to enjoy any toleration, nor would they
allow new religionists to go over to the Catholic faith.[1]
But, on the other hand, the Emperor and the Catholic
Estates in their territories were to submit to the free
exercise of the Protestant religion. When Maximilian
finally decided that an Electoral Diet should be held in
May 1575, and that it should meet at Ratisbon, Frederic
asked his son to draw up a memorandum of advice
respecting the conditions to be stipulated. Louis made
the following suggestions:—' For the benefit of the
spiritual Estates, the removal of the Ecclesiastical
Reservation must be aimed at, and for the sake of the
secular Estates the terms of the Religious Peace must
be corrected, explained, and extended; all towns,
parishes, and nobles, whether directly under the Empire
or not, must be allowed enjoyment of the Protestant
religion within the Catholic districts. Also, the burdensome oaths—made still more burdensome by the Council
of Trent—which the bishops were obliged to swear to
the Antichrist must be abolished.' All the old idolatries
and atrocities of Rome had been invested with additional force at this council by the Pope's bought servants,
slaves, and belly-worshippers. The Religious Peace
could not be maintained under such circumstances. In

---

[1] Moritz (p. 114) remarks, in opposition to Janssen, that the above
statements do not occur in the memorandum in Kluckhohn (see at p. 390,
note 1). This is correct, but Janssen has not made such an assertion.
Moritz himself remarks further on: ' At any rate the Palatine rulers
always avoid any statement as to how far they will go in the concessions
demanded of them towards the Protestants, and also to the adherents of
the old religion.' This silence (the correctness of which may be left alone)
and still more their proceedings against ' popish error, idolatry, and abominations,' prove only too well that they would show no toleration to the followers of 'Antichrist.' See vol. vii. pp. 125–127, 130–133, 316 ff., 319 ff.;
vol. viii. 50–51, 149–151.

addition to this the Council had given its sanction to
' a new and most pernicious vermin, the Jesuits.' ' How
much evil and iniquity this last new development of
ecclesiastical locusts and scorpions (of which mention
is made in the Revelation of St. John) have accomplished in Christendom in the space of a few years, their
own works sufficiently show.' [1] The Elector Frederic
adopted Louis's memorandum, and gave his ambassadors
still further instructions for the Electoral Diet. Among
other things he stipulated for the establishment of an
imperial council which should share the government
with the future Emperor; for the alteration of the
ancient form according to which the Emperor was
described as guardian (*Vogt*) of the Roman Church, and
for the retention of the Annates and Pallium fees
for the use of the Empire. He also enjoined his ambassadors to obtain from the Elector a formal declaration
that not only the inhabitants of the Palatinate, but also
their foreign Zwinglian and Calvinist associates, the
Swiss, French, English, Scots, Poles, Picards, and others,
should be expressly included in the benefits of the
Religious Peace.[2]

But the Count Palatine Louis, whom Frederic had
sent as his representative to Ratisbon, and the Palatine
councillors did not obtain a favourable hearing from
the Lutheran Electors of Saxony and Brandenburg.
' In all directions,' wrote a councillor of the Archbishop
of Mayence, ' there was great dread of the Calvinist
intrigues, and the Brandenburgers were no less vehement than the Saxons in their denunciation of Calvinism,
which aimed at turning everything topsy-turvy in the

---

[1] Kluckhohn, *Briefe*, ii. 804-811.
[2] *Ibid.* ii. 862-868; v. Bezold, i. 189.

Empire.' [1] The Elector Augustus spoke his mind
angrily to the Count Palatine Louis, telling him that
the Prince of Orange's second marriage, which had been
arranged at Heidelberg, had been planned with a view
to humbling the house of Saxony, and, as it were,
assailing his (the Elector's) honour; that the union of
John Casimir with his daughter had only been arranged
in order to unsettle his land and people; that by the
Flemish and French expeditions the Palatinate had
brought down on itself the Emperor and the Kings of
France and Spain.[2] 'We were treated with enmity and
contempt by nearly all of them,' wrote the Lord High
Steward, Count Louis of Sayn-Wittgenstein ; 'it came
pretty near to their turning us all out as Samaritans
from the Synagogue of the Pharisees.'

The Electors of Saxony and Brandenburg declared
themselves satisfied with the existing form of the electoral
capitulation; but they, in conjunction with the Count
Palatine, demanded that the ' supplementary declaration,' the *Ausnahmepatent* (the guarantee of exceptional
treatment), which King Ferdinand of the Augsburg
Diet of 1555 had granted the Protestant Estates with
regard to free exercise of the Augsburg Confession in
the territories of ' some of the Ecclesiastical Estates,'
should be incorporated in the Capitulation formula.
The Ecclesiastical Electors, however, would by no means
recognise the validity of this *Ausnahmepatent,* and at
first even disputed the existence of any such document ;
but at any rate—so they said in their declaration—they
could not do anything in so important a matter without

[1] *Bruchstück eines Mainzer Protocolls und einige Schreiben vom
Wahltag,* 1575.
[2] Louis's despatch of Oct. 12, 1575, in Kluckhohn, *Briefe,* ii. 878;
Senckenberg, *Sammlung von ungedruckten und raren Schriften,* iii. 8.

the concurrence of the other Estates.[1] Already 'the whole transactions concerning the election were threatening to fall through,' when the Elector Augustus, after an interview with the Emperor, declared himself ready (and won over Brandenburg also) to forego the incorporation of the patent in the formula of the capitulation on the strength of a promise from Maximilian 'to set the matter right at the next Diet.' [2]

In verbal promises the Emperor was munificent, 'but acting up to them was a very different matter.'

[1] More, further on, concerning the supplementary declaration in the chapter on the Ratisbon Diet of 1576 (pp. 353–359).

[2] Kluckhohn, *Briefe*, ii. 898–899. See the very full account of the Ratisbon Electoral Diet, derived from innumerable unprinted acts, by Moritz. *Wahl Rudolph's II*, p. 137 f. At pp. 167–168 there is an autograph *Aufzeichnung* from the Dresden Archives, in which the Elector Augustus records all the considerations which decided him to refuse his assent to the declaration of the election capitulation. 'They ought not,' so he reasoned, 'to let the whole business fall through on account of this disputed point, or there would be still more mistrust of them. If they dissolved without coming to a decision, there was no knowing when they would assemble again for the election. Opportunity would be given to enemies of peace to manœuvre for the throne, and there would be the very worst to expect if any disaster should befall the Emperor. The secular Electors should therefore represent to the spiritual ones, through some of the councillors, that out of consideration for the welfare of the Empire they were ready to consent to a postponement of the debate on the declaration to a general imperial assembly, but with the explicit reservation that thereby nothing should be lost to the Confessionists. For the present they were ready to go on with the deliberation respecting the election. As it were to justify his change of opinion, Augustus draws attention to these momentous points. 1st. The recognition of the declaration would in no way benefit those who had gone over to the Augsburg Confession since the Religious Peace. 2nd. If they attempted to carry their object through by force, they would place themselves in a very disagreeable position with regard to the Emperor and all the Catholic Estates, and would thus do themselves more harm than if they had altogether kept silence. Finally, there was no need to trouble themselves on behalf of others who did not belong to the Elector's council-board, and to sacrifice the general good to their interest; if they came themselves and advocated their own cause, he would be heartily glad to grant them what they wanted.'

This fact was discovered shortly before the Ratisbon Electoral Diet by the Bohemian Protestants, to whom he had made solemn assurances respecting free exercise of their religion, in order to accomplish the elevation of Rudolph to the throne of Bohemia.[1]

Rudolph was elected King of the Romans at Ratisbon on October 27, and on November 1, 1575, he was crowned by Daniel, Archbishop of Mayence, according to the ancient traditional forms.[2] 'It was most unwillingly,' Maximilian told the ambassadors of Aix-la-Chapelle, 'that he had fixed on Ratisbon as the place of election and coronation : he had had no intention of robbing the towns of Aix-la-Chapelle and Frankfort in any way of their privileges and traditional rights.' 'The alterations had been unavoidable, as was apparent from his Majesty's person and countenance, and had been approved of by the Electors.'[3]

The election capitulation to which Rudolph had to swear was precisely similar in substance to the one to which his father had pledged himself.[4]

During the election transactions at Ratisbon and at the Ratisbon Diet in the following year two important facts had come clearly to light. It had become apparent, on the one hand, to how great an extent the

[1] See Reimann, 'Der böhmische Landtag des Jahres 1575,' in the *Forschungen zur deutschen Gesch.* iii. 259-280. See also the articles by Swoboda in the *Innsbrucker Zeitschr. f. kathol. Theol.* xvii. 385 ff. ; xviii. 85 f.

[2] The reports of the Nuncio Delfino from Ratisbon from Oct. 7 to Nov. 5, 1575, in Theiner, *Annal.* ii. 463-470, are of great value. See Ritter, i. 463 ff. and Moritz, p. 173 f.

[3] Carl von Glauburg to the town council at Frankfort, Nov. 5, 1575, in the Frankfort *Wahltagacten*, 10, fol. 9. See Schneidt, *Gesch. der Königswahl Rudolf's II* (chiefly compiled from unprinted documents) (Würzburg, 1792), pp. 566 ff.

[4] See vol. vii. p. 339.

strength of the Protestants had been maimed by the antagonism between the Elector Palatine and the Elector Augustus, while, on the other hand, plain proof had been afforded of the strength and influence of a Catholic party in Germany which was doing its utmost not only to counteract the spread of Protestantism, but also to recover for the Catholics all the territory which they had been robbed of since the Pacification of Augsburg.

The Jesuits were rightly looked on by the Protestants as the chief source of this increase of papal power. According to the unanimous testimony of friends and foes this order was the actual mainstay of the Catholic faith in Germany.

The preacher Wilhelm Seibert, at the time of the Ratisbon Electoral Diet, wrote as follows :—' It is an undoubted fact that it is owing solely to the labours of the Jesuits that the preaching of the Gospel is at a standstill, and that in many places it is even on the retrograde. Before this brood of demons established themselves here and spread through the land, we had felt perfect confidence that the princes and magistrates, and the ministers of the Word, would succeed in rooting out the last remnants of antichristian, idolatrous popery.' [1] From the Catholic side, in the same year, we meet with the following expressions of opinion : ' Every Catholic who sets any store by his faith, and who joys in his union with the one true Church, and in the unity of the papal see, must be filled with deepest gratitude—both now and for all times— towards a society without which, humanly speaking, every vestige of Catholicism must have been obliterated

[1] Seibert, p. 21.

from the soil of the Holy Empire.' ' The Jesuits, during the last ten years, have rendered inestimable services, and it is patent to everyone that whatever the place which is the scene of their devoted zeal, their chief object invariably is to effect a true evangelical reform of life and character.' [1]

[1] *Christlicher Tractat,* 5, 7.

BOOK III

CATHOLIC REFORM LABOURS AND COUNTERACTING
INFLUENCES DOWN TO THE PROCLAMATION OF
THE FORMULARY OF CONCORD IN 1580

CHAPTER I

THE FIRST JESUITS IN GERMANY—'SPIRITUAL EXERCISES'

ALL work of Catholic reform that has had any permanence in it owes its origin to the exertions of the
first three Jesuits who laboured in Germany: Peter
Faber, Claudius Jajus, and Nicholas Bobadilla.

The first of these, Faber, born on April 13, 1506, in
the village of Villardet in Savoy, began his career in
1540 as a zealous missionary at Worms when the religious conference was going on there. He had not at
that time contemplated anything in the nature of a
struggle against, or refutation of, Protestant doctrine,
but merely a moral renovation of Catholic life.

' I observe with sorrow,' he wrote to a friend, ' that
the rulers and powers of this world labour for nothing,
think of nothing, consider nothing else necessary than
continued fighting against heresy and error. This
means, as I have said again and again, using both hands
to wield the sword against the enemy, whereas one
hand should certainly be employed in building up the
city of God.' ' Why do we not labour for a reform,
not of dogma and moral precepts, which is not wanted,

but of morals and of life itself ?   Why de we not return,
in the light of the old doctrines—which are both old
and new—to the earlier example and practice of olden
times and of the holy Fathers ?   But, alas, these my
complaints are of no avail whatever.' [1]   The moral
degradation of the clergy, to which he could not shut
his eyes, filled him with the deepest sorrow.   It was
only a wonder, he said in his letter to Ignatius of Loyola,
that the number of renegades among the people was
not far larger even, since conditions were everywhere
abundantly favourable to apostasy.   It was not falsification of the Holy Scriptures on the part of heretical
teachers, nor was it the plausibility of the new preachers
which were the cause that so many towns and countries
rebelled against the true faith ; the real reason lay in
the scandalous lives of the clergy everywhere.   ' God
knows whether here in Worms there are as many as
two or three priests who are not guilty of illicit connec-
tions, or else openly given up to other vices.   My heart
assures me that if there were but two or three zealous
pastors of souls in the place they would be able to do
what they liked with the good people.' [2]

Just because he knew so well what was the fountain-
head of the evil, Faber was full of mild and paternal
solicitude towards the new religionists.   His whole
being breathed forth love and tenderness.   ' I grieve with
deep, unceasing sorrow,' he wrote to the founder of the
Order, ' over the downfall of the noble German nation,
formerly the incomparable pearl of the Church and the
glory of Christendom.' [3]   ' Those who wish to be of

---

[1] Reiffenberg, *Mantissa*, p. 13.
[2] Bartoli, *Opere* (Torino, 1825), 5, 105.
[3] *Ibid.* 5. 110.   See 5 116.

service against the present-day heretics,' he wrote to
Father Lainez, later the General of the Order, 'must
above all things be distinguished by large-hearted
charity towards them, and must treat them with high
esteem, being careful to expel from their hearts all
thoughts which would tend in any way to lessen this
respect.   Furthermore, we must also endeavour to win
their hearts and affections, so that they may be chari-
tably disposed towards us in return, and cherish a good
opinion of us.   We should easily attain this end if we
carried on friendly intercourse with them, and confined
ourselves to discussing in an amicable manner, without
any rancour, those matters only concerning which there
is no dissension among us : we must begin, not with what
separates hearts in discord and schism, but with all that
draws them closer together.'

From the reform and requickening of practical morals
they might then proceed to the rectification of faith.
' If we have to deal with any who are infected with
erroneous opinions and who have degenerated in morals,
we must first of all endeavour, by all means of persuasion, to set them free from their moral infirmities,
before we say a word to them on the subject of their
errors.'   ' Whereas the Lutherans, among many other
mistaken tenets, all agree in the fundamental error of
refusing to ascribe any merit to human action, and,
with utter contempt for good works, place their reliance
on faith alone, it must be our aim, in our intercourse
with them, to pass on from works to faith, and always
at first to lay most stress on whatever may tend to inspire
them with love and zeal for good actions.'   ' Another
point also on which the teachers and preachers of
Lutheranism are wont to insist in defending their errors

respecting ecclesiastical laws and the injunctions of the Fathers, requires careful attention. They invariably refer to man's utter incapacity to obey the rules of the Church, and to endure hardship for the love of God ; they say that the laws and ordinances of the Church are far above human strength. It must be our endeavour therefore to set them right on this point, to encourage and inspire them with the hope and confidence that with the help of God they will not only be able to do all that is of obligation, but even to accomplish far greater things.' Those teachers who only speak to the wanderers of their obligation to lead a Christian life, of the beauty of holiness, of fervour in prayer, of the hour of death, of the eternity of hell, and other such subjects which tend to moral elevation, will do far more for their salvation than those who bring to bear on them all the weight of authority and a cartload of reasons. May Jesus Christ, the Saviour of all men, who knows that His written Word is not sufficient to move the human spirit, may He reach and soften their hearts by the power of His divine grace.' [1] 'Knowledge and learning alone,' Faber wrote from Ratisbon to the students of his Order at Paris in 1541, ' have very little power at present against erroneous doctrines. Under the existing condition of things no other proofs are efficacious but good works and self-sacrifice, even to the giving up of life. Labour zealously, therefore, to acquire the living *spirit* of science and learning, joined to a holy life in imitation of Christ, in order that you may be able to lead back to the truth those who are sunk in error. May the Lord grant you a spirit of

---

[1] *Memoriale*, pp. 378–383. See Cornely, pp. 68–71.

perseverance in the love of God and the patience of
Jesus Christ!'[1]

Faber's journal is a complete summary of his inner
life. In all his prayers he always especially included
Luther, Melanchthon, and Bucer. For seven towns
that had fallen into error, schism, or unbelief, Wittenberg, Moscow, Geneva, Constantinople, Antioch, Jeru-
salem, and Alexandria, he used to pray unremittingly
that either he himself or one of the members of his
Order might have the felicity of celebrating the holy
Sacrifice of the Mass within their walls.[2] 'Hitherto,'
wrote Peter Canisius to a friend in 1543, 'I have not
seen or heard any theologian who surpasses Faber in
profundity of learning, or any man who is his equal in
resplendent virtue. Nothing is so dear to his heart as
to co-operate with Christ in the salvation of souls; no
word ever escapes his lips, whether in intercourse with
intimate friends, at meals, or in society, which is not
redolent of God and of godliness. He has gained such
a reputation for piety that many members of religious
orders, many bishops and divines, have put themselves
under his spiritual guidance; among others Cochläus,
who declares that he can never thank him sufficiently
for all his instruction. Numbers of priests and clerics
of all classes have, under his influence, either given up
female companions of their sin, or turned their backs
on the world, or in one way or another become quite
reformed characters.'[3]

On one occasion in the year 1542, when he mounted

---

[1] *Memoriale*, pp. 370-376.

[2] *Ibid.* pp. 19, 22, 29, 30, 340. Concerning Faber and Melanchthon,
see *Cartas y otros escritos del P. P. Faber* (Bilbao, 1894), i. 32; *ibid.*
p. 295, Faber, *Ueber die Bekehrung der Irrgläubigen*.

[3] Riess, p. 33; Cornely, p. 125.

the pulpit at Aix-la-Chapelle, the fervour of his words penetrated so deeply into the hearts of his hearers, that an immense crowd followed him all the way to Cologne in order to get instruction from his own lips on the principal points of doctrine.[1]

Among Faber's most ardent desires was the conversion of heathen lands to Christianity. This work, as Ignatius unceasingly urged, the Order must, he said, consider one of its chief tasks.

And accordingly the first Jesuit who laboured on German soil represented the universal destination of the new Order, which was by no means to confine itself to combating the heresies of the day, but also to aim at extending the boundaries of Christendom, and reviving and intensifying Christian life among those who had remained true to the Church.

Claudius Jajus, who came from the diocese of Geneva, worked as zealously as Faber in the pulpit, in the confessional, and in imparting catechetical instruction. He, too, was firmly convinced that the schism in the Church was not to be treated as a mere learned controversy, but that what was most essentially needed was the conversion of the heart from which, much more than from the understanding, all this error and heresy proceeded. He was banished from Ratisbon in 1544. On being threatened that he would be thrown into the Danube he answered calmly: 'I hope to be able to rise to heaven even out of the waters of the Danube.'[2] He was quite ready, he wrote to an Italian marchioness, to give up his life, if only by so doing he could save the noble and mighty German nation from altogether losing

---

[1] Meyer, *Aachensche Geschichte*, pp. 447 ff.
[2] Agricola, i. 10 ; Boero, *Jaio*, p. 47.

the true faith.[1] At Worms he often watched by the
sick through whole nights, taking no money and living
in poverty.

' The first members of the new sect of the Jesuits,'
a Calvinistic preacher complained later on, ' seduced
numbers of people at Worms and in other places from
the Holy Gospel; one of them, especially, who led a
hypocritical life, spent half his days and nights in
churches and hospitals, ate and drank very little,
scarcely ever slept, and took care not to boast of good
works, as is the habit of all the other rascals of his
creed. This was well pleasing in the eyes of many,
and thereby they were seduced into falling back into
their popish idolatry, to the everlasting damnation of
their souls, all through this despicable, hypocritical
rogue and others of the tonsured gang.' [2] Such was
the judgment of Seibert on Claudius Jajus.

' Why should we grow bitter over the judgments
of men ? ' said Jajus; ' they pass by like spray in the
wind; only God's Word and commandment endure
for ever. To suffer persecution for the sake of Christ,
and to love poverty and abasement, this is an imperish-
able blessing.' When he heard that King Ferdinand
wanted to force him, through the authority of the
Pope, into acceptance of the bishopric of Trieste, he
implored Ignatius to do all in his power to prevent
such a measure ; he did not wish for any prelacy, and
considered it damaging to the efficacy of the Order for
its members to accept ecclesiastical dignities.[3] The
sphere of his ministrations was chiefly in Ingolstadt.

---

[1] Boero, p. 90.   [2] Seibert, p. 13.
[3] Fuller details in Boero, pp. 120-127. See especially his letter to
King Ferdinand himself, pp. 133-136.

The third of this trio, Nicholas Bobadilla, who came
from the diocese of Valencia in Old Castile, laboured
principally in Vienna. Ferdinand offered him residence at the court, but he preferred remaining in the
public hospital for the sick, where, like the rest of the
poor inmates, he lived entirely on alms. At no other
place in Germany, he wrote to Ignatius in 1542, 'is
there such a field for work as in this city. The King,
the court, and the apostolic nuncio are satisfied with
me. I generally preach every Sunday and on all
festivals; I hear confessions and dispense the other
Sacraments. The King solicits me daily to discuss
ecclesiastical matters and the affairs of religion with
him.' Although he was infirm and suffering, the Father
was anxious, in 1542, to join the camp in Hungary,
being ready to die in the service of religion.[1] In the
year 1544 he worked actively in a visitation of the
diocese of Passau, where he was successful in reforming
many priests of bad character.[2] During the Smalcald
war he devoted himself to the service of the sick and
wounded, and while engaged in this ministry he once
fell a victim to the plague, and another time was wounded.
To him also bishoprics were repeatedly offered; but
he refused them all for the same reasons that had
influenced Jajus, viz. that the acceptance of ecclesiastical dignity could not be beneficial either to himself
personally, or to the Order.[3]

These three men and their associates set the world

---

[1] Boero, *Bobadiglia*, pp. 16–17.

[2] Agricola, i. 9.

[3] Boero, *Bobadiglia*, pp. 43 ff.; Agricola, i. 15 ff. When Bobadilla
opposed the Interim as exceeding the legitimate power and prerogative of
the Emperor, the latter caused him to be expelled from Germany; see
Polanco, *Vita Ignatii Loyolæ*, i. 293, and Gothein, p. 682.

a shining example of devoted fidelity and self-sacrifice to the cause of the Catholic Church.

Their achievements in the amelioration of human life, conduct, and character, they attributed chiefly to the influence of a small volume compiled by Ignatius, the fruit, not of abstract study, but of his own personal life experiences. This little book, which Paul III., after repeated examination, ' approved, recommended, and praised' in an Apostolic Brief,[1] and which even its opponents pronounced to be a psychological master-piece of the highest class, ranks also as one of the most remarkable and influential products of later cen-turies in the field of religion and culture in Germany. ' Spiritual Exercises' is the shorter, popularly known title of this work ; the fuller one is ' Spiritual Exercises, by means of which man is helped to overcome himself and to reform his life, and to escape from the bondage of inordinate affections.' [2]

As regards form and style this little book cannot boast of any charm. In its artless simplicity it affords a striking contrast to the pretentious treatises of con-temporary humanists, and stands out as one of the plainest and baldest specimens of ascetic writing ever published, far removed from anything approaching to rhetoric or mystic extravagance.

In its substance also it did not at first sight appear to offer anything new and striking. It seemed a mere invitation to its readers to withdraw, for a few weeks or days, altogether from the world, its business, and its

---

[1] *Breve Paul's III* of July 31, 1548.

[2] *Exercitia Spiritualia S. Ignatii de Loyola cum versione litterali ex autographo Hispanico notis illustrata.* Lutetiæ Parisiorum, 1865. The introduction and the notes are the work of the General of the Order, J. Roothaan.

cares, to give themselves up, in complete solitude, to prayer and meditation, and to searching out the will of God, in order that they might bring their own spiritual condition into harmony with the requirements of divine law, and be led either to make choice of a definite vocation in life, or else to institute a thoroughgoing reform within the sphere of the calling they had already embarked on.

In their insistence on reform these Exercises chimed in with the universal cry of the age.

But the reform they laid stress on was not to consist chiefly in the alteration of external things—in changes connected with Pope, Emperor, bishops, and princes— but in a renewal of the inner moral life of individuals ; not in outward innovations, but in a return to the primitive fundamentals of Christianity, prayer, peni- tence, true sanctification, and perfection.

Like the principal and final object of the Exercises, the means thereto are things well known, practised by Christ and the Apostles, recognised and used for edifica- tion through all the ages of the Church, viz. the recep- tion of the Holy Sacraments, various kinds of prayer, examination of conscience, silence. The same remark applies to the subjects for meditation arranged for the soul's gradual purification, illumination, and union with God.

Another characteristic which, added to plainness of form, gave this work its peculiar stamp was the psychological reduction of the ages-old rules of Christian asceticism to a practical system—a uniform, methodical plan of action, as it were—a manual of tactics for spiritual warfare. Ignatius regarded the inward struggle of every human being as a part of the great world-struggle which has gone on between God and His sinful creatures ever since the fall of the angels, and in which Christ, as the general, bears the victorious banner. Ignatius joined himself to the glorious army of this King with the glowing enthusiasm, the high sense of honour, the heroic self-surrender of a gallant warrior. But as a genuine champion fighter he did not allow the sublime objects of the war to shut out from his view the grim earnestness of the struggle. With steady gaze he scrutinised all the weaknesses of his own character, sought diligently for the necessary counter-agents, and fought against himself with indomitable energy. The haughty, arrogant knight became transformed into the lowly-minded priest, who knew no other ambition than to suffer shame and persecution for the love of Christ.

The principal means put forward in this manual towards the attainment of perfection is mental prayer or meditation, which has served through all ages to build up the soul of every Christian life, especially of the monastic life. All the most important themes for meditation which revelation affords are at least touched upon, and they are arranged in four divisions called 'weeks.' The subjects of the first week relate to the fundamental verities which, being within the grasp of human understanding, form the reasonable, intelligible basis of every religion and of every religious life. There is no dallying with visionary ideas and sentiment; the reasonable, scientific development of the spiritual life is throughout considered. God is taken as the starting-point and the goal of this development. To serve God, and in the end to find beatitude in God, is the object for which man was created: man therefore must use all created things with a view to this end, and must free himself from all sinful and corrupt attachment to things of the earth. On this basis, which is the groundwork of every reasonable system of ethics, he constructs a series of meditations on the origin, nature, consequences, and punishment of sin, on its connection with human dispositions to evil (pride &c.), and with external and internal occasions (senses). The progression is arranged with a view to awakening genuine sorrow for sin and effectual penitential dispositions, which shall lead to complete cleansing and purification of the soul by means of a worthy reception of the Sacrament of Penance.

The second ' week ' deals with the practical reform of the inner life—that is to say, the acquisition of positive virtue. Christ, in His incarnate life, is set forth as the visible prototype of virtue, to which man should strive to conform. The remaining meditations follow quite simply the course of the Gospel narratives, from the Incarnation to the Last Supper. Only once, as a connecting link between the different points, the author introduces a ' meditation ' in which the spirit of Christ and of His kingdom is placed in sharp contradistinction to the power of the devil and *his* seductive arts.[1]

The third ' week ' is devoted to the sufferings of our Lord ; the fourth to the mysteries of His resurrection and ascension ; and this with the express design of ' strengthening more and more the resolutions that have been made for a reform of life.'

Finally, the concluding ' meditation ' on love gathers together the highest and most beautiful motives for

[1] In the original Spanish text this meditation is called ' de dos Banderas ' (of the two banners).

serving God, and as it were concentrates into one burning focus the sacrificial offerings connected with this service. Strengthened step by step in the imitation of Christ, growing more and more resolute in selfless, heroic renunciation for the love of Christ, he who trains himself in these exercises comes at length rejoicing to the goal, and gives up all things in exchange for ' the one treasure of love and grace.' [1]

Such in brief is the ground plan of the book.

The ' additions,' mostly in the shape of aphorisms, form partly a condensed method of mental and oral prayer, and partly a collection of hints and aids to greater facility and devotion in praying ; now supplying useful indications concerning different spiritual phases which occur in the religious life, now some short guide to the most effectual manner of carrying out the spiritual reform in question, now a few simple rules for outward life, and general principles by which to bring one's views into accord with the teaching of the Church.

These additional rules [2] are the only part of the ' Spiritual Exercises ' in which Ignatius in some measure assumes a position antagonistic to the novel doctrines of his age, though even here he proceeds quite indirectly and unobtrusively : for in this part he is addressing himself to Catholics only. On these, however, he inculcates most forcibly complete submission to the authority of the Church, recognition and respect for both scholastic and patristic theology, faithful observance of the whole system of Catholic worship (with

---

[1] The different subjects of the four weeks were distinguished with the words : ' Deformata reformare, reformata conformare, conformata confirmare, confirmata informare.'

[2] ' Regulæ aliquot ut cum orthodoxa Ecclesia sentiamus.'

obedience to ecclesiastical commands), humility and prudence in examining into different questions of theology—above all those of grace and predestination. The concluding words, however, are an exhortation not to forget the love of God and the humble, childlike fear of God which are always the beginning of all wisdom.

Neither superficial reading nor theoretical study will unlock the key to the full meaning of this little book. It is essentially a practical guide to show how the Spiritual Exercises may be made to bring forth effectual fruit.

As a guide to the Exercises, however, it has produced results which scarcely any other ascetic writings can boast of. All who have fully and faithfully followed its short rules of guidance have undergone the same or a similar transformation as that experienced by the author of the book, Ignatius. This was the case with his first associates, with secular clergy, monastic clergy, ecclesiastical princes, scholars, laymen of whatever class. All of them, by performing the Exercises, felt themselves transplanted into a higher spiritual atmosphere, removed from mundane cares, and placed in touch with higher things. Doubting spirits recovered full vigour of faith ; wavering, struggling souls attained to peace with God and with themselves. Pleasure-seeking worldlings were snatched out of the whirlpool of their passions and enticed into worthier modes of life ; thousands, tossed and buffeted amid the often selfish struggles of politico-religious strife, were recalled to earnest prayer and inspired with active love to God and man.

Faber, in describing his sojourn at Ratisbon, writes : ' It is to these Exercises, which many of the German

magnates performed, that we owe almost all the good
which was done in Germany later on.'[1]   The Carthusian
prior, Gerhard Hamont, drew up a report in 1543 on
the cases of Faber's missionary success in Mayence,[2]
brought about by the use of the 'Spiritual Exercises,'
and Jajus did the same for Augsburg.[3]   By means of
these Exercises, or spiritual retreats, as they are commonly called, the 'Society of Jesus,' at first only a
small band, gained fresh recruits every day ; from them
the disciples, ' schooled in warfare,' imbibed that
distinctive *esprit de corps*, that particular view of
the world in general which characterises the Order
always and everywhere.   These 'Exercises' were the
means of restoring hundreds of monasteries and convents to the primitive strictness of their Orders, of
converting clerics innumerable to a priestly mode of
life, of winning over to true evangelical reform countless numbers of the laity.   The Geneva bishop, Francis
of Sales, stated it as his opinion that ' the little book of
Exercises had saved more souls than there were letters
in its pages.'   'In practical value for genuine reform
of life among all classes, clergy and laity, learned and
unlearned,' no book, said the Viennese jurist Thomas
Scheible, in 1564, ' comes near the Exercises : none
who have proved their efficacy by personal experience
will hesitate to declare that they are a special gift of
grace from God in our disordered times, so fond of
discussion, yet so poor in the inner life of faith.'[4]

On the Protestant side there existed the most
remarkable ideas concerning these Exercises.

---

[1] *Memoriale*, p. 19.   [2] Serarius, p. 844.
[3] Boero, *Jaio*, pp. 243-244.
[4] *Epistolæ selectæ* (in a Mayence Dissertation of 1753), pp. 27-28.

One Calvinist, who figured in Catholic guise, called them ' occult, magic arts, by which the Jesuits, on certain days, performed heaven only knows what extraordinary feats, shut up in secret closets from which, having finished their sorcery, they emerged white as death, and with a look of having been terrified by a ghost.'[1] ' The Jesuits,' said a Calvinist preacher, ' seduce numbers of people into strange practices which they call spiritual exercises. Their victims, as is credibly reported, are intoxicated by fumes, and by other uncanny means, so that they believe they see the devil in living shape, and they begin to low like oxen, and are forced to abjure Christ, and to enter the service of the devil.'[2]

By means of these Exercises the Order, in 1543, won over to its ranks a man who figures among the most distinguished and influential Catholic reformers of the sixteenth century : Peter Canis or Canees, called later on Canisius, the first German Jesuit, the founder of Jesuit colleges at Vienna, Prague, Ingolstadt, and Freiburg, and the first Provincial of the Order for South Germany and Austria.

---

[1] *Prob. der Jesuiter*, p. 78
[2] Seibert, pp. 17–18. For the 'most extraordinary disclosures, of Gothein respecting the Spiritual Exercises of St. Ignatius,' see Paulus in *Histor. Jahrbuch*, 1896, p. 567 f.

CHAPTER II

CANISIUS came of one of the most influential and wealthy
families of the town of Nymwegen in the duchy of
Guelders, where he was born on May 8, 1521. His
father had several times filled the office of Burgomaster
and other places of trust, and it is attributed to his
influence especially that the Guelders Estates wished
to remain true to the Empire, and did not consent to
the treaty concluded by their Duke Charles with King
Francis I., according to which the country was to fall
into French hands.[1] Canisius received a careful education at Nymwegen and at the *Montau* gymnasium
at Cologne ; at this last place he came into intimate
connection with Nicholas van Esche, a priest from
Brabant, whom he praised in later life as a model
instructor. Van Esche, he wrote, taught him, ' both
by precept and example, to flee from and to abominate
moral transgressions more than barbarisms and sole-
cisms.' ' One thing only brings salvation,' Nicholas
was wont to say, ' and that is serving God : everything

[1] *Annales Noviomagenses* (Noviomagi, 1790), ad a. 1537, 1538, 1543.
The ordinary statement that the family of Canis was formerly called de
Hondt is doubtful.

else is illusion.' ' If you understand Christ aright, it
is sufficient, even though you should not understand
anything else.' Canisius was made to read a chapter
out of the New Testament every day, and to choose
for himself some specially pregnant text to keep in mind
and meditate on from time to time in the course of the
day.[1]

In the year 1536 Canisius was promoted to the
Baccalaureate of Arts at Cologne, in 1538 to the Licen-
tiate, and in 1540 to the rank of Magister of Philosophy.
Having heard great praise of the Jesuit Father Faber,
who was giving theological lectures on the Psalms at
Mayence, he made under his guidance, in 1543, the
Spiritual Exercises, and decided to join the Society of
Jesus. ' From that time forth,' he says in his spiritual
' Testament,' composed about a year before his death, ' it
was my one chief concern to follow Christ the Lord and
to tread as He trod, in poverty, chastity, and obedience,
the way of the Cross.'

What spirit it was that inspired him is seen from
the personal records he has left. ' When I took the
vows of my Order in 1549,' he writes, ' I seemed to hear
a voice saying : Go and proclaim the Gospel to all
creatures.' ' Thou, O Lord, didst as it were open Thy
sacred heart to me. From that fountain Thou badest
me drink; from Thy living waters, my Redeemer, Thou
taughtest me to draw my salvation. My most fervent
longing was that streams of faith and hope and love
might pour from Thy heart into mine. Thou didst

---

[1] *Confessiones* and *Testamentum Canisii* (there is a copy of the first
of these in the University Library at Munich, and of the second in the
imperial Archives at Munich). Now published by Braunsberger in
Epistulæ Canisii. The passages in question are at i. 17, 18, 19, 36.

promise me a cloak made of three pieces, fit to cover the
nakedness of my soul : these three were peace, love,
and perseverance. Clad in this garment of salvation,
I was full of trust that I should want for nothing, but
that all would fall out to Thy honour and glory.' All
his labours were to be devoted to the service of his
Fatherland. 'Thou knowest, O Lord, how repeatedly,
on the day of my consecration, Thou didst commend
Germany to my care, bidding me work wholly for her
after the example of Father Faber, bidding me to live
and die for her, and to join with her guardian angel in
protecting her.'[1]

Canisius, as his memoirs show, was always the advocate of the Germans with the Apostolic See.

In a letter to Lainez in 1559 he expressed his opinion
that Rome might do anything she liked in Germany
if only she knew the right way of dealing with the Germans.[2] With regard to Church penalties and the
fasting rules, he said, the Pope should proceed carefully with the people of this country ' so as not to extinguish the glimmering spark ; ' the index of prohibited
books, he said, required a milder tone.[3] 'There is no
nation on earth,' he wrote in 1568 to Duke Albert of
Bavaria, 'which ought to be dearer to the hearts of
us Jesuits, or which affords us wider scope for the exercise of patience, than the German nation.'[4]

[1] Python, pp. 57–59. *Beati Petri Canisii Exhortationes domesticæ,
collectæ et dispositæ a G. Schlosser* (Ruræmundæ, 1876), pp. 456–457.
Riess, pp. 78–80.

[2] '. . . modo Germanica hæc ingenia commode tractentur ' (Letter
of April 22, 1559). See preceding page, n. 1.

[3] To Lainez, April 29, 1564. To Hosius, Feb. 9 and Nov. 7, 1562, in
Cyprianus, *Tabularium*, p. 257.

[4] Python, p. 152.

'Italy and Spain,' he said to one of his fellow-workers, 'must be forgotten by us, and we must devote ourselves entirely to Germany, not for a period only, but for our whole lives. Here we must work with all our might and with indefatigable zeal, and, unless we are recalled, we must desire nothing so much as the improvement and the joyous prosperity of the harvest field of Germany, and abundance of good labourers to work in it, especially from the ranks of our own Order.'[1]

'How can we let ourselves be perplexed and disturbed in our efforts for the spread of the Gospel of our Lord and Saviour, by any reproaches we may encounter, any calumnies that may be circulated about us ? Have we not promised to suffer willingly all shame and ignominy for the glory and after the pattern of the Redeemer ?' From the lips of the founder of the Order himself, he said, he had received the injunction : 'It is an easy way to the attainment of perfection, when you endure much contrariety for the love of Christ ; it brings the joy of the Holy Spirit. Pray to God that this blessing may be vouchsafed unto you.' 'Overcome thine own self' was his favourite motto. 'Except a corn of wheat fall into the ground and die, it abideth alone.'[2] 'The Lutherans,' he wrote to Lainez, 'impute to me in their writings crimes of no slight nature ; they hope thereby to cloud my reputation, which I neither seek nor care to defend. All the

---

[1] To Pater Vittoria, Nov. 16, 1557, from Worms. See vii. 40, n. 3.

[2] Riess, p. 74. It was consideration and tenderness towards the heretics in teaching and preaching that St. Ignatius asked of the first Ingolstadt Jesuits in his 'Instructions' to them in 1556. See the important document (in Italian and German) by Pachtler, *Ratio Studiorum Societatis Jesu*, iii. 470–471 (No. 12) ; see *ibid*. No. 15 and pp. 474–475 (No. 6).

sectarians burn with hatred for the Jesuits. They load them with terrible calumnies, and from slander and abusive language they will doubtless soon come to blows and wounds. May we be enabled to love them more cordially even than they despise us! Even when they persecute us, they deserve to be loved by us, for the sake of the blood and the love of Christ, and also because the majority of them err out of ignorance.'[1] In his spiritual 'Testament' he says: 'The innumerable attacks, both secret and open, that have been made on the Society of Jesus have never disgusted me with my vocation; on the contrary, they have only increased my zeal and my delight in it, because I have rejoiced that I was counted worthy to suffer shame for the name of Christ, and to be slandered and maligned by the avowed enemies of the Church. If only I could bring salvation to their souls, were it even at the price of my own blood! I should esteem this indeed a gain, and I should thus, according to the commandment of the Lord, prove the sincerity of my love.'[2]

He considered Christian charity and tenderness the best means for winning back the Protestants.[3]

'There are an immense number of people in Germany,' he says in one of his letters, ' who err in religion, but they do not err from stubbornness or bitterness: they err after the manner of Germans, who by nature are generally honest-minded, firm, very receptive of all which they, born and bred in the Lutheran heresies, have learnt partly in schools, partly in churches, partly

---

[1] Sacchinus, *Vita Canisii*, p. 157.

[2] *Testamentum Canisii.* See above, p. 232, n. 1.

[3] To the legate of the Council, Hosius, from Augsburg, March 16, 1562, in Cyprianus, *Tabularium*, p. 222.

by the writings of false teachers.' [1]   By the simple presentation of Catholic doctrine, he said, greater and
better results would be gained than by controversial
attacks on the Protestants.   When, by desire of Duke
Albert of Bavaria, he held a mission for the people during
Lent, 1558, at Straubing in Bavaria, where Protestantism had gained a large following owing to the
apostasy of some of the priests, he did not dwell on the
subject of Luther and his adherents, but only on the
passion of Christ.   These sermons had great effect.
' Canisius,' wrote the ducal Vicegerent to the Bavarian
chancellor, ' is a most learned and eloquent man, and
he behaves with particularly commendable modesty in
the pulpit.' [2]   ' I pray that all the Fathers,' Canisius
said in a letter to Ignatius, ' who come to Prague for the
founding of the college may be fulfilled with holy
patience and with fervent resolution not to dispute
but to forbear, and to work for edification more by
deeds than by words, in order that after they have
sown in tears they may reap in joy and bring their
sheaves with them.' [3]

All sharp and bitter controversy was always ' repugnant to his inmost soul.'

' If ever I appear as an author,' he wrote to Lainez,
' I hope at any rate that I shall excel most of the trade
in charity and modesty ; for the violence of their style,
and the tumult of human passion that they bring into
their writings, tend much more to infuriate the Germans
than to heal the schism.' [4]   ' Men of distinction and

---

[1] *Gutachten für Claudius Aquaviva.*   See vii. 40, n. 3.
[2] Riess, pp. 242–244.
[3] From Vienna, Oct. 14, 1554. See Riess, pp. 130–131, and Braunsberger, *Epistulæ Canisii,* i. 498–499.
[4] From Augsburg, April 22, 1559.   See vii. 40, n. 3.

learning,' he urged on the controversialist William
Linder, then professor at Dillingen, later Bishop of
Roermond, ' agree with me in thinking that much in
your writings might be more suitably put : your *witti-
cisms* on the names of Calvin and Melanchthon, and
other similar things, may be suitable for a platform
orator, but conceits of speech do not become a theologian at the present day.   We do not heal the sick by
such medicine, we only render their disease incurable.
In defending the truth we must observe charity, con-
siderateness, and moderation, so that our temperance
may be manifest to all men, and that we may, if possible,
obtain a good testimony even from those who are not
of our party.'   ' The well-affected become disgusted
when affairs begin to smack of bitterness ; they like
to see discretion coupled with dignity and weighty
reasoning.' [1]

The Protestant polemical writings against Canisius
and against the Jesuits were remarkably wanting in
these last qualifications.

Melanchthon, in 1556, had no hesitation in calling
Canisius a cynic and in openly classing him with
those people who ' persecute truth against their own

---

[1] In de Ram's *Analectes pour servir à l'histoire de l'université de Louvain*, 1852, No. 15, pp. 144–152. The German Jesuit, Johannes Dirsius,
rector of the college at Innspruck since 1563, sent his superior at Rome
a memorandum on all the points to which all the Jesuits in Germany had
to pay special attention.   Among other things he says in it: ' The
members of our Order must be very careful in all their religious lectures
and discourses, both private and public, not to denounce our religious
opponents, whoever they may be, as heretics ; neither must they call
them good-for-nothing villains or devils, or hurl other odious terms of
abuse and calumny at them (*nec vocent eos nebulones nec diabolos vel
aliis vocabulis et calumniis odiosissimis*).'   The autograph MS. of this
memorandum is in the Roman Archives of the Society ; a copy of it is in
the library at Exacten.

consciences,' who ' persecute with malicious sophistry,
and strengthen the cause of error and idolatry.' [1]   The
preachers of the county of Mansfeld wrote in 1560 :
' The heretics, the Canists or Jesuits, have cast aside all
shame, like Canisius, who, by the way, gets his name
from a dog.' [2]

' Those Jesuits who are destitute of all shame, that
pestiferous swarm of vermin,' we read in a pamphlet
of 1561, ' have been well instructed by their houndish
Father Canisius, that gruesome persecutor of Christian
doctrine and of Christ the Lord, how to carry on
sanguinary intrigues against all the evangelicals.' [3]   The
theologian John Wigand asserted in 1556 that ' The
Jesuits are the most execrable and most thoroughgoing betrayers and persecutors of the Lord Christ, for
all that they call themselves Jesuits after the name
Jesus ; just as in former times the Roman lords were
called Germanicus, or Asiaticus, or Africanus, not
because they did any good to Germany, Asia, or Africa,
but, on the contrary, because they plundered and robbed
these countries, and did them incalculable harm.' ' With
wiles and sophistries these monks are deceiving the
poor Christians and leading them to everlasting hell fire.
Whoever likes may follow them there ; but all who
wish to be saved had better flee from such devil's nets,
snares, and huntsmen.' [4]

Six years later the theologian Martin Chemnitz, in
a Latin treatise entitled ' Concerning the new Order
of the Jesuits,' which was translated into German by

[1] *Corp. Reform.* viii. 688–689. See vii. 35.
[2] *Bekenntniss der Prediger in der Grafschaft Mansfeld* (Eisleben,
1560), p. 70.
[3] *Christliche Lehre von Rew und Busse* (Eisleben, 1561), p. 19.
[4] ' Verlegung des Catechismi der Jhesuiten,' N[3b], N[6].

the Brunswick preacher, John Zanger, descended to
even greater depths of coarseness in his language.
' Those scoundrelly knaves, the Jesuits, with malice
prepense and criminal pride begin by despising the
Holy Scriptures as the first rule of Jesus. Then they
speak of them not only jestingly and irreverently, but
even mockingly and abusively. Is it not, therefore,
natural and right that good Christian people should
raise the alarm, when they hear and see this new antichristian fry, these opponents of Jesus vomiting their
execrable lumps of blasphemy out of their stinking
mouths and bellies, and befouling, besmirching, destroy-
ing the holy, saving Word of God ? ' ' Take my word
for it, these men are no other than perjured, treacherous,
oath-breaking, dishonourable, disreputable, desperate
villains, against whom the German land ought to be
well on its guard.' Chemnitz smelt the ' Assafœtida,
the stinking Bisam, or Teufelsdreck which caused the
Jesuits to defend the " sacrilegious mass." They well
know that they have a good market with ready sale for
their masses to the living and the dead. That market
fills the kitchens and cellars of these lazy. . . . sows,
wherein they fatten until the devil kills them for his
own kitchen.' [1]

---

[1] What follows will not bear translation. Here is the text :—' Auch
durch die Lehre vom Fegfeuer wollen die Jesuiten ihre Küchen und Keller
füllen, und sind über die Massen sehr zornig, dass auch die Kinder
nunmals dasselbe ihr Fegfeuer Maculatorium heissen, damit man die
Hinteren pfleget zu wischen? ' Die viehsauische Gloss : Ich vertraue
auf den Herrn, heisst in viehsauischer jesuwitischer Sprach : Ich glaube
nicht dass es wahr sei, was Gott gesagt und verheissen.' ' Die anderen
Pultronen, oder Patronen sollt ich sagen, des päpstlichen sodomitischen
Frauenzimmers handeln die Sachen bescheidener, denn sie befleissen sich
ja, die gröbsten päpstlichen Fratzen zu versträuschen oder mit listigen
Geschwenken zu oberdrehen und vergabalisiren. Die Jesuwiter aber
haben sich gar ausgeschämt ' . . . Desshalb hatte ' die babylonische Hure

After this pamphlet by Chemnitz had appeared in Latin and German, Canisius, in spite of his strong objection to controversy, thought it advisable, in view of the high esteem in which Chemnitz stood in Protestant Germany, that a defence should be undertaken. ' I am certain,' he wrote to Lainez in May 1563, ' that it is a wise precaution on our side not to carry on disputations with those who hold erroneous beliefs. But love constrains us to come to the assistance of the weak brethren, and for this reason it is right that we should give an account of our faith, not for the sake of snarling and snapping back at our accusers, but in order to set forth the correctness of our teaching. Otherwise, as generally happens, many might think that what is imputed to us has a foundation of truth.' [1]

The more the production of Protestant polemical literature against the Church increased the more urgently necessary it appeared to Canisius that an exposition and defence of ecclesiastical doctrine and ordinances should be taken in hand by scholarly and authorised Catholic writers, who would execute the task ' not in a spirit of bitterness, or ambition, or from

genugsame und redliche Ursache, mit diesem neuen Otterngezücht schwanger zu werden.' 'O du zartes, feines Kind, wie bist du deiner papst-höllischen Mutter so gar ebengleich und ähnlich von Gestalt, Farben, Gliedmassen. . . . Du wirst deiner hursüchtigen Mutter ausgeschampftes Gestirn weit in aller unverschämten Unzucht übertreffen, wie es die Offenbarung Johannis 17 zuvor beschrieben ' (*Vom newen Orden*, 1562, *Vorrede*, Bl. A⁴, D³⁻⁶, E⁷˒², J¹˒², P⁷, Q², S⁷).

[1] Letter from Innspruck of May 8, 1563 (see vii. 40, n. 3). On May 31 he wrote that he was in treaty with a friend of the Society who, with the support of its members, would write a German refutation of Chemnitz's pamphlet. The friend was probably John Albert Wimpinensis, Professor at Ingolstadt, who published in 1563 his ' Bericht von der Gesellschaft Jesu ' (Report of the Society of Jesus) against Chemnitz and Zanger.

any other personal motive, but simply and solely out of disinterested zeal for a cause so sacred and of such vital importance to all Christians.' Again and again he represented most emphatically to the Generals of the Society that they would do well to select a number of Jesuits on whom the work of authorship should be imposed as a vocation for life, and that a kind of college of authors should be founded among the German Jesuits.

'I scarcely think,' he wrote to Francis Borgias, ' that our Order could undertake or carry out any work that would be more useful and more conducive to the general welfare of the Church. Fresh writings on religious questions make a great impression, and are a source of immeasurable comfort to the hard-pressed Catholics at a time when the writings of the false teachers are disseminated far and wide, and cannot be exterminated.' [1] 'I do beg of you,' he said to the General of the Order, Aquaviva, ' to choose out a certain number of our members whose duty it shall be to employ both speech and pen in defence of Catholic truth, to study intelligently the requirements of the age, and, filled with holy zeal, to bring the fruits of their studies to the aid of the Church in its present dire extremity. I do not doubt for a moment but that such a work of obedience and brotherly love would be equal in value to the conversion of the wild Indians.' [2] In this respect also he himself set a good example to his brother-members.[3]

[1] To Francis Borgias, from Dillingen, September 8, 1570; to Eberhard Mercurian, from Augsburg, May 5, 1571, and from Innspruck, September 1, 1574. See vol. vii., p. 40, n. 3.

[2] Sacchinus, pp. 361-362.

[3] More on this subject later on.

Canisius considered it one very important part of his work to found and promote colleges which should not only be centres of activity for the Jesuits, and educational institutes for the clerics of the Order, but should serve at the same time as public gymnasia, with free instruction, both for the training of the clergy and for the young in general.

The foundation of the first Jesuit college was laid in 1544 at Cologne, where, owing to the religious revolutionary agitations going on, intellectual and spiritual life had fallen into a woful plight. At the university, for want of good teachers—so the professors of theology complained in 1546—study had become almost extinct ; the prebends were bestowed by the Provisors on ' men unfitted for the chair, who were even unable to lecture.'   In the other faculties things were no better ; the Medical Faculty, for instance, numbered barely a dozen students.   The manner of life of the students was dissolute and extravagant.   In the ' *Dreikronen bursa*,' the inmates were guilty of such gross misconduct that the Council were obliged to evict all the pupils and to shut up the building for the time being.[1]

In the year 1555 Ferdinand addressed a request to the town council that for the benefit of ' Christian doctrine, discipline and unity,' they would entrust to the Jesuits the task of proclaiming the Divine Word and of educating the young ; and the result was that the following year the ' *Dreikronen Bursa* ' was handed over for two years to the charge of the Jesuit Johann von Reidt, the son of a Burgomaster of Cologne.   In 1557 some twenty Jesuit Fathers established themselves there.   ' Johann von Reidt,' says Hermann von Weins-

[1] Ennen, iv. 665–673.

berg in his memorandum-book, 'might easily have become a great prelate and lord, but he remained in a humble and plain condition, preached a great deal, and instructed the pupils ; he was eloquent and learned, and he set a good example.' [1]

By their self-sacrificing devotion at the time of the plague, the Jesuits had won the love of the people.[2] Already in 1558 their gymnasium counted nearly 500 pupils, sixty of whom were boarders.[3] The Fathers also held courses of lectures on theology, astronomy, and mathematics.[4] It was through their agency alone, wrote the papal nuncio Commendone in 1561, that the study of theology was kept up in Cologne. As educators of youth, as preachers and confessors, and as examples of blameless life and character, the Jesuits were altogether the most useful priests in Germany, and their colleges the strongest bulwark of the Catholic religion.[5]

[1] Ennen, iv. 696–700.   [2] Reiffenberg, p. 39.
[3] Reiffenberg, p 72.   [4] Ennen, iv. 707–708.
[5] Pogiani, *Epist.* iii. 307–308. For the beginnings of the Cologne Jesuit College, and the labours of the Fathers there, see also Pachtler, *Ratio Studior. Soc. Jesu*, i. 139–147, and Duhr, *Schulordnung der Gesellschaft Jesu*, pp. 79–80, and especially Hansen, *Die erste Niederlassung der Jesuiter in Köln*, 1542–1547, containing also a contribution to the criticism of the literature of the Order in *Beiträge zur Geschichte vornehmlich Kölns und der Rheinlande* (Köln, 1895), pp. 160–205. Here (pp. 185 f.) it is shown among other things that, when Faber came to Cologne, he found there a group of men who took up the cause of the old faith with warmth and enthusiasm—Gropper, Andreas Herll, Billick, Schotborg, Kalkbrenner. But (and in my opinion Hansen underestimates this fact) the danger for Cologne was by no means over. A principal part of this work of Hansen consists of criticism of the Jesuit historians, many of whom did undoubtedly greatly exaggerate. If, however, Hansen means that Faber too was not quite innocent in this respect, this is a charge which it would not be easy to substantiate. For correction of a complaint of Hansen against the literature of the Order, see also Braunsberger, *Epistulæ Canisii*, i. 110, note 1. While this work was in the press there appeared Hansen's *Rheinische Akten zur Geschichte des Jesuitenordens*, 1542–1582 (Bonn, 1896).

In the year 1560, at the behest of the Archbishop, the Jesuits began work in Treves, while at the same time they were admitted to the university of this place in the character of teachers. In 1561 they gained a firm footing in Mayence, and were also invited to Würzburg. In a protocol of the cathedral chapter of Würzburg, May 11, 1561, we read as follows : ' Whereas there are some very distinguished and learned persons among the Order of the Jesuits, it has seemed advisable to write to the cathedral preacher at Augsburg, Doctor Peter Canisius, to ask him if he would send one of them here. For this purpose our gracious Lord of Würzburg has addressed a letter to the said Peter Canisius.' The Prince Bishop, Frederic of Wirsberg, had also asked Canisius, on May 3, to send him a cathedral preacher : he was much occupied, he said, with the idea of erecting a college in his town for the Society of Jesus, which he had heard so greatly praised for its virtue and learning.[1]

When, in 1559, Canisius, at the request of the cathedral chapter, began preaching in the cathedral of Augsburg, his congregation numbered barely fifty, but with each sermon the attendance increased. He preached with so much fire and eloquence that his fame, according to the report of the Protestant physician Henry Pantaleon of Basle, spread far and wide : ' Among Germans and foreigners alike his name is in good repute.'[2] During the season of Lent he preached every day.[3] ' To-day we have been greatly encouraged,' he wrote on All Saints' Day, 1561, ' by seeing the people, contrary to their custom, flock in great numbers to the

---

[1] Wegele, *Universität Würzburg*, i. 109, note; ii. 34.
[2] *Prosopographia heroum*, &c. (Basileæ, 1566) pars 3, 501.
[3] Letter to Hosius of March 16, 1562, in Cyprianus, *Tabularium*, p. 223.

Holy Communion. The Word of God grows here in patience ; at the same time calumnies are circulated against the Society of Jesus. May we only prove worthy of this honour!'[1] 'At Augsburg,' he said in a letter to Lainez towards the end of the same year, 'abundant fruits are being reaped from the Jubilee indulgence, so that we have now plenty to do. The number of conversions is unusually large, and equally so the attendance at the Sacrament of Penance.'[2]

Similar results were accomplished by Canisius wherever he mounted the pulpit, and there were few large churches in Germany in which his voice had not resounded. He preached in turn in the cathedrals of Vienna, Prague, Ratisbon, Worms, Cologne, Strasburg, Osnabrück, and Würzburg.[3]

Canisius had directed his especial attention to Bavaria and Austria, ' on whose fidelity to the Church,' he wrote, ' everything depends.' If these two lands, which, if not the only ones, are nevertheless the principal ones retaining the name of Catholic, should fall a prey to the heretics, the downfall of the Church in Germany must inevitably follow.[4]

Duke Albert of Bavaria reverenced the Jesuits as being ' admirable preachers and instructors of youth, as well as shining lights of sacerdotal life,' and accordingly he bestowed his full favour on them even at the time when he still hoped to be able to heal the religious schism ' by temporising, and by a certain amount of

[1] To Salmeron from Augsburg, November 1, 1561. See vol. vii., p. 40, n. 3.

[2] To Lainez, December 20, 1561. Compare the letter to Hosius of December 29, 1561 ; in Riess, pp. 293-294.

[3] Riess, pp. 112-115, 134, 184, 207, 231, 235, 304, 349, 361.

[4] To Otto of Augsburg, January 17, 1556, in Riess, pp. 179-181 ; and Braunsberger, *Epistulæ Canisii*, pp. 595-597.

connivance.' Albert wrote to Ignatius on July 25, 1551, that Canisius was delivering a course of theological lectures which ' were meeting with very great applause, and producing equally great results,' and he ought, therefore, to be appointed vice-chancellor of the university.[1]

The Father accepted the post temporarily, but not the revenues and insignia belonging to it.[2] The year-books of the university praise him again and again in the strongest terms.[3] He revived among the students the frequent reception of the Sacraments, gave them a Latin address regularly every Sunday, and trained them to deliver discourses in Latin themselves. Every week he gave catechetical instruction to the people, and preached to them. It is significant of the religious conditions which he found existing, that it was said of him, among other wonders connected with his personality, ' When Canisius is in the pulpit the people stay to the end of the sermon, and even to the end of the Mass ; they do not hurry away, as the greater number used to do formerly in the middle of the sermon or immediately after the Consecration.' Even fasting came into vogue again.[4]

' After the "Catholic-evangelical freedom," which people had now enjoyed for so many decades, they were no longer accustomed, in Ingolstadt and other places, to such strange, out-of-the-way fellows as the Jesuits, and their mode of life attracted general notice.' Never-

---

[1] *Acta Sanctorum*, Julii (Antverpiæ, 1731), tom. vii. p. 501. See Polaneo, *Vita Ignatii Loyolæ*, ii. 256 f.

[2] Sacchinus, pp. 56–60.   [3] Mederer, i. 219, and ii. 150–151.

[4] Sacchinus, pp. 50–54. Letters of Canisius to Ignatius, November 2, 1550, and August 31, 1551. Braunsberger, *Epistulæ Canisii*, i. 337–341, and 379–384. See also pp. 315 f., 331 f., 392 ff.

theless, even their opponents among the Catholics
' could not but confess that the poor and the sick found
friends in the Jesuits, and were often maintained and
visited by them ; that their influence was often effectual
in reclaiming abandoned girls, in causing stolen money
to be given back, and in putting a stop to much discord among married couples. ' We do not interfere,' said
their opponents, 'with the fasting and church-going of
so many ultra-Jesuits, but we prefer our old ways.' [1]

' Jesuitical ' and ' strict Catholic ' came indeed to be
synonymous terms in Germany.

' It is the boast of the Society of Jesus,' we read
in a pamphlet of 1575, ' that everybody, lay or clerical,
who is in earnest about religion and the duties and
claims which the faith and the Church prescribe and set
up, is looked upon as a Jesuit.' [2]   ' Our foster-daughter
and my brother's wife and the young women,' says
Hermann von Weinsberg of Cologne, ' are good Jesuits ;
they go to church the first thing in the morning, and
fast a great deal ; ' ' my sister and the two young
women are jesuitish, and do not drink much.' [3]   When
Duke Albert of Bavaria was once told by his councillors
that his son Ernest was twitted with being ' too much of
a Jesuit,' the Duke answered : ' We can quite well put
up with his being too jesuitish—that is to say God-
fearing, honourable, learned, pious, and zealous—which
will not fail to bear good fruit, although not all the
children of this world approve of it.' [4]

---

[1] ' Ob die abgefeimten pharisäischen Jesuiter schier in allen Stücken
zu werwerfen ' (1569), C².

[2] *Christlicher Tractat*, pp. 6–7.

[3] Weinsberg's *Gedenkbuch*, in Falke's *Zeitschrift für deutsche
Kulturgeschichte*, Jahrg. 1872, p. 768, and 1874, p. 734.

[4] Lossen, *Kölnischer Krieg*, i. 558, note.

In the year 1556 Albert built a large college for the Jesuits at Ingolstadt, and three years later another one at Munich. In 1560 he requested the General of the Order, Lainez, to send some more Fathers to Munich, because those who were already there were labouring with such zeal that they were wearing themselves out.[1]

At Vienna, where a college and a gymnasium were founded in 1552, the number of pupils amounted in 1554 to 120 ; in 1558 it rose to nearly 500 pupils, who were all receiving instruction in Latin and Greek.[2] In 1554 King Ferdinand, in a letter to Ignatius, lavished immense praise on the labours of the Jesuits at Vienna, and asked for twelve Fathers for a college at Prague.[3] In this town, however, they encountered the fiercest opposition, and their lives were scarcely safe. ' At Prague,' Canisius wrote to Ignatius, ' I was greeted at the high altar with a huge stone which was flung through the window.' At the festival of the Ascension, while Pater Cornelius was reading Mass, after the Consecration he was accosted by a Bohemian who reviled him as though he were carrying on the worship of idols, and finally raised his hand to strike him a blow with his fist, saying in Bohemian : ' Ain't you going to answer me ? ' ' The Jesuits in their sermons proclaim the Catholic doctrine, and exhort to penitence and to pious works of Christian love and mercy ; they visit the sick in hospitals and private houses, catechise the people, and give them instruction also in the first elements of

---

[1] Adlzreiter, ii. 269.

[2] Canisius to Lainez, September 20, 1558.

[3] *Acta Sanctorum*, Julii 7, 498. See also Sommervogel, *Les Jésuites de Rome et de Vienne en MDLXI d'après un catalogue rarissime de l'époque* (Bruxelles, 1892).

learning ; they also collect alms for the needy inhabitants of the town. Under their influence many people who had before quite given up going to church now became zealous Christians again ; many of those who at first were enemies of the Fathers are now their friends.' With the Jesuit schools at Vienna and at Prague a boarding school was connected, and later on a seminary for poor theologians.[1]

But if here and there throughout Germany the establishment of the Catholic faith and the reform of moral and religious life had in some degree been effected, the Jesuits themselves were well aware that, as regards any permanence in their work, or any lasting preservation of the Catholic Church, an important factor was still lacking. It was above all essential to resort to that remedy which all religious-minded, well-intentioned people had for decades looked on as the chief means for asserting the faith, and for mending clerical abuses, viz. the holding and the conclusion of the General Council. Peter Faber, Claudius Jajus, Salmeron, Canisius, again and again gave utterance to the above conviction. The nuncio Commendone also, in 1561, after becoming more closely acquainted with the conditions of Germany, expressed the same opinion. ' We need good teachers and preachers,' he wrote, ' who, with patience and love, with true scholarship, and by good example, will deliver these people from their errors, will make known to them the Catholic truth, and lead them back to the Church, who will instruct the young in the schools, preach in the churches, and ad-

---

[1] Schmidl, i. 89 *sqq.*, 139. Riess, pp. 130 ff. Letters of Canisius to Ignatius of July 15, 1555, and May 17, 1556. Braunsberger, *Epistulæ Canisii*, i. 545 f. and 612–622; see p. 643.

minister the Sacraments. This work, at present, is
being done by the priests of the Society of Jesus, to
the salvation of many souls, and to the benefit of the
Apostolic See.' [1]   But he could not disguise from himself that, ' if the hopes of the Council were wrecked,
all would be at an end in Germany with the Catholic
faith ; any other means of instruction, exhortation, and
good example could only produce lasting fruit if the
Catholics were re-inspired with courage and stead-
fastness by the Council. If this event [the meeting of
the Council] were by God's grace successfully carried
through, then, even though men should doubt as to its
results or try to frustrate them, the Catholics, in Germany also, would stand arrayed in fresh strength and
unity, and that numerous class of " expectant " and
" neutral " persons, who for the moment attached themselves to no particular party, would know with certainty
what decision they ought to form. With a newly
assured basis to start from, and a firm, unalterable
goal to aim at, the work of reform, in all its various
branches, would be built up securely. We are dependent
in all respects on the issue of the Council.' [2]

It was therefore ' with constant anxiety that in
1562 and 1563 all faithful Catholics turned their gaze
to Trent, whence news poured in repeatedly, and from
different sides, that a sudden dissolution of the Council
was apprehended : Frenchmen and Spaniards were
everlastingly quarrelling about precedence, and there
had just been a bloody fray in the streets of the town ;
at the Council, inadmissible and self-contradictory

---

[1] Reimann, *Sendung*, p. 272.
[2] Aeusserungen gegen den Cölner Jesuiten Johann von Reidt nach
dessen Brief vom 24. April 1561. See vol. vii., p. 40, n. 3.

demands were put forward by the secular powers ; the princes saddled all the abuses and evils on the clergy alone, and would not hear of any such thing as reform in connection with themselves ; the papal legates and many of the bishops had spoken altogether despairingly of the situation.' ' How often we abandoned ourselves to desperation ! ' wrote the Viennese jurist Thomas Scheible (January 17, 1564) to a friend in Denmark, concerning the tidings that came from Trent ; ' I wonder, indeed, how many Catholics there are in Germany who were not in despair ? But all the greater is the present rejoicing over the successful termination of the Council. What infinite trouble it cost, only to get it started! What endless worry and dissension have gone on throughout the transactions, what struggles we have had to pull through ! But the Holy Ghost has decided. The Council has accomplished its task.' [1]

---

[1] *Epistolæ selectæ* (in a *Mainzer Dissertation* of 1753), pp. 28–29.

CHAPTER III

REFORM DECREES AND DOGMATIC DECISIONS OF THE
COUNCIL OF TRENT—CONCLUSION OF THE COUNCIL
IN 1563

It was not in the power of the Council to fulfil all the
expectations, all the hopes and wishes that had arisen
in the course of so many decades. The religious unity
of the Christian brotherhood on earth had been broken
up ; the gaping chasm had grown wider and wider in
spite of all attempts at closing it up. Abandoned by
the secular powers, the ecclesiastical authority could
make no further advances towards peace without sur-
rendering itself entirely.

Whereas the Protestant conception of the Church
as a state institution, subject to the control of the
reigning prince, had found friends also among the
Catholic powers, and whereas many ' theologising
statesmen ' considered the Council as little more than
an ecclesiastical Parliament, it is easily intelligible that,
side by side with unworthy derision, there should have
been loud complaints that the Council was not free.
Even the Emperor Ferdinand lent his ear for a time to
innuendoes of this sort from his diplomatic officials.
Again and again the legates found themselves compelled to remind the Emperor and the ambassadors of
the secular powers that they could only act in a representative character, that in matters of religion the Pope

was the chief teacher of the collective Church and the head of the Council, and that this position of his could not be circumvented in the case of dogmatic decisions.

Practically the Pope, for the furtherance of re-unification and in view of existing circumstances, had left the Council as much freedom in its transactions as was compatible with his position. In all questions of reform, and also in the matters of the lay chalice and the marriage of priests, the assembly was directed to decide without further appeal to Rome. If, however, still greater freedom was demanded, and the decisions in matters of faith were to be made without the con-currence or confirmation of the Pope, this would mean nothing less than the combined overthrow of the supreme papal authority in doctrine, and of the entire constitution of the Church, and the substitution of democratic numbers with a parliamentary rule-of-majorities for hierarchical unity. And to this neither the Pope nor the legates could consent.

In consequence of the many difficulties and differ-ences that had arisen, it had been impossible to arrive at a settlement, or at any rate a complete settlement, of some of the great doctrinal and practical questions which had engrossed so much of the Council's time.

In the decision on the position of the bishops, the long-debated question as to whether their jurisdiction proceeded directly or indirectly from Christ, was evaded by the following statement : the hierarchy, which con-sists of bishops, priests, and ministers, is instituted ' by divine ordinance.' A definition of the doctrine of the Primacy was not arrived at ; especially out of considera-tion for France, which threatened a schism if the papal authority over Councils was defined. With reference to this point, one of the most learned of the theologians of the Council, the Dominican Peter Soto, said in a letter to the Pope, which he dictated on his death-bed on April 20, 1563 : ' I testify both in life and in death that your Holiness is exalted above all Councils, and that you can in no way be controlled by them ; and I believe it to be of the highest importance that this should be settled dogmatically, for the opposite opinion only gives rise to disobedience, discord, and schism.' [1] But although no definite decision was formulated in this respect, the Pope did virtually exercise the rights of Primate at the Council, and his authority as such was practically acknowledged, seeing that the whole body of Fathers, with the exception of one bishop only, appealed for papal confirmation of their resolutions.

To the great detriment of the Church and the nation, the questions of ' Reform of the secular princes' and adjustment of the relations between Church and State remained unsolved.[2] But it was only through the consent on the part of the ecclesiastics to defer these points ' to less distracted times ' that it was possible to bring the Council to any satisfactory issue in agreement with the secular powers. The synod was obliged to confine its action ' to the restoration and safe-guarding of religious discipline among the people, and to reminding the secular princes of their obligations in connection therewith.' It renewed all the canons, conciliar decrees, and apostolic ordinances which had been framed at former Councils for the benefit of ecclesiastical persons and the freedom of the Church, and against the infringers of this freedom, and it ' admonished the

---

[1] Raynald ad a. 1563, No. 71 ; compare No. 118.
[2] See vol. vii., pp. 253–272.

Emperor, Kings, republics, princes, and all without exception, that 'the greater their worldly possessions and their power over others, the more conscientiously ought they to obey the laws of the Church, and honour them as the commandments of God,' and prevent these commands from being 'violated by their own ministers.' 'Each one of them should zealously fulfil his duty in this respect, and see to it that the public worship of God was carried on in a devout manner, and that the prelates and other ecclesiastics were enabled to remain undisturbed in their residences and their offices and free to work for the welfare and edification of the people.' [1] Two of the bishops disapproved of these admonitions, because they would be utterly fruitless.[2] And so indeed it proved. 'Even in the lands where the decrees of the Council were accepted, in spite of all papal orders, exhortations, and entreaties, the princes and their ministers, as well as the subordinate authorities, usurped more and more control and management in purely ecclesiastical affairs.' In Austria, for example, under Maximilian II., there arose, immediately after the conclusion of the Council, a system of Cæsaropapism destructive of all religious liberty and independence, almost unparalleled in history.

The attempt at reforming the princes failing, Morone's prediction to Ferdinand was verified : the decrees for reforming the clergy largely failed to attain the hoped-for effects.

The Cardinal-Archbishop Otto of Augsburg wrote as follows : 'Any prince who regards Church government as the province of the secular ruler is quite sure of

---

[1] Sessio 25, *Decr. de Reform.* cap. 20.
[2] Pallavicino, lib. xxiv. cap. 7.

finding, both among the higher and lower ecclesiastics, many docile servants, men with whom dependence on the favour of princes and the patronage of ministers and councillors almost amounts to a pleasure. Many such clerics will even incite and stimulate the secular lords to reduce the Church to bondage.'[1] 'We learn with profound regret,' said the Fathers of the Council, ' that some of the bishops, forgetful of their position, grievously dishonour the pontifical dignity, inasmuch as they show unbecoming subservience to the ministers of kings, to officials, and noble lords, both in and out of Church, and behave just as if they were the lowest ministers of the altar, not only giving precedence in a most undignified manner to these secular authorities, but actually rendering them personal service. The synod accordingly renews all the old ordinances relating to the maintenance of episcopal dignity, and it enjoins on the bishops to keep in mind the dignity and the rank which are rightly theirs, and always to remember that they are Fathers and Shepherds of the Church.'[2]

Very slight also was the effect on the princes and the military nobles of the decree relative to duelling, and the decree for the protection of freedom in contracting matrimonial alliances. ' The detestable practice of duelling,' so the Council prescribes, ' is to be entirely extirpated from the Christian world.'

Not only the actual combatants, but also their seconds, as well as the monarchs and secular lords who allowed the combat, were to be excommunicated; the duellists themselves were further to be punished by confiscation of goods and the brand of infamy, ' and,

[1] See vol. vii. p. 255, n. 1.   [2] Sessio 25, *Decr. de Reform.* cap. 17.

according to the canons, they should be punished like murderers, and if they fell in the duel they should be deprived of Church burial.' [1] A decree relating to marriage, framed for the protection of vassals, and the disregard of which was to be punished with excommunication, ran as follows : ' Whereas secular lords and rulers are often so much swayed and blinded by worldly considerations and ambition, that with threats and punishments they compel the men and women under their jurisdiction (especially the rich or such as have the prospect of wealthy inheritance) to marry against their will the husbands and wives whom they force on them ; and whereas it is wicked in the extreme to interfere with freedom of choice in marriage, and most disastrous that injustice and wrong should proceed from those to whom we look for justice, the synod hereby enjoins all and sundry, whatever their rank, condition, and dignity, under penalty of excommunication to be incurred *ipso facto*, that they do in no way whatever, either directly or indirectly, lay any compulsion on their subjects, or on any one else, to prevent their marrying according to their own free will.' [2]

But, whatever its failures and shortcomings, the Council fully justified its existence with respect to that which really was within its power, and which might truly be regarded as its legitimate work, viz. on the one hand to define in its full purity, against the multitude of novel sects at war one with another, the ancient teaching handed down from Christ and the apostles ;

---

[1] Sessio 25, *Decr. de Reform.* cap. 19.   Respecting the working of this decree von Below (*Hist. of the Origin of Duelling*, Münster, 1896, p. 23, note) refers to *Œuvres complètes de Branthôme*, tom. viii. (Paris, 1891) : *Discours sur les Duels*, p. 83.

[2] Sessio 24, *Decr. de Reform.* cap. 9.

and, on the other hand, to initiate the long-yearned-for
revival of spiritual life in the bosom of the Church itself,
both in its head and in its members.

The Council did not direct its reform labours firstly
to the secular princes and rulers, and the laity in general,
but it began with prescribing the strictest ordinances
for the whole episcopal body ; it kept the reform of the
hierarchy persistently in view as the crucial point of
religious renovation.

It was maintained by many of the Fathers that
' the greatest of all clerical abuses, and the one which
was the source of all others, was the non-residence of the
bishops.' ' The Churches complain,' said Bartholomäus, Archbishop of Braga, ' that they are abandoned
by their spiritual bridegrooms, some of whom treat
their flocks more like robbers than like shepherds and
fathers ; for they only come near them to take away
their goods, and then forsake them again, instead of
feeding, guiding, and comforting them.' The following
decree had already been issued during the first period
of the Council : ' Whereas the synod has taken in hand
to restore the discipline of the Church at present fallen
into such lamentable decay, and to improve the corrupt
morals of the Christian clergy and people, the said
synod is of opinion that it ought to begin its work with
those clerics who are placed over the higher Churches.
The bishops of all grades should be watchful over themselves and over the whole of the flocks which the Holy
Ghost has placed under their government. As, however, they cannot thoroughly fulfil these duties when
they leave the flocks entrusted to them to hirelings,
prefer earthly things to heavenly ones, become hangers
on at this or the other princely court, or occupy them-

selves with the cares of worldly business, the synod has
thought well to revive the old canons directed against
non-resident ecclesiastics.' [1]

Later on in the proceedings, the Council returned
to the question of non-residence, which was dealt with
very stringently, and, besides being declared a mortal
sin, it was made punishable by the confiscation of
property.[2] First on the list of episcopal duties was
placed the office of preaching ; the bishops were to
proclaim the teaching of Christ in person ; they were
also to perform the ordination of priests personally, to
provide for the religious instruction of the young, to
bestow especial care on the hospitals and poor-houses,
to welcome and entertain all who sought their assistance
as though they were entertaining Christ Himself, and
not to neglect pastoral visitation of the churches and
clergy of their dioceses.   Whenever it was a question of
inquiry into or reform of morals, no immunities or right
of appeal, not even to the Roman See, were to be allowed
to hinder or suspend the execution of the episcopal
decrees.[3] On pain of forfeiting their dignity, the
bishops were to receive consecration within six months
after their nomination.   The Pope alone, to whom they
had to swear obedience, had the right to depose them.

The reform of the priests was included in that of the
bishops. ' Nothing is so conducive to the stimulation
of continuous piety and reverence in others as the life and
example of those who have consecrated themselves to
the service of God.   The clergy ought, therefore, in all

---

[1] Sessio 6, *Decr. de Reform.* cap. 1, where the penalties are described
in greater detail.

[2] Sessio 23, *Decr. de Reform.* cap. 1.

[3] Sessio 24, *Decr. de Reform.* cap. 10.

respects to exhibit an earnest, exemplary character, permeated by religion, and even to avoid all those slighter kinds of transgression which in them would appear serious, in order that their behaviour and actions may inspire universal respect.' [1] The Council enjoined as special duties on the clergy to impart catechetical instruction, to preach regularly on Sundays and festivals, and to look after the poor and the suffering with fatherly solicitude.

With a view to the reform of religious associations it was emphatically represented to individual members of religious orders that all personal possession was unlawful for them ; minute regulations were laid down with regard to admission and vows, as also to the choice of the superiors ; the bishops were most strictly enjoined to exercise watchfulness over the enclosure of nuns ; in case of any refractoriness, they were to enforce ecclesiastical penalties, regardless of any sort of appeal. No convents were to be erected without permission from the bishops.   Under penalty of excommunication, it was enacted by the Council that ' prior to the novices taking the vows, no part of their fortunes was to be applied in any way to the convents, so that they might not be hindered from going out again if they wished to do so.'

One particularly severe decree, which points to the existence of very flagrant abuses, was enacted with regard to the celebration of the holy Sacrifice of the Mass.   The bishops were enjoined ' earnestly to interdict and abolish everything that savoured of greed, superstition, or a spirit of irreverence scarcely distinguishable from impiety : all haggling

[1] Sessio 22, *Decr. de Reform.* cap. 1.

with Masses, all raising of forced and involuntary alms, and other like practices which were not free from the taint of simony. Roving, unknown priests were not to be allowed to say Mass; no men of notoriously bad character were to officiate at the altar, or to be present at divine service. ' In order that no scope might be given for superstition,' it was forbidden to introduce any other than the recognised Church rites, ceremonies, and prayers at the celebrations.[1]

The deterioration of the clergy in respect of morals and learning was most closely connected, both in the Empire and in Austria, with the decay of the numerous educational and instructional institutions which the Church had formerly possessed in connection with her convents, cathedrals, and various corporations and colleges. In the universities which were still Catholic, there was general complaint that theological study ' had almost completely died out,' that the theological students ' were no less lawless, dissolute, and shameless ' than the other students. It was, therefore, imperatively necessary for the sake of the religious and moral training and culture of the rising clergy that fresh religious institutions should be founded.

The founder of the Order of Jesuits had declared such institutions to be ' the actual basis of all Church reform,' and this statement is fully corroborated by the Cardinal Otto, Bishop of Augsburg, in his remarks on the Jesuit colleges which had already been established before the opening of the Council. He draws attention to ' the large number of young men educated in these colleges who are now labouring as zealous, well-instructed priests, and bringing forth abundant

---

[1] Sessio 22, *Decr. de obs. et evit. in Celebr. Missæ.*

fruits in the pulpit, in the confessional, and by sick-beds in hospitals and poor-houses.'[1]

In conjunction with Ignatius, Cardinal Morone[2] had taken an active part in the erection of a ' German College ' at Rome, which college Pope Julius III. had called into existence, richly supported himself, and recommended also to the support of King Ferdinand.[3] In this college, for which Ignatius at the bidding of the Pope drew up the statutes, German youths, under the guidance of Jesuits, were to be instructed in humanistic studies, in philosophy, and in theology, in order to serve afterwards as secular priests and to preach the Gospel in their Fatherland. ' We use no harshness in our dealings with them,' Ignatius wrote to Canisius; ' we treat them with all possible kindness in order that they may lead edifying lives.' He requested Father Jajus and other Jesuits working in Germany to send to him at Rome suitable young men, who intended devoting themselves to the priesthood.[4] Twenty-five went there at once in the year 1552, and the following year the number rose to 52. When, under Paul IV., the college was reduced to extreme penury, Ignatius collected alms for the maintenance of the pupils. He wrote to the Cardinal Otto, Bishop of Augsburg, that, even if no one came to his aid, he should still go on helping and keeping up the college as long as he lived,

---

[1] See vol. vii. p. 255, n. 1.

[2] See Ignacio de Loyola, *Cartas*, iii. 524–528.

[3] Lämmer, *Zur Kirchengeschichte des 16. und 17. Jahrhunderts*, pp. 117–118. We are now admirably informed concerning the history of the German College by Cardinal Steinhuber's great work, based on a comprehensive study of old documents, *Geschichte des Collegium Germanicum Hungaricum in Rom* (Freiburg i. Br. 1895), 2 vols.

[4] Ignacio de Loyola, *Cartas*, iii. 395 (compare iii. 94). See Friedländer, *Beiträge zur Reformationsgesch.* pp. 275 ff.

and that he would rather sell himself as a slave than forsake the Germans.[1]

In England, too, Cardinal Reginald Pole had begun founding seminaries after the model of the German college, and indeed of Jesuit colleges in general. William Allen, later on promoted to the dignity of Cardinal, annexed an English seminary to the university of Douay.[2] At Rome, Charles Borromeus, nephew of Pope Pius IV., ' became enthusiastic over the idea that seminaries resembling the German college should be established in every diocese of Christendom ; after the re-opening of the Council, he laboured zealously, and with special support from the legate Morone and the General of the Jesuits, Lainez, to induce the Fathers to further this scheme.' [3]

At a solemn session of July 15, 1563, when, besides the legates and a few cardinals, there were present over 200 bishops, several Generals of religious Orders, a number of doctors, and also the Emperor's ambassadors and those of all the Catholic sovereigns assembled at Trent, the Council published, with regard to the seminaries, a strict code of regulations for the whole Church.

It was also settled that in connection with every cathedral there should be a training school for a certain number of young boys, the size to be determined by the respective extent and needs of the diocese. The conditions of admission were to be that the boys were so far uncontaminated by evil, that they had an adequate

---

[1] See Theiner, *Gesch. der geistlichen Bildungsanstalter*, pp. 88 ff.

[2] Fuller particulars in A. Bellesheim, *Wilhelm Cardinal Allen* (1532–1594) and the English seminaries on the continent (Mayence, 1885), pp. 26 ff.

[3] Letter of Otto of Augsburg. See vol. vii., p. 255, n. 1.

grounding of elementary knowledge, and that their circumstances and inclinations gave reason to hope that they would later on devote themselves to the service of the Church.   Precedence was to be given to the children of poor parents, but sons of wealthy people, who were ready to pay the costs of their education, were not to be excluded.   The whole external and internal management of the institution was to be in the hands of the bishop, who was to choose some of the canons of his cathedral chapter to assist him in the work of superintendence.   The subjects of instruction were enumerated, and for the defrayal of the expenses it was decreed that a tax should be imposed on all the benefices in each diocese, beginning with the incomes of the bishop and the chapter.[1]   At the end of the session several of the bishops expressed their opinion that even if the Council should have accomplished no other good work than the erection of seminaries, all its labour and trouble would have been richly rewarded by this one result.   For these seminaries were the most efficacious means for the restoration of Church discipline ; in every community the citizens were what they had been educated to be.[2]

As regards the settlement of dogmatic points the work of the Council was incomparably harder than had been the case with any one of the eighteen General Councils that had preceded it.   For the religious revolution of the sixteenth century had not only assailed separate articles of Church teaching, but had made a wholesale attack on the Bible, on tradition, on the Church and its constitution, on original sin and redemp-

[1] Sessio 23, *Decr. de Reform.* cap. 18.
[2] Pallavicino, lib. 21, cap. 8, No. 3.

tion, on justification and grace, on every single ecclesiastical means of grace—purgatory and veneration of
saints, confession and indulgence—in short, it had
threatened nearly the whole edifice of Christian teaching,
even the foundations of religion itself. As, however,
the worst consequences of the schism were at present
only apparent in isolated manifestations, the Council
was able to ignore them for the time being, and to start
its campaign against universal heresy from those great
verities concerning which the majority of the separatists
were in accord with the Church, viz. faith in Jesus
Christ and belief in His Gospel.

' The pure Gospel,' the then battle-cry against the
Church, was placed by the Council at the head of its
dogmatic decrees. ' The Gospel, promised in former
times through the prophets in the Holy Scriptures, and
first promulgated to us by the work of our Lord Jesus
Christ, and then at His command announced by the
apostles to all creatures as the source of all saving
truth and moral discipline,' shall, according to the
promise of Christ, be kept free from all error and preserved in its full purity by the Church for the benefit
of mankind. Christ's legacy to us, however, is not
exclusively preserved in written books, but likewise in
the living stream of tradition which accompanies the
written document from generation to generation. The
teaching body of the Church watches over the purity
of both. In the exercise of its teaching authority the
Council reaffirms the old canon of Holy Scripture, sets
up the Vulgate as a normal text, and makes provision
for its propagation and explanation. The Bible, lifted
from the confusion of the times and placed on the altar,
forms, under the light of tradition and the protection

of the living teaching authority, the firm foundation of all further transactions.

The Council then goes on to sketch in broad outlines the supernatural order of things which God called into being simultaneously with the creation of the first man, the disturbance of this order by the fall of man, the ruin worked by original sin on the whole human race, the restoration of mankind through Christ, who on the cross rendered full and perfect satisfaction, merited an abundance of grace for all men, and by His sufferings showed the way which mankind must henceforth follow in order to work out their salvation by personal co-operation with divine grace.

In consequence of original sin every human being enters life in a fallen condition, and from the first day of existence is in bondage to death ; the understanding is obscured, the will is inclined to evil, concupiscence is developed, but at the same time freedom of will is in noways extinguished. Only through baptism, real or of desire, is man freed from original sin, adorned with sanctifying grace, and made a child of God. But evil concupiscence is not removed by baptism : it is only by continuous, unremitting struggle with these desires and lusts, and aided by the constant help of actual grace, that the baptised Christian can reach his goal.

All justification and sanctification of man proceed from Christ, the only Mediator between God and man. Nevertheless, it is not by mere imputation of the merits of Christ, but by inward elevation and sanctification of spirit, that man is justified or made righteous. The salvation of each man and woman is, at its root, a freely given grace, because it proceeds from prevenient grace. It is in the power of every individual's free will either to reject this grace, or else to co-operate with it, and through fear and hope, through love of God and abhorrence of sin, springing from the root of faith, to fit himself for the reception of sonhood of God. The infusion of sanctifying grace is the work of God. Without special revelation none of us can acquire full assurance of possessing this grace ; but each one of us must persevere humbly in prayer and in work and in fighting against all that is evil.

But if nobody can be certain of being predestined to eternal salvation, neither has any one reason to doubt of God's love and pitifulness, since Christ died for all, and wishes all men to be saved, and every faithful believer in the efficacy of Christ's merits should feel unbounded confidence of attaining salvation through Him. A mere blind sentiment of assurance of being participators in the merits of Christ is not sufficient for salvation, but the justified co-operating with the proffered grace is able and bound to overcome temptations, to fulfil God's commandments, to accomplish really good works through the supernatural merits of the Redeemer, and thus to attain salvation.

Thus the doctrine of grace formulated by the Council, on the one hand, throws all the glory and honour of the work of salvation back upon Christ, who merited and dispenses all grace ; but, on the other hand, it credits man with freedom of will and action corresponding to his nature, and spurs him on to strive after closer spiritual union with Christ, the source of all supernatural life, by vigorous inward endeavour, by holy living, by true penitence, and by active imitation of his Saviour.

The proper complement of this doctrine is the life

of grace of the Church in the seven sacraments. These sacraments draw, in a marvellous manner, the earthly creation into the supernatural order. By them the spiritual and corporeal lives of individuals, from the cradle to the grave, are outwardly and visibly consecrated, inwardly and invisibly sanctified, and human society, in its two principal estates—marriage and priesthood—is most intimately connected with the life and rule of the Redeemer.

In consequence of the religious revolution of the sixteenth century this sacramental life of the Church seemed on the brink of complete destruction. While the cry rang out unceasingly that the honour of Christ and His pure Gospel were being threatened, the sacraments which He Himself had instituted were despised and even desecrated. Cut off from the fountain of grace, the masses sank into a state of wanton naturalism, which retained scarcely a vestige of the essential elements of Christianity, and Christian morality evaporated in mere sentiment.

In the midst of this general confusion of minds the Council reasserted the threatened ordinances of grace, established on a firm basis, in accord with Scripture and tradition, the sevenfold number of the Sacraments, their nature and form, their efficacy and the conditions of their efficacy, the properties common to all, and their differences.

Baptism elevates to a life of holiness the newly-born infant ; Confirmation strengthens the adolescent Christian on the threshold of life's battle ; Extreme Unction equips the dying mortal for the last struggles. The Sacrament of Penance restores to the truly penitent sinner the grace he has forfeited ; the Sacrament of

Matrimony invests the purely natural union with a supernatural consecration; the Sacrament of Order transmits the power necessary for the offering up of the Sacrifice and the administration of the Sacraments. But in the Holy Eucharist Christ is veritably and actually present among men, He becomes the food of their souls, and fulfils daily at the Holy Mass the prophecy of Malachi, that from the rising of the sun unto the going down thereof a pure sacrifice should be offered unto God. As the fulfilment of all the sacrifices of the ancient covenant, as the testament of the Saviour, as a bloodless renewal of the Sacrifice on the Cross, as the continued personal action of the eternal and only High Priest, the Sacrifice of the Mass constitutes the focus of the whole system of Christian worship.

The great brotherhood in which Christ unites mankind by means of the seven sacraments extends also to the life beyond this world, and the Council, accordingly, in the last session which it devoted to dogma, established the connection of the sacramental order of grace with the doctrines of purgatory, of veneration of saints and images, and of indulgences. Its decisions in this respect were as follows : The members of the Church militant on earth can, by their prayers and good works, help the dead who are still working out their temporal punishments in purgatory. The saints who are glorified in heaven pray for their still struggling brethren. The veneration of their earthly remains serves to nourish and keep alive, at one and the same time, the pious spirit of family feeling and all higher human aspirations ; Christian art finds in the representation of Christ, the Virgin Mary, and the saints the highest ideals for its creations. By indulgences the humble prayers of sin-purged mortals, the exercise of penance, and the practice of benevolence are brought into connection with Christ and with the common treasury of the merits of His saints.

And thus the dogmatic decrees of the Council, after the manner of the Apostles' Creed, conclude with the all-comforting doctrine of the communion of saints, which has its beginning here below, and finds its consummation in the life beyond.

Herewith the dogmatic work of the Council was finished. From out the well-nigh unravelable coil of reproaches, attacks, misrepresentations and calumnies, which half a century had wound round the Catholic Church, her likeness now stood forth pure and spotless, and in complete inner accord as to doctrinal and moral teaching, organisation, and worship. Her dogmatic connection with the apostolic past was clearly set forth at all points ; the reformation had been grounded, not on externals, but on the inward sanctification both of individual life and of the universal community of the Church.[1]

[1] The Protestant writer Marheineke, in his *System des Katholicismus*, says of the Council of Trent : ' However queer and wrong and undignified the proceedings frequently were, one can have nothing but respect for the perseverance and vigour displayed to save and strengthen anew the faith of the Church ; for the prudence and zeal evinced in the reformation of so many abuses and breaches of discipline ; for the piety and insight manifested in dealing with things of the holiest and highest order. No other Council lasted so long ; none deferred its conclusion so long in order to please its opponents ; none brought more learning and labour to bear upon matters of faith. No other Council ever counted among its crowd of mediocrities so considerable a number of the most learned theologians of the times. There were men assembled at Trent whose talents and genius, piety and knowledge of antiquity would have been an honour to any age, and who earned the right to be numbered among the most famous Fathers and schoolmen : Dominicus Soto, Bartholomew Carranza, Alphonsus a Castro, Melchior Canus, Ruardus Tapper, and many more.'

' All endeavours to draw the heretics to the Council have proved futile,' said the Cardinal-legate Morone at one of the last sessions; ' nevertheless, the assembly has accomplished admirable results in that it has given definite dogmatic shape to doctrines, and has contributed to the amelioration of Church discipline. Greater things were indeed to be desired; but the assembly was made up of men, not of angels, and we had to bow to circumstances and be satisfied with the best we could achieve, since we could not attain to the actual best.' [1]

The Council broke up on December 4, 1563, ' in universal concord of the Catholic world.' The goal which had scarcely even been hoped for by many, which in human estimation had so often been imperilled, was actually won.[2] The members, 250 in number, who had taken part in the proceedings, all signed the resolutions. Later on most of the envoys of Catholic powers added their signatures also.

Pius IV. informed the cardinals of the conclusion of the Council, and on December 30 his Holiness, who was still weak after a serious illness, delivered an address in Consistory overflowing with joy and gratitude. ' This day,' he said, ' ushers in new life and calls for new manners. By the authority of the Council, Church discipline, which had lapsed into decay among the masses, has been restored. But it is on the clergy

' Whosoever reads the Acts of the Council with a mind inclined to peace,' wrote the Protestant Hugo Grotius in his *Votum pro pace*, p. 682, ' will find that everything therein is explained widely and fully in accord with the teachings of the Scriptures and of the Fathers.'

[1] Pallavicino, lib. 24, cap. 3, No. 1.

[2] ' We can understand,' says Ranke, *Päpste*, i. 349, ' that the prelates, when they met for the last time on Dec. 4, 1563, were stirred with joy and emotion. Even those who till then had been enemies wished each other success. Many of these old men had tears in their eyes.'

above all that a new order of life has been enjoined, and from the regulations laid down they may learn that when once they have taken on themselves the dignity of Holy Orders, necessity is laid on them to shape their conduct according to the plan set forth with divine clearness in these most salutary decrees.' [1] Pius IV. gave orders to the Cardinal-bishops to repair to their dioceses and take up their residence in them. He announced that, in fulfilment of the resolution respecting seminaries, he intended at once to set them all a good example ; and he proceeded accordingly to erect ' the Roman Seminary,' which he placed under the direction of the Jesuits.[2] The excellence of the organisation of the new Order had been acknowledged by the Council,[3] and in the course of its different sessions several Jesuits had taken a leading part in the proceedings. When Ignatius, by desire of several of the bishops, ordered the Fathers Lainez and Salmeron to go to Trent in the quality of theologians, he gave them the injunction ' before all things to keep their own spiritual progress in mind, to speak with deliberation, and to behave with meekness and modesty at the Council.' ' Outside the Council you will, as far as lies in your power, lose no opportunity of making yourselves useful. You will, as occasion arises, hear the confessions of those who wish to unburden themselves to you ; you will preach to the lower classes, give Christian instruction to the children, incite people to strive after perfection by means of the Spiritual Exercises, you will visit the hospitals and administer loving help and consolation

---

[1] Pallavicino, lib. 24, cap. 9, No. 5.
[2] Raynald, ad a. 1564, No. 53.
[3] Sessio 25, *Decr. de reg.* cap. 16.

to the sick, and the more zeal you show in works of love and gentleness, so much the more abundant will be the outpourings of grace from the Holy Ghost on the Council. In your sermons you must be careful not to touch on any of the points on which Catholics and Protestants differ. The whole tenor of your preaching must rather tend to the improvement of morals and to leading your hearers into obedience to the Holy Catholic Church.' [1]

On January 26, 1564, the Pope ratified all the decrees of the Council in a bull signed by the whole college of cardinals.

All Catholics now felt once more reunited among themselves, and brought back also into close connection with their centre of unity at Rome; and from this central point itself new life streamed through the whole Church. 'Thousands, hundreds of thousands,' says a contemporary, 'are now once more setting shining examples of prayer, of renunciation and voluntary poverty, of the practice of every heroic virtue; numbers of saintly men show forth the eternal power of ministrations founded on the faith, and all classes of society are animated by zeal for ecclesiastical reform.' [2]

Four popes in succession came from the ranks of the people at this period. Pius IV. himself belonged to the humble condition of burgher; Pius V. (1566-1572) was of lowly origin; Gregory XIII. (1572-1585) was the son of a tradesman; Sixtus V. (1585-1590) the son of a gardener. Pius V.—a Dominican—continued, as Pope, to conform entirely to the strict rule of his Order, and was already looked upon as a saint

[1] Ignacio de Loyola, *Cartas*, i. 475–478.
[2] *De Reformatione Ecclesiæ* (Mediol. 1587), p. 5.

by his contemporaries : ' So pious a pope had never yet been known ' was the verdict of the people.

' Gregory XIII.,' wrote the Venetian ambassador Paolo Tiepolo in 1576, ' is certainly less austere than was Pius, but he does a great deal of good. It is a fortunate thing that two such pious popes should have followed one another ; for everybody has, or at least seems to have, become the better for their examples. The cardinals and prelates frequently say Mass, live devoutly, and in their households endeavour to avoid everything that might give offence. The whole city is transformed from its former demoralised condition ; everywhere it exhibits a marked improvement in morals and a distinctly Christian character, so that we may truly say : Rome leaves little more to be desired, as far as religion goes, and is approaching as near to perfection as is possible for human nature.' [1]

---

[1] In Albèri, ser. 2, vol. iv. pp. 213-214.

CHAPTER IV

THE ROMAN CATECHISM—THE CATECHISMS OF CANISIUS
AND OPPOSITION WRITINGS

AT the instigation of the Council and under co-operation
of some of its leading members, the compilation of a
manual of pastoral instructions for the clergy had been
begun at Trent, but the work had remained unfinished.
It was not till 1566, after several commissions appointed
by the papal chair had had a hand in it, that the
manual was published under the title of ' The Roman
Catechism.' [1]

This Catechism was not strictly speaking a ' symbolic
book '—that is, an authoritatively binding formulary of
faith—but it was nevertheless a text-book of theology
of the highest authority, inasmuch as it had been compiled under the auspices of a General Council, and besides
having been sealed with the approval of Pope Pius V.,
had been published by his orders. This work, in the
preparation of which the Dominican Order had had the
chief share, was not intended either as a compendium
of Christian instruction for the people, or as a complete
theological guide for students, but as a handbook for
pastors of souls, a manual in which the essential points
of doctrine were summarised for the use of the clergy

[1] 'Catechismus, ex decreto Concilii Tridentini, ad parochos, Pii V.
Pont. Max. jussu editus' (Romæ, 1566). See Streitwolf-Kleuer, *Libri
Symbolici Eccl. Catholicæ* (Gottingen, 1846), i. 105.

both as an aid to their own theological culture and also (chiefly indeed) for imparting religious instruction to others. The vast subject-matter was, with sharp preciseness of expression, put into a form both compact and appropriate ; knowledge deep and sound was set before the parochial clergy in the simplest form.

Among the Protestants, who had formed the most extraordinary conceptions of Catholic doctrine, this work caused no little sensation. Tilmann Hesshus wrote that the Catholicism contained in this catechism was not the same as that which Luther's Theses had attacked. It was the most artful book that had been written by the papists for centuries ; for the Pope and his consistory made it appear as if they were willing to do the right thing and to take up God's Word and the Catechism instead of befooling the people with Masses for souls, processions, indulgences, and idols. The authors of this book might almost pass as Lutherans. In the passages where they have occasion to praise the grace of God and Christ's ineffable merits, and the gift and power of the Holy Ghost, to exhort man to do good works and to keep him back from vice, the subject was treated in such a masterly manner that improvement was impossible. Nevertheless, Hesshus asserted, all this was not meant in good faith, but it was a subtle artifice whereby to ensnare the people. He was as fierce as he had been before in denouncing ' the execrable, scandalous crew of papists.' [1]

The Roman Catechism was rapidly translated into numbers of different languages, and the whole of the Catholic world greeted it with sincere delight. The

---

[1] Wilkens, pp. 127–128.

illustrious Charles Borromeus welcomed it as the realisation of one of his most cherished ideas. Many bishops, and synods innumerable, recommended the book, and before the expiration of the century twenty provincial synods had honoured it with their praise.[1]

The jurist and imperial councillor George Eder wrote in 1568, ' Verily the reading of this book hath greatly strengthened and confirmed one in the Catholic religion. Perceiving that a knowledge of it would be useful and necessary to the whole world, and as I considered it of the greatest importance that it should be circulated in all languages, I began at once to translate part of it into German, and I should have finished the translation some time ago if I had not been informed, on trustworthy authority, that Canisius, formerly my tutor and patron, had already embarked on this work. Not only was I delighted to make way for him, but I congratulated myself and the whole Church on his having undertaken the task.' [2]

At the time that the Roman Catechism appeared Canisius had already published several catechetical works of his own.[3]

[1] A complete list of these synods is given by the Dominican, A. Reginald, *De Catechismi Romani Auctoritate, bei Natalis Alexander*, suppl. i. 377.

[2] In the Dedication of his *Partitiones Catechismi Catholici* (Coloniæ, 1568) to the Senate and the University of Cologne. See Paulus in the *Histor.-polit. Blätter*, 115, pp. 26 ff. For the translation of the Roman Catechism by Canisius and Hoffäus, see De Backer, ii. 173; Riess, p. 382.

[3] Concerning the earlier Catholic Catechisms, among which that of Johannes Dietenberger stands out markedly, see Moufang, pp. 1 ff., H. Wedewer, Johannes Dietenberger (Freiburg, 1888), v. 198 ff., 416, and P. Bahlmann's bibliographical study : *Deutschlands katholische Catechismen bis zum Ende des sechzehnten Jahrhunderts* (Münster, 1894), a work as careful as it is industrious. See also *Die Ergänzungen von Paulus im Histor. Jahrbuch*, xv. 911 f. in the *Katholik*, 1894, ii. 185 f. See Falk in the *Katholik*, 1894, ii. 361 f.

The instruction of the young being looked upon by the Jesuit Order as altogether the most fruitful and profitable sphere of work, and at the same time as the occupation which gave most scope for the exercise of charity and humility, all those who were professed in the Order had to bind themselves by a special vow ' to instruct the little ones in the faith.' [1] Canisius began this work in the first years of his active career. ' The Apostle of the Germans,' it was said of him, ' is, like his Master, the warmest friend of children.' At the advanced age of fifty-six it was still his habit, on his frequent journeyings from Innspruck to Hall, to turn into the peasants' cottages and give instruction in Christian doctrine. The children used to run out to meet him in the distance, and when he took up his staff to go on further the little ones had to be dragged away from him. The peasants kept up the memory of the Christian teacher by having his picture painted on their walls.[2] ' We are busy teaching the children and the old people,' Canisius wrote but the year before his death.[3]

His first catechetical work, ' Summe Christlicher Lehre,' he published anonymously in Latin in the year 1555,[4] and a second enlarged edition, with his name, followed in 1566. Meanwhile, in 1556–1557, he had

---

[1] Institutum Societatis Jesu, *Constitutiones*, pars 5, cap. 3, No. 3.

[2] See Beda Weber, *Tyrol und die Reformation*, p. 380.

[3] Reifer, p. 14. See also J. Knabenbauer, *Canisius und die Schulfrage*, in the *Stimmen aus Maria-Laach*, xvii. 352–370. For what follows see the remarkably thorough work of Braunsberger: *Entstehung und erste Entwickelung der Katechismen des seligen Petrus Canisius aus der Gesellschaft Jesu* (Freiburg-i.-Br. 1893). See also small supplements in the *Histor. Jahrbuch*, xiv. 680, and xv. 912, and in the *Katholik*, 1894, ii. 191; 1895, i. 189 f.

[4] See Braunsberger, *Entstehung*, pp. 27–28.

brought out a Catechism of quite small size, both in
Latin and in German,[1] and this book was followed in
1558 by a rather larger volume, in Latin, an abridg-
ment of the 'Summe,' for the use of young students.[2]
His larger German Catechism, which came out at Dillingen in 1560, and which he commended to the use of
adults, especially fathers and mothers of families, was
an expanded translation of this abridged volume. He
appended to his larger Catechism, as he had done with
many other editions of his catechetical works, a prayer-
book, or a short selection of prayers, and also one of the
smaller catechetical treatises in which the more essential
points of Church doctrine were set forth in greater
detail.[3] ' How can we lay sufficient stress,' Canisius said,
' on the benefit and usefulness—nay, on the imperative
necessity—for all Christians to have in their minds a
clear summary of the Church doctrines on faith and
morals ? ' ' Is there any right-feeling man who would
not wish and advise that the rising generation should
learn these sacred things betimes ? Who can doubt
that our Christian youth would then grow up to be all
the more God-fearing, and that the whole of Christendom,
in all classes, would be made happier and better by such
pure and wholesome teaching ? '[4]

To impart this pure and sound instruction to the
country people round him was the one object of Canisius'
endeavours. ' What I have written here,' he says in
the preface to the ' Summe ' of 1566, ' I have not written
from avarice or greed of gain, not from love or hate of
any one person, but solely, as I can declare on my most

---

[1] Braunsberger, *Entstehung*, pp. 103–108, and *Epistulæ Canisii*,
i. 640, note 4.

[2] *Entstehung*, pp. 114–117.   [3] See Reifer, pp. 65 ff.   [4] *Ibid.* p. 72.

sacred oath, from the longing to spread the light of
religious truth, and in obedience to the command of the
Emperor. I have endeavoured by means of this book
to promote the general welfare of all Catholics, above
all of the German Catholics.'

The beginning and the end of Christianity, he
teaches in his Catechism, is to know Christ and to observe
all that appertains to Christian wisdom and righteousness. This wisdom, he says, consists of three parts:
faith, hope, and charity. Taking these three *seriatim*,
he first expounds the Creed, then teaches hope and confidence by means of the Lord's Prayer and the ' Hail
Mary' (Angelic Salutation), and finally leads up to
active love through the exposition of the ten commandments of God and the commandments of the
Church. But the Godlike life cannot exist and thrive
in the heart of man unless implanted and nourished by
the power of the sacraments, and so the Church teaching
on these follows next. Where there is life there is
activity. This activity shows itself in resisting and
struggling against all that is injurious to the Christian
life, and in seeking and protecting all that nourishes
and strengthens its growth. Canisius, accordingly, in
the second division deals with Christian righteousness
as the habit of resistance to evil and practice of good.
He delineates sin in all its different manifestations,
and shows how it is to be got rid of. He then enjoins
the performance of good works—especially works of
lovingkindness—discusses the cardinal virtues, the gifts
and fruits of the Holy Ghost, the eight beatitudes
and the evangelical counsels, and concludes with the
doctrine of the four last things: death, judgment,
heaven, and hell.

Throughout the whole work, from the first to the last page, Christ is preached as the beginning and the end, the root and the crown of human salvation. In the first edition of 1556, on the reverse of the title-page, there is a woodcut representing the cross, and in front of it the dead Saviour in His mother's arms ; above are the words of the prophet Isaiah spoken of the Messiah, ' Through whose name many shall be saved.' A second woodcut represents the Saviour as a teacher, surrounded by children, with the superscription from the Psalms, ' Hearken, my children, and I will teach you the fear of the Lord.' ' Christ's sufferings,' it is said in the fourth article of faith, ' Christ's blood, cross, wounds, and death afford to sinners continual consolation, health, vigour, and life, in so far as we obey Him as our head, and suffer with Him that we may be also glorified with Him' (Rom. viii.). ' The sign of the cross which we make on the forehead admonishes us to make the cross of our Lord our true and sacred boast and the anchor of our salvation.' [1] Before the section dealing with Christian righteousness there is also a woodcut representing the Saviour on the cross, with the following inscriptions above and below :

For Christ also hath once suffered for sins, the just for the unjust (1 Peter iii. 18).

That we being delivered out of the hand of our enemies might serve Him without fear, in holiness and righteousness all the days of our life (Luke i. 74).[2]

' It was in order that we might practise righteousness in both its forms, i.e. in avoiding evil and in doing good, that the grace of God has been merited

---

[1] The last statement of Canisius subjoined in the second edition of the *Summa* of 1566.

[2] *Summa*, 1556, fol. 117.

for us and promised us through Christ Jesus; this grace is necessary to us at all times. When it precedes and assists our actions the words of John are fulfilled: " He that doeth righteousness is righteous, even as he is righteous." " Without Christ," as Hieronymus says, " no man can be either wise or discerning, nor can any one know judgment, or be strong, or possess wisdom or piety, or be filled with the fear of the Lord." [1] " In what manner," he asks, " is sin to be rooted out ? " Here, if nowhere else, is a point of undisputed truth— namely, that Christ as man is the propitiation for our sin, and the Lamb of God who taketh away the sins of the world, and who alone can win for us forgiveness of and purification from sin. So then it is certain that God cleanses the heart through faith, as Peter says, because without faith, which is the gateway and foundation of human salvation, no man can attain or hope for forgiveness of or deliverance from sin.' [2] The edition of the ' Summe ' of 1556 ends with the words : ' To Jesus Christ, the crucified, who is the author and perfecter of our wisdom and righteousness, be eternal glory.'

In his catechetical works Canisius showed thoughtful care for every age and every degree of culture. His small Catechism, like that of Luther, was intended for young children. His ' Summe ' was on the lines of Luther's large Catechism, which was not meant to be learnt by heart, word for word, but was a collection of

---

[1] *Summa*, 1556, fol. 175ᵃ; *ibid*. 1566, fol. 177ᵇ–178ᵃ. For the illustrated edition of the Catechism see Braunsberger's exhaustive work, *Entstehung*, xxix. u. 155–160 ; *ib*. p. 85, on the wealth of quotations from Scripture and the Fathers. Braunsberger (p. 3 f.) criticises Canisius extremely well as a catechist in general.

[2] *Summa*, 1566, fol. 151ᵃ.

aids to religious instruction—' short sermons for children,' as Luther himself once called them. It also was
meant to be a guide and a model for religious instructors,
and a means of strengthening· and carrying on the
spiritual culture of the university students and of
adults. But between the great text-book and the small
child's Catechism Canisius inserted intermediary lesson
books. For the gymnasia, where Latin was the language in vogue, the ' Institutions ' was compiled ; and
for the higher classes of the German schools the larger
German Catechism was used. Both these books were
suited to the capacities of the young.[1] If to these are
added the translations of his Latin writings, Canisius
may be said to have presented the doctrine of salvation
to the German nation in at least six different forms,
each separate work being conceived in the same spirit
and cast in the same mould.[2] At this work he laboured
until his death, filling and filing, in order, as he said,
' to adapt it to the requirements of the age by making
it both shorter and clearer.' In the last year of his life
he edited his small Catechism with the words ' all
divided into syllables, to assist the dear young children
in learning to read, which will then be of great service
to them in learning to write.' [3]

The Catechisms of Canisius are entirely free from
the rabidly bitter polemical element which, after the
example of Luther, the Protestant catechists introduced into their works, and which by no means diminished the religious divisions of the German nation.

---

[1] See Reifer, p. 69.
[2] It was only the small German Catechism in which, later on, the
Roman Catechism was included.
[3] Reifer, p. 74.

He carefully refutes all the controversial statements of
the Protestants, but often only in an indirect manner
by means of a clear exposition and demonstration of
the Catholic doctrines.   In this way, for instance, he
deals, through several pages, with the Sacrament of
Extreme Unction, which the Protestants had rejected.
He proves the divine institution and virtue of this
sacrament from the Scriptures and from the belief of
the primitive Church, but never so much as mentions
his opponents.   Nowhere in the Catechism is there a
single spiteful or venomous word against the Protestants ; Canisius is altogether free from angry invective
or personal animosity.

And this absence of bitterness gives all the more
force and persuasiveness to his arguments.   Times out
of number, far oftener indeed than Luther, his words
are simply the words of Scripture.   But he is at the
zenith of his triumph when he makes Christian antiquity
speak through the mouth of its Fathers and Councils.
So plentiful is his store of evidence of this kind that in
hundreds of cases he can do no more than give marginal
references to the passages in question.   His brother
Jesuit, Peter Busäus, made later on a collection of all
these passages, and filled an imposing folio volume with
them.[1]

Luther's Catechism, however, could not have been
compiled on this principle, although even he cannot
wholly ignore the Fathers.   Thus, for instance, he defends infant baptism by appeal to ' certain fathers ' in
whom the Holy Ghost had been present—namely, Bernhard, Gerson, Johannes Hus, and others.

[1] See vol. vii. p. 6. See the various editions of this work by De Backer,
i. 975-976; iii. 2042.

No Catholic book of the sixteenth century caused so much agitation among the Protestant theologians and preachers as ' the accursed, blasphemous Catechism of Canisius.' The writings which were published against it deserve special consideration, as they reveal the particular method of controversy which so strongly influenced the popular life of Germany at that period.

The theologian John Wigand was held to be deserving of the highest praise because he had been one of the first who, in 1556, ' had sounded the trumpet of God's Word against the foul devil's excrements of the houndish Canisius, and had shown the world how to protect itself against his murderous demon's claws.' [1]

Wigand declared to the Protestant world that ' Canisius only carried on an empty sham fight with the name of Christ.' ' Just see,' he exclaims, ' how in this book this murderer of souls only preaches, to young and old, of good works, and does not say one word of the righteousness which the sufferings of Christ bestow on us through faith.' ' The Turk hacks off heads with his sabre, and there is not a creature who is not horrified at his deeds, especially among those who are on the spot and see with their own eyes how he has tyrannised over Hungary and other countries. But this murderer of souls has sharpened and drawn his sword in the production of this book, with which he will hack to pieces the souls of men, and destroy them eternally, and send them to the devil to perish in everlasting hell fire. Who would not tremble and flee before him while the soles of his feet were still left whole ? ' [2] In combating

---

[1] See pamphlet (8–9) quoted at p. 285, n. 1, of vol. vii.

[2] *Verlegung*, B²ᵃ–B⁴ᵃ. For the *Dialogus contra impia Petri Canisii Dogmata*, which appeared in Vienna as early as 1555, see De Backer,

the worship of the Virgin Mary Wigand delivers himself
as follows : ' What assurance can you have that Mary
hears your salutation or your invocation, when the
corporeal organs which she would need for hearing—
namely, her ears—are still buried under the earth, and
have undergone corruption, and will not come forth
again until the Day of Judgment ? ' [1] ' Let each one
consider for himself how idiotic it is to address Marys,
Annas, Catherines, and so forth, as Our Father. Are
these women indeed our fathers ? ' [2] ' The popish
Church is simply cramful of barbarous, monstrous,
worse than heathenish idolatry.' ' Whoredom is allowed
full swing and license by the Pope's own order or dispensation.' [3] . . . . ' Never since the world began has
greater blasphemy or outrage been committed against
Christ on earth than by the ceremony of the Mass, in
which the Pope has turned the Last Supper of the Lord
into a sacrifice for his oiled priests ; ' [4] and what a preposterous travesty of Christ's sacrifice on the cross this
Mass is ! In the first place the priest has the audacity
to present Christ to God the Father as a sacrifice, and
then he puts the sacrificial victim in his mouth and
eats it up ; whereas, if it was really a sacrifice, he ought
to leave it on the altar before God, and wait for God
to come and take the bread and wine which he places
there.' [5] In proof that the Sacrifice of the Mass cannot
be offered for the dead, he says, among other things :

i. 1064; Wiedemann, ii. 69–70, note ; and Braunsberger, *Epistulæ
Canisii*, i. 749 *sq.* ; see *ibid.* p. 755, for a satirical poem, of about 1556,
against the Catechism of Canisius.

[1] Bl. C⁸ᵇ, D²ᵇ–D³ᵃ.   [2] Bl. D⁸.   [3] Bl. E⁶ᵇ–E⁷ᵃ.

[4] Bl. G³ᵃ. On another occasion the Pope's priests are called ' shaven
(tonsured) stallions.' H³ᵇ.

[5] Bl G⁷ᵃ.

' The lips of the dead are frozen together, their stomachs are shrunken, and worms have devoured their bodies like cakes. Since, then, they can neither eat nor drink, but are themselves eaten up, torn and devoured by the worms of the earth, there can be no Sacrament of the Altar for them.' [1]

In auricular confession, he says, ' it is not the concern of the Pope to pronounce judgment on conduct, but to coerce people into forgetting Christ, to enable unclean priests to learn and practise all manner of wickedness, to betray and sell to the Pope in Rome all lords and princes and their transactions, and to make it easy for that devil's brood to vent their effrontery, tyranny, and violence.[2] The Sacrament of Extreme Unction Wigand calls ' the last smearing,' and he describes the oil used for the sick as ' the stinking oil which is used everywhere in the Popish Church, and which would be much more suitable for greasing rusty wheels.' [3] Canisius himself is honoured with the titles of wolf, soul-murderer, idolater, Pope's ass, maniac, blockhead, outrageous blasphemer, shameless, miserable devil.[4] ' That dog of a monk has made it his business to swallow all the excrements of the Pope or Antichrist.' [5]

Flacius Illyricus published a Latin treatise against the Catechism, in 1564, under the title of ' The Pagan doctrine of the Jesuits concerning the two principal articles of the Christian faith—viz. the blotting out and forgiveness of sins, and the justification or righteousness of Christ through which Christians are justified.' [6]

---

[1] Bl. H[2a].　　　　　[2] Bl. J[3].　　　　　[3] Bl. J[7b-8a].
[4] See Bl. B[5], C[5b], C[8b], D[3b], D[5a], D[5b], D[7a], D[8b], H[3a].　　　[5] Bl. H[3b].
[6] *Ethnica Jesuitarum doctrina,* &c. (without mention of place). At the end is the date 1564. See Preger's *Flacius Illyricus,* ii. 563-564.

In complete contradiction to the actual contents of the
Catechism, Flacius declares that the Jesuits ' teach precisely the same doctrine as the Pagans, Turks, and
Jews—viz. that it is by men's own works and merits
that they are justified in the sight of God.'   They
make ' the passion, the blood, the atonement, and the
righteousness of Christ completely and thoroughly null
and evil.   All Christ's sheep, therefore, must protect
themselves and cry out against these dangerous wolves.
Whosoever preaches a different gospel than that of St.
Paul, let him be Anathema, Maranatha.   Amen ! ' [1]
In justification of this curse Flacius quotes from the
' Summe ' of Canisius a few questions and answers which
relate to forgiveness of sins and Christian righteousness.
He does not, however, reproduce these passages word for
word, as he announces on the title-page, but gives
mangled versions of them.   For instance, after men-
tioning the Sacrament of Penance, almsgiving, forgiveness of injuries, the conversion of sinners, perfect
charity, and repentance as means for attaining remis-
sion of sins, Canisius says distinctly : ' Through these
and other kinds of exercises of true piety, we attain to
and perform, in Christ Jesus, all that to which the
Apostle, with the best of rights, exhorts us.' [2]   But
Flacius leaves out the words ' in Christ Jesus,' although
they are specially emphasised in the Catechism by being
printed in large type.   In the passage on ' Christian
righteousness ' he actually omits two whole sentences,
which certainly would interfere inconveniently with his

---

[1] Bl. 6.

[2] *Summa*, 1556, fol. 146[b].   In the edition of 1566, fol. 152[b], the statement is made still clearer by the words ' Christi gratia ' (' through Christ's
grace').

object—namely, those concerning the grace of God, obtained for mankind by Christ our Lord, and which, according to Canisius, is at all times needful, and which must precede and help the performance of good works.

In this same year, 1564, Tilmann Hesshus also issued a warning ' to the young and simple-minded against the godless, lying, and blasphemous Catechism of the Jesuit Canisius.' [1] He was exercised by the fear that this book might be prejudicial to the Catechism of the ' holy Luther.' ' By means of this work,' he said, ' the crafty, cunning enemy of our and all mankind's salvation is aiming at robbing us of this grand and priceless trea- sure ' (Luther's Catechism) ' and giving us in its place his own filth and poison.' [2] ' With this intention he has raised up the impious, execrable body of Jesuits and incited them to write a Catechism by which they pretend to instruct the young in the knowledge of God and the way of eternal salvation. . . . .' In spite of the new evangelical light that had dawned, Canisius per- sisted in defending ' the blasphemous papacy,' and ' the accursed Antichrist's kingdom of sin.' ' The shameless reprobate Canisius shuts his eyes wilfully, behaves as if he was ignorant of the fact that light had arisen, seems indeed rather to nurse the hope that, be the lies, blas- phemies, and errors of the papacy as great as they may, he will still find customers for his stock of falsehoods.' Among other things he ' forbids the priests to marry, although he knows full well that the world has been taught by St. Paul that such an inhibition is devil's

---

[1] In the preface (A^{vliib}) of his *Trewe Warnung für den Heidelber- gischen Calvinistischen Catechismum, sampt wiederlegung etlicher jrthumen desselben*, 1564 (no mention of place).

[2] Bl. C^{Iva}-C^{va}.

doctrine.   He even defends that horror of horrors—the
accursed sacrilege of the Sacrifice of the Mass.

The invectives of Flacius and Hesshus were credu-
lously reproduced by the Reuss preachers.[1]   Chemnitz
attacked the Catechism in the 'Hauptstücken der
Jesuiten-Theologie,'[2] the Heidelberg Calvinist, William
Roding, in a 'Pamphlet against the Jesuits,'[3] Douat
Wisart in his treatise 'Der Glaube Jesu und der
Jesuiter.'[4]

Another pamphlet particularly abundant in libellous
abuse was the 'Kurze und einfältige Widerlegung des
kleinen jesuitischen Catechismi Petri Canisii, aus heiliger
göttlicher Schrift und Catechismo Lutheri,' published
in 1568 by Paul Scheidlich, pastor at Nieder-Massfeld.
Scheidlich dedicated his work to the nobles, the episcopal councillors, and all godly Christians in Franconia
who were 'plagued by those heretical spirits,' the
Jesuits.[5]   The Jesuits, he declared, were 'the actual
hellish frogs that the hellish dragon had vomited forth.'
'In order to enlarge the empire of their father, the
devil, they have fastened themselves on the unfortunate
youth of Germany, and their patron and grandfather,
D. Petrus Canisius, has compiled a Catechism for children,
in which he teaches monstrous, abominable heresies and
idolatry, and, like a horrible basilisk, pours into the
ears of the poor ignorant young people the most
atrocious, diabolical poison.   Therefore it is impera-

---

[1] See their confession of faith in Köcher, pp. 284–287.

[2] Köcher, p. 59.

[3] See J. Perellius, *Ein Gespräch von der Jesuiter Lehr und Wesen.
Thun und Lassen*, translated by J. Götz (Ingoldstadt, 1576), Bl. Cl[3],
C[5]–C[6].

[4] Köcher, p. 68.   Christopher Pezel published a 'refutation' of the
Catechism in 1599.   De Backer, i. 1064.

[5] Fl. B[3a].

tively necessary that these simple-minded Christians—
above all the poor young children—should be faithfully
warned against these devilish larvæ and the diabolical
dirt and stink which they have disseminated among
the young, so that everybody may be on his guard
against them and flee from them, and shun them as
though they were veritable wolves.' [1]

Canisius did not allow himself to be disturbed from
his composure by attacks of this sort, and the Catholics
were by no means shaken in their love and appreciation
of the Catechism. Fresh editions of it followed in
rapid succession at Antwerp, Louvain, Liège, Cologne,
Basle, Lucerne, Dillingen, Augsburg, Ingoldstadt, Mayence, Hildesheim, Hanover, Douai, Herzogenbusch,
(Bois-le-Duc), Paris, Mantua, Venice, and other towns.[2]
Over 400 editions were counted up.[3] Many of these
were published in polyglot form, or illustrated with
pictures.[4] Every country of Europe had its own translations and editions. As early as 1623, Matthew Rader
wrote : ' Canisius has begun his message to the world
in almost every language under the sun, in German,
Sclavonian, Italian, French, Spanish, Polish, Greek,
Bohemian, English, Scotch, Ethiopian, and, as I am
informed by my brethren, in Indian and Japanese also,
so that it can truly be said now as then that Canisius is
the instructor of almost all nations.' [5]   In Germany

---

[1] Bl. H³ᵇ.
[2] See Reifer, pp. 62–75 ; Köcher, pp. 50–65; De Backer, i. 1053–1065 ;
iii. 2054–2055.
[3] Riess, pp. 121–122.
[4] See Reifer, pp. 66, 67, 75 ; De Backer, ii. 1180–1182, and iii. 2345.
[5] *Vita Canisii*, p. 58.   For the different editions and translations
which were already in print at the time of the death of Canisius (1597)
see Braunsberger, *Entstehung*, pp. 169–170. See also Gothem, p. 729.

especially the name Canisius was synonymous with
Catechism. 'Have you forgotten your Canisius?'
was as much as to say : ' Do you no longer know what
the Catechism teaches ? '   Bishops constantly reiterated
their conviction that the preservation of the Catholic
faith in Bavaria, Austria, Bohemia, Suabia, the Tyrol,
and Switzerland was in great measure due to the
Catechism of Canisius.[1]

---

[1] See Riess, pp. 532-533 ; Germanus, p. 118.

CHAPTER V

THE EMPEROR MAXIMILIAN II. OPPOSES THE DECISIONS
OF THE COUNCIL—COMPLETE COLLAPSE OF THE
CATHOLIC FAITH IN AUSTRIA

FOR the Catholics of Germany, those of Austria especially, the beneficial effects of the Council of Trent and the struggles of the Pope [1] and the Jesuits for reform, were materially counteracted by Maximilian's attitude towards the decisions of Trent. While to outward seeming the Emperor's position was chiefly equivocal and uncertain, it was in reality altogether hostile.

The Emperor Ferdinand had put many obstacles in the way of the Council, but had ended by agreeing to all its decisions, and, only a short time before his death, had declared repeatedly that he ' was ready to co-

---

[1] Concerning the labours and exertions of the Legate Commendone, the Venetian ambassador, Micheli, reports on December 23, 1568, that he left nothing undone which could contribute to the edification of the people; with his own hands he administered the Sacrament to a large number of communicants, among whom there were many Germans (Turba, *Venet. Depeschen*, iii. 465, note). Respecting Commendone's endeavours to reform the grossly licentious clergy, see Starzer, *Die Klöster- und Kirchenvisitationen des Cardinals Commendone in Niederösterreich, 1569*, in the *Blätter des Vereins für Landeskunde von Niederösterreich*, 1892, pp. 156 f., and M. Mayr, *Kirchenvisitationen in den Diöcesen Passau und Salzburg*, in the *Studien und Mittheilungen aus dem Benediktinerorden*, 1893, pp. 385 f. ; see also *Docum. inédit.* ciii. pp. 60, 62, 66, 67. The Spanish Minorite Michel Alvarez bestirred himself in 1579 to effect the reform of the convents of the Franciscan Friars Minor in Austria which had grown very corrupt. See the writings of Alvarez, published by Ottenthal in the *Mittheilungen des österr. Instituts*, xi. 322 ff.

operate, in the full spirit of the salutary reforms prescribed by the Fathers, in the advancement of the
Christian-Catholic faith among the people.' 'Jesus
Christ, Thou Son of God, have pity on me:' such was his
daily prayer. 'Have pity on the Church, which Thou
hast purchased with Thine own blood; restore to her the
loving concord which she has lost through the terrible
disputes on dogma; reunite her in the bands of peace
so that the ancient fear of God and the spirit of mutual
love may be hers once more. Uphold me, Lord, in the
true Catholic and apostolic faith.' [1] In one of his last
testamentary dispositions for his three sons—by which
Maximilian was to inherit Bohemia, Hungary, and
Upper and Lower Austria; Ferdinand the Tyrol and
the German *Vorlande* (territories beyond the dykes in
marshlands); and Charles, Styria, Carinthia, Carniola,
Görz, and Trieste—Ferdinand urged them most solemnly
to persevere in the faith of the Church.' 'When I
consider what the world is, and to what extent heresy
and sectarianism are gaining the upper hand, I cannot
but be anxious lest you, my sons, should be assailed
and led astray. For you, Maximilian, I am more
particularly solicitous, for I have always felt and
have been troubled with suspicions, lest you should
fall away from our religion, and should go over to the
new sects. I supplicate God fervently every day to
preserve you from such a calamity, imploring Him that,
rather than suffer you thus to desert the faith, He would
vouchsafe to take you out of this world while you are
still a good Christian.' [2]

[1] M. Citardus, *Ein christliche tröstliche Predigt über und bei der
fürgestellten Leiche des Kaysers Ferdinandi*, Bl. Q³.

[2] Bucholtz, viii. 753 ff.

Maximilian, however, did not openly apostatise from Catholicism; but he caused the deepest injury to the faith by his halting indecision, by his equivocal, uncertain position with regard to religion, his illusion as to the possibility of a union of the two parties, and by his whole system of government. In order to learn the manner in which he judged the Council, it is enough to read his letter to Duke Christopher of Würtemberg, to whom he sent, in 1564, a copy of all the decrees of the 'cunning Council of Trent,' not because he thought 'the Duke would derive any great comfort or instruction from them, but in order that he and his pious and excellent divines' should be made acquainted with the whole course of proceedings. At Trent, he says, 'nothing good has been accomplished.'[1]

The Council had ordained that the canons and decrees were to be subscribed to at the Catholic universities, and that all the different professors were to be bound by an oath to teach in a Catholic spirit.[2] Maximilian, on the other hand, allowed the university of Vienna, the first educational institution in the land, to 'develop into a perfect seminary of heretical innovations.' Immediately after his accession in the year 1564, he decreed, in opposition to the charter of the university, that taking the oath of conformity to the Roman Catholic faith should no longer be necessary for promotion, but that it would be sufficient if the candidate declared that he was a *Catholic* Christian. This distinction between Catholic and Roman Catholic produced great confusion, and opened up to the Protestants, who were very ready to call themselves Catholic,

[1] Reimann, *Religiöse Entwickelung Maximilian's*, pp. 63–64.
[2] Sessio 25, cap. 2.

free access to educational posts. In the year 1568, the
rector of the university, Caspar Piripach, erased the
word ' Catholic ' from the phrase ' Catholic faith ' in
Ferdinand's reform document of January 1554, and
substituted the word ' Christian.' [1] For the theological faculty ' no consideration ' was shown : when a
rector had to be chosen this faculty was coolly passed
over. The consistory of the university, so Melchior
Khlesl wrote from personal knowledge, ' is chiefly
formed of sectarian persons, who fill all the offices,
and outvote the Catholics in all matters ; the Bursas
are provided with sectarian superintendents, who only
bestow stipends on their own co-religionists, who
persecute the Catholics, inhibit the Catholic ordinances
of confession and communion, eat meat openly on fast
days and days of abstinence, and bring in Protestant
preachers. They deter the stipendiaries from going to
the Holy Mass, suppress the statutes, keep the stipends
in their own hands, and use the money to maintain
sectarians at Wittenberg, Leipzig, and Tübingen. They
appoint sectarian rectors who never take part in the
processions and who allow all sorts of pernicious and
disgraceful discourses to be held at St. Stephen's. The
professors weave into their lectures all manner of
doctrines injurious to the Church, and they often
spend the whole lecture hour in dilating on such matters ;
for instance, Doctor Benjamin, in a public discourse on
anatomy at which I was present, told an audience of
nearly 200 people that it was impossible to preserve

---

[1] Kink, i[a]. 308, 315. See Aschbach, iii. 105 f. Otto, *Gesch. der
Reformation im Erzherzogthum Oesterreich unter Maximilian II*, pp. 8 f.
Respecting Maximilian's attitude towards the Jesuits, see Hopfen, pp. 158 f.,
and also Paulus in the *Histor. Jahrbuch*, xvi. 603.

chastity.   He also spoke so scoffingly of religion that
no sectarian preacher could well have outdone him.' [1]

The bishops of Vienna were ' powerless against all
these things.'   Moreover, the bishopric had been un-
occupied for many years, and during the administration
all the revenues had gone into the imperial war coffers.
' All ecclesiastical matters had run riot.'   The new
bishop, Caspar Neubeck, who was consecrated in 1575,
wrote with deep emotion : ' The state of decay into
which divine worship has fallen is enough to make the
hearts of Christians bleed.   Parochial lands are split
up, church revenues are scattered in all directions and
withheld from the pastors, so that many parishes which
formerly stood in high repute, and were very prosperous,
are now incapable of maintaining an incumbent.   There
is lamentable dearth of priests and pastors, shameful
deficiency in every corner of parochial life and organisation, and in all ecclesiastical matters.'   The fasting rules,
he went on to say, had altogether ceased to be observed,
open market was held on high festival days, and in
many places servile work was also carried on at these
times.[2]   Burgomaster and town council took the lead
' in contempt for all that was Catholic.'   In the year
1569 there were only three members in the Council who
attended church on the highest festivals ; and none of
them would take part in the Corpus Christi procession.
It was considered a sign of an enlightened mind to
despise Christian interment, and to be buried without
the assistance of priests, without the tolling of a bell,
and without a cross.

At the imperial court ' almost everything had
become new-fashioned.'   When the Archduke Charles

---

[1] Kink, i[a]. 319 ; i[b]. 204.   [2] Wiedemann, ii. 163-164, 165, 173.

was at Vienna, it was thought quite an extraordinary thing that he should take part in the liturgic solemnities and attend Mass every day.[1] A special odour of repute hung round the 'Court Christians,' a set whom the imperial councillor Elder described as 'crafty, cautious gentlemen,' and of whom he wrote : ' Their game is to dissimulate and lie low, to find everything all right, and to conduct themselves in such a manner that nobody shall find out to which religion they belong. Some of them behave with such frivolity that they appear to treat the whole question of the religious quarrel with contempt, as of no concern to them ; they fancy they know well enough what to believe, and yet they borrow their tenets from high and low. Whenever the conversation turns on the damnable schism of the sects, they only make fun of it, and treat the whole subject with disdain.' 'Some of them are Lutherans at heart, but pose outwardly as Catholics.' ' Some of them are half Lutheran, half popish, and neither one thing nor the other, but change their coats according to the wind.'[2]

The number of unbelievers also became very large. As early as 1564 the imperial court preacher, Matthew Citardus, considered it necessary to preach in the pulpit at Vienna against the theory that ' when the body died it was all over with man.' He was obliged to remind his hearers that ' the bodies of Christians are the temples of God and instruments of the Holy Ghost. Why then were they to be cast aside and left to lie uncared for, as though they were the carcasses of dead carrion ? ' We had no right, he said, to cart away the bodies of our dead like dogs.   ' But there are people, some such indeed

---

[1] Wiedemann, ii. 126, 135, 137.
[2] Eder, *Evangelische Inquisition*, pp. 166–168[a].

in our midst, with godless hearts, slandering mouths, and wanton tongues, who despise all decent burial, who care not where their bodies are laid, whether in a field or a churchyard, whether in the carrion-pit or under the gallows ; they say : " Put me in the churchyard or under the gallows, among Christians or among brute beasts, when I am dead ; it's all the same." We ought not to regard burial-grounds as foul, execrable, stinking, corrupt places, but as holy sleeping-chambers, where the brethren lie side by side, as in the cells of monasteries, until they are awakened.' ' The lewd fellows, the infamous rogues and scoundrels,' he says in conclusion, ' who thus dishonour and abuse sacred burial-grounds, who degrade them to the level of dung-heaps, ought to be severely punished.' [1]

' While new teachers spring up every day,' said another preacher in 1567, ' and insist that they have found out a purer meaning in the Word of God, and curse all other teachers and consign them to the devil, the poor simple people are perplexed and bewildered in their faith and grope hither and thither, and know no longer where the door of entrance is ; and they fall into great sins and wickedness, such as was never heard of before, or only in rare cases which are recounted as terrible warnings, but which now are of almost daily occurrence. Thousands and tens of thousands in the towns—yea, even in the villages—no longer believe in God and in eternity.' [2]

---

[1] *Eine christliche tröstliche Predigt über dem Evangelio von dem erweckten Jüngling, der Wittiben Sun zu Naim* (Wien, 1565). See Paulus, *Der kaiserliche Hofprediger M. Sittardus*, in the *Histor.-Polit. Blätter*, pp. 116, 333.

[2] *Christliche Predigt von der Einigkeit im heiligen Glauben wider die Verächter des Glaubens und die gottlosen Ungläubigen* (Graz, 1567).

During the reign of Maximilian the secular authorities interfered ' resolutely, unscrupulously, and arbitrarily ' in all ecclesiastical matters, ever in purely spiritual concerns. The Catholic Estates of Austria complained later on that the Emperor had allowed himself to be talked round by Protestant councillors, who had told him that in his own kingdoms and hereditary lands he was sole patron and legal defender of all ecclesiastical property and benefices, and that by right of his sovereign authority he was free to deal with them as he liked without the knowledge or consent of the Pope and the bishops ; he could transfer, sell, give away and apply them as he liked. The Emperor accordingly had presented some of the convents to towns, and these towns used the revenues for their own purposes. Other convents he had mortgaged as government property to burghers and merchants, who often had placed Protestant preachers in the parishes belonging to the convents, by which means the inhabitants had been led away from the old faith. The head stewards, managers, and controllers whom the Emperor placed over the rest of the monastic property, and who were for the most part his Wittenberg doctors, had taken good care to appoint Protestant preachers. Acting under the guidance of his councillors the Emperor, in the reform ordinances drawn up for bishoprics, convents, and parishes, had laid down minute regulations as to the number of solemn Masses to be celebrated, and the manner in which the canonical hours were to be sung, the sacraments administered, and benefices disposed of. By these ordinances clergy and religion had been altogether subjected to the councillors in matters spiritual and temporal. All applicants for favour or promotion, all who needed protection in their own rights or possessions, were obliged to shape their religion to the wishes of the councillors. Hence the general apostasy from the Catholic faith both among clergy and laity.[1]

Bishop Khlesl, in an account of the condition of things under Maximilian, says : ' The result of this intrusion of the Emperor's councillors into all the innermost affairs of the Church, without regard for the bishops, was that all episcopal authority and prestige gradually disappeared.' ' On the other hand, freedom and licence gained dominion among the clergy, because the latter were protected by the court against the ordinary. The secular councillors having constituted themselves the heads and governors of the clergy in religion, the prelates and other ecclesiastics followed their example, and transformed the clerical estate into a thoroughly mundane business. The clergy married without any scruples or secrecy ; their children were considered legitimate, and right of inheritance was granted them by the secular magistrates. In the course of a few years the Lutheran Catechism, with all the rites and ceremonies enjoined by it, came to be taught, preached, and used in all monastic institutions and parishes throughout Austria.' It had come to this, ' that there was nothing in the whole country so detestable and so despicable as the Catholic religion and its

---

[1] *Schreiben der katholischen Stände in Oesterreich an den Erzherzog Matthias wegen ihrer Religionsvereinigung*, in Khevenhiller, *Annal. Ferd.* vi. 3151–3172. Raupach, *Evangel. Oesterreich*, 1, Beil. 8. For an account of the government dealings with church property, see Biedermann, *Aus der cameralistischen Praxis des 16. Jahrhunderts*, in Müller's and Falke's *Zeitschrift für deutsche Kulturgeschichte*, Jahrg. 1858, pp. 363 ff.

adherents; monks and nuns, and even prelates themselves, were hooted at as wolves in the public streets of Vienna by the lowest scum of the populace, and at the sessions of the provincial diet they were derisively called " Pilates " instead of prelates. Yea, verily, it has happened in the town of Vienna that priests carrying the Blessed Sacrament to the sick have been attacked and wounded.' [1]

In the year 1568 Maximilian gave permission to the lords and knights in the Archduchy of Upper and Lower Austria to introduce the rites and ceremonies of the Augsburg Confession in their country castles, houses, and domains, and in the churches under their patronage. This permission, as well as the later imperial ' Assecuration ' of January 14, 1571, did not include the towns and boroughs; burghers and peasants also were markedly excluded from the privilege which was confined exclusively to the nobles. As the Pacification of Augsburg had conferred on the princes alone freedom to adopt the Confession of Augsburg, while subjects still remained bound to conform to the religion of their sovereign princes, so now in Austria the ' Assecuration ' granted the adoption of the Augsburg Confession as a special privilege to the nobility. The lords and knights, on their part, pledged themselves not to assail the Catholic religion with abusive language, to undertake no operations of any sort against the Catholics, and not to deprive them of their incomes and their rights.[2]

Not one of these pledges was kept.

---

[1] von Hammer-Purgstall, 1, *Urkunden*, pp. 308–313.

[2] See v. Hammer-Purgstall, i. 16; Huber, pp. 233 f.; Hopfen, pp. 144 f. Otto, *Reformation im Herzogthum Oesterreich*, pp. 23 f., 43 f. Respecting the counter endeavours of Pope Pius V. and his legate Commendone, see Schwarz, i. 116 f., 119 f., 123, 127, 129 f.

In the year 1568 the lords and knights further promised, in a secret agreement, to refrain altogether from printing books, both within and without the country, to use no other creed than that of Augsburg, and to have a ritual drawn up by twelve theological experts. The Emperor reserved to himself the right of nominating six members of this ritual commission. As a matter of fact, however, it was not to a commission, but solely to the Rostock theologian David Chyträus, that the task of drawing up the regulations was entrusted.

On September 25, 1568, Maximilian wrote to the Dukes John Albert and Ulrich of Mecklenburg that he had granted permission to the lords and knights of the archduchy of Lower Austria to introduce the Augsburg Confession. ' This godly work,' he said, ' was very dear to his heart ; ' he therefore begged them to arrange for Professor Chyträus to come to Austria in order to draw up a pious code of Church regulations, and to take the lead in introducing the Augsburg Confession. Chyträus came, and on August 19, 1569, the Emperor, in a letter to the dukes, testified of him that he had shown admirable zeal in the work, and had merited the imperial gratitude.[1] But the code drawn up by Chyträus did not receive the approval of the wavering Emperor (still under illusion of the possibility of an amalgamation of Catholics and Protestants) until it had been in suchwise altered and reconstructed by the preacher Christopher Reuter that Chyträus did not recognise his work. When it was returned to him he expressed his astonishment that the Emperor should

[1] *Die Briefe* in Raupach, *Zweifache Zugabe*, pp. 103–106.

have granted the lords and knights a religious ' Assecuration ' based on so ' senseless and absurd a collection of Church ordinances.' Numbers of preachers
published opinions and pamphlets against the new
ritual ; many of them condemned it as godless and
contrary to Scripture : every preacher proceeded in the
matter according to his own liking.[1]

But ' this fresh outburst of general hatred and
strife did not hinder both the Estates in their vigorous
endeavours " to root out the popish idolatry." With
sublime unconcern the Protestant nobles ignored the
limits laid down by the Emperor's " Assecuration." Not
content with asserting their own and their subjects'
right to freedom of religion, they had recourse to every
possible means—even to violence—for spreading the
religious innovations further and further. They not
only cleared their own benefices and parishes of the
Catholic clergy, replacing the latter by Lutherans, but
carried on the same work of ejection in districts not
under their own jurisdictions ; they did not even
scruple to intrude on the domain of the sovereign
prince. They showed no sort of mercy in their proceedings. George of Lichtenstein actually caused a bed-
ridden priest, whose hands and feet were crippled, to be
turned out into the street, and also expelled the chaplain
and schoolmaster. Some of the nobles suppressed the
Catholic worship in churches outside their jurisdiction,
or at any rate forbade their subjects to attend them.
On one occasion when a farm-servant, on Good Friday,
in attempting to throw a stone at the Sacrament in
the holy sepulchre, struck the priest's head instead, the

---

[1] Wiedemann, i. 352–379.

offender's overlord, one of the Lichtensteins, and the land-marshal William of Rogendorf joined with the congregation in endeavouring to protect him. The Catholics were so greatly intimidated that in many places they did not dare show their faces in public.'[1]

It was ' quite heartbreaking,' wrote Bishop Urban of Passau to Maximilian, ' to see the poor inhabitants of the towns, boroughs, and villages belonging to these two Estates, often forced against their will to accept a new religion : the Emperor ought to decree that the new religion and regulations should not be established or practised anywhere but in the two princes' own houses, castles, and dwelling-places, and that the old Catholic religion should be preserved in the towns, boroughs, and villages.' The Catholic priests who would not swear allegiance to the Augsburg Confession were expelled by the lords and knights. As, however, there was a scarcity of preachers, men of all sorts were pressed into the service : bailiffs, farm labourers, strolling students and schoolmasters were sent to Tübingen, Berlin, and Rostock to receive ordination. From all the Protestant districts also there poured in ' worthless fellows of all sorts, who canted about the gospel, but were incapable of anything else than raging and reviling.' ' A few years ago,' wrote the preacher Christopher Reuter, on June 14, 1572, to Martin Chemnitz, ' we thought if only we could get leave from his Imperial Majesty to enjoy our own religion, all would be well. Now that our hopes have been fulfilled, we are faring worse than ever. One man comes from Wittenberg, another from Suabia, others from Bavaria,

---

[1] Huber, p. 238. Documentary proof in Wiedemann, ii. 521 f., 609 f. ; iii. 343, 361, 363, 578 ; iv. 6 f.

the Palatinate, Würtemberg, Meissen, Silesia, and each
wants to be cock of the walk.   And so there is nothing
but bragging, wrangling, and drunkenness all over the
land.' [1]

[1] Raupach, *Zweifache Zugabe*, pp. 116–118. ' Not only had Maximilian not realised the union of the different creeds,' says Huber, p. 238,
' but his attempt to restore religious peace in Austria by means of tolerance had completely failed.'

CHAPTER VI

CATHOLIC REACTION IN BAVARIA—ACCOUNTS OF THE
ACTIVITY OF THE JESUITS—MEASURES FOR CON-
SOLIDATING THE CATHOLIC RELIGION

WHILE in Austria, to quote Maximilian's own words,
' everything seemed on the verge of being turned upside
down,' and, as Canisius said, scarcely an eighth part of
the people could be regarded as ' genuinely Catholic,'
Bavaria had become the ' chief area' of Catholic
restoration.

The years 1563 and 1564 formed a turning-point in
the history of Duke Albert.

At a provincial diet held at Ingoldstadt in the spring
of 1563, the so-called ' elect children of God,' forty-three
in number,[1] began the work of introducing the Augsburg
Confession in Bavaria. ' At the very commencement
of the meeting, as soon as the order of the day had been
proposed'—so Albert, Archbishop of Salzburg, reports—
' some of the most distinguished of the counts, lords,
and knights stirred up a meeting among the lower
provincial Estates with the result that they would not
allow any committee to be elected, still less suffer the
proposed business to be discussed, until they should
have secured by all means freedom for every one to
adopt the Augsburg Confession. They behaved with

---

[1] Freyberg, *Landstände*, ii. 352, note.

so much violence and insolence, and had recourse to so
many wicked shifts and intrigues, that it is a wonder
they did not secure a majority among the two secular
Estates.' [1] The majority objected to the establishment
of the Augsburg Confession, but were in favour of the
general introduction of the lay chalice, and demanded
that none but clerics who did not oppose it should be
appointed to livings and benefices. Accordingly, all
priests who could not conscientiously agree to this
change were to be deprived of their posts. The Word of
God, it was said, must be preached ' in purity and
simplicity according to evangelical truth,' and those
priests ' who could not overcome human weakness '
must be allowed to marry. The avowed adherents of
Lutheranism, not satisfied with all this, protected
themselves by uniting, at the end of the diet, in a solemn
protest against everything that might be in opposition
to the Confession of Augsburg. They declared that
' they had nothing to do with any other Calvinist or
Zwinglian sect or with any species of fanaticism.'
During the debates the leaders of the party threatened
open rebellion if the Duke did not respond more
favourably to their claims. They pointed to the
Huguenots in France, and to the peasants of the Pinzgau, ' who had just taken up arms for the evangel.'
' What was now going on in the Pinzgau and in France,'
said Count Joachim of Ortenburg, ' would happen also
in other places.' [2] He called the Duke ' the leader of
the opposition against Christ in Germany.' [3] Pancraz
of Freyberg declared that ' he was determined to have

---

[1] v. Aretin, *Maximilian*, p. 92, note 17.
[2] Freyberg, *Landstände*, ii, 352.
[3] v. Aretin, *Maximilian*, p. 132.

the Augsburg Confession introduced, let the Duke say what he would : never mind about the Pinzgau peasants ; they knew very well what they were about.' Oswald von Eck ' spoke contemptuously, saying, " In the devil's name let go what you can't keep." ' He was determined, he said, to be free in the matter of religion ; ' the papacy was nothing but roguery.' [1]

In October 1563, Count Joachim of Ortenburg informed his vassals that he had been delivered ' through the Holy Ghost ' from popish darkness, and that he felt bound by gratitude ' to make them all also partakers of the same light.' His preacher mounted the pulpit ' clad in a coat of mail and holding an extended musket in his hand, and proceeded to denounce the Pope as Antichrist, the bishops, priests, monks, and nuns as the devil's courtiers, and complained that during several centuries they had had no really Christian Emperor, and had not got one yet.' ' The Count,' Duke Albert wrote to the Emperor, ' has stirred up so much sedition among my subjects for miles along the valleys of the Danube, Rott, and Vils, by distributing printed tracts and booklets, and setting schoolboys and others to read this rubbish to them in their homes and in shops, that they have become quite unmanageable ; they flock in crowds to hear his sermons—thousands of them together —like people who are out of their senses or bewitched, and they communicate and confess after the sectarian manner of the Duke. They are, withal, so daring, defiant, and violent that the cavalry I have told off to put them down cannot get the better of them by fair means or foul. They equip themselves with fire-arms, and pay not the slightest heed to my orders, mandates,

---

[1] Freyberg, *Landstände*, ii. 353-354.

inhibitions, and penalties.' Bavarian subjects were also compelled by the Ortenburg preachers to swear that in future they would not attend Mass any more, or receive the communion in one kind only. This, however, ' was dead against the Pacification of Augsburg,' which contained the stipulation that no one Estate of the Empire must dare to exert any influence over the subjects of another Estate in matters of religion. Albert would therefore have had good ground of complaint against the Count of Ortenburg, even—as was not the case—had he acknowledged the latter's claim to immediate membership of the Empire.[1] After vainly trying measures of gentleness, and making futile appeals to Joachim and his brother Ulrich to restrict the exercise of the Protestant religion to their own castles, he determined to resort to coercion. At the end of December 1563 he caused Alt-Ortenburg to be occupied, and a few days later Neu-Ortenburg ; and in consequence of a second invitation of his to Joachim to come to Munich producing no result, he confiscated the Duke's possessions in Bavaria. In the castle of Mattigkofen he unearthed the whole of the ' criminal correspondence ' of the Count with Bavarian nobles and foreign lords. A meeting of the most influential landlords of Upper and Lower Bavaria was convened at Munich, and the correspondence laid before them for investigation. ' It is not my wish,' Albert said to the assembly, ' that the accused persons and their letters should be condemned on account of their religious opinions. For, however glad and thankful I should be if I could keep my land and my people, all and every of them, in the

---

[1] v. Aretin, *Maximilian*, pp. 124 ff.

old Catholic faith, I do not insist on sounding and direct-
ing the heart and spirit of every one of my subjects :
that would be an impossibility, and indeed it is the
prerogative of the Almighty alone. But I am bound,
so it seems to me, to take care that, under pretence of
religion, the written edicts of canon and secular law,
the constitution of the Pacification of Augsburg, and
the rights and customs of the people be not violàted
and infringed. Of the above offence the persons
designated have been guilty, inasmuch as they have
attempted to make an arbitrary change in the religion
of the land, have assailed my princely authority, have
led others into insubordination, and have leagued themselves together for mutual support and succour, all
which is at variance with their duties to their natural
hereditary lord, to their feudal liege-lord, and to their
reigning prince.' After the letters had been examined,
the assembly gave the verdict that ' In the strict order
of the law there were grounds for criminal procedure,
but the Duke was recommended to grant the guilty
persons a preliminary trial and an opportunity for
defence.' This was done. The Duke was compared
in these letters to Pharaoh, and reviled as ' an appendage
to the devil ; ' the priests of the Catholic religion were
called ' devil's heads, who deserved to be punished with
hell fire.' The writers of the letters excused themselves
on the plea that all they had done had been prompted
by zeal for their religion, which in their opinion was
their first and highest concern ; of conspiracy, they said,
they had not been guilty. The charge of conspiracy
indeed was shown in the course of the trial to be
untenable. Nevertheless, in view of the conditions of
the time, Albert V. thought it necessary to secure his

duchy against further ' serious rebellious attempts.' [1]
At a diet at Munich he represented to the members that,
owing to the danger of war, invasion, and insurrection
which threatened the country from all quarters, it was
necessary to make becoming provision for the defence
of Bavaria.[2]

Having learnt from experience that he could not
maintain tranquillity in the country by kindness and
forbearance, the Duke now had recourse to stringent
measures in order to preserve the unity of faith among
his subjects by making them conform, as the Augsburg
Pacification expressly allowed, to the faith of the
ruling power.

The more Maximilian ' wavered in religion, the more
he connived, temporised, and showed himself neither
fish nor flesh,' so much the more resolutely did Albert V.,
with his rigidly Catholic chancellor, Simon Thaddäus
Eck, for counsellor, stand out as protector and defender
of the Catholic cause in the Empire. And a right
clever and skilful champion he was. He and his two
successors became the secular leaders of Catholic
Germany, while the influence of the imperial house of
Hapsburg grew continually less and less

Both in politics and religion the little duchy of
Bavaria acquired as much importance as if it had
ranked among the greatest powers of Europe.[3]

---

[1] Concerning the Ortenburg catastrophe, see Huschberg. pp. 378-399,
especially Buehl, *Das Verfahren Albrecht's V. gegen den Grafen
Joachim von Ortenburg und einige andere Landsassen, wegen Majestäts-
beleidigung und Meuterei, im oberbayerischen Archiv.* ii. 234-264. See
also v. Aretin, *Maximilian*, pp. 124 ff., and *Verhandlungen des histor.
Vereins für Niederbayern* (Landshut, 1894), pp. 30, 1-44.

[2] Freyberg, *Landstände*, ii. 359.

[3] The turn of affairs in Bavaria had been a gradual process. See above,
p. 173 ff. Among the latest accounts of the Catholic Restoration in Bavaria

The principal share in the revival of Catholic life in Bavaria must be ascribed to the Jesuits. ' In Austria,' wrote Canisius, ' matters stand with regard to religion almost exactly as in Saxony. If we do not concentrate all our energies on the defence of Bavaria, our poor Germany will have as good as nothing left that is orthodox and genuinely Catholic. The Duke must therefore be encouraged and stirred up to glowing zeal for the protection of religion ; he must be admonished not to remit or modify any of the Church's commands, if he wishes to maintain peace and loyalty among his subjects.'

' If the court set a good example of religious, upright, moral conduct, it would have an influence on the whole nation which would affect countless numbers in all classes.' ' God be praised,' said the Munich Jesuit Reinholt, ' there is much good to be said of the court at Munich. There is certainly, I own, too much love of splendour and ostentation ; greater economy and simplicity would be very beneficial to the nation, but scandals of other sorts are kept at bay ; any one acquainted with princely courts, lay and clerical, knows how much this means.' In respect of moral purity, Canisius called the Duke ' the lily among the thorns.' ' Genuine and exceptional Catholic virtue,' he said, ' shines brightly in his family.' The Duke made a great impression on the people by going frequently, at the head of his household, to the Holy Communion, to sermons on Sundays and festivals, and to other Church services. ' At the Corpus Christi festival,' Canisius wrote in 1565, ' the Duke, with his mother and

see that of Ritter, i. 303 f., which, it must be confessed, is often very one-sided. See also Hansen, *Nuntiaturberichte* xxxiv.

wife and all the nobles, accompanied the procession, carrying a lighted taper.' [1]

Canisius constantly alluded with joy to the fact that the Duke was in the highest measure favourable to the Jesuits : ' He helps on our colleges and schools, encourages us to hold missions for the people, and consults us in ecclesiastical matters.' At the same time Canisius firmly and persistently objected to the Fathers accepting any posts at court, or even becoming so-called spiritual councillors there, as Albert and his son William repeatedly urged them to do. There was great danger, he said, that such a step would lead the Order into too close connection with secular and political business. The Jesuits had no call to trouble themselves about the affairs of state, and, moreover, residence at court would in itself be prejudicial to the spiritual life of the members of the Order. ' Life at court,' he wrote to the General Mercurian in 1576, ' is dangerous for the priests, and dangerous for their companions who are obliged to live there without fixed rules, like fish out of water as the saying is, and to behave in many respects with greater freedom than the rules of our Order allow, or than appears advisable.' When Duke William V. wished to have a Jesuit as president of his council, and sent an envoy to Rome to obtain the Pope's order that his wish should be carried out, Canisius wrote a warning letter to Mercurian, saying : ' I scarcely think there is any conceivable measure which would more seriously impair the simplicity of our Order, or draw down on us

---

[1] Canisius to Hosius, Aug. 8, 1564. Letter of Sept. 20, 1564. Riess, pp. 330, 332. *Synopsis Catholica* (1568), pp. 27–28. Letter to the Cardinal-bishop Otto of Augsburg, Dec. 1, 1569. *Official Report to the General Francis Borgias*, July 1, 1565. See above, vol. vii., p. 40, note 3.

more odium, or bring us into greater danger.' ' The
Duke, in the first instance, for conscience sake as he
said, sought advice from our members in his private
affairs. Now he calls them to seats in the council of
state, requires them to put down their opinions on
paper, and to discuss and debate with the other councillors; to suit his pleasure they are to become his
privy councillors.' In this letter he goes on to beg
that the General will find some ' ways and means ' of
persuading the Duke not to burden the Fathers with
all this hateful secular business, ' but rather to leave
them to perfect themselves in their holy vocation, for
the edification of their fellow-creatures.' [1] The Order
issued a command that its members were not to mix
themselves up in any affairs of state. In consequence
of this, two Munich Jesuits refused to give the Duke any
political advice, whereupon William lodged a complaint
with the General Aquaviva.[2]

In remonstrating with the Duke on this matter,
Canisius told him that he ought to avoid even the
appearance of depending, in the government of his
people, on the advice of some favoured Jesuit; for to
expose himself to any such suspicion would imperil his
princely dignity.[3]

Not content with keeping the Fathers away from
the courts of the princes, Canisius insisted further that
they must, as far as possible, also avoid connection
with the palaces of the counts and noble lords ' for fear
that they might do more harm to themselves than good

[1] Canisius to Mercurian from Ratisbon, Aug. 18, 1576, and from
Augsburg, May 14, 1580. See above, vol. vii., p. 40, note 3.

[2] See Stieve, *Ursprung, Quellenbericht*, 36, No. 15 ; *Politik Bayerns*,
i. 417.

[3] Sacchinus, *De Vita Canisii*, pp. 296 *sqq.*

to others.' ' I entreat your paternity with all my powers of persuasion,' he wrote to the General Mercurian, ' not to let yourself be easily talked over by these great people when they want the Jesuits to come and stay at their palaces, and invite them to hold missions lasting over a month.' Mercurian answered : ' With regard to your urgent entreaty that we should keep the members of our Order away from courts, I can assure you, on my own part, that nobody is more strongly impressed than I am with the desirability of so doing. If all the members of our Order were filled with the same spirit as yourself, we should have no cause for the anxiety which, here and there, we suffer on account of our own brethren, and we should have little or nothing to do with the princes themselves.' [1]

' But, however careful we may be,' wrote a Father of Ingolstadt to a member of the Order at Rome, ' to keep aloof from mundane and political affairs, reports are nevertheless spread about by the opposite party that the Jesuits thrust themselves into everything, and are determined to rule everywhere. However, the founder of our Society predicted that we should have to suffer calumnies of all sorts. Let us not be troubled or daunted on this account, either in our own spiritual advancement, which is grounded on love and forgiveness, or in unrelenting activity for the spiritual welfare of the poor misguided people. Slanderers cannot hurt us in our souls—nay, rather, they greatly benefit us if we forgive them from our hearts.' [2] A calumnious report was even circulated and printed in different libellous pamphlets that a Jesuit had committed an atrocious

---

[1] Riess, pp. 467–468.
[2] Willemsen, *Erinnerungen an Rom*, pp. 19–20.

crime on a boy. 'Not far from the Bavarian frontier,'
Canisius wrote to the General of the Order on July 1,
1565, 'there are living a group of influential and powerful sectarians whose one aim and object is not only to
bring the Jesuits into ill odour, but to drive them out
of the country. A boy who had attended our school,
but had been expelled on account of his depravity, was
bribed to declare that he had been deprived of his
manhood by members of our Order. The statement
was repeated in all directions ; it was written about to
the Emperor and to several German princes, and envoys
were even sent to the Duke himself.' Albert sent for
the boy to Munich, had him examined by eight doctors
and six surgeons from Augsburg, Ratisbon, and Neu-
burg, and they all swore that ' the whole story was a
lie.' The Duke published the result of the examination
in a document signed with his own name and seal.[1]
But even after the lapse of decades the calumny continued to be repeated in numbers of libellous pamphlets.
Bartholomew Rülich, pastor of the evangelical church
at Augsburg, had the face to inform the German people
in a 'Jesuiterischen Newen Zeitung' ('new tidings of
the Jesuits') that the Jesuits of Munich had murdered
young women in their church, and that thereupon the
town council had apprehended five Fathers, and sentenced them to be burnt with red-hot pincers, having
strips of flesh cut out of their bodies.[2] 'Oh horror after

---

[1] Details in Agricola, i. Dec. 3, No. 150. Sacchinus, *Hist.* 3, lib. i.
Nos. 100–102. *Officieller Bericht an den Generalvicar Franz Borgias
vom 1. Juli* 1565. For the calumnious story about this boy see also
Katholik, 1895, ii. 459 f.

[2] A pamphlet was published against Rülich (who wrote as Baruch
Molitor) under the title : *Ausschütt und Steuberung der gueten Jesuiterischen Newen Zeitung, welche verschienes 1604 Jahrs Baruch (Molli) Thor-*

horror!' exclaims another preacher, ' the Jesuits are
murderers of young women and defilers of mankind, as
has just come to light at Munich, and, nevertheless,
these diabolical scoundrels are harboured and cherished
in the dear Fatherland; it is too abominable; in all
places where they nest their houses ought to be stormed.'[1]
In opposition to these statements the burgomaster and
the town council of Munich declared, in a document
attested by their seal, that the whole of the report was
downright deliberate falsehood. ' Far from there being
any truth in these reports,' they said, ' it is well known
to ourselves and to all the inhabitants and honourable
burghers of our town, as well as to all other residents of
whatever nation and religion, who have sojourned here
any length of time, what exemplary lives the reverent
Fathers of the laudable Society of Jesus have led here
for many years past, how great has been the renown of
their pious, upright, pure, and blameless priestly conduct. They have exercised an immense influence for
good, not only on us and our municipality, but also on
all other dwellers in the town, whether of high or low
degree, by their zeal in holding divine services, in
preaching, hearing confessions, teaching children, and
instructing the young in our schools. They show great
devotion also by day and night in tending the sick and
dying with fatherly care, and in short they behave in
all respects in such a manner as to gain the love and
esteem, not only of our most gracious sovereign prince

sonst Bartt Rulich . . . in Truck verfertiget. By Cleophas Distel-
mahr, *Ceremoniarum Minister* of the cathedral of Augsburg. Gräz,
1608. See Hueter, vi. 126, note 1.

[1] *Jesuiterische Mordthaten und andere manicherley Teufelspraktiken,
von einem Diener des Evangeliums allen friedliebenden Christen zur
Warnung vorgestellt* (1606), p. 9.

and lord, but also of ourselves and all our honourable citizens.' [1]

Among the crimes attributed to the Jesuits was the concoction of poisons, in which art they were said to be ' quite extraordinary masters.' The ' murderous agents and dare-devil rogues sent about by them '— so Magister Johann Pfeiffer of Altzen declared—' have orders and instructions to slay both Lutheran and popish teachers, and to accomplish this end by means of poison.' ' These villains have acquired consummate skill in this murderous art, and under their devilish treatment, dishes, spoons, basins, saucepans, salt-cellars, plates—in short, all utensils of daily household use—become so thoroughly impregnated with poison that no amount of rubbing, scrubbing, or cleansing will make them innocuous ; and the poison they have absorbed is so strong that it does not lose its efficacy before it has had time to cause a large number of deaths.' [2]

' We are quite accustomed,' wrote Duke Albert on July 19, 1573, ' to hearing startling things about the Jesuits : not only the most abominable reports, but also the most absurd and fantastic ones are spread about among the people, and too often these tales are believed,

---

[1] *Einblattdruck* of June 12, 1607, with the Munich State-seal.

[2] *Nova Novorum Jesuitica*: that is to say, *Historische und ausführliche Beschreibung, von den verborgenesten Geheimnüssen und schrecklichsten Thaten der Jesuwider, so sie bey Tag und Nacht in jren Speluncken treiben vnd vben. Newliker Zeit in lateinischer Sprach, durch einen mit Nahmen Johan Cambilhorn, welcher vnlangst auss jhrer Societet vnnd Collegio zu Graitz in der Stewermarck entsprungen, trewherziglich allgemeiner Christenheit zu einer Warnung gestellt, vnd zu Augsburg hinderlassen. Nun aber männiglich zu gutem, beydes Teutsch vnd Lateinisch in Druck verfertiget, vnd mit schönen Figuren gezieret. Durch M. Johan Pfeiffern von Altzen (Gedruckt durch Martinum Spiessen. Im Jahr M. DC. X.)*, p. 31.

untested, even by men of learning and high social standing. And yet, if truth be told, they are all scandalous
inventions, as everybody who takes the trouble to
inquire into them always discovers. It is the general
experience that the Fathers of the laudable society have
done, and are still doing, all in their power in these
miserable times to establish righteousness and justice,
and to build up a Christian people by means of instruction and preaching, by ministering in the hospitals, and
by kindly benevolence to the poor and to the lepers.[1]
This is all patent to every eye, but the strongest evidence
goes for nothing with the determined antagonists of our
holy religion. And if we protect the Fathers in their
laudable works, we become ourselves a stone of offence,
and they abuse us right and left; there is no saying what
lies they will not invent.'[2]

The turning-point in the religious reform in Bavaria
is the Recess concluded by Duke Albert on September 5,
1564, with the Archbishop of Salzburg and the other
bishops. By this compact the consenting parties

---

[1] See the praise which Albert bestows in 1576 on the many-sided
activity of the Jesuits, in the *Fundations-Urkunde des Jesuitencolleges*
in Ingolstadt, in Hund, *Metropolis Salisb.* ii. 278-279 (Mederer, iv. 346-
353). When the plague broke out in Munich in 1572 the Jesuits closed
their school, and the Fathers and the brethren nursed the sick day and
night (Agricola, i. 137). Concerning the loving services rendered by the
Jesuits of Vienna to the soldiers, the poor, &c., see *Monum. hist. Soc.
Jesu: Polanci Chronicon,* ii. 575, and *Mon. hist. Litteræ quadrim.* ii.
111-112, 376, 639.

[2] After Albert's death it was reported that a great stone 'with the
head of a Jesuit' had been found in his corpse. The Elector Augustus
of Saxony, who inquired of Duke William V. concerning this 'portent,'
was answered as follows : ' We are not at all surprised that such tales
should be got up by the opponents of our religion, for indeed much worse
things have been invented and given out about us before this ; however,
there is no truth whatever in this story of the head ' (v. Weber, *Kurfürstin
Anna,* p. 307).

pledged themselves to render willing obedience to the
salutary decrees formulated by the Council of Trent
and confirmed by the Pope, and to see that they were
properly enforced.[1]　On March 1, 1565, the Duke issued
a fresh stringent edict to the effect that ' no sectarian
books, tracts, libellous pamphlets or offensive carica-
tures were to be brought into the country, still less to
be sold and distributed there.　Later on he published a
complete list of forbidden publications, instituted a
strict inspection of book-shops, and mercilessly expelled from the country all booksellers who would not
conform to his orders.　To the catalogue of forbidden
books belonged ' all new small pamphlets which bore
the name of the devil on the title-page, such as *Hosen-
teufel*, *Spielteufel*, and so forth ' (devil-hose, games-
devil).　' For,' said the Duke, ' although these books
all have the appearance of having been written merely
for the sake of promoting good order and discipline, they,
nevertheless, must not be tolerated on account of their
scandalous stories and get-up ; and, indeed, their
character is almost such as to make them chiefly fit for
the service of him whose title they bear.' [2]

All ' sectarian teachers,' also, who ' showed themselves stubborn and obdurate,' were banished from the

---

[1] v. Aretin, *Maximilian*, p. 152, note 5.

[2] Sugenheim, *Baierns Zustände*, p. 81, note 94.　See Knöpfler,
Kelchbewegung, pp. 171 ff.　This new branch of ' Devil's literature ' was
especially taken up by the Frankfort book-dealers Han, Rabe, Feyerabend,
Hüter, and Schmidt.　In 1551 the *Saufteufel* (drinking devil) appeared, in
1562 the *Hofteufel* (court devil), in 1563 the *Wucherteufel* (usury devil), in
1564 the *Gesindeteufel* (servant devil), and the *Faulteufel* (idle devil).
In 1575 Schmidt & Co. published in a great folio volume, the *Theatrum
Diabolorum*, ' *eine allgemeine deutsche Bibliotek von lauter Teufeleien* '
(Moser, *Patriot. Archiv*, v. 285–286).　See our statement in the German,
vol. vi. 469 ff. ; thirteenth and fourteenth editions, pp. 487 f.

country like the contumacious booksellers. All children belonging to the duchy were strictly forbidden to attend Protestant schools and universities in other territories. In a school curriculum issued in 1569 for the elementary schools, religious instruction was put forward as the groundwork of all education. It was strenuously insisted on that none but truly God-fearing, earnest, Catholic men should be appointed as teachers, and that only Catholic lesson books should be used. In matters of religion young people must not be ' perplexed with recondite articles,' but they must be taught from the first to seek their souls' salvation more through the performance of Christian works and by conduct pleasing to God than ' by empty chatter and much disputing.' They must be made to understand ' that our holy religion is more concerned with lowly-minded simplicity than with arrogant, subtle, presumptuous learning.' Above all, ' children must be taught from their earliest youth the lesson of obedience, so that they may be able to practise it throughout their whole lives.' [1] For the sons of poor parents the Duke erected a seminary for boys at Munich, in which instruction was given gratis ; and for the sons of the nobles, a boarding-school at Munich and one at Ingolstadt, both under the management of the Jesuits. According to the decrees of the Council all the professors at the university of Ingolstadt were obliged to swear allegiance to the Tridentine Confession.[2]

Following the example of the Protestant princes who would not tolerate any Catholics in their dominions,

---

[1] *Schulordnung der Fürstenthumb Oberen und Niederen Bayerlandes* (München, 1569). See v. Aretin, *Maximilian*, pp. 178–179. See also Knöpfler, *Kelchbewegung*, pp. 189 f., and *Actenstücke*, pp. 93 f.

[2] v. Aretin, *Maximilian*, pp. 162 ff.

Albert resolved that 'all obdurate sectarians who persisted in their errors, after suitable previous admonition, should be expelled from Bavaria within a stated time.' 'If the Catholics,' he wrote to the Emperor Maximilian, 'are compelled on account of their religion to leave the territories of Estates adhering to the Augsburg Confession, why should not the opposite hold good in the Catholic territories?'[1] The Protestant party ascribed the Duke's harsh measures to the influence of the convert Frederic Staphylus, who was in high favour with Albert. In two tracts which appeared in the year 1564: 'Trost- und Vermahnungsschriften an die verjagten Christen aus dem Bayerland' ('Tracts for the comfort and admonition of the Christians expelled from Bavaria'), the author complained that 'Formerly, when Doctor Eck was still living and others also who were good papists, the Protestants were not so harshly treated; now, however, that the miserable Mameluke, Frederic Staphylus, had come into the country, he had qualified himself for the thirty pieces of silver better even than Judas, and he had not been able to rest until he had initiated and carried out the persecution that was now going on.'[2] According to the advice of the ducal councillors given in their memorandum of 1564, all persons were to be seized and sent across the frontier 'who were known to be ringleaders and seditionmongers, who had laid themselves under suspicion by contumacious language and treacherous, malign assignations, by erecting secret schools, by circulating venomous, noxious threatening letters—in short, who had been guilty in any way of open and

---

[1] Huschberg, p. 447, note.
[2] Schelhorn, *Ergötzlichkeiten*, ii. 287–289.

penal contempt of their spiritual and temporal rulers.'
The poor people who had been seduced and led astray
must be reformed and brought back by right instruction,
and threats of severe punishment must be held over
them in order to keep them up to attending Catholic
worship, the preaching of sermons especially.[1]   In a
similar manner, in the Protestant districts, the people
were compelled to attend sermons under pain of severe
punishment, and in the Saxon electorate the authorities
even went so far as to enforce participation in the
Lord's Supper under pain of banishment.[2]

It was regarded as an ' instance of special oppression
and injustice ' on the part of the Duke that he ' gradually withdrew entirely (except in the case of the nobles)
the permission he had formerly granted with regard to
the lay chalice, and on his own sovereign authority
ordained participation in one kind only.'   His reason
for issuing this decree, Albert said, was that he found
that ' with the greater number of the Utraquists there
was no question of reverence for the elements but merely
a desire to gain the carnal liberty for which they had
so long been striving, and obstinate determination to
carry their point, which they hoped to do on the strength
of his former declaration with regard to the Sacrament.[3]   The demand for the chalice had only been a
preliminary step to the complete decay of the Catholic
religion.   At a people's mission held, in the summer of
1564, at the request of the Duke by some Jesuits in
Lower Bavaria, it had been found that in the districts
bordering on the county of Ortenburg, among 8,000

---

[1] v. Aretin, *Maximilian*, pp. 147–148.

[2] See Carpzov, *Definitiones*, p. 453.

[3] v. Aretin, p. 155.   See Knöpfler, *Kelchbewegung*, pp. 201–211,
' Religionsvisitation und Wiederabschaffung des Kelches.'

adults, there were nearly 2,300 who would not communicate either in one kind or in both ; there were
about 100 who demanded the chalice.[1]   The Bishop of
Passau expressed the opinion that, judging from what
had taken place in his own diocese, one of the best
means for stemming further advances and encroachments on the part of the Protestants would be to re-
abolish the use of the chalice.[2]   As regards the Archbishop of Salzburg, Canisius wrote to Hosius, the result
of the concession of the chalice is ' that the peasants,
so we hear, are collecting in armed bands, and leading
their preacher round with them, ready for battle in case
the archbishop should oppose resistance to them ; the
chalice has now become a stone of stumbling and a
rock of offence.' [3]

' Whereas, through the use of both elements,' Albert
wrote to Wolf Dietrich of Maxelrain, on May 22, 1579,
' numbers of noxious old heresies and errors, which
have been condemned by the Council, have been re-
introduced, and whereas there are among the Protestants
as many different opinions about the Holy Communion
as there are men and women,' he had felt himself
obliged to abolish the lay chalice again ; and, moreover,
the spiritual authorities had enjoined this measure on
him as a duty.[4]   In many places it had been very
difficult to persuade the people—the women especially—
to give up the chalice : in some of the parishes of the
lordship of Waldeck, it had been necessary ' to threaten
them with incarceration in the Falkenthurm.'   In the
year 1583 numbers of the inhabitants were still leaving

---

[1] Riess, p. 331.   [2] See Wimmer, p. 38.
[3] Cyprianus, *Tabularium*, pp. 385–386.
[4] In v. Obernberg, pp. 56–60.

the country on account of their faith. The Catholic pastor installed at Miesbach was not sure of his life. The Catholics who attended sermons were pelted with stones.[1] In other places the end was accomplished more easily. For instance, in the town of Wasserburg, in the year 1569, nearly 250 people had wanted the chalice, while at Easter, in 1571, nearly all of these received the Sacrament in one form.[2]

In 1573 the work of Catholic restoration in Bavaria might have been considered virtually accomplished ; many years later, however, the inward decay of the Church, and of Christianity in general, was still manifest in the lives of numbers of priests, the tale of whose profligacy is verily appalling.[3]

---

[1] See v. Obernberg, pp. 32, 37.

[2] v. Aretin, *Maximilian*, p. 160.

[3] See especially the report of the Rentamt (tax-collectors' office), Burghausen to William V. in the year 1583, in Sugenheim, *Baierns Zustände*, pp. 542–563. Against these iniquities the nuncio Felician Ninguarda displayed the most bountiful and beneficial activity. See Schlecht's interesting narrative, based on the latest documents, 'F. Ninguarda und seine Visitationsthätigkeit im Eichstättischen,' in the *Römische Quartalschrift*, 1891, v. 62–81 and 124–150. See also an article by Schlecht in the *Jahresbericht des Histor. Vereins von Dillingen*, 1895, and the important 3rd vol. (just out) of the third division of the *Nuntiaturberichte aus Deutschland*, published by the Prussian Historical Institute ; K. Schellass, *Die süddeutsche Nuntiatur des Grafen Bartholomäus von Portia*, erstes Jahr, 1573–74 (Berlin, 1896).

CHAPTER VII

THE CATHOLIC RELIGION FIRMLY ESTABLISHED IN THE
ABBACY OF FULDA—OPPOSITION OF PROTESTANT
PRINCES—OPINIONS ON THE JESUIT SCHOOLS

ENCOURAGED by the example of Duke Albert of Bavaria,
the Prince-Abbot of Fulda, Balthasar von Dernbach,
also became a valiant defender of the Catholic cause. In
1570, at the ceremony of rendering homage to him, the
town council handed in a petition asking for a written
confirmation of their traditional rights, and for the
appointment of a Lutheran preacher and the abolition
of the Mass. The knights begged that a school might
be established in the empty building of the Barefoot
Monastery. Balthasar presented the burghers with the
usual charter of freedom, but would not consent to the
appointment of a Lutheran preacher ; on the contrary,
he said, he intended to exercise in his territories the
right of reform accorded him by the Pacification of
Augsburg. To the reiterated entreaty that, in view of
all existing difficulties, he would not interpret this
contract so literally as its wording might perhaps justify
him in doing,[1] he made no response. The abbot ' in complete understanding ' with the chapter, who undertook
to defray the third part of the expenses of a college,[2]

[1] See Heppe, *Katholische Restauration*, p. 29.
[2] Komp, *Fürstabt Balthasar*. pp. 10–12, from the sources mentioned
at p. 2.

began, in 1571, by summoning five Jesuits to Fulda for the purpose of founding a school. The knights, who had had in their minds the erection of a Protestant school, ' with the needed evangelical spirit, at once entered the lists against the Jesuitical rabble,' and ' speedily won to their side their fellow nobles in the aristocratic cathedral chapter.' The whole of the chapter, which consisted chiefly of laymen, yielded to the threats of neighbouring Lutheran princes, and not only withdrew their promise of help to the Prince-Abbot, but also refused even to sanction his maintaining the new Jesuit school at his own expense. The prebendaries became the enemies of Balthasar, who, being himself a model of priestly conduct, went in vigorously and resolutely for moral reform, insisted on the immediate abolition of concubinage, and actually caused ' the beautiful maiden ' of the Dean Hermann von Windhausen to be seized in the open street and removed from the abbey. ' Such a lord and Jesuitical hypocrite ' the prebendaries could not put up with. They also regarded it as unwarrantable impeachment ' of ancient custom ' for Balthasar to insist on strict choir-service, on ' church worship being conducted in an edifying manner,' and even on ' Christian attendance at sermons,' in all which matters he himself led the way. These new-fangled ' Jesuitical ways ' clashed with the habits of the noble lords. The abbot, Windhausen complained, was ' a thorough-going lackey of the Jesuits.' Balthasar increased the strictness of monastic confinement, visited many of the cloisters of his diocese in person, delivered exhortations .to the clergy and the people, revived pilgrimages and processions which had fallen into disuse, and endeavoured gradually to abolish the

practice, tacitly sanctioned by former abbots, of ad-
ministering the Sacrament in both kinds. He bought
up all heretical publications from the booksellers, and
forbade them in future to bring any such writings
with them from the Frankfort fair. All servants and
officials who refused to take part in the Catholic worship
he dismissed from his service.

All these measures, against which there was no
really tenable ground of opposition,[1] caused ' a tremendous sensation ' in the Empire. ' There could be
no doubt '—so the Protestants were heard to say—' that
the Jesuits were aiming at the complete overthrow of
the Pacification of Augsburg, and that they had found
in the abbot Balthasar an admirable tool for their
purpose.' [2]

In the autumn of 1573, at the request of the Protestant
burghers who had made constant but futile appeals to
the abbot that he would grant them liberty to conform
to the Augsburg Confession, the Elector Augustus of
Saxony, the Margrave George Frederic of Brandenburg,
and the Landgraves William and Louis of Hesse, began
to interest themselves in the affairs of Fulda, and proposed as a first step to ' turn the Jesuit rabble ' out of
the town. They informed the abbot that he must
grant the burghers the freedom of the Augsburg Confession, inasmuch as this creed had been freely professed
for the last twenty or thirty years, and even longer.
Delegates were sent by the four princes to exhort the
Protestant councillors and burghers to persevere faithfully in the acknowledgment of the ' Evangel,' and to
promise them support. A numerous body of knights

---

[1] *Urtheil von Moritz*, p. 21.
[2] Seibert, pp. 13-17.

told the abbot that if he did not forthwith accede to the demands of the princes, the latter, in accordance with the declaration of the delegates, would take into consideration by what means they could best defend their subjects who were adjacent to the abbey territory, ' from the accursed, ensnaring, and seditious sect of Jesuits, and rid themselves of the noxious brood : ' they advised the abbot to beware lest a small spark should develop into a large conflagration.

From fear of an investment of the abbey lands by the princes, the chapter also demanded the removal of the Jesuits, but finally, in conjunction with the knights, agreed to the abbot's proposal to refer the whole dispute to the decision of the Emperor and the Imperial Chamber.[1]

Nevertheless, on the following day, November 6, the canons, with their Dean Windhausen at their head, proceeded to arbitrary measures in the character of ' co-regents of the abbot.' They issued a proclamation to the Jesuits to the effect that ' within fourteen days the Fathers were to evacuate the diocese,' otherwise, said the canons, ' we shall, with the help of the knights, bethink us of the necessary means for getting rid of you Jesuits and all your followers out of the town and principality of Fulda : which dismissal will fall more heavily on you than at present you in the least imagine.' [2]

' The five poor Fathers caused terror to all.'

The abbot refused to be intimidated, and turned for

---

[1] Heppe, *Restauration*, pp. 39 ff.; *Instruction vom 24. Sept. 1573*, pp. 199–202.

[2] The best account is in Heppe, *Restauration*, pp. 231–234. See the report of the Prince-Abbot, Dec. 28, 1573, to Gregory XIII., in Theiner, *Annales*, i. 93.

help to the Imperial Chamber, with the result that an
order was issued by the court on November 13, enjoining the chapter, on pain of the imperial ban, to
refrain from all encroachment on the sovereign rights
of the abbot.[1]

On November 27, Duke Albert of Bavaria wrote to
the abbot to tell him of the great pleasure which his
courageous resistance to the attempts of the Protestant
princes had given him. He was writing to him, he
said, to comfort and strengthen him, that he might also
in the future protect his school for the maintenance
and establishment of the Catholic religion, and not let
himself be persuaded ' to put down the Jesuits, who in
these our later times have excelled all others in the good
they have done by preaching, giving Christian instruction to the young, and by their exemplary lives and
conduct,' as the Duke had experienced in his own duchy
of Bavaria. Whereas it was stipulated in the Pacification of Augsburg that ' no Estate should manœuvre
to bring over another one—or its subjects—to its own
religion, or should take the subjects of another Estate
under protection against their rulers, or champion them
in any manner whatsoever,' he felt certain that the
Protestant princes would not take any active measures
against the abbot and the Jesuits at Fulda. If, however, the abbot's own subjects should disturb the public
peace by force and violence, he (the Duke) would be
ready to give the abbot all the help guaranteed him by
the Pacification of Augsburg.[2]

The Protestants of Fulda and the Protestant princes

---

[1] Heppe, *Restauration*, p. 49.

[2] *Ibid.* pp. 238-240 ; Kluckhohn, *Briefe*, ii. 620 ; Gratiani's report
of Jan. 20, 1574, in Theiner, i. 412.

could not maintain that the exercise of the Augsburg
Confession had formerly been conceded to the burghers.
Communion in both kinds, the abbot said to the Burgomaster and the town councillors, and the use of the
German language in baptism, had certainly been allowed
by former abbots to their subjects, but it did not follow
from this that they had possessed the Augsburg Confession.   On his inquiry as to the contents and the age
of this creed, most of the town councillors were reduced
to pleading utter ignorance.

No Lutheran ministry had ever existed at Fulda.
The town councillors were actually unable to indicate
by name any single Protestant preacher who had
officiated under former abbots.[1]

Balthasar wrote to the Elector Augustus of Saxony
on December 4, 1573, that his statement that freedom
of adherence to the Augsburg Confession had been
enjoyed in Fulda for many years was based on error.
This was sufficiently proved by the fact—which any one
might verify for himself—that the burghers had again
and again appealed to his predecessors for freedom in
this respect.   But, even were this not the case, he, as the
reigning prince, had the indisputable right, according to
the terms of the Pacification of Augsburg, to re-establish
the Catholic religion in his own territory.

The Elector Augustus sent this letter to the Landgrave William of Hesse, and advised him to call on the
chapter to enforce the edict of banishment against the
Jesuits and to ' equip 500 or 1,000 horse ' for the support of the chapter in Fulda.'[2]

The Landgrave William signified to an envoy of the

---

[1] Komp, *Fürstabt Balthasar*, pp. 22-25.
[2] Heppe, *Restauration*, pp. 50-52.

abbot that the books of the Jesuits had found their way
even into his women's apartments, and that therefore
the Jesuits must be expelled from Fulda : ' if not, may
the beaker of wine I am drinking wrench my heart out
of my body !' [1]

In January 1574 William again besieged the knights
of Fulda with exhortations to use all their influence for
the suppression of the Fathers. He urged on the
chapter that they ought to treat the abbot as a lunatic,
and depose him and appoint in his place either the
Dean Windhausen or the young Protestant Count
Palatine Frederic. [2]

Admonished by papal and imperial despatches, the
chapter, however, did not act on this advice. On
March 1, 1574, the knights under the abbot's jurisdiction received a most stringent command from the
Emperor not to proceed to any active or violent measures
on account of the school which the abbot had established.
They were to obey the abbot, he said, as their reigning
prince, and if they had any grievances against him they
must follow the course of legal procedure, as Balthasar
consented to do. [3] The Elector Augustus of Saxony and
the Landgraves William and Louis of Hesse, who had
also been warned against violent procedure by Maximilian, brought their grievances against Balthasar to
the Emperor on May 1, 1574. They complained that
he had withdrawn from the town of Fulda its freedom to
use the Augsburg Confession and had also ' insolently
presumed' to criticise and condemn this said Confession (which was based on God's Word) in a public
pamphlet. The ' obnoxious sect of Jesuits' which he

---

[1] Komp, *Fürstabt Balthasar*, pp. 19-20 ; *Zweite Schule*, p. 23.
[2] Heppe, pp. 52-55.   [3] Heppe, pp. 235-237.

had introduced, and which had been quite unknown in
the town before, had had the effrontery to entice into
their school some of the boys belonging to the nobility
of their own principalities ' in order to train them up in
their own heresies.'   All this was at variance with the
Pacification of Augsburg and the Declaration of Ferdinand, and led to ' confusion and disturbance of the
general peaceful order of things ; ' and the Emperor
ought therefore to admonish the abbot to desist from
the course he had embarked on.[1]

Without help from Rome, Balthasar said to a papal
nuncio in March 1575, the melancholy religious conditions could not be improved.   The canons were very
ignorant men—so the nuncio reported to the Pope—and
their lives were so profligate that the very mention of
the word ' reform ' made them tremble.   A papal letter,
in which these ecclesiastics were sharply rebuked for
their immorality, had been welcomed gladly by the
abbot because it was in strict accordance with truth,
but he had not dared inform his chapter of it.   The
nuncio went on to suggest that for the moral improvement of the chapter it was necessary that the abbot
should have a certain number of young nobles, of
virtuous character, educated, and trained in piety, at
the German College at Rome, with a view to forming
future canons.   These ecclesiastics would then institute
reforms of their own accord, and by their own exemplary, priestly conduct would revive the manner of
life of the old Benedictines.[2]   The abbot himself, in a
letter to Gregory XIII. of September 19, 1575, pointed

---

[1] In the *Zeitschrift des Vereins für hessische Gesch. und Landeskunde,* neue Folge, ii. 187–192.

[2] *Bericht* Elgard's, March 9, 1575, in Theiner, *Annales,* ii. 75-76.

out that thoroughgoing measures of reform were almost impossible, because the spiritual jurisdiction within his own territory was divided between himself, the Archbishop of Mayence, and the Bishop of Würzburg, and that they scarcely knew, any of them, under whose judicial authority this or the other place came. It had therefore been very easy for the nobles to arrogate to themselves the control of ecclesiastical matters and to appoint Protestant preachers. Matrimonial conditions were altogether in confusion. Regarding the patronage, the revenues, the obligations and rights of the different benefices, it was impossible to obtain any trustworthy information. The Pope would do well to transfer the episcopal jurisdiction to the hands of a single individual, who would then be able to proceed zealously with the work of reform.[1]

The abbot's sole delight was the Jesuit school, which had rapidly risen to prosperity and which already reckoned hundreds of pupils drawn from different German districts.[2] The Jesuit schools at Treves and Mayence were equally thriving.[3] In the year 1567 colleges of the Order had been erected at Würzburg and at Spires ; in 1575 a college was founded at Heiligenstadt.

' The young people flock to the Jebusites from all quarters,' so the Protestants complained, ' and they are more devoted to them than the pupils of any other schools to their teachers. This result cannot possibly be accomplished by natural means.' ' Diabolical arts ' have a share in the game. ' The Jebusites deal in horrible spells and witchcraft ; they grease their scholars

---

[1] Theiner, ii. 77.   [2] Komp, *Zweite Schule*, pp. 13-24.
[3] At Mayence the establishment of a Jesuit college had followed in 1568. Gudenus, *Cod. Dipl.* iv. 721.

with secret salves of the devil, thereby alluring them so
that to tear them away from their charmers is difficult,
and a longing to return to them remains.' ' Oh, the
Satanic art that it is ! The dear evangel is quite help-
less against these agents of the devil, who start up from
the pit of hell to poison the whole youth of Germany, and
also the evangelicals, on whom they keep a special eye ;
and the evangelical schools have fallen into contempt
with many, not to mention that so little is done for
them by the evangelical party, because of the same
influence of the devil, who makes the young unruly, and
princes and magistrates careless in erecting good schools,
and so drives our boys and girls into the jaws of the
Jesuitical wolves.' The Jesuits, they said, must not
merely be expelled, ' they must be burnt to death like
sorcerers.' This was their ' well-merited punishment ;
in no other way could they be permanently got rid of.'
They were not only sorcerers themselves, but they gave
instruction in their schools in the art of necromancy.[1]
The Jesuits of Hildesheim, for instance, were accused of
teaching their pupils the incantations of poison mixers
and suchlike magic arts.[2] It was also asserted that the
Order made use of witchcraft and magic to accelerate
the progress of their scholars.[3] Protestant rulers and
theologians ' were thrown into tremendous but natural
consternation by seeing in all directions that numbers
of evangelical parents even—especially among the
nobles—entrusted their children for education to the
Jesuit wolves and furies.' ' The damnable devil,'
Joachim Mörlin wrote in 1568, ' does not allow the
unfortunate parents to understand what inhuman

---

[1] Seibert, pp. 27-28.   [2] See Pieler, p. 254.
[3] Sacchinus, *Hist. Soc. Jesu*, ii. 122.

monstrosity this is ; ' it is, however, ' unspeakably more wicked and cruel than if the poor, blinded people had offered up their children to Baal or to Moloch.' ' The Pope and his parasites,' Mörlin goes on, ' know that everything depends on the schools, and the devil, there- fore, artful rogue that he is, influences this sect to devote itself entirely to establishing and maintaining good schools, for which work they have indeed skill enough, and they bestow much more thought and labour on it than we, alas, do ourselves. In this way they not only snare the dear young people, but they also steal the hearts of their pious parents, so that the latter, without further reflection, send their children to school with them, knowing that in a very short time there will be some striking results to show.' [1] The indefatigableness of the Jesuits and their genius for instructing the young were never for a moment questioned. ' The Jebusites, or Jesuits, mean sneaks that they are,' said Nicholas Gallus in a sermon at Ratisbon, ' put on a Pharisaic semblance of sanctity before the world, prac- tise gentleness and zeal in teaching, especially with the young, and by this means they hope to train up a new world, and to reinstate and reinvigorate the fallen Empire.' [2]

The Landgrave William of Hesse was one among other Protestant princes who zealously opposed attend- ance at Jesuit schools. In 1573, at a general synod at Marburg, he urged the theologians who were present to make a public demonstration against the school ordi- nances issued by the Jesuits at Fulda. The theological

---

[1] Mörlin's translation of *Heshusii herzlicher Danksagung für die Bekehrung des Engländers Eduardi Thorneri* (1568), A³ᵇ, 4ᵇ.

[2] *Vom bäptischen*, &c. (1561), A².

professors, he said, were especially bound ' to cry out
against this wolf, and to take measures of some sort in
order to warn the people to beware of these heretics
and popish gins.' The pastors were to be enjoined to
preach with exceptional fervour against the papists.
The synod sternly inhibited attendance at Jesuitical
educational institutes, and had a warning against these
' ensnaring schools and teachers ' printed and circulated
through the land. The Jesuits were charged in this
document with teaching ' that sin was not atoned for
by the merits and satisfaction of Christ, but by the
individual's own works—almsgiving, confession, prayer,
and so forth. Moreover, in addition to the two future
states mentioned by Christ, heaven and hell, they had a
third—viz., purgatory.' ' People must be on their
guard against wolves such as these, and keep far aloof
from Babylonish impurity and the wiles of the Antichrist.' The Landgrave, however, thought this document much too mild ; he said it would be better that
the warning should be given to the people by the
pastors. The Church inspectors must make inquiries
everywhere as to whether ' any of the inhabitants, be
they nobles or others, of whatever degree, offered up
their children to Moloch—that is to say, threw them
into the jaws of the Pope by sending them to his institutions and schools.' [1]

The Elector Palatine Frederic III. had already
urged that the Protestants ought not to be less
assiduous than the Jesuits in ' founding fresh Christian
schools, and in improving those already in existence.
' I make daily experience,' he had said, ' of the diligence

---

[1] Heppe, *Generalsynoden*, i. 96, 98-99, 107. Heppe, *Kirchengesch.*
ii. 361-362.

and zeal displayed by this tonsured crew in setting up
their Jesu-Wider (anti-Jesus) schools in all directions,
and in forming learned men.'[1]   In the year 1575 William Roding, professor at the Pädagogium of Heidelberg, dedicated to the Elector a pamphlet entitled
'Wider die gottlosen Schulen der Jesuiten.'[2]   He had
written this pamphlet, he said in the dedicatory preface,
because he could not help seeing that large numbers of
people who, although to be reckoned among Christians,
had fallen to such a condition of madness and godless-
ness that they handed over their sons to the Jesuits for
education, and had no scruples in thus helping to
augment the kingdom of Satan.   The impious Jesuits
were the bitterest enemies of God and of Christianity,
full of blasphemy against Christ the Lord ; they were
wild beasts that ought to be hunted out of all Christian
towns.   But instead of doing this people handed over
their own children to these wild beasts, the Sowites, for
instruction, and allowed them to be driven into hell.
The excuse made was that the boys were still too young
to be influenced by the religion of the Sowites.   But
the Jesuits were accomplished and astute philosophers
whose object was to concentrate all their learning and
wisdom on the education of youth ; they were most
subtle and cunning instructors, and they knew how to
turn each pupil's natural proclivities to the best account.
This wisdom of the world came to them from their
author, Satan.   In their whole outward appearance and
demeanour they were simple, humble, humane, and well
behaved, but in reality they were furies and atheists—
far worse indeed than atheists and idolaters.   The

---

[1] Kluckhohn, *Briefe*, i. 696.
[2] *Contra impias Scholas Jesuitarum* (Heidelbergæ, 1575).

children entrusted to their care were compelled to join with their swinish instructors in grunting at the majesty of God.[1]

'Roding, so many think,' Perellius wrote in the year 1576, ' is much concerned about the evangelical schools ; and Sturm also, although the latter expresses himself with more moderation and reserve. They think that most of those schools are no longer so highly respected as they used to be, and also that the zeal and industry of the preceptors and schoolmasters, as well as of the papists, is growing daily less and less ; while, on the other hand, the schools of the Society—of which not a few flourish in Germany—lift their heads on high ; the preceptors and masters are exceptionally zealous and painstaking, and the number and fame of the pupils increase daily.' ' Our adversaries are well aware that the more the Catholics and their schools flourish and rise in fame, merit, and esteem, the more do their own go down in the scale.' [2]

An opinion expressed by the Protestant Nathan

---

[1] In the *Dedication* and on pp. 1, 2, 5, 7 ff., 28, 29, 31, 32. Some passages are quoted literally: p. 3, 'Excitavit igitur [Satanas] Joannem Petrum Carapham Romanum pontificem, ne dicam Christianorum carnificem, Paulum quartum appellatum, ex quo, ut constans fama est, tanquam ex matre procreavit Jesuitam Monstrum horrendum ingens &c. ad evomenda in Salvatorem Jesum convicia.' Pp. 5–6: 'Papa Romanus summus Jesu adversarius tibi pater fuit, impietas mater, obstetrix insania, morum et doctrinæ informator Satanas.' 'Jesuitas Suitas in posterum appellabo. Quemadmodum enim sus in stercore se volutat suoque rostro lutulento omnia contaminat, ita bestiæ istæ impurissimæ ac intemperantissimæ in impietatis cœnum se ingurgitant suoque ore impurissimo sanctissima quæque polluunt.' Then follows the evidence: 'Quid de simplicitate et habitu Furiarum dicam ? quodsi ora Suitarum, incessum, habitum et vultum, totius denique corporis gestus ac conformationes intueris, judicares, nihil istis hominibus (si homines dicendi sunt . . .) esse sanctius, nihil modestius, nihil humanius, nihil castius, nihil simplicius.'

[2] Perellius, Bl. H³.

Chyträus, professor at the university of Rostock, is worthy of notice. He often, he said in 1578, turned his mind to the consideration of what could be the reasons of the depravity and lawlessness into which, according to general complaint, the whole youth of Germany had fallen. He had come to the conclusion that one chief cause was the prevailing decay of home education. He considered it criminal to attribute all this anarchy and immorality to a divine judgment; for there were also a great number of prosperous and of admirably conducted schools. 'Leaving religion aside, there was much to be said for the schools of the Jesuits. And verily these schools, scattered about in so many different places, in all directions, at such distances from each other, could not invariably exhibit such high excellence of discipline, such diligence and perseverance in the performance of duty, both on the part of teachers and scholars, if all the surrounding lawlessness was the result of a divine dispensation.' [1]

[1] Rollius, *Memoriæ Philosophorum, &c.*, i. 105-106, quoted by Döllinger, i. (2nd edition), pp. 515-516.

CHAPTER VIII

PROGRESS OF PROTESTANTISM—PROTESTANT DEMANDS AT
THE DIET OF RATISBON IN 1576—DEATH OF MAXI-
MILIAN II.

WHILE in many districts of the Empire the Catholic
faith was gaining a continually firmer footing, in others
it still suffered constant fresh losses.   The bishoprics of
Meissen, Merseburg, and Naumburg-Zeitz, in spite of
the Pacification of Augsburg, passed gradually to the
electoral house of Saxony ; the bishoprics of Brandenburg, Havelburg, and Lebus to the electoral house of
Brandenburg.

In the year 1570 the administrator of the archbishopric of Magdeburg, the Margrave Joachim Frederic
of Brandenburg, had married a daughter of the Margrave Hans of Cüstrin, and, in spite of the Ecclesiastical Reservation, had remained in possession of his
bishopric.   The Emperor Maximilian was not willing to
interfere in favour of the Catholic cause at Magdeburg.[1]

The Archbishop Henry of Bremen, a Duke of Sachsen-
Lauenburg, had already, at the time of his election in
1567, been an adherent of the Augsburg Confession ;
but he had nevertheless represented himself to the Pope,
through Maximilian, as a loyal Catholic and a devotee
of the Apostolic See, hoping on these false pretences to
obtain papal confirmation.   In order also to be nomi-

---

[1] See Lossen, *Kölnischer Krieg*, pp. 138-139.

nated for the bishopric of Osnabrück, he had promised, in June 1574, that he would take holy orders and maintain the bishopric in the Catholic faith. Before his entry into Osnabrück, in May 1575, he pledged himself in his own handwriting to withdraw from his bishopric if he did not obtain confirmation from the Pope. Five months later, however, 'not possessing the gift of continence,' he contracted a secret marriage with his concubine, Anna von Broich. In the following year he renewed his hypocritical professions of entire fealty to the Pope.[1] Although he never obtained papal confirmation, he remained 'undisturbed in the possession of his bishopric.'

The bishopric of Minden had become almost entirely Protestant under the rule of Bishop George, Duke of Brunswick (d. 1566). The Duke's successor, Hermann, Count of Schauenburg, although he had subscribed to the Tridentine profession of faith, with its oath of unalterable fidelity to the Vicar of Christ, had nevertheless governed as a Protestant prince.[2]

The canons of the diocese had assured the papal nuncio Trivio, in 1575, of their entire devotion and loyalty to the Apostolic See, and had informed him of the violence and oppression which they had suffered on account of their Catholic faith; they were quite powerless, they had said; the town council allowed none of the burghers to attend a Catholic church, and even refused Christian burial to the parents of children who attended the cathedral school.[3]

At Lübeck Bishop Eberhard von Holle, who had been administrator of Verden as well since 1575, had

---

[1] Lossen, pp. 239, 256-259, 375-376, 385.
[2] Kampfschulte, pp. 259-260.   [3] Report in Theiner, ii. 471.

also become Protestant.   When, in 1575, on the day of
election at Ratisbon, the nuncio Delfino appealed to
the Emperor to take steps for the deposition of the
apostate bishop, he was answered : ' It was impossible
in those districts—the bishoprics of Lübeck, Merseburg,
and Halberstadt—to carry out all that was right; in
order not to incense the Protestant princes and stir up
worse evils, one must shut one's eyes to much.' [1]   The
chapter at Lübeck was Catholic, but the cathedral and
all the churches were in the hands of the Protestants.
So strong was the spirit of intolerance in the place that
in the year 1575, on the strength of a report that a sick
foreigner in Lübeck had received the Sacrament as a
Catholic, the preachers almost stirred up an insurrection
among the populace.[2]

As in many bishoprics, so in many of the imperial
towns, the stipulations of the Religious Pacification
were disregarded.

Strasburg, for instance, at the time of this treaty of
peace, was a ' parity' town.   The magistrates were
bound over to tolerate the Catholic faith, to allow
Catholic worship to go on in the cathedral and in three
other churches, which in the year 1555 were still in the
possession of the Catholics, and not to oppress the
small number of cloisters and religious foundations
which still remained unabolished.   In 1559, however,
the magistrates refused to protect the exercise of the
Catholic religion in their district, and in November of
the same year the populace, instigated by the preachers,
burst into the cathedral on a Sunday, while divine service
was going on, and committed sacrileges and abominations of all sorts.   It was with difficulty that the offici-

---

[1] Delfino's report in Theiner, ii. 467.   [2] Theiner, ii. 475.

ating bishop was able to save his life. For nine months long, after the expulsion of the Catholic clergy, the cathedral remained open day and night. It was not till August 18, 1560, that it was closed again in order that it might cease to be ' a public *latrine.*' [1] Regardless of the protestations of the bishop and the four parishes, the magistrates handed the churches over unreservedly to the Protestant worship. When, in February 1576, the nuncio Delfino urged Bishop John of Manderscheid to take steps for the recovery of religious freedom, the bishop declared all such attempts to be useless : imperial commands, he said, were despised by the people of Strasburg ; their territory, they said, certainly belonged to the Empire, but it was independent of imperial government.[2]

The magistrates at Hagenau had sworn to the Emperor in 1562 ' to remain, in future, faithful to the old, true, Catholic religion.' Three years later they sent for the Tübingen chancellor, Jacob Andreä, to assist in establishing the Augsburg Confession in the town. The Emperor, on July 27, 1566, reminded them of the promise they had made in 1562, and enjoined them to depose the preachers and to do away with all innovations. But their answer was : ' They had certainly made this promise, and they had not acted in opposition to it, for the Augsburg Confession was actually the old and true Catholic religion.' The Council had been primed by men learned in the Roman law to ' meet the Emperor with a " bold and spirited written document ; " for in matters of religion and faith there must be no

---

[1] De Bussière, *Hist. du Développement,* ii. 58, 65, 68 , 78–79. See Müller, *Restauration,* pp. 5 ff.

[2] Theiner, ii. 536.

question of cajolery and hypocrisy ; people were needed for the work who were born not in *Placentia* but in *Verona*.' An imperial commission, which had been deputed in 1572 to suppress the Protestant worship, had gone home without accomplishing anything. Since then Maximilian had left things to take their course. When, in 1574, Hagenau and other Alsatian towns appealed to the Pacification of Augsburg in justification of their proceedings, he answered that ' As regards the beneficial constitution of the Religious Peace, and the question who was and who was not included in it, His Majesty had no intention of disputing the interpretation of the said constitution, but would leave it as it stood.' This pronouncement gave the magistracy of Colmar also courage, in 1575, to suppress all ' popish idolatry,' and to complete the introduction of the Augsburg Confession. The Catholic clergy who appealed to the house of Austria for protection and defence, were declared to be traitors to their own native city.[1]

The magistracy forbade the chapter henceforth to keep their schools open ; preachers also were told off to work in the environs of the town for the abolition of the Catholic faith.   Pope Gregory XIII., on appealing to the Emperor for help, received an evasive answer.[2]

In this same year, 1575, the magistracy of the imperial town of Aalen also introduced the new doctrine, and they received special help in the work from Duke Louis of Würtemberg, the son and successor of Duke Christopher, who had died in 1568.[3]

In the Rhine district and in Westphalia, Calvinism

---

[1] Rocholl, pp. 140, 144, 165–168, 195, 206–207.

[2] Theiner, ii. 181.

[3] Zapf, *Sämmtl. Reformationsurkunden der Reichstadt Aalen* (Ulm, 1770 .

gained wider and wider footing. Wesel on the Lower Rhine became ' the mother of the Gueux ; ' the gymnasium at Duisburg developed into a centre of Calvinistic agitation. The county of Mark, the imperial lordship of Gemen, and the county of Rietberg were also invaded by Calvinism, and in 1574 the county of Wittgenstein fell a prey to Calvinistic iconoclasm.[1]

In a petition of grievances addressed to the Emperor in 1576, the Catholic Estates complained of continuous proceedings which were in opposition to the Pacification of Augsburg. The Confession of Augsburg was used as a cloak for covering all manner of sects and doctrines diametrically opposed both to this Confession and to the Catholic religion. Several of the bishops were in favour of the Lutheran Confession, and nevertheless they retained possession of their bishoprics. Since the signing of the Treaty of Passau many bishoprics had been unlawfully confiscated, and deprived of the Catholic religion ; the churches had been pillaged, the altars thrown down, the treasures carried off, the sacred hosts trampled under foot. Although, according to the terms of the Pacification of Augsburg, the free exercise of both religions had been established in imperial cities where they co-existed, it had nevertheless happened in many towns—among others at Mühlhausen in Thuringia, at Strasburg, Esslingen, Reutlingen, and Ulm—that the Catholics had been attacked by the Confessionists, and in some towns, as for instance at Ulm, Catholic sermons had been prohibited. The town council of Ulm had actually caused a priest in the house of the Teutonic Knights to be seized before the altars and dragged through the streets to the tower amid the jeers of the populace. In the

[1] Kampschutle, *Einführung*, pp. 232–242.

towns where religious foundations possessing imperial privileges still existed, the municipal authorities had taken upon themselves to deprive the Catholics of their schools, thus striking at the roots of the Catholic religion.

The Bishop of Eichstädt informed the other Catholic Estates that the Lutherans had forced their own preachers on the villages and parishes of his diocese, had drawn away his subjects from him in violation of the Religious Pacification, had taken away ecclesiastical privileges, tithes, and advowsons, and had actually gone the length of stripping a priest of his Mass vestments before the altar, and thrashing him out of the church. The Bishop of Ratisbon complained that the town council had turned cloisters and churches into drinking taverns and coal-cellars.

In their petition to the Emperor the Catholics made a general complaint that ' the Confessionists, while themselves allowed unrestrained liberty to make whatever religious regulations they like in their own lands, are intruding in the internal affairs of our territories, and, both by open and secret measures, strengthening the hands of those of our subjects who will not conform to our religious decrees, and encouraging them in their resistance. In the Protestant territories the loyal Catholics are held in bad repute, plagued, and persecuted ; the preachers are even enjoined by the ruling authorities to denounce them from the pulpit and make them hated by the people. They are not only excluded from all honours and offices, from weddings and baptisms, but in many places they are even condemned to suffer imprisonment or to pay heavy fines, the moment it becomes known that their wives and children have attended a Catholic sermon or received the Holy Sacrament in a strange church. If they protest that all they ask for is that without loss of honour they may be allowed to forfeit their goods and chattels and seek refuge under a Catholic ruler, even this is not granted them ; and such treatment is more unkind, unchristian, and much harder than if they were ordered to leave the country.' [1]

This petition of grievances was handed in to the Emperor at the Diet of Ratisbon, at which assembly most of the Protestant Estates, under the leadership of the Count Palatine, attempted to carry such comprehensive measures that Duke Albert of Bavaria wrote to Cardinal Morone : ' It is evident that the policy of the opposite party aims at nothing less than the complete overthrow of everything that remains of Catholicism in Germany.' [2]

The Diet of Ratisbon was opened on June 25, 1576.[3] The Emperor had mentioned, as the most important point for consideration, the threatened danger from the Turks. He now stated that the eight years' armistice which he had secured from the Sultan for the Hungarian dominions had been of little profit to himself and his subjects ; for in spite of it the Turks had possessed themselves of one spot after another on the frontier, had captured several strong places, had burnt and devastated the country, and had carried numbers of Christians into captivity. If they wished to keep away from German soil the arch-enemy who would soon

---

[1] In Erstenberger, pp. 90ᵇ–96; Lehmann, pp. 165–171.

[2] v. Aretin, *Maximilian*, p. 217.

[3] For the Diet of Ratisbon, see now, in addition to Ritter, i. 479 ff., 500 ff., and Hansen, *Nuntiaturberichte*, ii. p. xiii. ff., 1–192, Moritz's remarkably exhaustive narrative, entitled *Wahl Rudolf's II.* pp. 261–431, compiled from a wealth of unprinted material from the archives of Munich, Marburg, Wiesbaden, Frankfort, Dresden, and so forth.

have conquered the whole of Hungary, it was imperatively necessary that they should contribute not only
immediate and temporary, but also permanent aids.
The imperial appeal was supported by the Estates of
Styria, Carinthia, Carniola, and Görz, who all implored
the Diet for help in order to save Hungary from falling
into complete bondage to Turkey.[1]

'The Emperor'—so the Frankfort delegates reported
on July 4—'is keen on permanent aid, but, as it seems
to us, the rest of the Estates are as little in favour of
it as are the honourable cities : be this as it may, however, the towns will make as much opposition as possible.'[2]

The Elector Palatine Frederic considered the present
opportunity a favourable one, not only for obtaining
recognition of King Ferdinand's 'Supplementary Declaration,' but also and above all for carrying through
the measure of 'episcopal enfranchisement,' i.e. the
abolition of the Ecclesiastical Reservation. He hoped
that in the Rhine district, 'as had been the case in
Saxony and other places,' some of the bishops might
be persuaded to adopt Protestantism, in which event
it would be necessary to give them support. 'It does
not seem to us,' he wrote to the Landgrave William of
Hesse, 'that the question is so great and difficult a one
as might be supposed, especially in the present situation
of Germany.'[3] Anyhow, the Estates must grapple

---

[1] Häberlin, x. 18 ff.; Moritz, pp. 280 ff. See the report of the Venetian
ambassador, Giovanni Correro, on the conditions of the Empire and the
Turkish danger in 1574 : Le forze dell' Imperio per ogni ragione dovria
S. M. averle pronte, perchè trattandosi di perder l' Ungheria si tratta
insieme della sicurezza di tutta Germania. Albèri, ser. 1, vol. vi.
pp. 168–169.

[2] Reichstagsacten, 76, fol. 17.

[3] Kluckhohn, Briefe, ii. 926, 933.

' manfully ' with the question of enfranchisement, and
before entering into deliberation on any other subject
they must obtain from the Emperor a plain written
statement on the matter, and they must also intimate
to his Majesty that they would not withhold advice
and succour from any ecclesiastical elector or any
prelate who should come over to their religion. Episcopal enfranchisement was necessary because ' the
advancement and spread of the evangelical religion
depended chiefly on it.' By the Ecclesiastical Reservation the children of secular electors, princes, counts, and
nobles of the Augsburg Confession were debarred from
holding benefices, and the result of this would be that
in time to come all the principalities and counties would
be more and more cut up by division and subdivision,
and would utterly decay.[1] Let them only consider, he
said, with what zeal and earnestness the Pope and his
followers ' were busying themselves to promote idolatry.'
The Cardinal-legate Morone, whom Gregory XIII. had
sent to Ratisbon, was ' a thoroughgoing manœuvrer.'
When he had endeavoured to get off the journey to the
Diet, the Pope, according to trustworthy report, had
said to him : ' Either Morone goes to Ratisbon or else
I shall have to go myself.' From this it was easy to
conclude what was in prospect. The Archbishops of
Mayence and Treves had already had the audacity to
celebrate the papal jubilee year with unwonted magnificence, and they had carried on unheard-of ' monkey
tricks and jugglery ' at the processions. In both these
archbishoprics a large bull of indulgence had appeared
in print, and in golden letters the public attention had
been directed to ' the unity of the Christian princes, the

---

[1] Friedrich's *Instruction*, in Häberlin, x. 16, 236 ff.

extirpation of heresy, and the exaltation of the Holy Mother, the Christian Church.' [1]

Everywhere the Pope was endeavouring to hinder the course of the ' Evangel,' and finally to crush it out altogether. This end he was compassing by all manner of artifices, notably by the introduction of that ' mischievous sect ' of Jesuits, who ' were taking deeper and deeper root in the Empire, and who were enticing the innocent young nobility into their traps, and infecting them with their poison.' These iniquitous proceedings were carried on with special vigour in the bishopric of Fulda and on the Eichsfeld, where, regardless of all petitions and complaints, the public profession of the Augsburg Confession had been suppressed. In the margravate of Baden the same state of things prevailed, and the administrator of the diocese of Hildesheim— so the Elector had learned—had undertaken both to encourage the Jesuits and to prohibit the Confession of Augsburg. The evangelical burghers of Cologne, Hagenau, Wimpfen, Biberach, and other towns, had long ago brought forward their religious grievances, and enumerated the enormities to which the Augsburg Confessionists in Bavaria, in the archbishopric of Salzburg, and in the territories of Archduke Ferdinand of Austria, had been subjected in the way of oppression and violence, were universally known. Until redress had been secured for all these grievances, the Elector reiterated, they must not embark on any other transactions at Ratisbon—above all they must not vote any Turkish aids.

After hearing the Elector Palatine's proposal, the Protestant Estates present at Ratisbon drew up a

[1] Kluckhohn, *Briefe*, ii. 960, 969, 971, 973, 979.

petition to the Emperor, demanding in the first place, as a condition of granting a Turkish subsidy, that the ' Supplementary Declaration ' of King Ferdinand should be incorporated in the Recess of the Diet, and that it should be taken into account by the Imperial Chamber in all the judgments they pronounced. For had not Maximilian promised the Protestants at the election of King Rudolf that he would ' put right ' the question of this Declaration at the next Diet, and that meanwhile he would address himself to the spiritual princes with regard to freedom of religion for their Lutheran subjects ? [1]

Ferdinand's Supplementary Declaration had been drawn up at Augsburg on September 24, 1555, on the day before the conclusion of the Religious Pacification, and it was to the effect that ' all knights, towns, and parishes under the jurisdiction of ecclesiastics, and having for a long time past adhered to the Augsburg Confession, professed its religion and openly practised its rites and ceremonies and ordinances, must not be forced, either by the clergy or by anyone else, into giving up all these privileges ; but that, pending a Christian reconciliation of religion, they must be left unoppressed and undisturbed in the exercise of their religion.' To all this —so the document asserted—the Ecclesiastical Estates had agreed. ' In order to safeguard our Declaration from attacks, all the Ecclesiastical Estates present, and the councillors and delegates of the absent, agreed, for the honour and satisfaction of their subjects, that the

---

[1] Kluckhohn, *Briefe*, ii. 898–899; Moritz, pp. 285 ff. See above, pp. 210, 211, n. 2. Burghard, in the *Zeitschrift des histor. Vereins für Niedersachsen* (1890, pp. 21-67, and 1891, pp. 1-60), has lately given an exhaustive, though in part extremely biassed, account of the *Gegenreformation* (counter-reformation) on the Eichsfeld from 1574-1579.

derogation set forth at length in the treaty of general Religious Peace concluded at this Diet, viz. " that no declaration contrary to said Religious Peace, or anything else which might obstruct or alter it, shall be made, demanded, or accepted, but shall be null and void," shall have no invalidating effect upon our above-mentioned Declaration and decision.' [1]

In King Ferdinand's lifetime there had never been any mention of this Declaration. It had first been discovered in the spring of 1574 in the chancellery of the Saxon Electorate, and then published in print. According to the statement of the secretary of the imperial court council, Andreas Erstenberger, it had been published at the instigation of the Elector Augustus of Saxony, who hoped thereby to counteract what he feared would be the effect of the Ecclesiastical Reservation, viz. the complete restoration of the Catholic faith in the bishoprics of Meissen, Merseburg, and Naumburg-Zeitz. Such a contingency would have thrown great obstacles in the way of his long-cherished plan of gaining these bishoprics, and possibly Magdeburg also, for his electoral house. The Declaration—so Erstenberg stated—had been a reward to the Elector for his conciliatory behaviour in matters connected with the Ecclesiastical Reservation, and Ferdinand had had it drawn up in the form of a private document for the use of Augustus, who was the only person possessing an authentic copy. In the Acts and protocols of the Augsburg Diet—so Erstenberg writes—' there is no mention of anybody who applied for the said decretal, except the Saxon councillors. They alone, moreover, received the document into their own hands straight from the chancellery.

---

[1] Erstenberger, p. 81; Lehmann, pp. 55–56.

It is only to be found in the Elector of Saxony's chancellery, and not in the possession of any other elector or prince. It is not even in the imperial chancellery, where all other State papers and resolutions are preserved.' [1] The above statement is quite as incorrect as the explanation which makes out the Declaration to be a 'Supplementary Recess' emanating from the new religionist princes. For the document had not come into existence by the regular process of deliberation at imperial council boards, and at these with the King, but by private arrangement. On the other hand, however, it was in no way a private document for the use of the Elector Augustus, but a royal ordinance drawn up at the wish of the new religionists. The consent of the Catholics had only been given in a passive, and so far still an unbinding, form. They had assented to the document on the express condition that it should not be published. For this reason the Imperial Chamber, to which the Pacification of Augsburg, like all other imperial decrees, had been presented as a future rule for its decisions, had not been informed of the Declaration. Consequently the document did not possess full legal authority.[2]

At the election day at Ratisbon, therefore, in 1575, the three Protestant electors had put forward the demand that the Declaration of Ferdinand, which had been proclaimed so long ago, and which had such an important bearing on the proceedings in Fulda,[3] should be embodied in the capitulation of the new King, and should be ratified in a manner which would make it binding both-on Emperor and people. The ecclesiastical

---

[1] Erstenberger, pp. 389-393.
[2] Moritz, *Wahl Rudolf's II.*, pp. 21-32.   [3] See above, pp. 333-334.

electors, who till then had had no official intimation
of the Declaration, disputed, not its legality only, but
also its existence, which they would not believe in until
the Elector Augustus laid before them the original
document, signed and sealed by Ferdinand.

When at the Diet at Ratisbon the Protestant Estates
demanded that the Declaration should be inserted in
the imperial Recess, the Catholic Estates ' unanimously
and angrily repudiated the improper proposal.' Of the
said Declaration, they declared, they had known nothing
till the year 1575 ; some of the Estates who had formed
part of the Government as long ago as 1555, and a
number of councillors and delegates, still living, who
had been present at the Diet in question from beginning
to end, could remember nothing about any such transaction or Declaration. Besides which the document
was of earlier date than the Religious Treaty of Peace, in
which all stipulations that were opposed to this peace
had been cancelled and annulled, with the knowledge
and consent of all the Estates, and in the best possible
manner. They were all the less willing to enter into
any transactions or dispute with the Augsburg Confessionists concerning this Declaration, because that
Declaration was in direct opposition to their official
duties, to their calling, and their consciences, and would
occasion nothing but disturbance, disobedience, and
refractoriness among their subjects.[1]

Among the Protestant Estates, the Elector Augustus,
in spite of the positiveness with which he had vouched
for the Declaration before the meeting of the Diet, had
nevertheless not been willing to urge ' its incorpora-

---

[1] Erstenberger, pp. 86ᵇ- 88. See Lossen, *Kölnischer Krieg*, pp. 318–
319 ; Moritz, p. 314.

tion in the Recess,' and to make participation in the transactions of the Diet and the grant of a Turkish subsidy conditional on the acceptance of this document. He had enjoined his councillors to give to the Confessionists, at their special committee meetings, detailed reports as to the treatment of subjects differing in religion from their rulers. These reports, however, do not tally with the statement in the Declaration that the Ecclesiastical Estates had agreed to the document. The ecclesiastics, Augustus said, ' have never been willing to let themselves be dictated to with regard to their subjects.' ' It was in this spirit of independence that, at the Diet at Spires in 1544, and again in 1555, and at other Diets they had inserted the following clause in the Recess : ' ' Moreover, no Estate must coerce or entice another Estate, or its subjects, into its own religion, or in any way take these subjects under their protection in opposition to the rulers of said subjects.' ' And over and above this,' the Elector goes on, ' in the Recess, Anno 55, it is further stated that nothing in the Articles of this Treaty of Peace is to be altered or eliminated, nor is any subsequent declaration to be made in opposition to it.'

To all this the Estates professing the Augsburg Confession had given their consent.

' Nevertheless,' they said, ' they could not be otherwise than grateful to the Emperor Ferdinandus for having drawn up this Declaration ; at the same time they must be careful to take it *cum grano salis*, and not to allow it to be the cause of disturbance in the Empire, or of the entire overthrow of the Religious Pacification, especially as it was a matter that did not concern the Augsburg Confessionist Estates, but only foreign subjects.'

' To smuggle the said Declaration into the Imperial
Recess, and to get it introduced into the Imperial
Chamber,' was not in the power of the Emperor, because
the consent of the ecclesiastical Order was necessary.
The Estates ' should consider—and, as members who
attended the Diets, they must know—that nothing
could be inserted in the Recesses but what had previously
been discussed at the imperial councils and passed by
all, or by a majority of the Estates, or else left to the
Emperor's decision.' ' With regard to the insinuation
of the Declaration into the Imperial Chamber, the consent of the Estates was also necessary for this.   It was,
moreover, an unprecedented thing in the Empire for a
supplementary declaration, drawn up independently of
any Recess, to be made binding on the Imperial Chamber.'
Altogether the Estates must bear in mind ' that matters
were not exactly on a right and unquestionable footing.'
The Elector Augustus, on October 1, 1576, in com-
municating to Duke Julius of Brunswick the remonstrances he had made to the Confessionists, wrote as
follows : ' We cannot find that in the Holy Empire there
is authority or justification for claims and threats such
as these : " If this, that, or the other is not conceded on
behalf of foreign subjects, we would see the Empire
disintegrated, the religious pacification overthrown, one
Estate after another swallowed up by the Turks, and
the whole of the Holy Roman Empire made subject to
the Ottoman power, rather than give a farthing for the
maintenance of the Empire and the prevention of
the great danger which threatens it." ' [1]

On the other hand, the Landgrave William of Hesse
admonished Duke Julius to hold out valiantly, both in

[1] Schmidt-Phiseldek, ii. 102–122. See Moritz, pp. 459–460.

the matter of the Declaration and of the Ecclesiastical
Reservation which the Catholic Estates had refused to
abolish ; to make a fresh united stand, and to refuse
the Emperor any grants of money if their demands were
not fulfilled. Some of the Estates professing the Augsburg Confession were, indeed, of opinion that the
Pacification of Augsburg should not be overthrown for
the sake of the evangelical subjects of the papists ; but
it was not justifiable to God and to posterity that so
many Christians ' should be driven into the jaws of the
devil.' William was delighted, he said, that Julius also
was ready to ' prove himself a valiant Christian and a
staunch old German prince : ' if all the Estates were
like-minded ' we should soon,' he said, ' be quit of the
cunning intrigues by which the opposite party endeavour
to hinder the progress of the Gospel, and we should be
secure in the possession of our traditional German
liberties, and in no danger of sinking to the condition of
tributaries.' [1]

The commander-in-chief, Lazarus von Schwendi,
whose influence with the Emperor was very great, also
urged on the Protestant Estates to proceed ' manfully
and undauntedly.' ' They were behaving too sluggishly,'
he said to the Protestant delegates ; Maximilian was
' on the right road, but he had got the notion that the
Confessionists were not greatly concerned about the
needs and the danger of the poor subjects : they ought
to throw more zeal and vigour into the cause.' [2]

Schwendi addressed a memorandum to the Emperor,
begging him to introduce ' liberty of conscience ' throughout the whole Empire. The Catholic Estates would, of

[1] Schmidt-Phiseldek, ii. 77–87.
[2] Lehmann, p. 143.

course, oppose the step with all their might, but they had no valid ground for so doing ; for it was a matter that rested wholly with imperial authority, sovereignty, and office. The Pope also had nothing to do with the matter, as he had no authority in the affairs of the Empire. If the Emperor did not grant freedom of conscience, the clergy would have ' the very worst to fear from civil wars ; ' he himself would not be likely to obtain a Turkish subsidy from the Protestant Estates, or, even if aid should be volunteered, he would not be able to reckon on it with any certainty ; grave political troubles would await him in the future, and ' ruin would threaten him on every side.' [1]

The liberty of conscience claimed by Schwendi related chiefly to a ' franchise ' which the majority of the Protestant Estates in their supplication to the Emperor had made a further condition of a Turkish grant. They demanded, namely, that the Protestant counts and barons should also have free access to the higher benefices, without being obliged to change their religion.

This demand had been put forward at the Diet of Augsburg in 1566, by a number of counts from the Rhine district, from Franconia, Thuringia, Harz, and Wetterau, who had been instigated to the step by the Counts John of Nassau and Louis of Wittgenstein. The Emperor at the time had answered that he would consider by what means these and other ' disputed points of religion could be brought to a godly, Christian settlement.' [2]

[1] *Gutachten ' gestellt auf dem Reichstage zu Regensburg,* 1576,' in the Letters of L. Schwendi, from 1568–1583. Roll in the Frankfort Archives, fol. 45–50. See Moritz, p. 361.

[2] Lossen, *Kölnischer Krieg*, pp. 300–301. The ' Supplication ' in Erstenberger, pp. 44–46.

Since then Louis of Wittgenstein had become the Grand Chamberlain of the Elector Palatine, and under his influence Frederic III. had developed into a most zealous advocate of the ' Franchise.' At the time of the election at Ratisbon, in 1575, the Landgrave William of Hesse and the Count Palatine Richard von Simmern had also promised their help to the counts. By Richard's advice a petition to the secular electors had been drawn up at that time. The actual object which the associates aimed at through this Franchise— and which they openly acknowledged among themselves—was ' the extirpation of popish idolatry ' in the ecclesiastical territories. This, however, they naturally did not proclaim publicly, as they did not wish to ruin their chances of influencing this or the other ecclesiastical elector or bishop in favour of the measure. ' When you want to catch birds,' said the Count of Winneburg, ' you must not throw stones among them.' [1] The Catholics were to be decoyed into the trap. They were to be made to believe that the Protestants were not aiming at the suppression of their religion, but only at putting matters on a footing of equality and justice in order thereby ' to establish genuine confidence, free from all hypocrisy, between the members of both religions, lay and clerical.' At the same time they did not refrain from attempts to intimidate the Catholics by threats. In the petition they addressed to the electors it was urged that if the counts who adhered to the Augsburg Confession were debarred by oppressive oaths and statutes from procuring for their numerous offspring any portion among the higher benefices, they would be driven to constant subdivision of landed

[1] Lossen, *Kölnischer Krieg*, p. 317.

estates and territory, which would result in the dying out of the Order of Counts. Moreover, the children and successors of these counts would feel very hotly and bitterly on the subject; they would remember that their forefathers had given largely of their wealth to these bishoprics, and they would dare the uttermost rather than allow themselves to be ousted from their rightful heritages, because they were not adherents of the papacy. All this, it was to be feared, might occasion troublesome and extensive complications and the ruin of all peaceable existence in Germany.[1]

The petitioners, however, did not obtain a hearing from the Electors of Saxony and Brandenburg on the election day, and they then indulged the hope of carrying their measure through at the Diet. Frederic of the Palatinate and William of Hesse again offered their support. But men of insight did not reckon on any success. 'If I speak the real truth,' wrote the Hessian Chancellor, Reinhard Scheffer, on January 1, 1576, to Burkard von Kram, Stattholder at Marburg, who was pushing on the matter zealously with his friends among the counts, 'the whole business is so thorny, intricate, and complicated, that, under the present condition of affairs, and unless some other medium intervenes, I have not the slightest hope of any good result. The clerics cannot support the measure on account of the oaths and obligations by which they are bound to the Pope. Nor do they wish to do so. They want to preserve their own popish religion, and if once this franchise is obtained, the papacy will be lying in the mud.' 'The bishops' terror of confiscation,

---

[1] *Die Supplication*, Erstenberger, pp. 47-53.

disintegration, and spoliation, no amount of caution and no imperial decree would be able to overcome.' ' Besides which the wider the doors of the bishoprics were thrown open to the princes, counts, and nobles of the Augsburg Confession, the more tightly would they be closed against popish princes, counts, and nobles. The latter would never willingly forego their advantages. And, therefore, at the present juncture all our trouble and labour would certainly be thrown away. Preparation of another sort was requisite; but this must not be talked about.'

Concerning a wedding at Hanau, which, it was thought, would have been an opportunity for furthering this matter with the counts who were present, the following communication was made to John of Nassau, in February 1576, that, ' what with gorging and swilling, nothing profitable could be thought of or planned ; we are going on in such a manner that God has good reason to punish us with blindness.' [1]

The Protestant knights shared the conviction of the Catholics, that in agitating for this Franchise the princes and counts were not concerned about religion, but merely about the confiscation of ecclesiastical property, and that the disintegration of the bishoprics would be the inevitable consequence of the passing of the measure. At two general congresses of knights, at Worms and at Frankfort on the Main, the knights of the Rhine resolved not to give their consent to the Franchise, and they made known this resolution to the Franconian and Suabian imperial knights.[2] Delegates from the three bodies of

---

[1] Lossen, *Kölnischer Krieg*, p. 394, notes 1 and 2.
[2] Erstenberger, pp. 73–75. See Lossen, *Kölnischer Krieg*, pp. 303, 393, 395.

knights handed in to the imperial councillors at Ratisbon a petition in which they expressed themselves decisively against the ' extremely dangerous and pernicious ' Franchise, which had already been the cause of ruin to many important bishoprics in numbers of places. They begged that, whereas this measure would be specially prejudicial to the bishoprics and other ecclesiastical foundations, and to the nobles, the Emperor would put a stop to it altogether, and let everything remain in accordance with ancient tradition and with the terms of the Pacification of Augsburg.[1]

By the Catholic party a ' Franchise ' of another sort was recommended as ' useful and desirable ': namely, ' that the cathedral chapters and the episcopal and archiepiscopal offices should not only be open to princes, counts, barons, and nobles, but that virtuous, learned, and efficient men of all classes should be eligible for them.' [2]

In the days when this ' primitive equality of persons ' was in vogue, better order, they said, was maintained in the Church. ' Love, humility, wisdom, are the means used by the Spirit of Christ for preserving the Church of God ; Christ does not care for nobility of birth, and therefore He chooses in a different way from that of the men of the world.' ' Christ examines His disciples as to whether they are able to drink the cup of suffering ; He asks if Peter's love is greater than that of the others ; and before entrusting him with the keys He caused him to make profession of his faith.'

---

[1] *Die Supplication vom 9. October, 1576,* in Erstenberger, pp. 71–72.
[2] *Von der hoch berümpter Religionsfreistellung ein kurzer Bericht, &c. Autore Andrea Dorkenio.* Printed at Cologne, 1576 ; see p. 39. See Stieve, *Die Politik Bayerns,* i. 157, and Moritz, p. 406.

But if the advocates of the Protestant ' Franchise' were to get their way, the entrance examination of the Church would have to be on very different lines—namely, ' whether the candidates could ride well, fence, tilt, play tennis, and romp!' 'Moreover, even supposing that they only took into account the temporal possessions of the Church, it would still be found that honourable, legitimate, able burghers and burghers' children were just as much entitled to admission to the colleges, to the higher benefices, and to Church government as men of noble birth, seeing that it was their God-fearing ancestors rather than the wealthy who, according to St. Luke's testimony, endowed the churches, and who still nowadays, by their bitter toil and sweat, earned the tithes from their own possessions.' 'If the low-born be excluded from Church benefices and the clerical beneficiaries turned into lay and political canons, then the tenants and estates will also be exonerated from rents and tithes to which political canons have no right.' 'Finally, all our ancestors, in all places, were guided by the usages of the Roman Church, and although the overseers and bishops of the Church of God have generally been chosen from imperial, royal, noble or other distinguished classes, it is, nevertheless, known to everybody that no one, because he is not of noble birth, is ever excluded by the consistory either from the election or from the higher offices.'

The Roman Church has always admitted to her consistory and her government men of all nations, classes, and clerical orders. And consequently all other Churches, institutions, and colleges throughout Christendom are bound to follow her example and to admit all suitable persons, without distinction of class. Such a

Franchise as this would be a godly and a glorious one, in accordance with Holy Scripture, with councils, canons, and imperial law, with the teaching, the endowments, the last testaments of our parents—indeed with everything that is right and reasonable, and it would be injurious neither to the nobles nor to any one else, but, on the contrary, beneficial to all classes.' [1]

But for all its Christian merits and its usefulness to the Church, the great Catholic lords would have as little to say to such a Franchise as would the Protestants. The Council of Trent, indeed, owing to the strong opposition from the powerful magnates among the clergy and the laity, had been obliged to withdraw the measure for admitting the burgher class to the cathedral canonries. [2]

While ' an incredible spirit of acrimony was apparent among the delegates of the different Estates assembled at Ratisbon, [3] the religious episode of Fulda was threatening to provoke a disastrous war even during the sitting of the Diet.' Shortly before the opening of the Diet, in consequence of a conspiracy of the chapter and knights of Fulda, the Prince-Abbot, Balthasar von Dernbach, had been deposed and compelled to sign a capitulation making over the administration of his diocese to the Bishop of Würzburg, Julius Echter of Mespelbrunn. [4] In a mandate of June 28 the Emperor, under Morone's influence, [5] had annulled the enforced contract and decreed that the abbot should be rein-

---

[1] Pp. 10–28.   [2] See above, vol. vii. p. 267.

[3] Report of the Brunswick chancellor, Mutzeltin, October 1, 1576, in Schmidt-Phiseldek, ii. 101–102.

[4] Further details in Kamp, *Fürstabt Balthasar*, pp. 106–133. See also Egloffstein, pp. 41 f. Bishop Julius played a far from honourable part in the conspiracy.

[5] See Hansen, *Nuntiaturberichte*, ii. p. xxviii; Moritz, p. 410.

stated. But the conspirators would not submit to the imperial decree. The Estates of the realm were 'inundated with despatches' from both sides. These despatches were so numerous, the Frankfort delegate, Carl von Glauburg, reported on September 13, 'that six weeks will not suffice to copy the whole lot of them. In order to save time, the Mayence chancellor has had them read out at the imperial council, and it has taken three days and a half to do it, giving at least five hours a day to the work. Glauburg feared that this business might be the beginning of a dangerous disturbance and insurrection in the Holy Empire.' [1] In order to avert such a calamity the Emperor allowed 'Balthasar's case to drop.' He sequestrated the abbacy, ordered both parties to bring the matter into the courts of justice, and appointed the grand master of the Teutonic Order, Henry of Bubenhausen, administrator.[2]

When a Bavarian ambassador remonstrated with the Emperor, saying 'how dangerous it would be if it became the rule everywhere that "right must succumb, that might was right," Maximilian answered : "Nothing can be done, and I am weak and ill." '

'Devoid of inward fortitude, because of the uncertainty of his faith, suspicious alike of Catholics and Confessionists,' a victim, moreover, to liver complaint and stone, the Emperor ' all through the Diet was in a constant state of perturbation and distress such as words are powerless to describe.' The position was indeed a critical one. While the Protestants, on the one hand, persisted in making the grant of Turkish aids

---

[1] In the Frankfort *Reichstagsacten*, p. 76, fol. 40.

[2] Komp, *Fürstabt Balthasar*, pp. 187–208, 288–299. It was not till twenty-six years later that the abbot recovered his rightful possession.

contingent on the fulfilment of their demands, the Catholics, on the other hand, declared that ' they would contribute nothing to the subsidy unless it were agreed to abide by the Pacification of Augsburg, and to reject all the objectionable proposals of the Protestants respecting the Declaration of King Ferdinand, the abolition of the Ecclesiastical Reservation, and the Franchise for the counts and lords.' The Cardinal-legate Morone, who was at Ratisbon, was working most energetically to keep the Catholic party unanimous, and in several conversations with the Emperor he took care to let his Majesty know clearly what his policy was. ' Just see what a miserable plight I am in,' Maximilian said one day to a councillor of the Elector of Mayence whom he had received in bed, being laid up with a sharp attack of stone ; ' I do not know where next to turn. There is nothing but suspicion and mistrust everywhere, while the Turk is on the point of breaking into my hereditary dominions, and attacking the heart of my Empire.' ' Everybody,' the councillor replied, ' must feel pity for your Majesty and for the danger of the Empire, and the Estates of the true religion are ready and willing to give manful succour ; but they cannot allow enemies, by whom they are no less hated than by the Turks, to grow up in their own lands.' ' The principal cause,' he said, ' of the general confusion and anarchy which was yearly increasing, was the religious schism which embittered hearts and minds, and drove the Estates further and further asunder.' For many years past too much had been ceded to the Protestants, while the small band of Catholics had been too long oppressed ; the latter, however, had at last ' roused themselves to some degree of manliness,' and

they were now resolved ' to be masters, at any rate in
their own territories, just as the Protestant Estates were
determined not to be dictated to in any way in matters
of religion in *their* lands.' Just as the Protestants,
on the strength of the Pacification of Augsburg, refused
to tolerate any religious schismatics in their domains,
and denounced everything Catholic as ' idolatry and
devil's work,' so too the Catholics had made up their
minds ' henceforth to avail themselves of the rights
conferred on them by the said Pacification, and not to
tolerate any other religion than the Catholic one among
their subjects and adherents, and to punish with all
needful severity any revolt and mutiny which are the
natural sequence of the agitation.' ' The Catholics had
slumbered too long, and for all their sitting still and
giving in, they had gained nothing more than constant
fresh oppression ; fresh devices and pretexts had been
incessantly invented for crushing and ruining them ; it
was high time for them now to awake and strive at any
rate to save the small remnants still left in their hands.' [1]
The Archbishop of Cologne, Salentin von Isenburg, who
had been for many years past on a friendly footing with
the Protestants, now spoke at Ratisbon in favour of
unconditional rejection of their demands. He had
become the leader of the Catholic party.[2]

It was to the exertions of Duke Albert of Bavaria
that the Catholics were chiefly indebted for the fact that
the Elector Augustus of Saxony assumed a conciliatory attitude and refused to associate himself with the

---

[1] *Kurmainzischer Bericht vom Tage zu Regensburg*, 1576, contributed by Böhmer from the papers bequeathed by Habel. Morone's
reports from Ratisbon dated June 19 and July 4, 1576, in Theiner, ii.
524–525.

[2] Morone's report, dated July 13, 1576, in Theiner, ii. 525.

Protestant demands, saying rather that they ought to abide by the Pacification of Augsburg. He said to Duke Albert, who paid him a visit at Dresden after the opening of the Diet : ' If only your Majesty remains firm, we shall manage to keep things as they are.' [1] He acknowledged emphatically the binding character of the Ecclesiastical Reservation, and sent word through his ambassadors to the Protestant Estates at Ratisbon that its abolition would be a breach of the Pacification of Augsburg.   The Elector wished the ' urgently needed Turkish subsidy ' to be granted forthwith, without further stipulations.   ' Even supposing the Religious Peace were to be overthrown,' Augustus wrote, ' would this justify his Imperial Majesty's Estates in refusing help against the Turks, and in looking calmly on while one corner of the Empire after another was being swallowed up ? ' [2]

In a ' Kurmainzischer Bericht ' (Report by the delegate of the Elector of Mayence) we read as follows : ' It was chiefly owing to the unanimity of the Catholics, who from the very first stood out like one man against the demands of the Count Palatine and his Calvinistic followers,[3] and to the astuteness of the Lutheran Elector of Saxony and Brandenburg, who plainly saw to what confusion and anarchy the Calvinistic manoeuvrings

[1] v. Aretin, *Maximilian*, pp. 213–215.

[2] Kluckhohn, *Briefe*, ii. 965–967.   Ritter, *August von Sachsen*, p. 360.

[3] On July 4, 1576, Morone had already written concerning the Catholics : ' Tutti però si mostrano unitissimi a non voler consentire a queste loro esorbitantissime petitioni ' (Theiner, ii. 525).   Archduke Ferdinand II. of the Tyrol was also one of the princes who held the Emperor back from concessions that would have been fatal to the Catholics ; see Hirn, ii. 129–130.   Concerning Morone's exertions during the Diet see (now) especially, besides Hansen's *Nuntiaturberichte*, ii. 50 ff., the account of Moritz, pp. 292 ff.

would lead, that these said demands and manœuvres were, for the time at least, overthrown.'[1]

The Emperor lived to enjoy the gratification of being promised, ' at least on paper,' sixty *Römermonate*, payable within six years, for help against the Turks. As for ' actual payment' of the subsidy, however, ' in the case of very many of the Estates, the old habit of dogged indifference was kept up.' Even in the case of Frankfort on the Main, which had boasted on former occasions that ' its council showed greater promptness and punctuality than many others in sending in its contribution,' not a single farthing had been paid up by September in the following year.[2]

On October 12, when the Estates were assembled for the reading of the Recess, the news was brought them of the Emperor's death.

After the doctors had given up all hope of Maximilian's recovery, ' the Empress '—so the Spanish ambassador at the Viennese Court wrote to Madrid—' appeared, on October 6, at the bedside of the dying man, armed with all the courage of religion. She fell on her knees before him, and implored him with scalding tears to send for a priest of the Catholic Church, on whose wisdom and piety he could place reliance. The Emperor answered that his priest was in heaven. " Quite true," replied the Empress, " but the heavenly Priest has appointed His servants on earth to minister to the salvation of souls." Once more she implored him to with-

---

[1] In the Report cited at p. 369, note 1. Respecting the attitude of the Elector of Brandenburg's representative, which is not quite correctly described in the report in question, see Moritz, pp. 396–397 and 405.

[2] *Kammergerichtliche Citationen und Ladungen an den Rath vom 5. September, 1577*, in the Frankfort Archives, *Kaiserschreiben*, 15, fol. 10, 11. See Moritz, p. 454.

draw into himself, to confess, and to receive the Body of
the Lord. The Emperor answered: "Very good;
he would think about it." More than this the Empress
could not effect. All further efforts on her part were
fruitless.' Equally futile were the exhortations of
the Cardinal-legate Morone. Maximilian's sister, the
Duchess of Bavaria, also 'made a vain attempt, on
October 10, to open her brother's eyes to the danger of
his condition, and to persuade him to seek salvation in
the truths of religion. The Emperor put them off with
general remarks and reassurances, but at last he became
so exasperated that he would no longer suffer either
the Empress or the Duchess to come near him.' Not
till the night before his death did he send for his court
chaplain, the Bishop of Neustadt, to whose questions
whether ' he repented of his sins and hoped for forgiveness, and whether he believed and held as truth all that
the Church had taught since the days of the apostles,
and whether he wished to die in this faith,' he
answered : ' Yes.' [1] ' In confidence I must tell you,'
Duke Albert of Bavaria wrote to the Elector Augustus
of Saxony on November 5, 1576, ' that his Majesty, as
I understand from my wife, behaved in his last moments
as he had done all his life, so that no one actually knows
whether he died as a Catholic or as a Confessionist ;

---

[1] d'Almazan's Report, dated October 13, 1576, in Koch, *Quellen*, ii
101–107. See also the Report of the Lord of Dietrichstein in Gindely,
Gesch. der böhmischen Brüder, ii. 225 f. These two reports agree in the
essential points. For Maximilian's last illness, see Becker, *Die letzten
Tage und der Tod Maximilian's II.* (Wien, 1877), pp. 7 f., 29 f., 39 f.;
Hopfen, pp. 173 f. and 413 f.; and Moritz, pp. 433 ff. Respecting Maximilian's
physician in ordinary, Crato of Krafftheim, see, in addition to Gillet's
Monographie, Otto's *Reformation im Erzherzogthum Oesterreich*, p. 30,
and Beer in the *Beilage zur Zeitschrift für praktische Heilkunde*
(Wien, 1862), p. 8, No. 38. Hansen, *Nuntiaturberichte*, ii. 169 f.

he did not confess either to one or the other opinion,
but departed this life with but very few words.'[1]

To his son Rudolf, a young man of four-and-
twenty, Maximilian bequeathed his Empire in the
most hopeless condition of anarchy. His own wavering
and equivocal position in matters of religion, and the
inevitable duplicity of language consequent thereon,
had rendered the Emperor 'equally despicable to
Catholics and to Protestants.' The Venetian delegate,
Giovanni Correro, said of him in 1574, that he was
neither loved nor feared, and therefore very little
obeyed.[2] During the Diet of Ratisbon, the Brunswick
chancellor, Mutzeltin, was full of apprehension that
'they would soon have the French King in German
territory.' At the end of his report on Maximilian's
death, he added : 'We have now a young and insignificant monarch.'[3]

Rudolf II. was not equal to his task. At the time
of the election at Ratisbon, the Nuncio Delfino had
written : 'The King, in all modesty, shows that he is
incapable of bearing the heavy weight of government.'[4]
He was possessed of great talents and much knowledge,
he spoke six languages, was a lover of the fine arts,
collected art-treasures of all sorts, and gathered at his
court scholars of the highest merit and distinction.
But his character was weak and irresolute, suspicious
and mistrustful ; and the melancholy of his disposi-
tion speedily developed into morbid inactivity.   The
Emperor—so people said—' occupies himself as an astro-
nomer with the harmonies of heavenly constellations,

---

[1] Weber, *Des Kurfürsten August Verhandlungen*, p. 337. See p. 338.
[2] Albèri, Ser. 1, vol. v. 170.
   Schmidt-Phiseldek, ii. 101, 123.   [4] Theiner, ii. 463.

but from the un-harmony of earthly things it is his
habit to escape ; he is frightened of all affairs of government, and appears to have no confidence in his own
judgment.' 'Rudolf is a good, pious prince, who,
methinks, would gladly act rightly,' said Duke Albert of
Bavaria shortly after the Emperor's accession, 'but after
he has spent a short time in business of state, he becomes
worried and anxious, and places himself entirely in the
hands of the old privy councillors,' [1] many of whom
were in favour of the religious innovations. Hubert
Languet, on the other hand, wrote simultaneously
from Ratisbon, on October 18, 1576, to the Elector
Augustus of Saxony that 'the new Emperor appears
only to listen to popish counsellors ; many people are
beginning to fear that great changes are at hand in
religion, not only in Austria, Hungary, and Bohemia,
but also in the Empire.' [2]

Rudolf II. brought on himself at the outset the
charge of 'popish tyranny' through certain measures
instituted against Protestant extravagances in Austria.

---

[1] v. Aretin, *Maximilian*, p. 221. See Huber, pp. 284 f. and the
literature there cited.

[2] *Epist. Secretæ*, 1ᵇ, 242. See Moritz, p. 443.

CHAPTER IX

PROTESTANT EXCESSES IN AUSTRIA—PROTESTANT RF-
PORTS ON THE MORAL AND RELIGIOUS CONDITION
OF THE PEOPLE IN AUSTRIA

WITH a view to restoring to order the utter chaos of
their Church affairs,[1] the lords and knights of the
archduchy of Upper and Lower Austria had implored
Martin Chemnitz, in 1572, to take pity on their Church
and to undertake the office of superintendent, for one
year at any rate. Chemnitz had expressed his readiness
to do this, but only on condition of their adopting a
particular scheme of dogma, which neither the Estates
nor the priests had been willing to sanction. In 1573
the Estates turned for help to David Chyträus, who
had already before rendered them faithful service,[2] and
who was again at the time labouring zealously and
honestly for the removal of ' clerical abuses which had
become almost irremediable.' Chyträus held consultation with some of the deputies from the Estates, and
some of the theologians, and they came to the conclusions that ' It must be insisted on that henceforth no
one shall be appointed to the office of preacher unless he
has first been pronounced orthodox by the superintendent, still to be appointed, and unless he pledges
himself to conform to the Ritual; and preachers
must be bound over to abstain from all unnecessary

---

[1] See above, p. 300.   [2] See above, p. 302 f.

disputations.' Chyträus, however, expressed his opinion
at the outset that, in the present lawless state of things,
when every preacher was determined to be Pope and
Emperor in his own Church, it would be very difficult to
carry out these regulations. The holding of a synod
was also urgently necessary, but at the same time im-
practicable, on account of the ' many seditious, stuck-
up, pig-headed, arrogant fellows who would not agree to
anything that was not exactly in accordance with their
own ideas.' A convention of preachers which was
summoned in July 1574 only led to increased bitterness
and schism, and verified afresh the words spoken by
Maximilian to Chyträus : ' I see fresh schisms springing
up day after day, and the dogmatic quibbles in your
Church are so enormously increased by colloquies, that
I despair of any healing.' [1] Every preacher in Austria—
so Polycarpus Leiser, pastor of Göllersdorf, wrote from
long experience—' inveighs and preaches against his
neighbours openly from the pulpit, insults his rulers
in the most disgraceful manner, and rates and abuses

[1] See Wiedemann, i. 382–387. In the year 1573 the Estates of Styria
had sent the chairman of their Estate, Bernhard Lerch, to Rostock and to
Berlin, to fetch David Chyträus, Professor at Rostock, and George
Cœlestinus, Provost at Cölln-on-the-Spree, in order that these two men
might organise ' the evangelical church-system ' in Styria. Lerch had
left Berlin on December 1, but had soon left Cœlestinus behind, because,
as he wrote to the Styrian Estate (provincial council), ' the provost was a
good-for-nothing fellow, thirsting only for gold and glory, a conceited,
worthless adventurer, a quarrelsome, insolent fool, a godless, usurious
man.' While Chyträus was content with only two servants, Cœlestinus
had a retinue of five or six, and two private saddle-horses which followed
his carriage for his sole use (Lisch, *Jahrbücher*, xxiv. 87, 119–123). The
physician of the Elector of Brandenburg, Leonhard Thurn von Thurneyssen, pronounced equally severe judgment on Lerch ; he called him ' a
rogue and a villain,' and said that he had shown him much friendship
and kindness at Berlin, and that Lerch had rewarded him for it by
cheating him of 300 florins (Thurneyssen, *Ein durch Noth gedrungenes
Ausschreiben*, &c. (1584), 2, lv).

his hearers if they will not conform exactly to his notions.' [1]

The only thing in which the preachers agreed was in hurling the most virulent invectives at all that was sacred to the Catholics. The concessions made by Maximilian to the Estates were, as they themselves allowed, ' far greater than what any single Protestant territorial lord had granted to his own Catholic subjects.' Yet, not content with all they had obtained, the preachers stormed and raged about ' inhuman oppression ' because forsooth ' popish idolatry ' was still allowed in the land. Although the Emperor had repeatedly declared that free exercise of the Protestant religion must not be extended to the towns and boroughs belonging to reigning princes, he had nevertheless acquiesced silently in the erection of a Protestant chapel at Vienna in the building where the provincial Estates held their meetings. ' After this, conventicles sprang up like mushrooms at Vienna.' ' At the " Golden Angel," where Count Nicholas Salm lives,' wrote the Court Councillor Eder, ' noisy orations are delivered every day. It is also said that the Mass has already been celebrated there according to the new ordinances. The burghers take part in these proceedings.' [2] The preacher Lorenz Becher, of the sect of the Flacians, was heard to say from the pulpit of the House of the Estates . . . that ' Rome was Babylon ; that the Pope insisted on being worshipped ; that he forbade marriage, as if the conjugal state was in itself sinful and impure ; that it was stated in the Decretals that even if the

---

[1] Raupach, *Erläutertes evangelisches Oesterreich*, i., Beilagen, pp. 149–150.

[2] Wiedemann, ii. 138, 206–207.

Pope did lead thousands of souls into the abyss of hell, nobody had a right to ask why he did so. Becker also, it was said, abused and slandered the regular authorities. Therefore, ' everybody ought to beware of the Pope and his phantasmagoria as of the devil incarnate, and of the papacy as of the kingdom of Antichrist, and no parents should allow their children to be baptised, no papists should be allowed Christian burial, neither should they be chosen as God-parents, nor invited anywhere as guests ; in short, there should be no fellowship whatever with them ; they should be placed outside the pale of civilisation, and prayers should be offered up against them.' [1]   Another Flacian preacher, Joshua Opitz, ' thundered ' more vehemently still in the same house. ' For,' writes his eulogist, Michael Eichler, ' he had been commissioned by God to denounce Pope, Jesuits, monks, priests, nuns, and all the atrocities of the papacy, and all the ungodly ways and all the wickednesses of mankind.'   His numerous listeners thronged from all classes of society, in direct defiance of the imperial injunction that Protestant services were to be held exclusively for the members of the provincial Estates present at congress. The effect on many of his hearers of his anathemas against those who professed a different religion was to rouse them to such a pitch of excitement and fury that ' whenever they came away from listening to his sermons, they were ready to lay violent hands on the papists whom their preacher had just been condemning as idolaters and consigning to the devil.' [2]

[1] Wiedemann, ii. 139–141.
[2] Raupach, *Erläutertes evangelisches Oesterreich*, i. 285. See Eder, *Warnungsschrift an den vierten Stand der Städte und Märkte in*

There were numbers of such ' storming, peace-hating preachers as Becher and Opitz in Austria.' The pastor of Langenlois, for instance, told his congregation that ' the Pope and his followers were altogether diabolical; that the Mass was the devil's phantasmagoria; that it was devilish to receive the Sacrament in one kind only, ' like rats and mice, which only eat and don't drink.' The preacher at Hadres had one only theme for all his sermons: ' All Catholics are devils; whosoever hears Mass and confesses and clings to rites and ceremonies is given up to the devil; the bishop is the devil-in-chief; they must all of them be stabbed to death.' [1]

We find the following acknowledgment from the preacher George Pfinzing, in July 1576: ' In many sermons in the Austrian lands I have heard strange and startling things from the mouths of men who professed to be proclaiming the Gospel. Abuse, curses, maledictions against the papists, in coarse and swinish language such as one hears nowhere else but in taverns, is, so to say, the only food which they set before the people. The shoals of unattached preachers who perambulate the towns and villages, Flacians, Spangenbergists, Osiandrists, or by whatever name they are pleased to call themselves, more than others bring the dear Gospel into lamentable shame and disgrace by their never-ending scolding and reviling, and by their lewd, disreputable behaviour, and they provoke the arm of the law to interfere against them.' Again he says: ' It is all very well to inveigh against the papists,

Oesterreich (Ingoldstadt, 1580), Bl. G²ᵃ. See also Wiedemann, ii. 204, and Huber, pp. 289–290.

[1] Wiedemann, iii. 119, 154. See pp. 136, 146, 150, &c.

but we ought first of all to testify our horror at all the
abominations which numbers of preachers, who boast
that they are proclaiming the pure Gospel, pour into the
ears of the people.' [1]

It was reported, for instance, that at Pirawart, near
Weimar, the pastor and his wife got drunk together,
and quarrelled and fought to such an extent that it
was feared they would kill each other; ' the people of
the parish go about like brute beasts.' In the year
1576, the town council of Weissenkirchen made serious
complaint of the preacher Matthew Rueff, deposing
that ' he and his whole family led the most disgraceful
lives, and were given up to immoderate drinking,
dancing, and fiddle-playing; the father was in the
habit of taking his daughters to bad houses in the company of profligate young men; the mother offered to
sell her daughters for a *thaler.* It is stated, among other
things, in a report of the town council of the year 1577,
' Vice, diabolical superstition, contempt of sermons and
Sacraments, quarrelling, hatred, enmity, gambling,
gorging, drinking, adultery, and prostitution are gaining
the upper hand.' [2]

Andreas Lang, who was appointed preacher first at
Chemnitz, then at Colley in Carinthia, then in Klagen-
furt, and finally at Wülfferstorf in Austria, expressed his
regret, in the year 1576, that the people who had been
Protestantised spoke more favourably of the municipal
and moral condition of things in former times than in the
present. Those who think like this, he said, are ' worldlings.' ' When worldly-minded people look back with
regret at the days of our ancestors and think they were

---

[1] *Von den wahren Feinden des Evangeliums* (1576), G³, H².

[2] Wiedemann, iii. 15–16, 133, 338–339.

better off than we are, it is because in those days wine, corn, meat, fish, and all the necessaries of bodily existence were plentiful, and could be had in abundance for very little money, and not for this reason only but also because [so these 'worldlings' say] in those days people were pious, upright, industrious, friendly, peaceable; not as they are nowadays, knavish, crafty, and cunning.' 'On the other hand, they complain of the present times, that everything is deteriorating, and withal that prices are everywhere rising, and that everybody is growing more wicked. Consequently they look upon us preachers as sinful people, and lay the blame of all that is wrong on the blessed Gospel, saying that since it came into vogue there has been no good anywhere, and that things are growing worse day by day.' That these complaints were justified, Lang by no means denied. 'It certainly is the case,' he confessed with sorrow, 'that at present the majority of people do become worse after adopting the pure teaching of God's Word.'[1]

At first 'everything in matters of religion remained *in statu quo* under Rudolf II.' But the raving and ranting of the Flacian pulpit-demagogues against the 'popish idolaters and blasphemers' led to such excesses among the people that in the interests of public order[2] it was necessary to proceed to serious measures. In Vienna itself, in 1577, a nobleman insulted the officiating priest during divine service in the church of St. Stephen, made use of the foulest language against the women who were praying, and brandished his dagger at a burgher. Two archers who were present joined in these

---

[1] Lang, *Von der Seligkeit* (Frankfurt a. M., 1576), Vorrede, A², pp. 223, 258, 260.

[2] Huber, p. 290.

proceedings, and were on the point of falling on the dean with naked sabres.[1] The following year, on the occasion of the Corpus Christi procession, in which the Emperor, the Archdukes Ernest and Maximilian, and Duke Ferdinand of Bavaria took part, there was such an alarming rising of the people that it became necessary to stop the religious solemnities. In consequence of this disturbance the preacher Opitz, on whom fell ' the brunt of the blame of embittering spirits and belittling the ruling authorities,' was expelled from Vienna with two of his associates. Opitz was compelled to leave the imperial dominions. The two other preachers were allowed to remain in the country, but only on condition that they did not go into any towns or markets under the jurisdiction of the sovereign.[2]

This decree was denounced through the whole of the Empire as ' an atrocious piece of popish tyranny.' Resentment and opposition bordering on insurrection were aroused by Duke Ernest, whom the Emperor had appointed governor of Austria, because he was unwilling to allow the Protestants any privileges beyond those granted them in Maximilian's ' Concession ' and ' Assecuration.' All rights that they had ' unlawfully exercised, over and above these, were to be taken from them.' The two Estates were forbidden ' to admit any besides their own subjects to the Lutheran services; ' the towns and boroughs subject to the sovereign received strict orders to put a stop to Lutheran church-worship, to remove the preachers, and to return to the Catholic religion. The towns and boroughs addressed a petition to the Archduke against this order, and called on the

[1] Wiedemann, ii. 164–165.
[2] v. Aretin, pp. 222–223 ; Wiedemann, ii. 207–208; Huber, p. 291.

two Estates to intercede for them; but they were answered, in January 1579, that the Emperor Maximilian had persistently refused permission to his towns to adopt the Augsburg Confession, and had always rejected the intercession of the two Estates. The towns had themselves to thank for the present interference of the Government; for they had not been content to remain undisturbed in the secret exercise of their faith, but had made wider and wider encroachments, had openly established the service of the new religion, had expelled the Catholic priests and appointed Protestant preachers, had taken possession of the benefices and converted them to the evangelical faith, and had made glaring encroachments on the province of the spiritual Estate.

In this same year 1579 a new code of school regulations was published for Austria. It was thereby decreed that none but Catholic teachers should be appointed, and none but Catholic books used for instruction. The pupils were to be taken to Mass, and to hear sermons regularly on Sundays and feast-days, and to be kept up to observing the fasts; the teachers, before being appointed, were to undergo an oral examination from the Official (judge appointed by the bishop) at Vienna, and the Dean of the theological faculty, and to be presented to the board of magistrates; the schools were to be inspected twice a year by school inspectors appointed *ad hoc*, and reports of their condition were to be drawn up. All harmful and suspicious books were to be removed from the book-shops.[1]

The resolute behaviour of the Government afforded

[1] These regulations were by no means universally carried out. See Huber, pp. 293 f., where also are fuller details respecting Khlesl's labours.

encouragement also to the hitherto 'oppressed and timid order of prelates.' When the other Estates, at the provincial Diet of 1580, had refused to vote any subsidies for the Turkish war unless they first obtained from the Emperor a favourable decision concerning free exercise of religion, the prelates had protected themselves against the setting aside of the governor's proposals on the pretext of a religious discussion by declaring that the urgency of the Turkish question would not allow of much disputation on religion at present. 'Besides which,' they had said, 'religion nowadays is no longer an influence that binds men in united efforts, but it is the cause of most disastrous and pernicious separation and division among the laudable Estates : one of them wants this religion, the other that, the third, fourth, fifth something else, and all have their own different ideas on the subject, so that for many years past it has been impossible to effect any kind of reconciliation or unity. If, however, we are ever to arrive at a common understanding, it must be achieved in some other place, at a different time, and by a different method of procedure ; the Catholics must also be allowed to speak and make known their requirements ; they must be listened to and not contemptuously ignored, as though it were quite the proper thing to pay attention to one side only, and to refuse the opposite party any recognition whatever : not only to oppress, but also to condemn it.' Their ecclesiastical fiefs, they urged, were becoming enormously curtailed, their subjects were forced into strange religions, against their conscience and their duty ; all who attended Catholic worship were punished as evil doers and driven out of house and home. 'Furthermore,' they went on, 'on the strength of the imperial concession the country is filled with all sorts of sectarian preachers, men not of one but of many religions, who most slanderously defame the prelates, and who poison the people with all manner of execrable errors and heresies. May God Almighty forefend that such Babel-like confusion should be dignified with the name of religion and tolerated among Christians!' [1]

In order to put an end to this state of confusion, the existence of which nobody could deny, the two Protestant Estates summoned to their aid the Rostock theologian Lucas Backmeister, and requested him to undertake an inspectoral visitation of all the churches in the land, and to take active measures for an amicable settlement of the Flacian dissensions. On the part of the Government not the slightest hindrance was opposed to the scheme. Archduke Ernest, who asked to be more fully informed on the subject, expressed his approval, saying that the inspectoral visitation had no other object than to establish righteous government, discipline, and unity in the churches of both the Estates.[2]

The hindrances came from another quarter.

At a series of preliminary meetings which had been held in the castle of Horn after March 1580, Backmeister being present, the debates on doctrine and ceremonies had led to so much disagreement and dissension, that before the beginning of the inspectoral visitation, Backmeister had notified to the Estates that ' If it were not that he felt so much pity for this distressed and disordered Church, he should beg for his discharge.' A document was sent up to the assembly at Horn by eleven Flacian preachers, in which they

---

[1] Wiedemann, i. 388-392, and ii. 213-214.
[2] Raupach, *Erläutertes evangelisches Oesterreich*, ii. 13.

threatened all 'prophets of peace' with God's terrible punishments, because the true Church on earth had no business to be in any way at peace, seeing that man was by nature a seed of serpents and a lump of sin.

The inspection 'brought very melancholy circumstances to light.' The majority of the preachers were found to be inexcusably ignorant. Some of them had never even seen the Augsburg Confession, much less read or studied it. Some could not even repeat the *Symbols*; some took care not to show themselves; others formally opposed the inspectors. In consequence of the Church patrons having confiscated the Church property and the foundations, the parsonages and school buildings were on the verge of ruin; the schools themselves had completely collapsed.[1]

At the first preliminary meeting at Horn, it had been proposed to appoint a superintendent and a church council ' in order that the chariot of Israel, which had sunk so deep in the mire, might be drawn out again.' Backmeister had refused to accept the post of superintendent, and the Estates had therefore bestowed the office, in 1582, on the theologian Conrad Becker of Brunswick, who, however, soon after returned to his own home. There was little hope left of establishing any organised Church government in Austria.

The Flacians, backed up by a certain number of the Estates, maintained the upper hand, and kept up in their sermons and writings an uninterrupted fire of invective against all their enemies, denouncing them as papists, sacramentarians, sham Lutherans and peace-brothers. Almost every parish was pitted against another in open combat. For even among the Flacians

---

[1] Raupach, *Erläutertes evangelisches Oesterreich*, iii. 194 ff.

themselves most dreadful dissensions had broken out. Some of them exaggerated their master's teaching by adding to it the statements that ' Original sin derives both from God and the devil ; the devil is the creator of souls. Women in a state of pregnancy carry within them the devil incarnate, for fallen and unregenerate man is a creature of Satan.' Those among the preachers who, ' out of consideration for the people, would not perpetually discuss such subjects in the pulpit,' were denounced by ' the undaunted ' as ' miserable cowards, mercilessly criticised in sermons, and even consigned to the devil.'

One of the chief agents in raising these pulpit-storms was Joachim Magdeburgius. He had previously been preacher at Salzwedel, and had been sentenced to death on the gallows, in 1551, for having defied the Church ordinances of Joachim II. The sentence of death had afterwards been commuted to banishment from the Electorate of Brandenburg.[1] He had first of all taken refuge with Rüdiger of Starhemberg, at Eserding in South Austria, but in 1564 he had been appointed preacher to the German horse-soldiers at Raab by the the General Hans Ruber. In this place, and also in Grafenwerth and elsewhere, he had preached, both verbally and in writing, an ' expanded form of Flacianism.' He taught that the bodies of Christians continue, after death, to be in substance original sin ; that sin and the wrath of God remain in them until the Day of Judgment ; that not till His second coming to awaken and regenerate the mortal bodies of believers will Christ

[1] Raupach, *Presbyterologia*, p. 104. The pass-word of the ' Substantialists ' on meeting was : ' God greet thee, original sin,' and the answer was : ' Original sin thanks you ' (Raupach, *Erläutertes evangelisches Oesterreich.* ii. 130, note).

remove original sin. This doctrine met with staunch
supporters among the Flacians, but also with decided
opponents, and ' fierce contention was carried on
respecting the relation of corpses undergoing decom-
position, and those already decomposed, to justification
and salvation.' One party pronounced the doctrines
of Magdeburgius to be contrary to Scripture, and
declared that they cast odium on the passion and
death of Christ, and were heresies which would undermine the true faith, and called those who accepted these
tenets grave sinners, grave prophets, dead original
sinners, cadaverists, bone polluters, corpse polluters,
midnight ghosts and hobgoblins. The other party
answered that their opponents had no understanding
of Holy Scripture, that they were corpse-lauders, Antinomians, Epicureans, deniers of the imputed righteousness of Christ, repudiators of original sin.[1]

But the fight was not only waged in pamphlets and in
pulpits ; it penetrated also among the people, and led
to sanguinary brawls in streets and in public-houses.
The old-school Flacians, Spangenberg, Opitz, and others,

---

[1] Among others the theologian Christopher Irenæus concentrated
all his ingenuity on demonstrating that · original sin is something living,
rational, intelligent, and ruling, as Paul and Luther show. Since, now,
the soulless body of a believing man is dead, is without reason or understanding, and has no ruling power, this body can neither be, nor be called,
original sin.' ' Original sin exists, lives and commits all other sins,' so
Luther says ; ' but the soulless body has no life, commits no sins, and
therefore cannot be original sin.' He compared a dead body to a disturbed den of robbers. ' Such a den,' he said, ' is no longer a den of
robbers, but only a heap of stones, and just because it was a den of
thieves and in order that henceforth no more robberies should be
committed from it, for that very reason was it destroyed and turned into
a heap of stones.' *Von dem neuen Dogmate der todten Erbsünder und
der seelig im Herrn verstorbenen Leichnamsschender* (1583), A[3a], A[4b],
C[b]; see E[4b]. This pamphlet of Irenæus was celebrated in verse, in a
Latin elegy, by Christianus Gerhardi, exile, on March 25, 1583, H[4b].

who attempted to mediate, were reviled as fools and
heretics, were anathematised, banished, and ' consigned
to the jaws of Satan.' But when matters went to the
length of a preacher actually refusing to administer the
Sacrament to the wife of Rüdiger von Starhemberg,
who was pregnant, unless she acknowledged before the
whole congregation that she was ' sin,' and that she
carried the devil within her, Rüdiger, who for many
years past had been the champion of the Flacians, withdrew his favour from them. Rüdiger thought of
removing the Flacians from his dominions. But ' he
came off badly in consequence, and suffered extreme
disgrace.' The Flacians denounced him as a tyrant, a
persecutor of Christian preachers of pure doctrine, a
champion of unclean, popish, godless, seducing hypocrites, hirelings, and ' accident priests.' Rüdiger's
brother, Gundacar, expelled the preachers from his
territory by force, regardless of the ban which they had
pronounced against him.[1] It was a bitter humiliation
for the Protestant Estates to be reduced to appealing
for help to Archduke Ernest to rid them of the Flacians,
whom they had themselves patronised and encouraged
for so many years, and whom they now described as
' a venomous sect.' [2]

In temporal matters, also, imperial commands met
with no obedience. When Rudolf ordered that Pope
Gregory XIII.'s improved calendar should be adopted
in his hereditary dominions, it was the signal for ' fresh

[1] Concerning the expulsion of the Flacians, see Raupach, *Erläutertes
evangel. Oesterreich*, ii. 130, note; iii. 49 ff. Double supplement, pp. 25 ff.
Presbyterologia, p. 109. *Die neuen Propheten und flacianischen
Schwärmer aus ihren Predigen und Famosschriften gezeichnet* (1584),
pp. 13, 27–35. Wiedemann, i. 392–428.

[2] Wiedemann, i. 426–427.

vehement invective and abuse ' from Protestant pulpits.
Seven preachers of Lower Austria expounded in a
special pamphlet the reasons which prevented their
adopting this ' accursed calendar,' this ' abominable
dragon's tail.' The Pope, they said, was ' proved to be
the Antichrist of Revelation,' and whosoever mixed
himself up with this calendar was guilty of the most
criminal ingratitude to God the Lord. If the Emperor,
or any other secular authority, sanctioned the calendar,
it would be tantamount to ' paying court to the execrable
Antichrist.' No Christians should have any part in
such abominations ; they should remember the terrible
threat in the Apocalypse that ' Those who received the
mark of the Antichrist on their foreheads or on their
hands should be tormented with fire and brimstone in
the presence of the holy angels, and in the presence of
the Lamb.' It is impossible for us to obey the Pope or
the devil—for it is the same thing—even should he
order us to say the Paternoster, or to receive the Sacrament in both kinds, or to do anything else that is in
itself right.' ' It is just as impossible for us to admit
this calendar into our Church, and to remain at the
same time Christians, even though it does not come to
us direct from the Pope, but through his agents, as it
would be to accept something sent from the devil, and
still to call ourselves Christians.' As Doctor Luther has
said in one of his own books : ' Whoever obeys the Pope
cannot be saved ; whosoever wishes to be saved must
shun, flee from, and curse the Pope as though he were the
devil himself.' These words of Luther contained the
highest wisdom and piety, they said. To accept the
calendar would be to incur everlasting damnation.[1]

[1] Wiedemann, i. 438–456. See our fuller statements on the Calendar

Among the people ' everything was out of gear.'
' God's Word is trampled under foot,' the preachers
complained in a pamphlet to the Protestant Estates,
' the Sacraments are despised ; flagrant crimes such as
adultery, usury, oppression and extortion of subjects
and of the poor, increase from day to day, so that things
can scarcely go any further ; ' many of the nobles come
hardly once or twice in the whole year to hear a sermon.[1]
The Protestant nobles in Austria—so Polycarpus Leiser
said in 1580—were divided either by public or private
hostility, they were not even united in their religious
creed, and they were given up to drink and voluptuous-
ness. ' Alas, what a string of complaints I could bring
forward against their intemperance, and the debauchery
of their lives ; they are turning our religion into a
laughing-stock for our adversaries.' ' Profligate living
and the decay of all moral discipline,' the preacher
Hofmar at Horn wrote to Leiser, ' will bring down on
us either the Turkish yoke, or complete annihilation.' [2]

' Things have become altogether chaotic and lawless
among the evangelicals, and as a rule the preachers take
the lead in setting a bad example.' Good, upright
preachers—so David Schweizer, preacher at Schön-
graben, reported—were not to be had in Austria, ' only
drunkards, and grinners and ruffians, who are fit for
nothing, or else dissolute Flacians who deceive everybody.' [3] There was no exaggeration in the statement
of the Catholic Estates that ' the evangelical Estates
have no preachers who expound the doctrine of the
Augsburg Confession purely and correctly ; they appoint

dispute, Vol. 5 (1st–12th edition), pp. 346–356 ; (13th and 14th edition),
pp. 361–375.
[1] Raupach, *Erläutertes evangel. Oesterreich*, iii. 70 ff.
[2] Döllinger, ii. 652.   [3] Raupach, *Zwiefache Zugabe*, p. 74.

a set of ranting agitators, who are not in agreement with any Lutheran community, but who have been expelled on account of godless teaching.' [1]

Consequently, doubts arose among the Protestants themselves as to the possibility of preserving the exercise of the Augsburg Confession intact in Austria. ' Our godless preachers,' said the Baron von Hofmann, a most zealous Protestant, ' will go on till they have caused us to lose all our churches, schools, and pulpits.' [2] In the eighth year of the Emperor Rudolf II., the preacher Haselmeyer gave a description of the distracted state of things among the Austrian Protestants, to Duke Louis of Würtemberg, by whose permission he had accepted a post at Eferding. ' The Flacian sect,' he said, ' give each other the most hateful and scandalous names, but towards the Lutherans they pose as friends, like Pilate and Herod, and call us robbers of God and murderers of souls.' ' In Lower Austria the brood of vipers has taken such deep root that both among the people and among the upper classes the best and the most distinguished persons do not know what to make of it. And whereas, under his late Imperial Majesty's rule, we enjoyed wide tolerance, it is now to be feared that this schism will result in the banishment of the Augsburg Confession, as from Vienna, so from the whole of Austria.' [3]

While the Protestants of Austria were striving ' to restore some slight degree of order, at any rate, in their convulsed Church organisation,' in the Empire also the Protestant princes and theologians ' had recommenced with fresh vigour their oft-repeated attempts at

---

[1] Raupach, *Evangel. Oesterreich,* i. 162.
[2] Hurter, iii. 194.   [3] Raupach, *Zwiefache Zugabe,* pp. 29–31.

unification.' They were now at last determined to
establish ' a uniform code of doctrine' as an ' evangelical
counterpoise to the damnable Conciliabulum of Trent,'
' in order, on the one hand,' said Nicholas Selnekker, ' to
stem the constantly increasing moral depravity among
the evangelical people, and, on the other hand, to fight as
a united band of valiant brothers against the idolatrous
papacy and its fiendish satellites, the Jesuits, with all
their rabble of followers.' [1] It was, therefore, a significant event for Lutheranism that the Prince Elector
Frederic of the Palatinate, who died in October 1576,
and who had been for years past the most zealous
servant and promoter of the Calvinist party of action,
was succeeded by a Lutheran-minded elector. ' Through
the death of Frederic,' Augustus of Saxony wrote,
' the Calvinistics have indeed lost a good man from
their chess-board.' [2]

[1] Quoted in the *Beiträge zur evangelischen Concordie*, pp. 42–43.
[2] Kluckhohn, *Briefe*, ii. 1014, note.

CHAPTER X

SUPPRESSION OF CALVINISM AND RESTORATION OF
LUTHERANISM IN THE PALATINATE—PROTESTANT
REPORTS ON THE MORAL AND RELIGIOUS CONDITION
IN THE SOUTH OF THE EMPIRE

THE Elector Palatine Louis, hitherto governor of the
Upper Palatinate, successor of the Elector Frederic III.,
began his rule in the year 1576 with the openly avowed
object of re-establishing Lutheranism in his land,[1]
regardless of his father's will and testament by which
he was enjoined as a sacred duty to maintain the
existing Church doctrine and organisation. ' Now the
wolves will come down from above' (from the Upper
Palatinate), preached the theologian Olevian at Heidelberg, ' and devour the sheep.' [2] On the entry of the
new Elector into Amberg, all Calvinists who had joined
in the proceedings were ordered off with the intimation
that ' so pious a prince would be dishonoured by their
presence.' [3] All preachers who refused to make public
recantation in church before the whole congregation, of
all the tenets they had hitherto held, were mercilessly
expelled with their wives and children ; all laymen also,
of whatever creeds, if they did not fall in with Lutheranism, were compelled forthwith to leave the country.[4]
The number of ejected preachers and schoolmasters

---

[1] Pressel, *Kurfürst Ludwig*, pp. 5 ff.   [2] Wundt, ii. 125, note 10.
[3] Wittmann, p. 66.   [4] *Ibid.* pp. 67–68.

amounted to 500 or 600.[1] ' The successors of the ejected clergymen '—so the theologian Ursinus informed his friend Crato on June 20, 1577—' are mostly, as I am told, ignorant and immoral men, who flock from all quarters like vúltures on their prey. It has come to this that worthy men no longer wish to take office, but only good-for-nothing fellows whose one thought is to plunder right and left, and to get everything into their own possession : hypocrites, flatterers, harpies, all of them.' [2] In the year 1579 the Elector issued the decree that ' all premeditated sedition and all crafty enticement into damnable heresies and false doctrines, contrary to the Word of God, were to be treated as criminal cases.' [3]

The same sort of complaints that had been uttered by the Lutherans at the time of Frederic III.'s innovations were now made loudly by the Calvinists : ' The changes in religion are robbing the people of all religion.' [4] The result of successive church visitations went to show that among the preachers as well as among the laity there existed an almost incredible amount of ignorance in religious matters ; while the general coarseness and profligacy of language and conduct was so terrible that the reports on the subject are too shocking to reproduce.[5]

[1] See Wundt, ii. 126–129. The clergy of Neustadt wrote, in December 1577, to the town council at Schaffhausen, that over 500 ministers of the Church and schoolmasters had been dismissed (v. Bezold, *Briefe, J. Casimir's*, i. 289, No. 89).

[2] Sudhoff, pp. 426-428. Among the people Calvinism had made very little way. On November 24, 1577, Ursinus wrote to an unnamed friend : ' Nobilitas, præfecti, magistratus, major pars populi sunt nobis infensi, alii neque intelligunt neque curant religionem, pars minima nobiscum gemit et ea, quæ nihil potest ' (v. Bezold, i. 221, No. 8).

[3] Wittmann, p. 67.

[4] Sudhoff, p. 426.

[5] Says Wittmann, who saw the documents, p. 69.

The people had sunk into a state of semi-bestial savage-
ness, ' the result of hearing' nothing but abuse and
malediction in the churches, and because ' all law and
discipline were trodden under foot.'   In an address to
the Estates of the Upper Palatinate in 1577, the Elector
mentioned, among the reasons which entailed considerable additional expenditure, ' the enormous increase of
vice, notwithstanding all the penalties that had been
decreed, the maintenance of the criminals and the law
expenses, incumbent by custom on the lord of the land,
whereby the revenues of the domain were perceptibly
diminished.' [1]   Respecting Amberg, we read in an
official report of 1581 : ' What sort of doings go on
among the burghers is seen by day and by night, for
day and night they sit swilling in taverns and drink-
ing-houses, where you will meet many more people
during sermon-time than in church. Copulation before
marriage is common, and the most shocking wantonness
of behaviour is seen at weddings. Blasphemy of the
name of God has become so habitual among children
and others that it would be no wonder if God were to
open the earth and swallow up such people.' [2]   At
Pfalz-Zweibrücken similar complaints had been loud
for a long time past. ' Diabolical and unchristian
blaspheming, cursing, and swearing,' wrote the lord
of the manor, the Count Palatine Wolfgang,
' are increasing more and more.' It was imperatively
necessary, he said, to enforce the most severe penalties.
Everybody who blasphemed against God, as though He
were not almighty and all just, or against the ever-
blessed Humanity of Christ, and against the divine
Sacraments, must be punished either by death or ' by

[1] Wittmann, p. 70.   [2] *Ibid.* p. 71.

loss of some limb.' 'Curses and oaths, such as were
never heard formerly, and which were too awful to
repeat, had now become quite customary.' This evil
must be met by imprisonment or money fines. The sin
of adultery was 'treated quite lightly and committed
without any shame.' Adulterers must be punished by
imprisonment, and condemned on four successive
Sundays 'to carry the two sinners-stones ('Lastersteine')
which ought to be found hanging outside every church,'
three times round the church. On a second offence
they should be expelled from the country.[1] 'Brotherly
love and pity for the poor,' the preacher Carl Sander
declared in 1577, 'are no longer met with among these
savage, licentious people; beggars loaf about the towns
and villages in hunger and want: verily, under the
papacy there was nothing of this sort to be seen.'[2]

The theologians Olevian and Widebram, who had
been banished from the Palatinate, had found refuge
with Count John of Orange-Nassau, and since 1577 they
had been engaged in establishing Calvinism in his
territory. The movement was begun at Diez, and
initiated by the destruction of the images of Christ and
the Saints; the count himself laid violent hands on a
life-sized gilt statue of Our Lady, of great artistic
value: he struck the statue a blow on the forehead with
his sword.[3] Throughout the whole county of Hadamar,

[1] In [Faber] Stoff, ii. 126–127, 129–133.
[2] *Beiträge zur evangelischen Concordie*, p. 39. See the statements
of the superintendent Culmann Flinsbach in [Faber] Stoff, ii. 51.
[3] Mechtel in the Pagus Loganæ, in Marx, *Gesch. von Trier*, 2ᵇ, 163.
In 1590 the order was issued for the county of Diez that 'the altar-
stones were to be hewn in pieces; all works of idolatry (*i.e.* the images
which the inhabitants had concealed in their houses) were to be dragged
out from their hiding-places under roofs and in cellars and carted off.'
At Ems, in 1599, 'the large stone crucifix in the churchyard had to be

all altars that had been left standing were pulled down,
and the images and pictures were smashed in pieces or
burnt in front of the church.[1] In the year 1572, the
Lutheran church inspectors had complained that the
preachers were despised, and the church goods squan-
dered, and that blasphemy of God was a universal
habit.[2] Matters were not improved by the introduction
of Calvinism. In 1580 the preachers complained as
follows : ' The more we attempt, at the divine bidding,
to root out popish idolatry and all traces of it that are
left in the reformed religion, the more the people shows
its ingratitude to the Holy Evangel by contempt of all
clerical ministrations and all divine service in the form
of preaching and catechising ; so that on the high
festival days there are not even ten people to be seen
in church ; the world is leading a dissolute, bestial,
heathenish existence of drunkenness, profligacy, blaspheming, and profanation of the Gospel.' A decade
and a half later, William Zepper, professor of theology
at Herborn, wrote : ' People of the lowest classes, tailors,
shoemakers, soldiers, idiots of all sorts who have
learnt nothing, are stuck up in the pulpits ; Schwenckfeldians and other heretics, atheists even, and mon-
sters who teach the most abominable errors, start up
in the churches as if from hell ; the poor common

smashed to pieces.' It was decreed at the same time that 'during the
sermons some one was to walk round the church with a stick and prevent
people going to sleep.' Among ' abuses not to be tolerated ' were classed :
' sticking crosses on graves, and the habit of saying of a deceased person :
"God have mercy on his poor soul," for Scripture says nothing whatever
about wishes and prayers on behalf of the dead, and it is not proper to
mix up anything of our own with our prayers ! ' See *Beiträge zur
Nassauischen Reformationsgesch.* in the Mayence *Katholik*, 1886, i.
541-557.

[1] Wagner, i. 255-258.

[2] *Ibid.* i. 238-241.

people are left to fare no better than cattle, whether in life or death.' 'Everyone can see how scandalously the schools are neglected and despised; with what coldness and indifference any still extant studies are pursued; how churches and school-buildings, colleges, hospitals, and sick houses have either already lapsed into ruin or are rapidly approaching it.'[1]

Conditions of this sort were universally complained of in the Southern districts of the Empire. In 1575, for instance, the preacher Christopher Marstaller wrote: 'Under the dispensation of the Holy Gospel the churches are all falling into ruin. Our parents reared these edifices from their foundations upwards, and showed themselves ready to give lavishly towards the building and adornment of temples, and they did not suffer want in consequence; they were blessed with years of plenty, with prosperous days and hours, and with peaceful lives. Nowadays the churches are so ruthlessly plundered by the ruling authorities that it is no longer possible to keep the roofs over them; the rain and the snow pour in at all cracks and corners, and many churches look more like stables for horses than like temples of God.' 'Nowadays we cannot rob the dear Gospel of many chalices in the churches; for they have already, almost all of them, been polished off by the administrators of these same churches. Our forefathers supplied the churches with beautiful, exquisite chasubles of velvet and silk, adorned with pearls and coral, and we now carry off these treasures and convert them into hoods and bodices for our wives. So poor, indeed, have most of the temples become under the sway of the

---

[1] *Zepperi Politia eccl.*, in Grosch, *Vertheidigung wider Arnold*, p. 497.

Gospel, that we cannot even afford to give our ministers a surplice to wear in the pulpit.' As for the ministers themselves, Marstaller goes on, they were very lightly thought of by the evangelical lords and princes. ' When a lord goes out hunting, the parson too, just as though he were one of the jockeys, must be in attendance with his boar-hound, and he must yell and halloo like the rest of them ; yes, the poor pastor and shepherd of souls must play the part of dog-keeper, bellow like a quack dentist, and submit to threats such as : " Parson, if you lose my hound I shall not lose you ! " '

' The vulgar populace, who know and understand as little about the blessed Gospel as a cow does about the dinner hour, cry out : " Ever since Lutheran doctrine has come in, and the new Gospel has been preached, there has been no luck or prosperity, and no good stars have shone since that time ; we have had nothing but war, pestilence, famine, and failure of crops, and one misfortune has followed after the other." ' [1] James Andreä, ' the much-travelled man,' who had been provost and chancellor at Tübingen since the year 1563, was accurately acquainted with the moral and religious conditions among the Protestant people. Although a vehement opponent of the papacy and the Catholic Church, he did not deny that since the preaching of the new doctrine the ancient virtues had disappeared from among the people, and that many vices, formerly unheard of in the nation, had come into vogue. ' In the ranks of the Lutherans,' he preached in the years 1568 and 1569, ' no sort of improvement is perceptible ; they are given up to a dissolute, epicurean, animal existence of eating and drinking, greed and arrogance,

---

[1] *Pfarr- und Pfründebeschneiderteufel* (Ursel, 1575), J. J.[3-5].

and blasphemy of the name of God. The Protestants, like the papists, think they are to go unpunished in their idolatry ; any efforts after strict Christian discipline, such as God has so strongly enjoined in His Word and exacts from all His children, are looked on in the light of a " new papacy " and new " monkery." ' ' We have learnt,' they say, ' that we can only be saved by faith in Jesus Christ, who by His death paid the penalty for all our sins ; we have learnt that we cannot pay the debt with our own fasts, alms, prayers, and other works. Let us, therefore, be content with the work accomplished for us ; we can all be saved by Christ.' And in order that all the world may see that they are not popish, and also that they do not rely on good works, they take care to do nothing good. Instead of fasting, they eat and drink to excess ; instead of alms-giving, they rate and fleece the poor ; instead of praying, they curse, slander, and blaspheme the name of God in a way that even the Turks are not guilty of. Instead of humility they exhibit pride, ostentation, arrogance, extravagance, and extreme immodesty in dress. And all this, forsooth, is to be regarded as evangelical. ' These unhappy people actually persuade themselves that their hearts are full of true faith in God—in a God of mercy—and that they are better than the idolatrous apostolicity-shamming papists.' ' The vices of gluttony and drunkenness,' he goes on to say, ' have increased from day to day. Our dear forefathers, as I have frequently heard the old folk tell, would not suffer drunkards and wine-bibbers to hold any public offices, or to take part in any social gatherings, or to be present at weddings. And, nevertheless, our parents did not enjoy so clear a gospel light as we do ! How,

then, are we going to justify ourselves before God, we
on whom the Lord has allowed His light to shine so
brightly ? ' It was the devil, he said, who was the
chief author of this constantly increasing curse of
drunkenness. ' In so far, however, as man has anything
to do with the spread of the evil, the reason is that as
a rule intemperance is no longer regarded as a disgrace
either by the upper or the lower classes, and that those
who ought to put a stop to it, both by good example
and by stringent punishment, are themselves the worst
offenders. When a Christian fast is mentioned to us
it sounds like an invitation to return to papistry.'
Next to drunkenness came ' the frightful sin of blasphemy against God.' ' This offence is common among
high and low, among women as well as men, among
young and old, and even among little children who can
scarcely speak plainly. Such was not the case in the
days of our forefathers. For oaths and imprecations
such as are quite common nowadays were never even
heard in their time. And if any chanced to be overtaken by this sin—in far less measure even than is
usual nowadays—the transgressors were sent to prison
and tortured.'

' Since the revelation of the Antichrist, epicurean
living prevails under the name of the Holy Gospel ; for
while with their lips men magnify the Gospel and the
truth, in their actions they contradict and oppose these
with all their might, as though their one aim and object
were, not to follow after piety, uprightness, chastity,
temperance, faith, and Christian love, but to act in
direct opposition to all these virtues, and to abandon
themselves to all manner of wantonness. With all
of us, alas, it has come to this, that, to our perdition,

we have one and all set ourselves up as prophets. For whenever two or three of us come together and lament over the sad state of the world, especially of our own Germany, we say all at once : It can last no longer, it must break, for things have come to a climax ; the fear of God, faith, and faithfulness have gone from the people, injustice has the upper hand ; we are bound to be punished—there is no other way out of it.' [1]

Andreä saw the chief cause of the increasing corruption in ' the contentions and religious divisions among the evangelicals of the dear Fatherland,' in ' the abusive vociferations which evangelical theologians and preachers hurled at each other,' ' in consequence of which the people were perplexed and bewildered and hardly knew what they ought to believe.' He represented to the Prince of Anhalt, in 1570, that the Protestant churches were all in turn cried down, far and wide, by calumniators in their own bosoms, and that they were bringing on themselves the reproach that there were scarcely a couple of preachers among them who did not disagree about some article or other of the Augsburg Confession. Andreä was indefatigable in his endeavours to bring about unification, and with a view to this he altered his own theological position. Immediately after the convention of Zerbst [2] he had broken with the Wittenberg ' Philipists,' and he now considered Melanchthon's code of doctrine, which he had formerly declared to be quite orthodox, ' stained with a multitude of heresies.' In a course of six sermons published in 1573, he held up Luther's Catechism as a standard for all

---

[1] *Erinnerung nach dem Lauf der Planeten gestellt* (Tübingen, 1568), pp. 22, 49, 140, 146, 181, 191, 202. *Dreizehn Predigten vom Türken* (Tübingen, 1569), pp. 106 ff. Cf. Döllinger, ii. 375-378.

[2] See above, p. 172 f.

disputed points of belief, and denounced all doctrines opposed to this code as undoubted heresies. At the wish of Martin Chemnitz, with whom he had again become associated, he published these sermons in the form of doctrinal articles under the title of ' Schwäbische Concordie.' He gained the interest of Duke Julius of Brunswick in this matter, and through the efforts of the Duke combined with the support of Chemnitz a ' union of the Suabian and Nether-Saxon Churches ' was accomplished.[1]

The reintroduction of Lutheranism in the Palatinate was looked upon as ' an event ordained by God for the accomplishment of universal concord.' Under the rule of the Elector Louis, the religious feud of so many years' standing between the Palatine electors and the electors of Saxony came at last to an end, and Louis and the Elector Augustus ' trod side by side the same pathway with the same ardent enthusiasm for the true faith.' In conjunction with the Elector of Brandenburg they directed their whole energy and activity against Calvinism, and they laboured zealously to ' bind all the adherents of the Protestant religion in one body by means of a new code of belief.'

Augustus became ' the foremost patron and manager of this scheme,' but Andreä was ' the true spiritual father of the " Concord." '

[1] See Döllinger, ii. 379-380. Heppe, Gesch. des Protestantismus, iii. 9-73.

CHAPTER XI

FRESH EFFORTS AT UNIFICATION AMONG THE PRO-
TESTANTS—THE TORGAU AND THE BERGEN BOOKS
—FRIENDS AND OPPONENTS OF THE CONCORD FORMULA
OF 1580

'THOUGH all rulers must shrink,' wrote the Elector
Augustus of Saxony, in November 1575, to his confidential councillor, 'from mixing themselves up with
the tangled web of theological disputes,' he nevertheless feared that, as there was no Pope among those
dissentient divines, the quarrels would only grow worse
and worse if sovereign authority did not assert itself
in all directions. As there was no longer any room
for hope that the theologians, left to themselves, would
come to any agreement, or even compromise, at a
colloquy or a convention, or that they would even
listen quietly to each other's arguments, it had occurred
to him (Augustus) that it would be well to convene an
assembly of the Estates of the Augsburg Confession,
and that each sovereign lord should bring with him to
the meeting his own code of doctrine. From all these
different formulas they would then, with the help of
a few amicable theologians and political councillors,
construct a general code which should be printed, and
should be considered binding on the whole body of
preachers.[1] Augustus was of opinion that there was

---

[1] Hutter, pp. 271-273. See Planck, vi. 437-438.

more chance now than of old, that a convention of
princes might have beneficial results as regards the
healing of dissensions because 'Flacius and other
cantankerous theologians were dead, and the rest of
them had worn themselves out with scolding and
scribbling.' [1]

He intended to establish ' peace once for all through
his princely dictum ; ' for it grieved him sorely, he
wrote to the Landgrave William of Hesse, that God
' had let the devil go unbridled to kick up one disturbance after another.' [2]

At the instigation of the Elector a convention was
held at Torgau in June 1576, and, in addition to twelve
theologians of the electorate of Saxony, the following
five foreign ones were also present : James Andreä,
Martin Chemnitz, David Chyträus, Andreas Musculus,
and Wolfgang Körner.   The Saxon theologians, some of
them the same men who had formerly been champions
and patrons of the school of Melanchthon, had already
in February declared themselves against Melanchthon's
Corpus—which had become the established creed of
Saxony—and against the Dresden Consens, and had
expressed themselves in favour of the sole authority
of Luther's creed.   At the convention of Torgau a
new Formula of Concord called the ' Torgau Book '
was now drawn up, and in this, as Chemnitz
boasted, ' the memory of Melanchthon was wholly
obliterated.' [3]

The whole of the Torgau work, Andreä wrote to

[1] Despatch to William of Hesse, dated Dec. 19, 1575, in Heppe,
Gesch. des Protestantismus, iii. 325-329.

[2] Heppe, ii. Beil. p. 110.

[3] Heppe, Gesch. des Protestantismus, iii. 111, 116.

Hesshus and Wigand on July 24, was compiled in the spirit of Luther, which was the spirit of Christ.[1]

Andreä went to Wittenberg in the official character of visiting inspector of the electorate of Saxony, and in an address to the Senate of the university he declared that ' the Christ who was omnipresent both in His humanity and in His divinity, had chosen him as an instrument for the restoration of the pure doctrine.' Against Melanchthon he uttered all manner of calumnies in private conversation.

All opponents of Christ's ubiquity were in his eyes ' stiffnecked heretics, with whom the ruling authorities should have recourse to strong measures.' A fierce conflict arose between him and Lucas Major, the superintendent at Halle. Andreä asserted that everybody who would not allow that ' the human nature of Christ is omnipotent and omnipresent ' must be regarded as a Calvinist : ' The Turkish Alcoran teaches more truly concerning Christ than such preachers ; we are bound to believe that Christ in His human nature is present in every stone, plant, and rope.' Major retorted angrily that ' Christ must be sought for in His words and sacraments, and not in ropes and stones ; thieves and

---

[1] ' Nihil hic fucatum, nihil palliatum, nihil tectum est, sed juxta spiritum Lutheri, qui Christi est, candide, aperte, pie, sancte ad veritatis illustrationem et propagationem omnia geruntur ' (Heppe, iii. 111, note). According to a report of the theologian Nicholas Selnekker, Andreä said of Chemnitz that he ought not to be retained in Saxony, for he was ' black and false and he would bring Hesshus and all the Flacians into the land.' Selnekker writes : ' Andreä did nothing but rail against Chemnitz, and yet all the while he addressed to him the most flattering language, which seemed to me very strange.' Chemnitz, on his part, said of Andreä : ' He did not see what good this man was likely to do. If I say what I conscientiously think, it would be best to send him home again ; we shall have no peace and unity otherwise ' (Pressel, *Andreä*, pp. 239, 240, 241, 248).

rogues who ought to be in ropes may seek him there :
he was not going to let himself be caught by Andreä,
who himself, formerly, had taught and subscribed to
a very different doctrine on ubiquity. He hoped that
the signatures demanded for the new book might produce better fruits than former visitations and sub-
scriptions to articles : in Thuringia alone he had already
witnessed five similar attempts, each one of which had
in turn undone the work of the foregoing one. From
none of them had any good resulted, and the inspectors
had been driven out of the land.' [1]

The Torgau Book met with full recognition in
Würtemberg, Baden, Brunswick, Brandenburg, Mecklenburg, and in the towns of Lübeck, Hamburg, and
Lüneburg. The ministers of these three towns insisted
that this new formula must be imposed on all teachers
by public State authority, and that one and all of them
must be required to assent to it in plain, unequivocal
language. Anyone who should attempt to evade it by
subterfuges and artifices must be treated as a base turn-
coat, and, without respect of person, be dismissed from
his office. In concert with the opinions of the Bruns-
wickers they demanded that no theological pamphlets
be henceforth printed without censorship ; further,
that no bookseller should be allowed freedom to introduce all sorts of foreign publications among the people.
To prevent such an occurrence proper superintendents
should be placed over the book-shops.

The Prussian theologians also assented to the Torgau
Book and denounced Melanchthon, openly and unreservedly, as a heretic and a misleader of the people.

On the other hand, the Pomeranian theologians

---

[1] Heppe, *Gesch. des Protestantismus*, iv. Beil. pp. 50–59.

rejected the book, and would by no means consent to accept all Luther's writings as authorised doctrine. Of the three Dukes of Holstein, two refused to pledge themselves to the new formula of faith. The theologians of Anhalt made objections of various kinds. From the large number of different sentences pronounced on errors and heresies in the Torgau Book, they wrote, the enemies would be able to make out triumphantly that ' in the course of forty-seven years the Protestants had split up into at least a hundred different sects.' ' Let them beware,' they said, ' of covetous, unhallowed, sacerdotal strife, and not uncover their own shame before their enemies.' [1] It was both dangerous and disgraceful, Joachim Ernest, Prince of Anhalt, wrote to Andreä on March 23, 1577, to set up so many new creeds, and ' to be always inventing fresh equivocal, ambiguous, pliable phrases, many of them repugnant and unheard of : this sort of thing not only served to strengthen the hands of the enemy, but also brought ruin on the churches and schools.' ' If discord arose out of this so-called work of concord, and persecution followed, the originators of the work would alone be responsible for the mischief.' [2] In Andreä's conversations with the Anhalt clergy, Joachim Ernest wrote to the Landgrave William of Hesse, ' all manner of things were said which we should be ashamed to write.' [3]

In Hesse also the Torgau Book met with opposition. Of the three Landgraves with whom Andreä negotiated concerning the adoption of the book at Ziegenhain, the Landgrave William was especially zealous in the pursuit of theological matters.

At a discussion on the doctrine of the Sacrament

---

[1] Heppe, iii. 139 ff.   [2] *Ibid.* iii. 186–187.   [3] *Ibid.* iii. 188, note.

of the Lord's Supper he once called on his four-year-old
boy Maurice to give his opinion also. 'Whereupon
the infant lord,' Andreä wrote to the Elector Augustus
on August 8, 1576, 'said : "I advise that we should
abide by the letter in the Word." When at the evening
meal the Landgrave related how Maurice had said that
they ought to abide by the Word, the little lordling
corrected his father and said : "No, I said : *in* the
Word." ' 'This verily,' Andreä remarks, 'did not
happen by accident, and without doubt this little child
was set in the midst, as in Matthew xviii., to teach that
we should hold to the simple Word.'

At a synod called together by the Landgrave at
Cassel for consultation over the Torgau Book, the
Superintendent Meier, among others, remarked emphatically that a long time ago the Elector of Saxony had
caused the Augsburg Confession and several pamphlets
of Melanchthon to be published as an authoritative
code of doctrine, and that the theologians of Jena had
also brought out a separate code.[1] If the Torgau Book
was also to be regarded as a 'Corpus,' it would seem
as if they were to have a fresh creed every day. Moreover, in the Torgau Book Luther's private and controversial writings were both printed as authoritative
doctrine, whereas none but public writings 'published
in the name of the whole Church could by right belong
to it.'[2] 'Everybody knew '—so the synod declared—
'that Luther's writings exhibited differences of opinion,
that others besides the papists had produced evidence
against us from these writings.' Luther's small Cate-

---

[1] Commonly called Corpus Thuringicum, of the year 1571. Walch,
Religionsstreitigkeiten der evangel.-lutherischen Kirche, v. 65.
[2] Heppe, *Generalsynoden*, i. 198-218.

chism was the only volume of his that ought to be
considered authoritative; the writings of Melanchthon
and the amended Augsburg Confession must not be
rejected; the way might be prepared for a Christian
reconciliation with the Calvinists.[1]

The Saxon court theologians were very angry at
this verdict on the Torgau Book, which was communicated to them by the Elector Augustus. They begged
the Elector to admonish the Landgraves of Hesse to
keep better watch over the proceedings of their theologians; the altered version of the Augsburg Confession
was a falsification of the genuine one; those who did
not publicly denounce the Calvinists as slanderers of
the Sacrament had better 'take care that they were
not themselves reckoned among the blasphemers who
called the Sacrament a piece of cyclopean flesh-eating,
an excrement of Satan.'[2]

On the other hand the Landgrave William declared
most positively that he would not suffer the doctrine
of ubiquity to be taught at the university of Marburg.
'I cannot see,' he wrote, 'how it can be an honour to
Christ, as some seem to think, to believe that He is also
corporeally present in the devil; likewise, that hell is
contained in God, and that Heaven—namely, the abode of
the blessed—has no fixed locality, and has not yet been
created by God, and whatever other propositions follow
from this absurdity. We are not aware that there has
ever been a demon in hell audacious enough to advance
such a theory as this.'[3] 'The whole body of evangelical
doctrine,' William had already before written to Andreä,

---

[1] In Hospinian, cap. xii. 65-68ᵇ.
[2] Heppe, *Generalsynoden*, i. Urk. pp. 30-54.
[3] *Ibid.* pp. 75-78. See Müller, *Denkwürdigkeiten*, ii. 417-420.

' is made contemptible and hateful in the ears and the hearts both of sovereigns and people, because almost every theologian presumes to correct the writings of the others and to condemn them on his own private authority.' [1]

In consequence of the adverse judgments pronounced against the Torgau Book in different directions, the Elector Augustus, in March 1577, summoned a fresh convention in the monastery of Bergen near Magdeburg. Andreä, Chemnitz, and Selnekker took part in this, and later on also Chyträus, Musculus, and Körner. Many alterations in the Torgau Book were proposed at this meeting, especially in the article on original sin and free-will.

Concord did not reign among the ' Bergen Fathers.' ' Many people,' Chyträus wrote later on to Marbach, ' compare these wretched, discordant colleagues of Bergen to the Aristotelian company of eight robbers. In order to arrive at unanimity, first of all, four of them slew the other four ; then, out of the surviving four, two slew the other two ; and finally out of the two, one slew the other. And thus unity was established.' [2]

The authority of Andreä was decisive in determining the adoption of the Torgau Book, which, under the title of ' Formula of Concord,' was now to become a theological law-book for all the Protestant churches.[3] The

---

[1] Calinich, *Kampf*, pp. 305–310.

[2] Planck, vi. 547.

[3] Selnekker asserted that Andreä himself was not satisfied with the book: 'On Dec. 6, 1577,' he says, ' Andreä argued angrily with me at Leipsic *de communicatione idiomatum*, and with sneers and laughter twitted me and Chemnitius with not rightly understanding what it was. Old Dr. Musculus, he said, is but so and so—a man to whom I could prove that Barthel [Bartholomew] is a cow's name ; but I must handle

idea, originally contemplated, of summoning a general evangelical synod for the formal adoption of the book, was given up because Chemnitz predicted that ' nothing but schism and confusion in the work' would be the result of such a step. The princes, he said, ought to ' demand, and take down categorically, the signatures of all preachers and school officials.' [1]

The commissioners appointed to collect the signatures in the electorate and in the duchy of Saxony were the three ' genuine supporters' of the book, Andreä, Selnekker, and Polycarpus Leiser, who, on Andreä's recommendation, had been nominated superintendent at Wittenberg. The superintendents, preachers, and school teachers were all summoned to assemble at stated places ; ' Not one of them,' Andreä said, ' was allowed to give his signature in private ; all had to be done under the open sky, in the same way that the *Landsknechts* are reviewed.' Not one of them was ignorant of the means by which the Elector ' was wont to cleanse

him carefully. Among other things he said : " Do you think that I am satisfied with this Formula of Concord ? It was Chemnitius who introduced into it the *tria genera communicationis de persona Christi* ; this, however, was done against my wishes, and in my opinion what stands in the book is not a correct statement of truth." To which I answered : " Lord God, what do you mean ? All the way here you have done nothing but declare that there was not a letter in the book which had not been weighed in the balance, and that if you had ever taught or written anything that was opposed to this book, or ever did so in the future, you wished it to be condemned and cursed through all eternity." Then he became alarmed, and answered that he would discuss the matter with Chemnitius in my presence ' (Pressel, *Andreä*, pp. 245–246). Chyträus refused to be classed among the composers of the Formula of Concord. He wrote : '*Nihil enim omnium quæ a me dicta, acta aut scripta essent, Jacobus Andreæ Aristarchus noster probabat, ita ut ne verbum quidem a me scriptum libro Concordiæ insit*' (*Chytræi epp.* p. 873).

[1] Bertram, *Evangel.* Lüneburg, Beil. p. 365. Heppe, *Gesch. des Protestantismus*, iii. 205 ff.

the Church from all the vermin that refused to be converted;' of the manner in which he had proceeded first against the Flacians, then against the crypto-calvinists; or of Peucer's tortures in prison.

The companies assembled to inscribe their signatures were informed by the commissioners that the 'Corpus' of Melanchthon, which had till then been the authoritative code of doctrine for Saxony, was now entirely superseded; for in many of its articles it was quite false, and it served merely as a mantle for Sacramentarians and other factions. It had happened with Melanchthon as with King Solomon, who also at first had written good books, but had later on established idolatry and false doctrine.

The Book of Concord alone contained the true doctrine.

They were told that they were all in duty bound to subscribe to it, and not with their hands only, but also with their hearts, or they might come to share the fate of certain 'doctors' of Wittenberg and Leipzic, some of whom had had to escape with evil consciences, while others had been sent into perpetual exile. They were advised to take special warning by the death of Doctor Stössel, who had simply succumbed to despair—to such despair as had overtaken Cain and Judas.'[1]

---

[1] Heppe, iii. 219–223. The commissioners of the electorate of Saxony were not on friendly terms with each other. Selnekker complained that Andreä, after a disputation, called out after him: 'You damned rascal, you good-for-nothing scoundrel, you arch-villain, you hellish thief,' &c. The next morning Andreä declared that he had been speaking to his servant. 'I was obliged,' Selnekker said, 'to let the matter rest there. Afterwards, at table, he began such a scene with Dr. Maximilian Mörlin that I got up and went away; but Dr. Maximilian wept bitterly and lamented over the condition of the churches, which was being aggravated by Dr. James.' 'On Sept. 17, 1577, at Berlin, Andreä, in the

The commissioners for the electorate of Brandenburg encountered great opposition in the course of
collecting signatures.

The preachers of the Neumark thought it strange
that so many academies and churches in Germany
should have been passed over, and the settlement of the
disputed questions left to six theologians, some of whom
had formerly been champions of the doctrines they
now rejected : this nominal concord would only serve,
they said, to augment schism and confusion. Numbers
of the Brandenburg pastors expressed their disapproval
of the articles on original sin and free-will in the Book
of Bergen. Musculus could only obtain the signatures
of these men by promising them that he would make
the Elector acquainted with the objections they had to
the book.[1]

In some districts, however, the work of collecting

presence of distinguished councillors from the electorate of Brandenburg,
in prandio, spoke ill of the Consistory, and said that no theologian ought to
have anything to do with matrimonial matters; that a theologian, after
dealing for two years with such matters in the Consistory, was fitted to be a
brothel-keeper.' 'Mense Novembri 1578: The way things go on in the
Synod at Dresden is heart-breaking. God preserve me and all lovers of
peace from a synod in which Doctor James rules supreme and lays down
the law for dead and living, great and small, not even sparing our dear
sovereign lord. . I know nobody in these lands (with but one sole
exception) of whom he thinks well, and yet from his talk you would
imagine just the opposite, and swear that he means all he says truly
and sincerely; but it all goes for nothing. Virtutes ipsius: Wantonness,
avarice, ambition, duplicity, insolence, vindictiveness, hypocrisy, fair words
and false faith, contempt of all others ' (Pressel, *Andreä,* pp. 244–247).
Andreä, on the other hand, complained of Selnekker's diabolical tricks.
He said that this Saxon theologian, and others also, would be delighted to
see him, the Suabian, hanging on the gallows (Döllinger, ii. 337–338). The
university of Wittenberg deteriorated greatly in consequence of these
religious controversies. On Sept. 14, Paul Franz wrote thence to
Hieronymus Schaller : ' Status scholæ et civium est tristissimus. Auditoria
ubique vacua,' &c. (In Riederer, i. 367 ; see i. 244.)

[1] Heppe, iii. 246-247.

signatures went on smoothly, as in the duchies of Würtemberg, Brunswick, and Mecklenburg, and in the towns of Nether-Saxony, with the exception of Bremen, whose citizens would not submit to the prescriptions of men 'who had set up certain dogmas and paradoxa on their own authority after the manner of Roman Prætors and Dictators.' [1]

'In a considerable number of places the signatures were extorted by measures of force.' This was the case in Anspach, where the Margrave George Frederic threatened all obstreperous persons with merciless compulsion. At Kitzingen he would not even accede to the request of the assembled chapter ' to be allowed to look through the Book of Bergen once more after it had been read out to them.' Those who had asked this favour ' fell under no slight suspicion of Calvinism.' ' So then,' we read in a report, ' all of them gave their signatures without further parleying or opposition. If any one of them had persisted in refusing, he would forthwith have been stigmatised as a Calvinist and expelled from the country with his wife and children. But where in these times could anyone have taken refuge ? ' [2]

Flacianism was hunted down as mercilessly as Calvinism. Even the mother of the Margrave was accused of being a ' Flacian woman.' [3]

Count John of Oldenburg also followed the Margrave's plan, and gave out that all persons who refused to subscribe to the Bergen formulary of faith, approved by him, would not be tolerated any longer in the land. [4]

---

[1] Pressel, *Kurfürst Ludwig*, pp. 43 ff.   Heppe, iii. 252.
[2] Heppe, iii. 252–254.   [3] Lang, *Baireuth*, iii. 378.
[4] Heppe, *Gesch. des Protestantismus*, iii. 255.

At Magdeburg the book was first of all rejected, but afterwards accepted, owing to the influence brought to bear by Duke Julius of Brunswick.

The theologians of the Count Palatine, John of Pfalz-Zweibrücken, decided, in August 1577, that the Book of Bergen was in accordance with Scripture, and declared their resolution to ' stand firmly by it till their death.' In July 1578, however, at a fresh convention, they flatly repudiated it. In Pfalz-Neuburg the preachers signed because the Count Palatine, Philip Louis, required them to do so, and because the Superintendent Tettelbach assured them that ' the book was compiled exactly in the style of Melanchthon.' [1]

The Elector Palatine Louis, although a zealous Lutheran, would not accept the new formulary of faith at once, because he did not agree with its doctrine on the Sacrament and on the person of Christ, and he also wished for alterations in other points. ' We fail to see,' he wrote on October 17, 1577, to the Electors of Saxony and Brandenburg, ' with what semblance of reason or justice we princes and Estates can be expected to subscribe to this Book of Bergen, when the above-mentioned points have not been altered in accordance with our opinions.' [2]

William of Hesse adhered ' doggedly to the determination to do everything to oppose the Torgau Book, and its altered version, the Bergen code of belief, and all tyrannical imposition of creeds.'

Through the doctrine of ubiquity and the terrible deductions following from it, ' the simple, ignorant laity,' he wrote to the Elector Augustus of Saxony, ' were likely

---

[1] Heppe, iii. 256-271.
[2] Pressel, *Kurfürst Ludwig*, pp. 36-38.   Heppe, iii. 263-266.

to end in complete atheism.'[1] He drew up a long
catalogue of ' contradictory opinions of Luther on the
Sacrament' in proof that appeal could not be made to
the latter in respect of this doctrine.[2]

Prince Joachim Ernest of Anhalt caused it to be made
known by his theologians that ' The Book of Bergen, with
its rambling diffuseness and hopeless perplexities, was not
a means to peace, but a new apple of discord, by which
old, extinct quarrels would be revived. Andreä had
stolen into these lands like a wily fox, and his feminine,
wanton inconstancy had acquired world-wide notoriety.
For a long time past he had been ingratiating himself
first with one side, then with the other : formerly he had
declared with unction that all that he did was done for
the honour and glory of Melanchthon, for whose Corpus
he was ready to die ; and now he was decrying Melanchthon openly as an idolatrous Solomon.'[3]

At a colloquy held at Herzberg in August 1578 on
the subject of the Book of Bergen, between the theologians of the electorates of Saxony and Brandenburg,
Melanchthon was stigmatised as the principal author
of all heresies, and Andreas Musculus moved a resolution that his corpse should be disinterred and burned
with his writings.[4] The result of this colloquy was
still wider estrangement between the dissentient parties.[5]

---

[1] Feb. 3, 1577, in Heppe, *Generalsynoden*, i. *Urkunden*, p. 81. See
William's letter to the court preacher of the Elector of Saxony, Martin
Mirus, of Aug. 13, 1577, in Pressel, *Kurfürst Ludwig*, p. 59.

[2] Heppe, *Gesch. des Protestantismus*, iii. 271–290.

[3] Pressel, *Kurfürst Ludwig*, pp. 69–71. Heppe, *Geschichte des Protestantismus*, iii. 292–299. See H. Duncker, *Anhalts Bekenntnissstand
während der Vereinigung der Fürstenthümer unter Joachim Ernst und
Johann Georg* (Dessau, 1892), pp. 10 f.

[4] Thus wrote Paul Franz to Hieronymus Schaller, according to the
report ' of a thoroughly trustworthy man,' on Sept. 11, 1578.

[5] Beckmann, ii. 117; Salig, i. 499. Pressel, *Kurfürst Ludwig*,

It came to the knowledge of the Elector of Saxony that Joachim Ernest of Anhalt was denouncing him to other princes as ' a Mameluke who had apostatised from the true religion of the Augsburg Confession and had adopted new, erroneous doctrine.' He accordingly threatened the princes, on June 26, 1579, that if he was not in future spared such attacks on his honour, he should find himself compelled to take steps ' which might result in very scant friendship between them.' [1]

After lengthy negotiations the theologians succeeded in persuading the Elector Palatine Louis to sign the Book of Bergen. This result was achieved by means of a ' preface ' in which the points which Louis objected to were ' modified or altered.' The attempt to win over Joachim Ernest on the strength of this preface proved a failure. To the prince's question, ' Why the alterations suggested by him were not made in the book itself ? ' Andreä answered : ' The only place where anything could be added to or eliminated from the book was the preface ; the body of the work must not be touched, for in this the theologians were the spokesmen ; but in the preface, which was the utterance of the princes, anything which the latter considered desirable might be introduced.' ' By which we are to understand,' wrote Joachim Ernest to William of Hesse on November 16, 1579, ' that the theologians cannot err, and that they will not allow anything they have said to be corrected ; but that what the princes say is not of so much importance.' [2]

The Landgrave William at the time had just

pp. 268–284. Concerning the transactions at Herzberg, H. Moller wrote to J. Monau on Sept. 22, 1578 : ' *Res tota magnis clamoribus acta est septem quibus convenerunt diebus* ' (Gillet, *Crato*, ii. 222, note 26).

[1] Heppe, iv. 125.   [2] *Ibid.*

' vehemently declined to recognise the preface.' In October 1579 an influential deputation from the Electors of Saxony, Brandenburg, and the Palatinate had come to Cassel for the purpose of obtaining William's signature. The envoys agreed with the Landgrave that it was certainly most desirable that all subtle points of controversy should be put aside, and that the Holy Scriptures should be recognised in the Formula of Concord as the sole standard of doctrine. When William asked, ' Why then did they not alter the Formula in this sense ? ' the chancellor of the Elector of Saxony, Haubold of Einsiedel, and Diestelmeyer, the chancellor of the Elector of Brandenburg, answered that the book had already been signed by so many Estates and Churches that no further alterations must be made in it. On the Landgrave's asking further, if they did not think it would be time and money well spent to send round the book in an amended form ? the answer was : ' It was to be feared that if this were done most of the Estates would refuse to sign. The Landgrave stuck to the statement that the Book of Bergen deviated from the true faith : he had grown too old to learn a new religion, and he was not going to let himself be led astray by two or three all too sapient priests ; he challenged them to show him where, in the Scriptures, it was said that the body of Christ was not in Heaven, that the Virgin Mary did not bring forth like another woman, that the human nature of Christ was omnipresent. ' Such statements as these were all new-fangled dogmas, however much they might smear and daub them over with Luther's excrements.'

' Before and at dinner,' the envoys reported, ' William rated the parsons who set the lords by the ears, and of

Luther he said: "Luther had written contradictory things in the other pamphlet; the poor old spoon-bill goose had not known what it was penning." '[1]

'I verily believe,' William declared to the Elector Palatine on October 19, 'that if the book is published with the *Grillomatibus* (eccentricities), as it stands now, it will not only be the ruin of peace in church and religion, but also in politics and affairs generally; and the distortion of the important article on the person of Christ, which is the groundwork of the Christian faith, and in which we have always been at one with the papists, will give the latter good reason for denouncing the Pacification of Augsburg.'[2]

Besides the Landgrave William and the Prince Joachim Ernest of Anhalt, many others refused their

---

[1] Report of the ambassadors of October 30, 1579, in Hutter, pp. 215–216. See Heppe, *Gesch. des Protestantismus*, iv. 142.

[2] Pressel, *Kurfürst Ludwig*, p. 474. For the language in which the Landgrave and Andreä mutually condemned each other, cp. Pressel, p. 508; Heppe, iv. 258, note; cp. also Heppe, *Kirchengeschichte*, i. 409 ff.; Pressel, *Andreä*, p. 247. As reasons for the withdrawal of William and of Prince Joachim Ernest of Anhalt, Andreä stated to the Elector Augustus: 1, Both of them retained heretical teachers near them; 2, 'Both persist in this wrong course because they maintain that each of them has the *donum dijudicandi spiritus* and the *donum prophetiæ*, in which idea both are egregiously mistaken; for the Holy Ghost not only distinguished between gifts of this sort, but also gave them in different measure to different people, so that inequality of this sort is found even among our teachers; and for this reason prophet must be subject to prophet, and one must give way before the other when he sees that the other speaks with greater weight' (Pressel, *Kurfürst Ludwig*, p. 497). The Elector Augustus also consulted his puncture-books in October 1579, and asked: 'What is it that keeps the Landgrave William back from agreeing with us in the work of concord?' From the figures he made out the answer: 'Nobody else holds him back from us but wicked, false, dishonest people, and his own crack-brained head, by which, however, few people let themselves be guided; and, besides this, the demon of pride tempts him with the notion that he ought not to be guided by other people' (Richter, *Die Punctir-bücher*, p. 29).

adhesion to the Book of Bergen and its preface : the three Hessian Landgraves, Louis, Philip, and George; the three Palatine Counts, John Casimir of Neustadt and Lautern, John of Zweibrücken, and Richard of Simmern ; and the two Dukes, Hans Friedrich and Ernest Ludwig of Pommern-Stettin. In Holstein the Superintendent-General, Paul von Eitzen, in the name of the clergy of the place, made the following declaration to the Elector of Saxony :

' We have reason to thank the good God that three years ago we promptly and plainly refused to subscribe to the Torgau Book. For had we then let ourselves be drawn into signing this book, and had afterwards seen how much the authors themselves corrected in it— even wiping out nine and twenty whole pages—before the Book or Bergen was concocted out of it, we should verily not have had much to boast of in our consciences.'

Among other things, von Eitzen pointed out that the teaching of the Torgau Book in the article on good works had been correct, whereas in the Book of Bergen this point of doctrine had been explained away and set aside. On the other hand, the Book of Bergen had omitted two flagrant errors contained in the Torgau Book concerning the Sacrament, the statements, namely, that ungodly communicants could also be recipients of the Spirit of Christ, and that Heaven had no fixed locality ; to set against this, however, Pelagian and Manichean errors had been introduced into the article on original sin.[1]

The numerous opponents of the Book of Bergen received an unexpected addition to their numbers in the person of Duke Julius of Brunswick, ' the actual

[1] Pressel, *Kurfürst Ludwig*, pp. 504-509.

originator of the *Concord,* who had devoted endless
time and trouble to correspondence, negotiations, and
journeyings on its behalf,' besides having spent more
than 54,000 thalers in the cause.[1] As lately as August
1577 he had required his preachers and schoolmasters
to sign the Formula of Concord, and on April 23, 1578,
during the fruitless negotiations with Hesse, he had
written to Chemnitz : ' Let who will among the Electors
and princes bend or break, cool down, or desert as
regards the Formula of Concord, I cannot feel any
alarm, for God is powerful enough to manage His own
work.' [2]

' A dreadful incident,' however, did before long
occur.

Henry Julius, the Duke's eldest son, born in 1564,
had, in the lifetime of his grandfather, the Catholic
Duke Henry, been elected Bishop of Halberstadt, on
condition that he was to be brought up in the Catholic
religion, and that he should continue in this faith,[3] and,
moreover, that the government of the diocese, which
at that time was entirely Catholic, should remain for
twelve years in the hands of the chapter. In spite of
the first stipulation, Duke Julius had brought up his
son as a Protestant. In 1578, when the twelve years
in question had elapsed, and the chapter were preparing
to oppose the actual installation of the Bishop designate,
the Duke met the difficulty by having his son consecrated bishop by the abbot of the monastery of Huys-
burg, and had him installed according to Catholic usage,

---

[1] From his own statement. See Bodemann, *Julius von Braun-
schweig,* p. 219.

[2] Rehtmeier, *Braunschweigische Kirchengeschichte,* iii. 464. Stübner,
Histor. Beschreibung, pp. 75–76.

[3] Bodemann, *Weihe und Einführung,* p. 241.

he himself being present at the ceremony with his two younger sons. These two sons also, at the Duke's wish, received the minor orders, in order to make them eligible for ecclesiastical benefices. ' Clad in papistical habit,' says a report, ' the son, Henry Julius, was placed in the midst of the priests at Halberstadt, and with crosses and banners, and much screaming or singing, he was led by them into the choir and seated on their altar— the altar on which they daily perform their godless Mass—in order to show that he (Henry Julius) was to become the chief head of the execrable idol-worship.' His father, by his presence, ' confirmed the worship of Baal.'

The next day, however, after the installation of the Bishop, when the cathedral chapter invited him to attend Mass and take the customary episcopal oath, Julius bluntly declared that he and his son ' would neither hear nor look on at the Mass, or take any part in such an abomination.' He caused it to be proclaimed openly that, in spite of his having put on the episcopal habit, Henry Julius would not associate himself with the papacy, but would adhere to the Augsburg Confession and maintain and propagate it in the bishopric.

The chapter and the Catholics of the diocese had been disgracefully trapped. But the whole of Protestant Germany also was roused to extreme indignation by this proceeding.

' There is no place, banquet, or assembly of any sort,' wrote the Lübeck superintendent, Pouchenius, to Martin Chemnitz, ' however insignificant it may be, where the talk does not incessantly turn on the unchristian, unevangelical conduct of your most august prince, who, as if forgetful of all fear of God and all respect for his own good name, has handed over his three sons in a body to the Roman Antichrist; just as in Old Testament history the impious kings sacrificed their children to the idol Moloch.' The theological faculty at Helmstädt informed the Duke that the Pope was the Beast described in the Revelation of St. John, that tonsure was the mark of the Antichrist, and that those who received it would suffer everlasting damnation; Christ must have no fellowship with Belial, nor believers with unbelievers; to march in a procession with the popish clergy, carrying crosses and banners, was equivalent to being yoked together with unbelievers.

Chemnitz spoke even more strongly in a letter to the Duke. 'It is plain and certain,' he said, 'to all honest-minded Christians among the Evangelical Estates that the Roman Pope, with all his officials and subordinates, is the veritable Antichrist, revealed in and through God's Word, and that his whole religion is a monstrous collection of damnable idolatry, superstition, and abuses. It is the solemn command of God, spoken in the Apocalypse, ch. xviii.: 'Come out of her, my people, that ye be not partakers of her sins, and that ye receive not of her plagues.' To receive popish consecration and tonsure, which are the marks of the Beast, is described in the Apocalypse as committing fornication with the Babylonish whore in order to become rich. If the Duke should retort: 'He had not wished to sanction and confirm popish idolatry by his behaviour, he had only made use of outward means through which, later on, harm might be done to the papacy,' such answer would not save his conscience before God nor entirely remove the given scandals. One cannot, at the same time, have part with God and with the devil.[1]

Not content with giving this letter the widest publicity, Chemnitz and the Brunswick preachers instituted a campaign against the Duke from the pulpit, denounced him as unchristian, called him an apostate and a Mameluke who ' had offered up his son, an innocent, dear youth, to Moloch.' They grew still louder in their invectives against Julius when, on August 12, 1578, he issued a mandate granting the Jews free residence in Brunswick.[2]

The courts of the Protestant princes joined the preachers in indignant outcries against the proceedings at Halberstadt. The Electors of Saxony, of Brandenburg, and of the Palatinate addressed letters of strong remonstrance to Julius, and Duke Louis of Würtemberg also informed him of his intense displeasure.[3]

The Duke was roused to violent anger by all these remonstrances and admonitions, especially as he was little edified by all the ' drinking, gambling, and carousing' that went on at the Protestant courts.[4] When in the autumn of 1579 the three electors made a fresh appeal to him respecting the conclusion of the business of the Concord, he refused to have anything more to

[1] Bodemann, *Weihe und Einführung*, pp. 251–271.

[2] See *Die Juden unter den braunschweigischen Herzogen Julius und Heinrich Julius*, in the *Zeitschrift des Histor. Vereins für Niedersachsen*, Jahrg. 1861, pp. 244–306. See also Hachfeld, pp. 123–130; Henke, *Helmstädt*, p. 17, note 2. Chemnitz was dismissed from his post of ecclesiastical and consistorial councillor to the Duke; and when his son Paul was chosen by the magistracy to be abbot of St. Giles's monastery in Brunswick, Julius refused to ratify the appointment, and confiscated the property of the monastery for the benefit of the university of Helmstädt (Bodemann, p. 289).

[3] Bodemann, pp. 272 ff.

[4] See Bodemann, *Weihe und Einführung*, p. 278.

do with it, and warned the princes against ' the quarrelsome, covetous theologians ' who were chiefly actuated by ' personal interest.' He alluded bitterly to the fact that some of the doctrinal statements in the Formula of Concord had been altered by the very persons who had originally drawn them up and subscribed to them. He spoke his mind as follows to the theologian Timotheus Kirchner, professor at Helmstädt, who had been discharged from his post for having added his signature to the letter of the theological faculty concerning the mark of the Antichrist : ' We find that the theologians themselves are as far apart from one another as heaven and earth ; for, alas, they can none of them live together in peace, love, and unity ; they are all chiefly concerned about a handful of earthly honours, and, indeed, in many things they are solely influenced by human thought and opinion.'

He was determined, he said, not to put himself under the feet of the theologians : ' In Brunswick they had all been in corners and in the dark with their preceptor and wet nurse, Chemnitz, and to whatever he had proposed one had said " Yes," another " Amen," and they had all followed his lead like schoolboys.

' He hoped that other princes also would take care not to fall in with them so as to bring about " another Protestant war and another ' blood bath ' for Christianity."

' For the Church could not be built up and maintained by means of envious, conceited pates. The theologians want to prescribe a Formula of Concord for others when all the while they are at deadly feud among themselves. By what means the Formula of Concord was concocted, and how one signed to please another, and so on, you and others will come to know in the future ; we learnt all this to our bitter cost.' [1]

On June 25, 1580, the fiftieth anniversary of the day on which the Augsburg Confession had been handed in to Charles V. and to the Estates, the Formula of Concord was proclaimed at Dresden amid loud rejoicing.

John Hainzel, burgomaster of Augsburg, called it ' the last miracle before the Day of Judgment.' [2] It was stated in the preface that by special grace of the Holy Spirit the theologians had brought everything into good order. Not only were all the errors of the adversaries condemned in this book, but the adversaries themselves were repeatedly charged with wilful lying.

The Book of Concord gave to the Lutheran Church its final constitution, and raised an indestructible wall between it and Calvinism.

The number of Protestant Estates (as the Elector Palatine Louis remarked to the Elector of Saxony) who severed their connection with this book exceeded the number of those who had associated themselves with it.[3]

Besides the many princes already mentioned, the Count of Hanau-Münzenberg, the Counts John of Nassau and Louis of Wittgenstein, the Counts of East Friesland, and most of the Counts in the Wetterau and in Westphalia, refused their signatures. Among the towns that were firm in opposition were Nuremberg, Frankfort on the Main, Spires, Worms, Bremen, and Dantzic. At Nuremberg the booksellers were forbidden ' to exhibit

---

[1] Bodemann, *Herzog Julius*, pp. 219–220. See Bodemann, *Weihe und Einführung*, pp. 294–296. See also Bodemann's article on Duke Julius in the *Zeitschrift des Histor. Vereins für Niedersachsen*, Jahrg. 1887, pp. 42 f.

[2] Gillet, *Crato*, ii. 243.

[3] Pressel, *Kurfürst Ludwig*, p. 562. See Möller-Kawerau, *Kirchengeschichte* (Freiburg, 1894), iii. 267 ff.

the book in their shops.' The students of Altdorf fired
off their jokes on the doctrine of ubiquity.[1] Andreä had
vainly endeavoured to get the people of Nuremberg to
go through the form of signing the book, assuring them
that ' they would not thereby be prevented from con-
tinuing in their former opinions.' [2]

Fierce and degrading conflicts raged in Strasburg in
consequence of the Concord question.

The preachers of the town, with Doctor Pappus at
their head, were in sympathy with it ; the magistracy,
on the other hand, backed up by the university and its
rector, Johann Sturm, rejected it wholesale. The burghers and students broke up into ' knots of furious dis-
putants, and fought over their respective tenets with
savage shouts and insults, or even with blows.' In the
space of three years the different parties hurled at each
other well-nigh forty controversial pamphlets, full of
malice and bitterness, coarse insults, and odious misrepresentations. Riots of armed mobs occurred repeatedly. Andreä importuned the town councillors no
longer to tolerate the Rector Sturm with his ' devil's
doctrine,' and he was accordingly dismissed from his
post on December 7, 1581. Sixteen years later, however, the Formula of Concord was officially recognised
by the magistracy.[3]

The Lutheran King of Denmark, Frederic II.,

[1] Heppe, *Gesch. des Protestantismus*, iv. 271–277. Tholuck, *Das
kirchliche Leben*, i. 24–26.

[2] Heppe, iii. 299–307.

[3] *Beiträge zur evangelischen Concordie*, pp. 47–51. Röhrich, ii. 158 ;
Salig, i. 453 ff. ; Heppe, iii. 314–322, and iv. 313–315. Bussière, *Déve-
loppement*, ii. 167–188. See W. Horning's *Dr. Johann Pappus von
Lindau, 1549–1610, Münsterprediger, Universitätsprofessor, und Präsi-
dent des Kirchenconvents zu Strassburg*, from unprinted documents and
MSS. (Strassburg, 1891.)

brother-in-law of the Elector Augustus, threw the presentation copies of the book which were sent to him straight into the fire with his own hands. ' At first great things had been expected from the Book of Concord,' so the Danish ambassador, von Danzay, wrote from Hamburg to Duplessis-Mornay in November 1580 ; but after it was published everybody ridiculed it ; the King of Denmark forbade the sale of the book in his kingdom on pain of death ; anyone found possessing it was to be executed.[1]

Andreä, ' the father of the Book of Concord,' had not enjoyed many pleasant days in Saxony. In his capacity of inspector-general and superintendent of the Saxon churches and the three universities of Wittenberg, Leipsic, and Jena, he had been directed by the Elector to revive the ' pure, unfalsified doctrine,' in opposition to the existing Church organisation, and ' to reinstitute the right sort of instruction from the Word of God, for the perverted young of these districts.' At Wittenberg he was to have been abundantly helped in this work by the professors Polycarpus Leiser and Johann Schütz, whom the Elector had nominated. On April 23, 1577, the Elector had severely reprimanded the university of Wittenberg because it had set itself against this praiseworthy undertaking, thereby showing that it was still tainted with the venom of Calvinistic fanaticism, and that it led the young astray. 'If any one of the professors in future refused his support to the three men in question, the Elector declared that, in spite of the liberties and statutes of the university, he would make such a signal example of such mutinous Calvinists that the others would have a wholesome

---

[1] Duplessis-Mornay, ii. 110-113. See Pontoppidan, iii. 483.

horror of acting likewise.'[1]   At Wittenberg, on the first
Sunday after Trinity, in the year 1579, when Andreä was
reviling Melanchthon and his books in a sermon, 'he was
hooted down with so much uproar that numbers of people
fled out of the church, and a tumult was apprehended.'[2]

In October of the following year, after the Formula
of Concord had been publicly announced, Andreä brought
out 300 theses on the Person of Christ, and 285 on the
Lord's Supper, and he held a disputation on them at
Wittenberg during four successive days.

When on this occasion—so the Wittenbergers report—
he called Melanchthon a shining light and ' our common
teacher,' he was ' loudly hooted and hissed by the
students, because, in a sermon preached a year before,
he had denounced Melanchthon's writings in the strongest
terms, and had called his code of doctrine a " scoundrelly
book." '   During his defence of Christ's ubiquity he was
' hooted five times running,' and later on ' coughed
down ' twice.[3]   Andreä, on the other hand, wrote to
the Elector of Saxony that he had ' come off con-
queror in his disputation, and had proved unmistakably
to the perverted youths what blasphemous doctrine
concerning the Person of Christ and the Sacrament the
former Wittenberg theologians had read into the Word
and the Scriptures.   ' Down to the present day, he said,
the professors of this university had dealt in deceit and
falsehood ; in particular, one of them had instilled into
the minds of the students such enthusiasm for Melanchthon, " the mainspring of all this tribulation," that, as

---

[1] In Löscher, *Hist. Motuum*, iii. 231–233.

[2] Letter of Sebastian Leonhart, in Müller, *Staatscabinet*, viii. 331.
On May 18, 1580, Leonhart wrote concerning Andreä : this man is ' in
odio apud omnes in tota aula et regione,' p. 333.

[3] In Heppe, *Geschichte des Protestantismus*, iv. Beil. pp. 14–29.

often as his mere name was mentioned, they would all
take off their birettas with special reverence ; but when
the name of Jesus was spoken, their birettas or hats
remained on their heads.' [1]

The Tübingen theologians treated the Wittenberg
report that Andreä had been hooted at by the students
as ' a flagrant, shameless falsehood.' They declared, on
the contrary, that Vitus Winshemius, the rector of the
university, had been the general butt of the students'
ridicule.[2]

The opinion pronounced by thoughtful men was
that ' all subtle disquisitions of this sort, in which the
noise and tumult of the students was taken as a sign of
victory over the opponent, were in no way conducive
to Christian discipline in the universities; but, on the
contrary, were very prejudicial to serious study and
Christian behaviour, for it was a well-known fact that
turbulence was the constant result of this practice of
disputation, and that brawls and frays were of daily
occurrence among those who engaged in controversies
on things divine and Christian.' [3]

Anyhow, Andreä's supposed victory bore no fruit
whatever. The university remained at daggers drawn
with him, and took a lively part in the outcry
of the Anticoncordists, who, according to a report of
Selnekker, of January 25, 1582, declared that ' the
" Concord " was from the devil, and they wished that
they might be the executioners when the parsons who
had compiled it were burnt to death.' [4]

[1] Pressel, *Andreä*, p. 62.

[2] *Gründlicher Bericht*, Tübingen, 1585, p. 666.

[3] Letter of Doctor Balthasar Huber of Jena, dated June 23, 1586, in
the Mayence Dissertation, pp. 13–14, quoted above, p. 222, note 4.

[4] *Forma Concordiæ*, A².

In the immediate neighbourhood of the Elector, also, Andreä had encountered violent antagonists. His inspectoral visitation of churches—so the court preacher, George Listenius, wrote to the Elector—had so greatly incensed and embittered the clergy and laymen, nobles and commoners, pastors and chaplains, that there was even danger of a serious rising, as both among the clergy and the laity hostile parties might easily be formed. 'For it is well known that, in the Hartz district, there are starving counts, with their accomplices, the seditious substantialists, and that debts, suretyships, and *corvées* have reduced the power of the nobility to extreme want, so that they can scarcely get bread to eat.' Everybody has some personal grudge against Andreä, and all ' have the greatest loathing for him on account of his profligacy.' ' *In summa*,' says Listenius, 'his oath on every occasion is that the devil may take him, or that he may not see the face of God in eternity.' ' By this means he deceives the people. He abuses and slanders your Grace's councillors, calls them bagpipes, drummers, and shawm-players, and brags of having given to their business the turn he liked.'

' He was bound in duty, honour, and conscience,' the court preacher told his sovereign lord, ' to divulge all this to him, although Andreä was his especial friend and favourite.' [1] Selnekker handed in a document to the Electress, in which, among other charges, he maintained that Andreä had said : ' I do not care for the Elector ; I did not care for him before, and it's all the same to me whether I am in or out of favour with him.

---

[1] Pressel, *Andreä*, pp. 210-214. See the letter of Listenius to Chemnitz, dated March 16, 1578, in Leuckfeld, *Hist. Hesshusiana*, pp. 127-128.

The Elector must be well aware how matters stand with
himself, for he has said to me more than once that he
has not a single loyal councillor, and that he cannot
trust anybody.' [1]

Andreä's dismissal from Saxony took place at the
end of 1580, in a manner little flattering to himself,
even though there was no outward evidence of disgrace.[2] It was made by his enemies a welcome target
for their attacks. They poured out against him and
' his diabolical, so-called Book of Concord ' a plentiful
shower of satires, pasquils, epigrams, and parodies—for
which last purpose they selected portions of Scripture,
such as the Gospels, the Church Creeds, the Psalms
and hymns, and even the Lord's Prayer. Here is

---

[1] The document in Pressel, *Andreä*, pp. 239–249. ' By this document,'
says Pressel, ' we gain a melancholy insight into the unhappy state of things
at the court, where all were against all, and a hateful system of spying
and denouncing poisoned everything.' The following anecdote is told of
Andreä's private life :—' In the monastery of Bebenhausen he swallowed
a tall goblet of wine at one gulp, so that his eyes filled . . . and he said :
'' I shall certainly be hanged in the end ; I feel the rope in my breast.'' '
In the monastery of Heilsbronn he drank to confirm the assertion that
' the Turkish Alkoran would be taught openly in the pulpits of Nuremberg.'
He called for a drinking-vessel ' and emptied the wine at one gulp, saying,
'' if he was not speaking the truth might this beverage stop the beat-
ing of his heart.'' Then he leaped round the room, exclaiming : '' You
see I did speak the truth, the wine has not hurt me ! '' He actually
boasted of this disgraceful drinking, in print, to Sturm : even to this day
he said he was none the worse for his excess in drinking. Sturm replied :
'' The Devil entered into Judas Iscariot as soon as he had eaten the sop,
but his accursed belly did not burst, nor did his treacherous, robber heart
break until he had hung himself on the rope which he had carried long
before in his bosom '' ' (Altenrath, pp. 63–64).

[2] Details in Pressel, pp. 240–264. Heppe, *Gesch. des Protestantismus*,
iv. 259–270. In Peucer's *Historia Carceris* a despatch of the Elector is
quoted in which he complains of Andreä : ' He is accused of denying all
the infamous things that he has been charged with saying of other people,
both of high and low degree. And this is scoundrelly behaviour, and does not
proceed from the Holy Ghost, but from a lying devil's parson ' (Heppe, iv.
264, note). See v. Bezold, *Briefe J. Casimir's*, i. 424, No. 269, note 2.

an example : 'Devil Jacob, which art in the devil's
heaven, dishonoured be thine accursed name ; may thy
ubiquity kingdom be destroyed ; thy will be done
neither here, nor at Wittenberg, nor down at Leipzig ;
steal not from us our daily bread, but pay our debts
for us, so that we may not have to pay a penny to any
of our creditors ; lead us not into thy damnable Formula,
but save us from thy blasphemous book. Thou sacrilegious Jäckel [old Nick], hell fire is thy power, sulphur
and pitch are thy might, a cord round thy throat is thy
honour, the shambles and the gallows are thy glory,
from eternity to eternity, and through all eternity.
Amen.'[1]

The Bremen theologians were specially infuriated
with Andreä. 'In Andreä,' they wrote in 1583, 'Satan
has transformed himself into an angel of light ; Eutyches
and Schwenckfeld are also reincarnated in him.' With
good reason and truth it could be said of him that ' he
mocked at God and at the world, that he had no shame
and no conscience, that he was a roguish juggler, and a
raging, devouring wolf.' The theologians published a
poem against Andreä and all the ubiquitists, those
' enemies of God and of all Christians,' from which we
quote the following lines :

> . . . They think the clear, pure truth—
> And all good Christians, too, forsooth—
> To root out, kill, exterminate,
> By raging, wrangling, and debate :

---

[1] Further documents in Heppe, *Gesch. der Concordienformel*, in the
Zeitschrift für die Histor. Theologie, 1857, pp. 465–493. The following
is an extract from a parody on the *Te Deum* directed against Andreä :

Te per territoria principum Germaniæ sancta abominatur ecclesia,
Patrem nefandæ Eslingæ perpetratæ cum duabus ancillulis turpitudinis,
Detrudendum in carcerem . . .
Tu devorator multorum millium grossorum, &c.

In Heppe, *Gesch. des Protestantismus*, iv. Beil. pp. 43–45.

By slandering and falsehood weaving,
By tricking, shamming, and deceiving;
By scolding, damning, giving men
Sectarian names, by prison den;
By ban, by persecution sore,
And other tyrannies galore.[1]

Among the most serious refutations of the Formulary of Concord was a pamphlet which the Count Palatine, John Casimir, caused to be written by his theologian, Ursinus, and which was ratified by the clergy of his land and published in 1581. It went by the name of the ' Neustadt Admonition.' It was stated therein that there was no warrant for attributing to the Augsburg Confession an authority which outweighed that of all other creeds. At the time when this Confession was drawn up, it had not been possible, as Melanchthon himself had shown, to arrive at a full comprehension, and to make a complete and perfect statement of all the different points of doctrine under consideration. The Confession had been drawn up hastily, and it was almost solely the work of Melanchthon. Moreover, the original authors and first adherents of this creed had themselves altered much of its contents, had even added entirely new statements of doctrine, showing thereby that they considered the first version of the creed incomplete and faulty. In the earliest text there were statements which even the most zealous defenders of the Confession no longer accepted. For instance, the tenth article, in its original form, by no means excluded the Catholic doctrine of Transubstantiation, and had consequently not been attacked in the Catholic ' Confutation.' Now, however, the Concordists themselves were the fiercest antagonists of Transubstantiation.

---

[1] *Abfertigung der berühmten Widerlegung*, L³ᵇ-4ᵃ.

Luther was idolised by the Concordists. It was only nominally that his writings were subordinated to Scripture in the Formulary of Concord. In reality they were exalted into Gospel truth and treated as a standard of doctrine and a rule of faith. Experience, however, had long since shown that in the controversies of the Augsburg Confessionists all parties alike appealed to these writings, and their many errors, exaggerations, antilogies, and recantations made it possible for the most opposite opinions to be supported with equal plausibility by Lutheran statements. Above all, Luther's controversial writings, to which the Concordists attached the most extreme importance, could not claim any authority. ' In these, as his own followers were obliged to confess, he had been carried away, into excitement and passion which exceeded all bounds, and had been guilty of assertions which contradicted his own earlier declarations, and which he himself in disputation had often been obliged to withdraw or to modify.'

From the Book of Concord itself the ' Admonition ' cited a whole series of statements which were in opposition to the Holy Scriptures and to the old formulas of faith, and which even made the book contradict itself. Finally, it was declared that the book had come into existence in an altogether illegitimate manner, and that schism and anarchy in Church and State—certainly not unity—would be the result of the whole business.[1]

The Concordists had hoped that the work they had undertaken would ' unite all evangelical Christians in one body,' that, as a uniform body of doctrine, it would form a counterpoise to the damnable ' Conciliabulum of Trent,' and would be the strongest bulwark against ' the

---

[1] Johannsen, pp. 461-476. See Gillet, *Crato*, ii. 230.

idolatrous papacy and its diabolical satellites, the Jesuits, with all their rabble of followers.'[1] This hope did not meet with fulfilment. On the contrary, as John Casimir's admonition predicted, the 'work of concord' only intensified and embittered the religious controversies among the Protestants. 'In particular,' wrote a contemporary, 'the chasm between the Lutherans and Calvinists had been so enormously widened and deepened that there could be little doubt left but that open war and bloodshed must be close at hand.'[2]

In the Empire the Calvinistic party of action gradually gained the upper hand.

---

[1] See above, pp. 392, 393.
[2] In the *Beiträge zur evangelischen Concordie*, pp. 49-50.

INDEX OF PLACES

INDEX OF PERSONS

END OF THE EIGHTH VOLUME

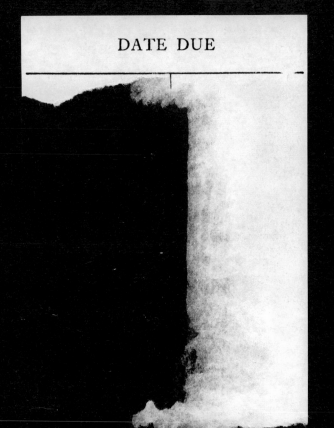

DATE DUE